Hope and Kinship in Contemporary Fiction

Hope and Kinship in Contemporary Fiction

Moods and Modes of Temporality and Belonging

Gero Bauer

BLOOMSBURY ACADEMIC
NEW YORK • LONDON • OXFORD • NEW DELHI • SYDNEY

BLOOMSBURY ACADEMIC
Bloomsbury Publishing Inc, 1359 Broadway, New York, NY 10018, USA
Bloomsbury Publishing Plc, 50 Bedford Square, London, WC1B 3DP, UK
Bloomsbury Publishing Ireland, 29 Earlsfort Terrace, Dublin 2, D02 AY28, Ireland

BLOOMSBURY, BLOOMSBURY ACADEMIC and the Diana logo
are trademarks of Bloomsbury Publishing Plc

First published in the United States of America 2024
This paperback edition published in 2025

Copyright © Gero Bauer, 2024

For legal purposes the Acknowledgements on p. vii constitute
an extension of this copyright page.

Cover design: Eleanor Rose
Cover image © Getty Images

All rights reserved. No part of this publication may be: i) reproduced or transmitted in any form, electronic or mechanical, including photocopying, recording or by means of any information storage or retrieval system without prior permission in writing from the publishers; or ii) used or reproduced in any way for the training, development or operation of artificial intelligence (AI) technologies, including generative AI technologies. The rights holders expressly reserve this publication from the text and data mining exception as per Article 4(3) of the Digital Single Market Directive (EU) 2019/790.

Bloomsbury Publishing Inc does not have any control over, or responsibility for, any third-party websites referred to or in this book. All internet addresses given in this book were correct at the time of going to press. The author and publisher regret any inconvenience caused if addresses have changed or sites have ceased to exist, but can accept no responsibility for any such changes.

Library of Congress Cataloging-in-Publication Data
Names: Bauer, Gero, 1986- author.
Title: Hope and kinship in contemporary fiction : moods and modes of temporality and belonging / Gero Bauer.
Description: New York : Bloomsbury Academic, 2024. | Includes bibliographical references and index. |
Summary: "Explores the emphasis that contemporary novels, films and television series place on the present, arguing that hope emerges from the potentiality of the here and now, rather than the future, and as intimately entangled with negotiations of structures of belonging"– Provided by publisher.
Identifiers: LCCN 2023029724 (print) | LCCN 2023029725 (ebook) |
ISBN 9798765104194 (hardback) | ISBN 9798765104187 (paperback) |
ISBN 9798765104200 (epub) | ISBN 9798765104217 (pdf) | ISBN 9798765104224
Subjects: LCSH: Kinship in literature. | Hope in literature. | Belonging (Social psychology) in literature. | American fiction–21st century–History and criticism. | LCGFT: Literary criticism.
Classification: LCC PS374.K545 B38 2024 (print) | LCC PS374.K545 (ebook) |
DDC 813/.609–dc23/eng/20230828
LC record available at https://lccn.loc.gov/2023029724
LC ebook record available at https://lccn.loc.gov/2023029725

ISBN:		
	HB:	979-8-7651-0419-4
	PB:	979-8-7651-0418-7
	ePDF:	979-8-7651-0421-7
	eBook:	979-8-7651-0420-0

Typeset by Integra Software Services Pvt. Ltd.

For product safety related questions contact productsafety@bloomsbury.com.

To find out more about our authors and books visit www.bloomsbury.com
and sign up for our newsletters.

CONTENTS

Acknowledgements vii

Introduction: Hope and kinship 1

Part I What comes after: Temporality and belonging in contemporary post-apocalyptic fiction 43

1. Radical solidarity: The (anti-)futuristic politics of Cormac McCarthy's *The Road* 51

2. 'No more kid stuff': Monstrous kinship in AMC's *The Walking Dead* 77

Part II Beyond time and space: Queering hope and globalizing kinship in contemporary speculative fiction 103

3. 'What is an ocean but a multitude of drops': Metafiction and universal kinship in David Mitchell's *Cloud Atlas* 113

4. 'I am also a we': Affect, simultaneity, and the global imagination in Netflix's *Sense8* 139

Part III Hysterical pessimism: Contingent hope and the proliferation of the present in the novels of Hanya Yanagihara 167

5. Moral matters: Power, coloniality, and narrative in *The People in the Trees* 175

6 Beyond repair: Friendship and the end of hope in
   A Little Life 201

Coda 231

References 239
Index 255

ACKNOWLEDGEMENTS

I began thinking about this project several years ago while immersed in the reading and watching of generous amounts of recent and, in many cases, very popular novels, films, and television series. These texts began to suggest lines of thinking which slowly converged into an argument about temporality and belonging. It seems terrifyingly fitting that I wrote the bulk of the book during the first wave of a global pandemic which radically contracted temporal horizons, suddenly restricted my own movements to a fairly small radius, and made encounters with other people outside the virtual space of Zoom rare and precious. These circumstances inevitably had an impact on what this book has become, and they make it all the more necessary to acknowledge the people who provided material, intellectual, and emotional sustenance in the process.

Ingrid Hotz-Davies and Regina Ammicht Quinn not only created and maintained a professional environment which allowed me to work on this project, but were also incredibly enthusiastic, productively critical, and immensely supportive first readers and conversation partners. Corey McEleney and Carl Fischer extended much appreciated academic and personal invitations, and Corey pointed me in the right direction. Astrid Franke provided an extremely supportive space in which I could discuss this work, and gave generous feedback. Lukas Häberle, Mrunmayee Sathye, and Fanni Weber shared exceptionally helpful advice while also being wonderful and meticulous proofreaders. Special thanks to my mother Sonja Bauer for compiling the index.

In the process of writing this book, I became unusually mindful of the wonderful networks of friends, family, and kin who make up my world. It would be impossible to mention them all here. I do, however, want to explicitly thank the members of my book club – Rebecca Hahn, Stefan Heck, Susanne Jung, and Miriam Wallraven – whose taste in literature, joy of reading, and intellectual companionship have crucially determined my choice of material for this book.

My mother and father, as always, have been an invaluable source of emotional comfort and support, and continue to show an unwavering interest in my sometimes eclectic academic endeavours.

Finally, the most wonderful encounters happen when you least expect them to, and some moments of joy extend into something longer. Endless thanks for this go to Jakob.

Introduction: Hope and kinship

In 2011, one decade into the new millennium, communist philosopher Franco 'Bifo' Berardi takes stock of the contemporary moment in western[1] societies, and comes to the conclusion that 'the future is over' (2011: 3). One century after the heyday of futurist trust in progress and human advancement through technology and knowledge that characterized the first years of the twentieth century, Berardi faces a sober realization: '[t]he idea that the future will be better than the present is not a natural idea, but the imaginary effect of the peculiarity of the bourgeois production model' (18). Confronted with the dissolution of the future as the realm of utopian projection, he discovers hope in the possibility of the present moment: '[w]e sing to the infinity of the present and abandon the illusion of a future' (166). Strikingly, Berardi associates both the loss of the future and the rediscovery

---

[1]Throughout this book, I understand 'the west' as denoting both a geographical and a cultural sphere of influence mainly originating in and focused on Europe and North America, and those countries and regions that inherit their global economic privilege, cultural self-image, and epistemological authority and dominance from the historical hegemony of European colonial powers. As such, 'the west' is a contingent category, an idea which, like 'the Orient', as Edward Said observes, 'has a history and a tradition of thought, imagery, and vocabulary that have given it reality and presence in and for the West' ([1978] 2003: 4–5). As Kwame Anthony Appiah argues, the concept continues to produce exclusions along historically grown lines of demarcation: '[w]e have used the expression "the west" to do very different jobs ... Often, in recent years, "the west" means the north Atlantic: Europe and her former colonies in North America. The opposite here is a non-western world in Africa, Asia and Latin America – now dubbed "the global south" – though many people in Latin America will claim a western inheritance, too. This way of talking notices the whole world but lumps a whole lot of extremely different societies together, while delicately carving around Australians and New Zealanders and white South Africans, so that "western" here can look simply like a euphemism for white'. My usage of the term despite these pitfalls is meant to reflect the ongoing political, cultural, and social efficacy of framings of dominant thinking emerging from anglophone academic cultures in Europe and North America as institutionally and genealogically tied to specific histories of scholarship.

of hope in the epistemological indeterminacy of the here and now with the condition of the social fabric. Hyper-capitalism, he contends, has led to 'a reduction of the capacity for empathy' (68). In consequence, 'there is no longer time to get close to each other … no more time for caresses, for the pleasure and slowness of whispered words' (95). However, in 'the consciousness and sensibility of social solidarity, of human empathy, of gratuitous activity' (163) also lie hope and potential.

This book is about the loss of the future and the possibility of hope in the here and now. It asks what happens to the social imaginary and the cultural (and critical) imagination when the present is experienced as an ongoing state of crisis and the future is framed as unattainable, undesirable, or unsustainable; when hope emerges not from individual and collective projections of and into a better future, but in the shape of acts of solidarity, provisional communities, and structures of belonging that provide care and concern along both predictable and unexpected lines. Over the course of the following chapters, I consider how contemporary fiction engages the shifting nexus of time and belonging that Berardi captures in his diagnostic take on the historical now. Taking the tension between a disillusionment with narratives of progress and a continued commitment to the affect of hope to be a strong mood in the contemporary cultural landscape, my aim is to move along the blurry middle ground between dominant expressions of anxiety and feelings of crisis, and equally persistent calls for a renewal of the utopian imagination. I want to disentangle this utopian spirit from prevalent associations with futurity in order to identify a theme in fictional production since the turn of the millennium that responds to the contemporary zeitgeist by imagining hope as firmly embedded in the present moment, and as emerging in renegotiations of structures of care and belonging. I will trace this nexus of hope and kinship in recent popular narratives that all speculate about a world in a state of global or local crisis, and which suspend their characters in a present haunted by unspoken pasts and faced with impossible futures. In this way, I intend to map a particular mode of contemporary fictional production that imagines hope and kinship in unexpected ways, and which emerges from more general cultural concerns with time and belonging.

There seems to be, by now, a consensus in cultural studies, history, and sociology that cultural attitudes towards the future – and to time in general – have been changing in western societies since the last decades of the twentieth century, but particularly since the turn of the millennium. And this change is regularly brought into conversation with equally fluctuating conceptualizations of the social, and of the making of community. Writers as methodologically and ideologically diverse as Aleida Assmann, Lucian Hölscher, and Zygmunt Baumann all propose that we have arrived at a moment in which disillusionment with the future prevails, and hope for social cohesion rests on calls for global responsibility.[2] All three take their cue from the observation that our understanding and lived experience of temporality has been – and still seems to be – in a state of crisis, while the future becomes increasingly untenable as a realm of utopic affective attachment; and all three foreground shifting notions of community and belonging as intimately intertwined with the temporal reconfigurations they attempt to analyse and systematize. My own project inscribes itself into these debates, but explicitly positions itself tangentially to them. Where Assmann argues for the social importance of cultural memory, I intend to take seriously the implications of forgetting and cultural amnesia I find in my corpus of texts. Where Hölscher ultimately arrives back at a call for new utopias, I want to stick with the implications of a lack thereof. And where Baumann bemoans a sense of 'tribalism', I will trace the diverse meanings of kinship that emerge in the fictional worlds under discussion in this book. Such a stubborn focus on the present and on forms of improvised sociability that abstains from proposing any grand utopian narrative or political vision might go against the grain of current theoretical trends, but that is precisely my point. I believe that we can only understand certain themes and tendencies (however minor) in the contemporary cultural imagination if we ask ourselves why stories that embrace negativity and pessimism and look for connection and solidarity in provisional structures of care and concern enjoy such enduring popularity.

---

[2]Assmann demonstrates how, since the 1970s, the future has lost its appeal as a time of promise and positive affective identification, and how time itself has become a category in crisis (cf. 2011: 10, 247). She critically examines recent scholarly tendencies to foreground an increasingly extending present, arguing instead for a renewed focus on cultural memory. Hope, for Assmann, lies in a confrontation with the painful past, which, if properly integrated into the present, can enable a society's future; and this identification with the past requires that we learn to be truly empathic (cf. 318). For Assmann, the future gets realigned from an association with progress and teleology towards a sustainable extension of a present which continues to learn from a past made productive for critical collective identification (cf. 322). Like Assmann, Lucian Hölscher approaches the future as a historically emerging category, and homogenous, teleological time as a specifically modern phenomenon (cf. 2016: 10). He, too, points out a shift in perspective in the 1970s, when, in the context of early debates about climate change, the future of humanity as such became contingent (cf. 308). But it is the early years of the new millennium, Hölscher argues, which saw a definitive association of the future with fear, anxiety, and unpredictability, and thus foregrounding of what he calls 'negative' futures (cf. 318, 322). Hölscher historically locates hope in political and social commitments to global collective responsibility and in a politics for future generations (cf. 307, 308). Zygmunt Baumann, finally, diagnoses the contemporary moment with a collective rejection of utopian thinking in favour of increasingly emerging '"retrotopias" … : visions located in the lost/stolen/abandoned but undead past, instead of being tied to the not-yet-unborn and so inexistent future' (2017: 5). In this context, Baumann laments, among other things, the 'rehabilitation of the tribal model of community' (9), and closes his analysis with a plea for a recovered sense of global humanism in the face of accelerating crises: 'we face joining either hands, or common graves' (167).

Any project addressing contemporary culture inevitably faces the challenge of conveying a convincing idea of the usefulness of the term 'contemporary', which, as Theodore Martin points out, seems to designate 'something still moving through history' (2017: 4). What is the relationship between the 'being with time' implied by the word's etymology and our everyday associations with the idea of a recent past or a simultaneous occurrence? Giorgio Agamben usefully complicates common notions of contemporariness by tying it to a particular attitude in an observer or reader: contemporaries are those who have a 'relationship with time that adheres to it through a disjunction and an anachronism' (2009: 41). Similarly, my own approach to contemporary fiction in this book assumes that the texts under discussion negotiate investments in temporality – within their respective fictional words *and* with the wider context of their historical environment – that are fragmented, provisional, and out of joint, producing a notion of what Caroline Edwards calls '*non-contemporaneity*' (2019: 9, emphasis in original).³ They are contemporary in the sense that they self-consciously reflect attitudes towards the (fictional and historical) present of their own genesis to the effect that these attitudes themselves emerge as a '*strategy of mediation*' and 'a critical concept' (Martin 2017: 5, emphasis in original).

The contemporary focus of this book is thus twofold: I am interested in the fictional foregrounding of a sense of an extended present, but I also look for these processes in very recently published works of fiction, which arguably present something like a properly contemporary cultural mood. As Peter Boxall argues, in twenty-first-century fiction, '[t]here is a persistent fascination with the shifted temporality that characterizes the new century, with a time that passes in a way that we cannot quite capture, that eludes our narrative grasp' (2013: 9). The contemporary novel, in particular, is often shaped by a 'fascination with the passing moment, with speeded, slowed, stalled, uneven time' (10), and by an 'awkward relationship to the present, to a present moment that will not yield itself to any available vocabulary' (17). At the same time, the twenty-first-century novel is 'engaged in an extraordinarily intimate refashioning of the ties which bind us in our environments' (14). It is exactly these uneven temporalities, the present

---

³While Edwards' and my critical interests align in our concern with the dramatization of the experience of time in contemporary fictional narrative, her argument leads her to conclusions decidedly more optimistic than my own. Her observation 'that the utopian imagination is making a distinct return in the twenty-first century' (2019: 19) is based on an engagement with a fictional archive quite similar to mine, and her argument that many twenty-first-century texts 'interrogat[e] forms of intersubjective, if not properly collective, encounters through new temporal engagements' (24) aligns with my own understanding of the entanglement of hope and kinship. However, my take on the prevalence of hope – not 'utopia' – in the contemporary cultural imagination puts less emphasis on the future-oriented potential of the utopian spirit than on the provisional potentialities of the present.

moments rendered in contemporary fiction, and the diverse articulations of the binding ties that permeate fictional landscapes which I want to address in this book. These ties emerge as dynamic nodal points around which affects of hope and despair, optimism and pessimism are negotiated in the context of a devastated present in a state of ongoing crisis. I ask what kind of agency and what unexpected lines of connection arise from contexts in which the past only intrudes upon the present in traumatic ruptures, and where there is no future on the horizon. And I am interested in the capacity of fiction to speculate about what happens to the ties that bind us to each other and to our environments in times of crisis, and in making this fictional rendering of affect available to readerly identification. Like Benjamin Bateman, who engages with a much older archive of queer modernist texts, I discover in my fictional examples the entanglement of hope and kinship as a '[l]iving and growing inside of one another rather than determining to live and grow apart' which is 'not necessarily oriented to the future' (2018: 10), and I turn my critical attention towards 'an overdetermined present' (17) that emerges from fictional texts published after the turn of the millennium.

As such, my argument also resonates with debates about the limits of deconstruction and literature 'after' postmodernism. Irmtraud Huber suggests that what is often framed as a return to realism, sincerity, and authenticity in contemporary fiction is, in fact, a 'shift of interest' away from 'postmodernism's constant endeavours to disrupt, to alienate and to subvert' (2014: 6), and towards a new commitment to affective readerly investment. Contemporary fiction, viewed from this perspective, 'attempts to bridge the rupture (not to cover it), to be accessible (though not transparent), to create (but not to posit). After and because of deconstruction, it seeks to reconstruct' (6–7). Huber acknowledges that this turn to reconstruction can 'seem blatantly anachronistic, desperately futile, hopelessly naïve or embarrassingly optimistic', and 'that it is a tentative but pervasive optimism concerning the impossible possibility of communication that ultimately emerges as the essential qualitative difference of the emerging literary trend' (24, 36). For Huber, the central characteristic of the literature of reconstruction is 'the return to a commitment towards communication, connection and responsibility' (48). In this book, I take these observations about the reconstructive quality of contemporary writing as a starting point to think about the thematic concerns of recent narrative fiction (not just novels) more generally, but also about their intersections with theoretical debates about the way we read fiction as critics. In the close readings that make up the bulk of this book, I explore how the optimistic mood which Huber finds in recent novels counterintuitively emerges, in my own case studies, against the backdrop of a pervasive pessimism in setting and characterization, and in a thematic focus on temporality and belonging that posits hope as bound to the here and now, and as contingent upon iterations of care and belonging. In the context of my more theoretical concerns in this introduction, I contend that debates about reparative and postcritical reading in literary and cultural theory provide a productive echo chamber for my thematic interest in hope and kinship. The epistemological concerns raised within these debates are best understood, I think, as expressive of the same cultural shifts that characterize the literature of reconstruction: both discourses (theoretical and fictional), in their respective registers, are preoccupied with questions of temporality in times of crisis, and with the work of turning towards reconstructing lines of connection and the ties that bind us to the world.

Over the course of the following chapters, I engage a small selection of recent fictional narratives across different media: novels (Cormac McCarthy's *The Road*, David Mitchell's *Cloud Atlas*, and Hanya Yanagihara's *The People in the Trees* and *A Little Life*), films (John Hillcoat's adaptation of *The Road* and The Wachoswskis and Tom Tykwer's adaptation of *Cloud Atlas*), and television series (AMC's *The Walking Dead* and Netflix's *Sense8*). I will attempt to trace a mood, in the contemporary cultural imagination, that performatively thinks about hope and kinship as entangled concepts. My aim is not to delineate the boundaries of any kind of closed system, or to argue that the texts under consideration form a coherent canon of sorts. Instead, I offer my analyses of individual narratives to illuminate, in exemplary fashion, different spaces within recent fictional discourse where questions of temporality and belonging and a pronounced emphasis on the present become particularly virulent. I move from the more obvious nexus of post-apocalyptic fiction via speculative and metafictional storytelling, and end up with two works by a single author. Both the choice of examples across media and the varying logic of the textual pairings are deliberate: they are intended as an attempt to combine the patient indulgence in close readings of a small sample of material with the tracing of a more general cultural tendency across a range of contexts and genres. With this approach, I hope to do justice to the complexity of the examples at hand, and to put into conversation an abundance of theoretical, critical, and fictional voices that negotiate the place of hope and kinship in the contemporary cultural imagination. My approach attempts to bring together insights from a long-standing conversation about temporality and kinship in queer theory with debates about critique and criticism in literary theory. Given the wide theoretical reach of the concepts I engage with, I also draw on more general work in philosophy, cultural theory, anthropology, science studies, and the new materialisms to further contextualize my argument. At the heart of my elaborations lies a concern with tracing a line of thinking that attaches the affect of hope to a temporal mode which privileges the present as a space of potentiality over the future, and which contemplates inventive possibilities of making kin under devastating circumstances.

Now or never: Hope

In the context of this book, I understand hope as a strong affect and as an organizing temporality. Hope attaches subjects to the possibility that things could be different from what they are. It is a cognitive and emotional investment in objects, people, ideas, ideals, practices, and narratives that positions and arranges individuals vis-à-vis one another and the world. In a basic sense, hope most often invokes a future not yet here, and 'educated hope' draws attention to the lessons that we can learn from the past in order to be better judges of what can realistically be hoped for. While hope thus reaches towards a future horizon and may be called upon to learn from the experiences of the past, the present moment becomes the contested ground that takes on varying meanings in different conceptualizations of hope. Major crises and the prospect of global (social, political, environmental) collapse regularly raise urgent questions about the place of hope in times of uncertain futures. Against the backdrop of the crisis discourses of the early twenty-first century, contemporary fictional texts ask what happens to a future-oriented understanding of hope when it appears that the future has always already come, and that it is not better and most likely will never be. As if in answer to a pervading cultural pessimism, these texts negotiate the place of hope in disillusioned times, where the horizon is dark and the possibility of reparation lies in the potential for care and responsibility in the present. In this temporal shift of perspective, hope also emerges as a practice, as the concrete business of forging connection in risky, contingent, and improvised encounters.

One of the aims of this book is to question and complicate the usefulness and productivity of hope for readings of fiction. It asks what hope can do for a criticism invested both in holding on to the political, cultural, and critical potential of hope as affect, and in acknowledging its potentially detrimental effects when it does not engage with the temporal slippages and stumbling blocks in naively optimistic narratives, especially as they are tied to normative and conservative kinship discourses of family and reproduction. I examine contemporary fictional texts that reconfigure hope so that it is bound to some reparative vision (sometimes, if not always, of a future), while not subscribing to a simplistic optimism. Hope, in my analysis, is thus neither fully opposed to nor fully synonymous with optimism. While I understand both concepts as affective orientations towards the world that forge attachments, hope, more than optimism, lends itself to the kind of pragmatic work of connection I emphasize in my argument.

Two of the most influential considerations of the temporality of hope and hope's place in history are Walter Benjamin's aphoristic defence of historical materialism, and Ernst Bloch's opus magnum *Das Prinzip Hoffnung*. Although vastly different in scope, both usefully foreground the tension between hope's futuristic tendencies and its rootedness in the here and now. Benjamin contrasts the messianic time of historical materialism with the homogenous and empty time ('homogene und leere Zeit', [1940] 1992: 150) of historicism, which, through its belief in progress and history's inevitability, makes the people oblivious to their revolutionary potential. As an antithesis to the 'angel of history's' witnessing of the catastrophic piling up of history's debris Benjamin posits a powerful 'Jetztzeit' (150), a messianic now in which time itself comes to a standstill to unfold a revolutionary chance in the fight for the oppressed past ('revolutionäre[] Chance im Kampfe für die unterdrückte Vergangenheit', 152). Understanding the present as *Jetztzeit*, and thus as full of potential and possibility liberates the historical narrative from the corset of historicism's preservation of the status quo. While my own argument is much less concerned than Benjamin with attitudes towards the historical past, his foregrounding of the revolutionary now is an important source of inspiration for my engagement with the material under consideration. Only by turning away from the seeming inevitability of capitalist teleology and its attendant insistence on more of the same, and by turning, instead, to the potential of the here and now, Benjamin suggests, the working classes – and society as a whole – can achieve real revolutionary momentum; that is, society's hope lies in the possibility of the now.

Sharing Benjamin's socialist agenda, but much more outspoken about the fundamentally futurist orientation of hope, Bloch's authoritative account of utopia as a principle of human existence is nevertheless instructive for a project invested in the embeddedness of hope in the present. Bloch emphasizes that if hope is to serve a higher good, it must become manifest as a concrete, educated hope, as a '[w]issend-konkrete Hoffnung' ([1954] 2016: 3) or '*docta spes*' (8, emphasis in original), which is both firmly grounded in the possibilities, the 'Noch-Nicht' (8) or not-yet of the present ('noch ungewordene Möglichkeit' (5)), *and* oriented towards the future ('*Gewissen des Morgen, Parteilichkeit für die Zukunft*' (5, emphasis in original)). Hope, in Bloch's account, is the affect that mines the present for its futuristic potential. As such, it is ambiguously teleological: dissatisfied with the present, it always gestures towards a future, but its ultimate goal is a contentedness and sociability in the present, which Bloch calls 'Heimat' (1628).

While both Benjamin and Bloch evoke the concrete utopia of a socialist future, which they insist we should work towards in order to become fully human, Benjamin's *Jetztzeit* and Bloch's *Noch-Nicht* also serve as reminders of the importance of the here and now for conceptualizations of hope's relation to temporality. Over the course of the following chapters, I want to pay close attention to this presentist dimension of hope, and not yield to the pull of the future, which, for Bloch, Benjamin, and other socialist thinkers, gives pride of place to the telos of revolution and socialist liberation. While their utopic thinking remains a powerful source of inspiration for more recent theoretical projects of liberation and emancipation, their ultimately optimistic trust in social betterment and the dawning revolution, and their categorical rejection of pessimism[4] seem somewhat out of tune with a contemporary cultural mood dominated by the impeding climate catastrophe, hyper-capitalism, and ongoing global conflicts and social inequality. In order to arrive at a nuanced understanding of how the contemporary cultural imagination negotiates the affect of hope under conditions which, more often than not, do not see a future for humanity at all – never mind for a socialist revolution – we should, I believe, neither dismiss the bleakness of much contemporary fiction as mere fatalism, nor measure it by conventional understandings of hope that reduce it to its future-oriented tendencies. Instead, the body of works discussed in this book requires an approach that addresses hope as it emerges in the potentialities of the present moment, less in Bloch's sense of the teleological *Noch-Nicht*, but in true acknowledgement of the radical openness of the *Jetztzeit*, which cannot yet know where it is headed, but which unfolds its potential in acts of solidarity and the acknowledgement of pain and loss.

I find further inspiration for this kind of investigation in the productive tension between negativity and utopianism that has characterized the field of queer theory for the last two decades. Negotiating the place of queerness within different configurations of temporality and the social, arguments have recently been shifting away from negativity and what has been called the 'antisocial turn'[5] in queer theory towards more reparative theoretical and critical projects. On the whole, these debates have been conducted in terms of an unnecessarily stark opposition between paranoia and the reparative, the antisocial and optimism. In contrast, the novels, films, and series I engage with in this book try to navigate between a commitment to hope and a rejection of naïve optimism, while foregrounding the present as a temporal plane of reparative and queer affective investment. Going against the grain of current theoretical trends, I want to insist on the ongoing relevance of queer-negative thinking for an understanding of the contemporary cultural imagination, arguing for a disentanglement of queer negativity from antisociality as such in order to preserve the potential of queerness to sidestep dominant narratives of family, generation, and what it means to be and act together in the present. In this respect, my project

---

[4] Bloch calls pessimism the paralysis par excellence ('die Lähmung schlechthin', [1954] 2016: 518).

[5] The 'antisocial thesis' in queer theory is most often traced back to Leo Bersani's (1987, 1995) framing of homosexuality in general and homosexual sex in particular as politically unacceptable because they are, in a psychoanalytic sense, fundamentally opposed to relationality, community, and sociality. Only about a decade after Bersani's contributions, queer theorists began to bemoan what came to be perceived as a dominant association of queerness as such with negativity, anti-futurism, and the shattering of community and the political order (cf. Caserio et al. 2006, Halberstam 2008).

inscribes itself into debates surrounding queer temporality, and engages queer negativity to make an argument about hope in contemporary culture more generally.

Time and temporality and their relation to the politics of identity and representation have long been a central concern of queer theorizations. At the heart of these conversations lie questions of the (non-)normativity of linear and circular notions of time, and the relation of queerness with the temporality of reproduction and with structures of kinship.[6] At the same time, queer temporality, especially after the historical experience of the impossibility of a future for queer lives in the context of the AIDS epidemic, gets associated with 'a new emphasis on the here, the present, the now, and while the threat of no future hovers overhead like a storm cloud, the urgency of being also expands the potential of the moment and ... squeezes new possibilities out of the time at hand' (Halberstam 2005: 2). Hope for the queer subject, in this logic, must lie outside and beyond the linear temporal framework of a long and healthy life within the scripts of reproductive futures. These considerations of the shortened horizon of queerness strongly resonate with a wider contemporary cultural mood in which the climate emergency and a global pandemic seem to uncannily generalize the queer-temporal experience of 'no future'. Taking this observation as a starting point, I argue throughout this book that queerness' scepticism of reproductive futures and of optimistic framings of hope becomes a fundamental feature of contemporary cultural expression and facilitates the movement of queer subjectivity and its attendant temporalities into the popular mainstream. The texts I enter into conversation with negotiate affective investments in different notions of time under catastrophic conditions, entangling questions of hope with the formation, dissolution, and re-emergence of structures of care and belonging, while the heterosexual, nuclear family often remains a prominent (if damaged) frame of reference.

As such, these texts heavily resonate with queerness' embracing of negativity and non-reproductive temporalities prominently articulated by Lee Edelman in *No Future*, his polemic against 'reproductive futurism' (2004: 2). Edelman takes seriously the suggestion that, in a Lacanian framework, queerness emerges as that which the symbolic frames as fundamentally opposed to the order of the social. If queerness thus figures the death drive of the social – the impossible and transgressive desire for the pain of pure *jouissance* – then queerness cannot and should not aspire to integration into the social. For Edelman, the figure which epitomizes the drama of this antithetical relation between queerness and the social is the Child, 'whose innocence solicits our

---

[6]As Jack Halberstam proposes, '[q]ueer uses of time and space develop, at least in part, in opposition to the institutions of family, heterosexuality, and reproduction ... [Queer time] is also about the potentiality of a life unscripted by the conventions of family, inheritance, and child rearing' (2005: 1, 2).

defense' (2). The abstract Child – which never comes to mean actual children – is symbolically invested to be 'the emblem of futurity's unquestioned value' (4), and this future necessarily excludes the queer. Since abstract queerness is thus forced to signify the flipside of the social, the concrete homosexual, Edelman concludes, must do away with hope, which is only an affective and collectively obsessive investment in a future which, for him, will never come. He recommends, in playful reference to Lacan, to all '*sinthom*osexuals who figure the death drive of the social' (153, emphasis in original) and the unmaking of the heteronormative social order 'to refuse the insistence of hope itself as affirmation, which is always affirmation of an order whose refusal will register as unthinkable, irresponsible, inhumane' (4), and 'to insist that the future stop here' (31). Hope, for Edelman, thus figures as a mere affirmation of heteronormativity's ultimately harmful investment in a teleological fiction of fulfilment in a future in which the queer will be dead and the Child will be safe.[7]

I want to take Edelman's employment of the figure of the Child as a starting point for thinking about the ambiguous relationship between the powerful and paranoid narrative of reproductive futurism, and those elements that disturb, distort, and complicate the linear streamlining of narrative's relation to temporality in contemporary fiction. Where Edelman's *No Future* exemplifies queer negativity's embrace of the antisocial, and of queerness' seemingly necessary commitment to anti-futuristic temporalities, José Muñoz' evocation of queer utopianism powerfully argues for a queer reclaiming of the future. Muñoz rejects the proposition that if there is hope for queers, it cannot lie in the future, and argues instead that 'the future is queerness's domain … The here and now is a prison house. We must strive, in the face of the here and now's totalizing rendering of reality, to think and feel and *then and there*' (2009: 1, emphasis in original). Muñoz explicitly orients his argument by Bloch's concept of a concrete utopia as 'the realm of educated hope' which is opposed to 'banal optimism'; and, in parallel to Bloch's *Noch-Nicht*, he posits hope as an 'affective structure' that is 'anticipatory' (3). My critique of Muñoz aligns with my critique of Bloch: I do not think that the anticipatory nature of hope and its characteristic potentialities and possibilities absolutely necessitate a commitment to futurity. Muñoz' argument, however, resonates with my own in that he emphasizes hope's structural alignment with the making of community. Like him, I understand 'queerness as collectivity' (11); but where he insists that queerness and community are structurally opposed to singularity and negativity, and that 'queerness is primarily about futurity and hope' (11),

---

[7]Although, to an extent, Edelman's nuanced engagement with rhetoric and psychoanalysis resists reductive receptions such as mine (cf. McEleney 2019), I deliberately foreground a thematic reading of his argument to make it available to my own tracings of the nexus of negativity and kinship in contemporary fiction.

I argue that the hope and the commitment to the idea of community which queerness entails can emerge from the very negativity and anti-futurism Muñoz and other queer utopianists argue against.

Hence, in this book, instead of rejecting 'the stultifying temporal logic of a broken-down present' (12), my aim is to delve into this very broken present, and to demonstrate how an acknowledgement of its pains and losses can open up possibilities and potentialities which, perhaps counter-intuitively, emerge as a kind of hope in times of no future. I ask how fictional texts can simultaneously be invested in teleology and make futuristic notions of hope impossible through temporal distortions, dialectical characterizations, and specific kinds of fictional setting. I look for the disturbances in the grand narratives, the moments of weakness and liberation that appear against the foil of naïve hopefulness in popular fictional narration. Together with Jack Halberstam, I ask: 'what comes after hope? ... What is the alternative ... to cynical resignation on the one hand and naïve optimism on the other?' (2011: 1). And like Halberstam, I commit to literary and critical reading practices that engage with both high-brow and popular texts to discover that 'to live is to fail, to bungle, to disappoint, and ultimately to die' (186–7). Criticism of this polemically anarchic kind obviously raises questions of hierarchy and privilege, both on the level of academic discourse (What kind of position enables someone to 'embrace' failure?), and in the fictional material itself (Is reparation a luxury of the powerful? Are the weak condemned to paranoia?). While I intend to address these questions in this book, I also want to take seriously the implications of the consequences of the potential failure of hope and kinship.

Generally speaking, then, my understanding of hope is emphatically distinct from common conceptualizations of optimism, and more akin to a – albeit very sober – version of Bloch's *docta spes*. Hope's relationship with optimism, however, deserves some further consideration, because recent critical debate has productively revolved around the positive and negative affective properties of optimism, and its relevance for an engagement with both literature and emancipatory politics. Michael Snediker argues for a reconceptualization of a specifically *queer* optimism not as future-oriented, but as concerned with drawing attention to our affective investments in the present: '[q]ueer optimism ... is not promissory. It doesn't ask that some future time make good on its own hopes. Rather, *Queer Optimism* asks that optimism, embedded in its own immanent present, might be *interesting*' (2009: 2, emphasis in original). Queer optimism, in Snediker's sense, is 'immanently rather than futurally oriented' (3). As such, it is less associated with the affective horizon of futurist hope than with affects like shame, which draw the subject into the experience of the present moment. Like Snediker, I am interested in how to think and conceptualize anti-futurism without giving way to destructive negativity and nihilism; and like him, I take hope's temporalities to emerge as more interesting, layered, and nuanced once they get dissociated from the predictable scripts of teleology. Where Snediker speaks of optimism, however, I prefer to speak of hope, which, I believe, is semantically more open to ambiguous associations, and less determined by the upbeat thrust of its everyday usage.

In this sense, this book is committed to fleshing out the ambiguously hopeful intensities of the here and now as they emerge in contemporary fictional narration. With Lauren Berlant, I assume that many of the attachments that make up the affective registers of hope and optimism are 'cruel' in the sense of not necessarily being enjoyable or even sustaining, and that these affects are best understood by turning to 'the production of the present' (2011: 4) and to the dynamics of 'the emerging event' (5), that is, to instances of agency and occurrence that rely on spontaneity and improvisation in the here and now. This kind of attention to affective structures of attachment enables an understanding of the present as 'immanence, emanation, atmosphere, or emergence' (6). It is in these structures of potentiality that I locate hope – a hope that manifests itself in the context of catastrophic temporalities, where the present appears as 'a moment in extended crisis, with one happening piling on another' (7). Like Berlant, I understand hope as 'manifest[ing] in attachments and the desire to sustain them', while these attachments remain ambiguous in effect and can range 'from the romantic to the fatalistic to the numb to the nothing' (13). Berlant here already points towards what will be central to my own argument: the close affinity between hope and the structures of belonging and care that I will be referring to as kinship. Where hope's investment in the potentialities of the present emerges as a dominant modality of crisis narratives, 'the often cruel promise of reciprocity and belonging' (21) appears as that which sustains the attachments that bind subjects to the world and to each other.

My theoretical interest, then, lies in an insistence to not let go of the epistemological and experiential insights that negativity can provide. Attention to the ambiguous temporal and social attachments that characterize the contemporary fictional imaginary can yield important insights when the negativity inherent in these narratives is not simply denounced and rejected as a perverse indulgence while, allegedly, what we 'really' need is a turn away from the depressing present towards a renewed investment in stories of better futures. I want to insist that a critical engagement with the pains, temporal ruptures, and social devastations at the heart of the texts I enter into conversation with is a worthwhile task, and that moments of reparation and sustenance emerge from these sites of crisis in unexpected ways. In this sense, I take my cue from the insight that, as Alexis Lothian puts it, '[t]he end of the world as we know it seems continually imminent' (2018: 2). Lothian goes on to engage a corpus of 'old futures', texts from the past that imagine a future horizon which she activates for our present, arguing, against Edelman, for a more nuanced account of different possible futures (some of them reproductive) in queer cultural production. Her effort to complicate binary understandings of the relationship between queerness and futurity is an important contribution to queer theory's positioning within wider contemporary crisis narratives. And her engagement of 'the dense futurities of the present' (21) in an attempt to 'resist[] and challenge[] the logics of progressive developmental time' while 'acknowledg[ing] the impossibility of letting go of them entirely' (24) inspire my own thinking about the queer potentialities of the here and now. Where Lothian's interest, however, lies in locating queer reproductive futures that escape the logics of normative time and a futurity that is 'dissipated among moments of joy, pain, sex, love, oppression, and resistance' (28), I explicitly depart from her argument in stubbornly sticking with the anti-futurist hopes emerging from many popular contemporary texts which firmly locate the possibility of reparative hope in their 'implicit present potentialities' (29).

In order for queer theory to resonate with other strands of contemporary thinking that acknowledge the devastating realities and temporal consequences of current social and environmental crises, it must be patient enough to engage the darkened horizons of these times in order to see what still becomes possible, how hope and kinship intersect in the storm clouds of the here and now. This kind of thinking is, I believe, less akin to naïve optimism than to a *docta spes* appropriate for our times.

A mutuality of being: Kinship

Throughout the following chapters, I argue not only that the fictional texts under consideration locate hope in the present moment, but also that kinship – in the sense of structures of belonging and care that bind individuals to one another and to the world – becomes a site on which hope plays out in the form of (positive or negative) affective investments in mutuality. 'Kinship' is a contested and controversial concept. Forever tied to naturalizing and universalizing notions of the heterosexual, patriarchal family,[8] and intimately

---

[8]In the introduction to a classic volume on *The Family in History*, Charles E. Rosenberg, for example, observes about the cultural, social, and economic efficacy of the family that it 'is a primary reality not only in terms of individual emotional development but in terms of social and economic organization as well. The family functions as a mode of structuring sexual relationships, kinship relations, and child rearing – but also as a source of labor and capital accumulation, as a mechanism for the transmission of property and the imposition of social control' (1975: 8). Marilyn J. Coleman and Lawrence H. Ganong, too, in the introduction to their much more recent *Social History of the American Family*, maintain that '[a]s a fundamental unit of society, families exert powerful influences on virtually every aspect of the culture' (2014: xxxii). At the same time, historians have established that 'the family as a form changes over time' (Rosenberg 1975: 8), and with it the meanings, realities, and contexts associated with it. Most crucially, although the 'nuclear family' (father, mother, children) – what, in a US context,

associated with western imperialism and the history of slavery,[9] kinship has nevertheless been an integral part of queer, feminist, and critical race theory. Despite its semantic awkwardness and its violent historical legacies, kinship, as a critical concept, remains productive for thinking about the modes of belonging I explore in this book. With Tyler Bradway and Elizabeth Freeman, I want to consider the forms of relations I trace in the following chapters in terms of their '*kincoherence*', the ambiguous flow of 'forces, desires, practices, relations, institutions, and forms that render kinship a horizon of violence and possibility' (2022: 3, emphasis in original). In the context of this book's argument, I am interested in the ways contemporary fiction explores notions of kinship that position themselves against and alongside notions of the family as 'nuclear', heterosexual, and reproductive, without idealizing the ostensibly 'liberating' potential of such notions. As Judith Butler points out, kinship is always politically regulated, bound to 'social, legal, and economic powers and institutions' (2022: 26). But it also always bears potential for 'unexpected filiations' (47). Bearing this ambivalence in mind, in my readings of the material under discussion, I trace the tensions between narrow understandings of kinship and wider, more improvised, less established, queerer, and more diverse conceptualizations of structures of belonging and care that emerge under precarious circumstances as places from which hope becomes possible. Acknowledging that the trope of the nuclear family alone cannot adequately capture the dynamics of attachment, inclusion, and exclusion unfolding in contemporary crisis narratives, I foreground an understanding of kinship as first and foremost a concept that describes and denotes the emerging and performative nature of relationality and belonging. Kinship's conceptual 'affinity to a larger community than that of the family' (West-Pavlov 2020: 37) makes it an extremely useful category for an analysis of contemporary culture's reconfigurations of care and belonging under precarious circumstances. These reconfigurations, in a lot of contemporary fiction (and theory), oscillate between holding on to the structures and fantasies attached to the nuclear family, and acknowledging that, in the final analysis, '[t]he populations of the globe are irreducibly related to one another and that interrelatedness, that vast kinship, has been

---

is often referred to as the Standard North American Family (cf. Coleman and Ganong 2014: xxxi) – is still often assumed to be 'a universal human social grouping' (Murdock 1949: 2) that exists across cultures, its ideological primacy in western societies is a historically fairly recent phenomenon, which carries implications of nation, economic organization, and the institutionalization of reproduction and care. Brigitte Berger (1998), for example, demonstrates how the nuclear family and the capitalist system that was the prerequisite for European imperialism and western dominance are mutually constitutive historical developments.

[9] As Christopher Chamberlin observes, '[s]lavery is essential to the structure and historical formation of modern kinship … Slavery compels the defensive invention of conservative notions of kinship' (2022: 217, 223).

the driver of cultural history' (ibid.). Definitions of kinship are thus also determined by questions of scale: the usefulness of the concept hinges upon the tension between very narrow and very broad understandings of who can conceivably be taken to be each other's kin. In my own analysis, it is precisely the tensions between biological and social, and between very local and very global notions of kinship that animate the stories I engage with in this book.

Within anthropology, the discipline most readily associated with the study of kinship and its relevance for different societies, the term has always been ambiguous. While early studies tend to privilege specifically biological kinship ties, scholars have increasingly emphasized the social and cultural nature of kinship systems.[10] For my own analyses in this book, Marshall Sahlins' argument in favour of a wide and performative notion of kinship proves to be particularly productive. Sahlins rejects the possibility that kinship can have any fundamental or essential grounding in biology which exists somehow prior to or beyond the social and ever-emerging notions of affective relationality that any group or individual ascribes to it. In consequence, he argues for an understanding of kinship as a '"mutuality of being": kinfolk are persons who participate intrinsically in each other's existence; they are members of one another' (2013: ix). This definition of kinship includes all forms of socially meaningful belonging, be they based on lineage and procreation, or on ritual and performative ascription. Kinship is thus never a fixed or permanent state that an individual or group find themselves in; instead, it emerges over time in contexts of care and concern, is subject to change, and carries the potential for growth or diminishment. Sahlins' elaborations allow for an understanding of kinship that can capture vastly different scales of relationality, since its definitional basis rests solely on mutual affective investment and responsibility. As such, kinship as 'mutuality of being' can account for the varying iterations of notions of care and belonging that characterize, as I will go on to demonstrate, a lot

---

[10]As Gayle Rubin puts it, 'a kinship system is not a list of biological relatives. It is a system of categories and statuses which often contradict actual genetic relationships' (1975: 169). Beginning with Lewis Henry Morgan's 1871 *Systems of Consanguinity and Affinity of the Human Family*, early studies of human kinship systems were based on the assumptions that the development and maintaining of stable social structures were unique to humans, and that all humans shared an inherent valuation of specifically genealogical ties. At the same time, however, Morgan himself and later scholars always already found evidence across societies of the usage of kinship terminology to describe social bonds beyond the immediate family. Over the course of the second half of the twentieth century, anthropologists such as David M. Schneider contributed to a general shift towards seeing kinship as primarily constructed, symbolic, and performative, rather than based on any 'natural' preconditions. Scholarship thus increasingly acknowledged that, in many if not all social contexts, who or what counts as kin and who or what does not, more often than not extends far beyond the sphere of lineage and marriage.

of contemporary theory and fiction. These iterations unfold on a spectrum that reaches from the enduring economic, emotional, and ideological relevance of the reproductive human family to the increasingly urgent foregrounding of multiple and unpredictable lines of connection across time, space, and species.

While more radical theorizing importantly deconstructs the anthropocentrism at the heart of many more conservative understandings of kinship in order to emphasize humanity's embeddedness in larger structures of responsibility, my own interest in the particular kind of fiction I engage with in this book entails a certain anthropocentric bias. My analyses are concerned with how, in fictional worlds that put the *human* experience of major crisis at their centre, a detachment of hope from futuristic investment aligns with inventive reconfigurations of structures of care and belonging under conditions of social, environmental, and personal devastation. Queer theorizations of kinship prove particularly productive for this line of argument. Where queer theory has long been fundamentally concerned with conceptualizing the relationship between affect, attachment, and temporality, scholars of LGBTIQ history and subjectivity have also crucially contributed to analysing the workings of kinship in contemporary society. Taking their cue from the empirical observation that queer emancipation has often come along with conflicted relationships with and renegotiations of networks of care and support, scholars of queer kinship have foregrounded the individual stakes in queer subjects' search for structures of belonging in urban communities, the ongoing relevance of families of origin, and the difficult conceptual relationship between queer anti-normativity and state-sanctioned forms of sexuality and care. Studies of gay and lesbian communities, from Kath Weston to Heather Murray, have complicated easy assumptions about the relationship between 'chosen families' and 'families of origin'.[11] While my own analyses of contemporary fictional texts put less focus on fully established queer identities, tracing instead a variety of kinship dynamics

---

[11]The central finding of Weston's research is that, contrary to the clichéd expectation that all queer subjects experience ostracism from their biological families and, as a consequence, seek out alternative kinship networks, 'chosen families do not directly oppose genealogical modes of reckoning kinship. Instead, they undercut procreation's status as a master term imagined to provide the template for all possible kinship relations. In displacing rather than disallowing biogenetic symbolism, discourse on gay families moves obliquely toward the future, responding to hegemonic forms of kinship not with a defensive countermove, but by deftly stepping aside to evade the paradigmatic blow' (1991: 213). Murray makes a similar point about the historical development of queer emancipation in the United States: 'families were always integral to these developments ... The family remained a symbol of care, intergenerational ties, and eternal relationships that shaped the revelations of gay selves, even amid anxieties or ideas about family excommunications' (2010: x, xi).

under socially, culturally, and individually precarious conditions, these arguments are important frames of reference. The texts I enter into conversation with, while engaging to varying degrees with questions of sexual identity, all foreground the precarious symbolic status of the heterosexual family and, in particular, the figure of the Child, and propose reconfigurations of kinship that respond to the different catastrophic scenarios that draw these stories and their protagonists into the present moment.

Apart from the everyday relevance of conflicting conceptualizations of kinship for queer subjects and their lives, queer theorists have also highlighted the tension between emancipatory politics aimed at the recognition of non-normative forms of kinship by the state and the antinormative thrust of queerness that recognizes the exclusions produced by what Lisa Duggan (2002) calls 'homonormativity' – the attainment of 'equal' rights for those queers who can reproduce heteronormative (gendered, racial, economic) ideals at the expense of those who will not or cannot live up to these ideals. As an alternative to the lure of kinship normativity, Judith Butler considers a radical understanding of kinship as 'relationships of various kinds which negotiate the reproduction of life and the demands of death', and kinship practices as 'those that emerge to address fundamental forms of human dependency' (2002: 15). Butler's analysis of the mutually constitutive dynamic of inclusion and exclusion in queer emancipatory politics is instructive for my readings in the following chapters. While social and political authorities and institutions are largely (and conspicuously) absent from most of these stories, much of the narrative suspense they produce arises from negotiations of who gets recognized as kin and who as 'other', and under which circumstances, while those in the inevitable residue get pushed to the margins of signification and lose their status as humans deserving of care and concern.

The processes of inclusion and exclusion implied in questions of queer kinship have long discursive ties with the relationship between kinship and race, especially in an American context. As Saidiya Hartman puts it, 'slavery is the ghost in the machine of kinship' (qtd. in Butler 2002: 15). Since Carol B. Stack's 1974 study of poor Black communities in the United States, in which she insists on the centrality of extended kinship networks for the creation of mutual support systems among African American families, scholars of the history of slavery and racism have emphasized both the systematic and violent ruptures of lineage in the slave trade, and the ongoing vital importance of *both* social *and* biological kinship ties to families and communities of colour in a racist society. Theorizations of queer kinship, too, have been grappling with the tension between a glorification of improvised urban gay families and the social, cultural, and economic realities that have queer subjects of colour continue to depend on their families and communities of origin.¹² While race and racism are no primary points of reference for my own argument, the fact that I engage mostly with US-American fiction and theory necessitates a basic awareness of the intersections between (queer) kinship and race. The centrality, in these texts, of renegotiations of family and belonging itself cannot be fully understood outside of their particular cultural context.¹³ Over the course of the following chapters, and in my readings of texts that imagine the family in crisis and kinship as determined by both economic circumstances and the politics of inclusion and exclusion, I want to bear in mind the specific histories and legacies of kinship in Anglo-American culture. In all the stories under consideration, even if they do not foreground race as a primary concern, these histories are present in the post-apocalyptic, global, humanist, and hopeful imaginaries that unfold in these narratives.

While centuries of dominant thinking in the west have worked to eclipse long and vital histories of lived kinship that have always extended beyond the patriarchal family, the logic of human ownership of the earth, and the domination of one race over the other, critics of colour and indigenous theorists have highlighted existing traditions of kinship in non-western worldviews. Daniel Heath Justice, for example, proposes a decolonial

---

¹²David Eng draws attention to the historical racialization of the spheres of family and kinship in the United States, arguing that 'queer liberalism relies upon the logic of colorblindness in its assertion that racial difference has given way to an abstract U.S. community of individualism and merit' (2010: 3), and that 'queer liberalism is predicated on the systematic dissociation of (homo)sexuality from race as coeval and intersecting phenomena' (4). He goes on to insist that 'we must resist the idealized notion of family and kinship relations as somehow removed from or eccentric to the racial tensions, cultural differences, and national conflicts that continue to define our domestic and global political economies and conditions of existence' (8), and that we need a language of kinship that can account for the queer diasporic experience. Along similar lines, Richard T. Rodríguez contends that, in the context of Chicano/a queer politics, the family of origin remains a central frame of reference, and 'reconfigured kinship arrangements need not be established in mutual exclusivity from biological relations ... For Chicano/a queers ... disinheriting one's biologically given family is a near impossible task considering how blood ties often prove invaluable' (2013: 324–5).

¹³As Holly Jackson demonstrates, rhetorics and ideologies surrounding the family have been at the heart of US-American national identification since the early days of the nation. The nineteenth century saw debates between those who considered the domestic family and genealogical thinking as detrimental to the republican project, and those that idealized the family as a nationalist cornerstone (cf. 2014: 4). At the same time, genealogical pride was ideologically transferred from old-world aristocratic dynasticism onto a narrative of 'nationalism as a modern blood identity' (6), which, at the same time, reinforced racist exclusions: '[w]hite Americanness emerged as a modern form of citizenship by excluding peoples constructed as genealogically determined, even while the conceptual roots of nationalism in ancestry and blood relation were disavowed' (13). In the long run, these ideologies 'gave rise to what we now call "family values" political rhetoric: the strength of the nation-state depends on the health of the family, a vulnerable institution that must be protected at any cost' (14).

understanding of kinship, arguing that the project of decolonizing knowledge and knowledge practices must incorporate specifically indigenous experiences and understandings of kinship, which then, in turn, materializes not as an epistemological or ontological category, but as an emergent practice.[14] My point is not to disingenuously appropriate indigenous theories of kinship for other projects. However, for anyone concerned with notions of kinship beyond the scope of the heteronormative and patriarchal, it is crucial to acknowledge that practices of kinship which manifest themselves as reparative processes in the contemporary political, social, and cultural landscape are not 'inventions' of western (post-)postmodernity. Rather, rigid notions and classifications of kinship as exclusively denoting blood relations and heterosexual lineage are fundamentally colonial knowledge projects that we need to unlearn in order to arrive at a more open and liberated perspective on kinship. A critical framing of kinship which takes into account the term's intersections with histories of racism and colonization might enable new and better understandings of contemporary literary and cultural practices and the lived realities of many people, and lay bare the stakes implicit in shifting notions of community and belonging. Resisting simplistic perspectives on kinship and human relations also means resisting both a narrowing of the hermeneutic potential of kinship and an impoverished understanding of lived and shared experience and practice. Such thoughtful resistance can enable better and more inclusive knowledge about shared pains and shared responsibilities. With these considerations in mind, I take my cue from Justice to understand kinship first and foremost as a verb, a doing, a process, something that emerges, in the fictional material I engage with in this book, as a sustaining and hopeful mode of existence in contexts of individual and collective precarity.

The study of kinship – queer and otherwise – is always political, not least because the concept itself moves across shifting definitional terrain. Arguments addressing specific configurations of kinship will also always inevitably

---

[14] As Justice puts it, 'it's not about something that *is* in itself so much as something we *do* – actively, thoughtfully, respectfully ... [K]inship is best thought of as a verb rather than a noun' (2008: 148, 150, emphasis in original). At the same time, kinship, for Justice, is also an 'interpretive concept[]' (149) that emerges as part of the project of developing a Native literary criticism, and which is thus key to an understanding of indigenous literatures. He explicitly pits an indigenous understanding of belonging and community against 'the individualist ethos of Eurowestern academe' (153), and argues that established western epistemological frameworks and traditions are inadequate for indigenous criticism. Politically speaking, Justice's emphasis on kinship also works towards more effective agency for indigenous peoples within a racist context. The expansive and embracing scope of kinship, he argues, has the potential to unite indigenous nations in their fight for survival and cultural expression, whereas debates about racial purity and originality only lead to separatism 'in a country that prizes blood purity above kinship obligations' (158): '[k]inship is adaptive; race, as a threatened constitutive commodity, always runs the risk of becoming washed out to the point of insignificance' (159).

argue for a narrower or wider understanding of who and what should count as kin. Most often, arguments in favour of a narrow understanding of kinship will also tend more towards privileging the family, the clan, lineage, and reproduction as primary points of reference. Tendencies towards wider and more inclusive notions of kinship can be found in projects which have political stakes in disabling the heteronormative, nationalist, and racist implications of an exclusive focus on family and descent, and in emphasizing instead the 'mutuality of being' shared by all humans, and by humans and non-humans on this planet. These latter arguments often emerge from a sense of urgency in the face of social inequality and ecological devastation. As Russell West-Pavlov speculates, 'we may need to begin to think in terms of a planetary kinship in which each member is related to all the others, and each plays a part in securing the wellbeing of all others' (2020: 40). His call for recognizing kinship as a global category of the Anthropocene and as an 'irreducibly ethical' (ibid.) principle echoes Donna Haraway's urgent contention that, in times of planet-wide ecological devastation, we need 'to make kin in lines of inventive connection as a practice to live and die well with each other in a thick present' (2016: 1). In contrast to West-Pavlov, however, Haraway explicitly grounds her argument in the present: instead of 'succumbing to abstract futurism and its affects of sublime despair and its politics of sublime indifference', she argues for a stubborn presentism that arises out of the urgent insight that 'we require each other in unexpected collaborations and combinations, in hot compost piles. We become-with each other or not at all' (4).

While my own argument in this book ultimately remains focused on *human* communities and the inventive itineraries of *human* kin-making, Haraway's insistence on mutual responsibility and creative connection in the crowded present provides useful guidance for my attempt to conceptualize hope and kinship as entangled concepts. My readings of the body of material under consideration are inspired by the realization that, in times in which the horizon has darkened, 'we succumb to despair or to hope, and neither is a sensible attitude' (4). Throughout the following chapters, I argue that, in contemporary fictional negotiations of time and belonging, a kind of hope emerges which turns away from the future, speaks to the urgencies of the present, and finds expression in 'lines of inventive connection'. Taking my cue from Haraway, I engage hope as an affect that animates the present in troubled times. My corpus of novels, films, and series proposes speculative answers to her observation that 'we need stories (and theories) that are just big enough to gather up the complexities and keep the edges open and greedy for surprising new and old connections' (101). I am interested in practices of inventive kin-making that do not necessarily follow the scripts of reproduction and genealogy, and my analyses in the following chapters will resonate repeatedly with Haraway's proposition to 'Make Kin Not Babies!' (102). The texts under consideration locate hope not in futuristic projections that often align with fantasies of reproduction, but instead in the practices of care and concern that make a good life (and a good death) in the present possible.

Overall, then, my analytical sympathies lie with broader understandings of kinship. However, for the purpose of this book, and to do justice to the specificities of the individual fictional texts, instead of absolutely opting for one particular definition, I want to primarily foreground the inventive, performative, contextual, and ambivalent nature of kinship, and the tensions of scale that emerge from the literature dealing with the concept. All of the texts under consideration in the following chapters position themselves, in one form or another, vis-à-vis the ideal of the heterosexual family, and most of them contain child characters that occupy sometimes predictable, sometimes surprising positions in relation to the ideological baggage of Edelman's figurative Child. These stories also all, however, present alternative visions of care and belonging under devastating circumstances.

How to read: Postcritique, reparative and hopeful reading

Where hope and kinship emerge as dominant themes in contemporary narrative fiction, these themes – and their attendant tensions between teleological and non-teleological notions of time, and narrow and wide notions of kinship – are also intimately entangled with theoretical concerns about epistemology and method. Recent theorizations of reparative and postcritical reading in the humanities provide important methodological inspiration for a project concerned with dynamics of temporality and belonging in contemporary literature and cultural theory. Over the course of the last few decades, debates about the merits and limits of dominant methodologies and about the state of critical theory have animated scholarship in the humanities. Several theorists have questioned the seeming ubiquity of what Paul Ricoeur (1970) calls a 'hermeneutics of suspicion', a tendency of contemporary critical theory to place all its bets on interpretative acts of unveiling, exposure, and ideology critique. Increasingly, the question arose whether this understanding of critical thinking in general and literary criticism in particular does not ultimately exhaust itself in tautological acts of writerly self-aggrandisement, instead of providing valuable insights beyond the mere confirmation of presupposed knowledge. Critical engagement with questions of inequality, power relations, and the workings of ideology – whether Marxist, Freudian, or Foucauldian – has certainly contributed (and continues to contribute) to enabling literary criticism and critical theory to ask questions about the social world, where earlier forms of criticism 'proper' often remained within the limits of aesthetic inquiry. Eve Kosofsky Sedgwick (2003), Bruno Latour (2004),[15] Rita Felski (2015), and others ask, however, what gets lost when suspicious reading and theorizing become the *only* mood recognized as legitimately 'critical'. Although 'suspicious' or 'paranoid' epistemologies are effective – and in certain contexts undeniably necessary – when the critical (and political) task at hand demands the reiterative laying-bare of structures of violence and oppression, critical thinking should not (and does not), these scholars argue, restrict itself to such modes of inquiry. Instead, they call for 'reparative' and 'postcritical' moods and modes of thinking and writing that enable epistemological effects and affects other than those achieved by the self-affirming search for hidden meanings.

My interest here does not primarily lie in participating in the postcritical debate – in offering a fully fledged methodological alternative to critique, or in even positing critique and postcritique as mutually exclusive. Instead, my own concern is twofold. On the one hand, I want to consider how reparative epistemology productively aligns, on a methodological level, with cultural reflections about non-teleological and non-linear conceptualizations of time and generation, and with an interest in notions of care and belonging. On the other hand, I suggest that reparative and postcritical hermeneutical *attitudes* lend themselves particularly well for the project at hand, which thus inscribes itself both into a cultural conversation about the limits of narrow notions of hope and kinship, and into a critical tradition that calls for a reconfiguration of hermeneutics along lines of creative connection.

Although Sedgwick's essay on paranoid and reparative reading, first published as part of the introduction to *Novel Gazing* in 1997 and then as a full chapter of *Touching Feeling* in 2003, is regularly credited with introducing the postcritical discussion into both literary and queer studies, her choice of vocabulary, taken from Melanie Klein's writing on psychoanalysis and Sylvan Tomkins' on affect theory, is now often dismissed

---

[15]Although, not primarily aimed at literary studies, Latour's call for a turn towards '*matters of concern*' (2004: 231, emphasis in original) in critical inquiry is instructive for thinking about a hermeneutics most appropriate for a project interested in hope and kinship. He asks the critic to move beyond suspicion and deconstruction to see their object of study as a rich assemblage, as a thing that only comes into being through various forms of kinship and connection: '[t]he critic is not the one who debunks, but the one who assembles. The critic is … the one for whom, if something is constructed, then it means it is fragile and thus in great need of care and concern' (246). Latour's critic approaches their material with openness, a careful interest in detail, with attention to the affective economies involved in the act of encountering an object of inquiry, and with the aim of opening up rather than closing down chains of association in the act of interpretation, so that critique becomes 'associated with *more*, not with *less*, with *multiplication*, not *subtraction*' (248, emphasis in original).

as too closely situated in the vicinity of the psychopathological.[16] I myself, however, find Sedgwick's framing of the two critical moods she contrasts enduringly productive. While she clearly distinguishes her understanding of critical paranoia from clinical psychiatric phenomena, taking her cue from Klein enables her to theorize paranoid and reparative critical modalities as co-existing in a text, and as enabling different effects and affects on different local levels of production and reception of the same material. Most crucially for my purpose, Sedgwick foregrounds paranoid and reparative modalities of reading and knowing in terms of their different relations to temporality and belonging. Instead of contrasting paranoid and reparative critical projects in terms of their political value, she foregrounds their different scope and orientation. Paranoid and reparative hermeneutics, she argues, generate, among other effects, contrasting frames of temporality and kinship. The anticipatory character of paranoia, for example, entails a 'unidirectionally future-oriented vigilance' (2003: 130) which forecloses the possibility that the present might bear the potential for something other than paranoia's worst fears; it being reflexive and mimetic does not allow for agency that takes into consideration the benevolent embrace of the 'other'; and as a strong theory of negative affects, Sedgwick proposes, paranoia as critical method reduces the local nuance and ambiguous dynamics of scholarly inquiry to tautological and teachable reiterations about the 'truth' of pain, loss, and oppression. Strikingly, for Sedgwick, a reparative critical position would not necessarily be more optimistic about the state of the world than paranoia. However, while 'both epistemologies are likely to be based on a deep pessimism' (138), reparation's search for pleasure invests its energies in critical impulses that generate sustenance and connection. Where paranoia places its bets on exposure, reparative critical projects sidestep the knee-jerk impulse to know in advance all the horrors that are to be discovered. Instead, they complement the predictable mechanisms of unveiling with local strategies such as 'tonal nuance, attitude, worldly observation, performative paradox, aggression, tenderness, wit, inventive reading, obiter dicta, and writerly panache' (135–6).[17] Sedgwick thus frames paranoia as a strong theory that positions the writerly subject 'in the know' in opposition to some

---

[16]Felski, for instance, while acknowledging Sedgwick's important influence, 'prefer[s] ... to avoid terminology that conjures up the picture of a clinician peering suspiciously into the soul of a recalcitrant patient' (2015: 35).

[17]Some critics have argued that Sedgwick's heavy emphasis on readerly disposition is ethically and politically suspect. Carolyn Laubender, for example, in returning to Klein's theories, posits that reparative endeavours potentially silence the object of inquiry because they almost exclusively rely on the subject's/critic's own attitudes towards their object, which might have 'little to do with the status of the object as the (potentially unwilling) recipient of such assignations of injury and repair' (2019: 53). David Eng goes a step further in calling the

ignorant 'other', and as heavily invested in a teleological progression from knowable past to predictable future. In contrast, she proposes reparative reading as a set of hermeneutic practices that acknowledges the need, in literary criticism, for both 'strong' (global, overarching) and 'weak' (local, detailed) theory, and for a critical language which relates differently to temporality:

> [T]o a reparatively positioned reader, it can seem realistic and necessary to experience surprise … Hope, often a fracturing, even a traumatic thing to experience, is among the energies by which the reparatively positioned reader tries to organise the fragments and part-objects she encounters or creates. Because the reader realises that the future may be different from the present, it is also possible for her to entertain such profoundly painful, profoundly relieving, ethically crucial possibilities as that the past, in turn, could have happened differently from the way it actually did. (146)

Where hope here manifests itself as a critical temporality that sidesteps the paranoid logic of knowing in advance what the critic might find, Sedgwick also associates reparative epistemologies with queer and non-reproductive forms of kinship that live and think outside the 'Oedipal regularity and repetitiveness' characteristic of paranoia: 'isn't it a feature of queer possibility … that our generational relations don't always proceed in this lockstep?' (147). In her own queer friendships, shaped by queer sexuality and determined by the temporal logic of terminal illness, Sedgwick discovers ways of being and thinking that are painfully aware of 'the present fullness of a becoming whose arc may extend no further, who we each must learn best to apprehend, fulfil, and bear company' (149). For Sedgwick, a reparative critical mode thus emerges from an existential need for ways of knowing, thinking, and being which account for the knowledge and insight of those who 'know there isn't time to bullshit' (149), and which recognize the immediacies and potentialities of the present moment, without prematurely resorting to grand narratives of paranoid prediction.

---

affective economies he finds in theories of reparation 'colonial object relations' (2014: 3). Also returning to Klein, Eng points out how her reliance on affective attitudes in the subject '*produce* good and bad objects in the first place, valued and devalued objects worthy and unworthy of repair' (6, emphasis in original), thus 'proleptically dissociat[ing] reparation form morality and justice' (9). While I would still insist that Sedgwick's nuanced elaborations on different kinds of reading remain extremely useful – and I believe that, to an extent, this kind of criticism emerges from a lack of differentiation between Klein's and Sedgwick's understanding of the reparative position/impulse – these critics helpfully point out the power imbalances inherent in any interpretive project.

Although Sedgwick refrains from prescribing a concrete methodological recipe, apart from promoting the value of 'imaginative close reading' (145), her elaborations are an invaluable starting point for thinking about hermeneutics and method in the context of a project on hope and kinship in fiction. Her exploration of paranoid and reparative critical positions both provides a useful set of terms for reading different epistemological modalities that works of fiction themselves produce, and encourages this particular reader to put less emphasis on catering to the protocols of paranoid exposure – although I will not fully refrain from ideology critique – and more on exploring what kinds of connection, association, and worldmaking a particular piece of fiction enables. With Rita Felski, I understand all forms of critical reading as manifestations of moods and sensibilities, and a reparative – or, in Felski's terminology, 'postcritical' – readerly attitude as a commitment to entering into a conversation with the text, 'reflecting on what it unfurls, calls forth, makes possible' (2015: 12). Where Felksi associates suspicious critique with the teleological drive of utopian thought, because critical 'affirmation can only exist in a radically disjunctive relationship to a fallen present, i.e. in a far distant future' (189), postcritical reading places its bets with 'attaching, collating, negotiating, assembling – of forging links between things that were previously unconnected' (173); that is, it focuses on the multiplicities of a text's connections, associations, and entanglements in the past, present, and future, and across and to the side of such temporal divides.

While this book takes its cue, among other influences, from the pessimism and negativity of a certain stand of queer theory, and argues for not prematurely letting go of the energies that can unfold from anti-futuristic perspectives, I firmly locate this kind of negativity on the side of the reparative. While I agree that queer theory might have unfortunately and prematurely associated negativity with the antisocial, I argue that it is precisely in the vicinity of the negative, understood as a reparative positionality that sidesteps the automatized logics of both cultural (reproductive, progressive) and critical paranoia, that hope and kinship, as critical lenses, generate affirmative knowledge about the dynamics of connection and sustenance within and in conversation with literature.[18] As such, this book aims to inscribe itself into an understanding of fiction – in its various forms of expression – which emphasizes 'that art's distinctive qualities do not rule out social connections but are the very reason that such connections are forged and sustained' (Felski 2015: 165).

---

[18]While Felski explicitly distances herself from a formulation of queer negativity in the form of the 'antisocial thesis', she points out exactly the connective energies that negativity itself can unwittingly call forth: 'such a thesis can only sustain itself by enlisting allies, generating attachments and connecting to networks ... Negation thus collides with the ubiquity of relation' (2015: 76-7).

Hope and kinship, then, as this book's main points of reference, emerge not only as conceptual frameworks guiding my analysis of the texts under discussion, but also as methodological commitments. I understand reparative reading as an ethical standpoint that calls for an awareness, on the side of the critic, of writerly positionality, the affects of reading and writing, and for a mode of criticism that is attentive to the reconstructive potential of critical practices. As such, this modality of reading is not primarily tied to one particular kind of approach to text and interpretation, but rather to a *mood* of reading and writing that attaches itself to affects other than the ones Christopher Castiglia associates with what he calls 'critiquiness': 'a combination of mistrust, indignation, ungenerosity, and self-congratulation' which lacks 'ethical positioning' (2017: 214). Castiglia frames the other, reparative kind of critique in terms of the affects and temporalities of hope in the sense this book also uses them: this kind of critique would 'measure[] the present or the past against the imagined alternatives generated from a radically insufficient *now*. It is that combination of critique and imaginative idealism that ... I call *hopefulness*' (216, emphasis in original).

Following Castiglia, my interest in fiction is, to a large extent, driven by the belief that literature (like other forms of imaginative storytelling) 'is a training ground in the unreal, and hence a powerful partner in the work of critique aimed not *at* the text but alongside it' (218, emphasis in original); and like Castiglia, I believe that 'criticism, too, can be an imaginative space coexisting with and perpetually troubling the imperative here and now within which new ideals, new versions of the real, can be envisioned' (218). Hope, in this sense, becomes disentangled from the narrow confines of paranoid projections of the ever-same pasts, presents, and futures, where there can only be one dominant narrative of how things *must* proceed, of what is inevitable, and what *must* be done. Instead, hope emerges as a critical mood that pauses to observe the present moment, to add reality to it, to enrich it with all its inherent potential for connection and kinship – or the necessary letting go of the same. Hopeful reading[19], in this sense, corresponds to the affect of hope as an 'itch that refuses to be soothed, an ongoing discontent that is not reducible to the dead end of suspicion ... [I]ts necessarily unfinished business is what keeps the real in an ongoing state of un- and remaking' (222, 224).

---

[19]My sense of 'hopeful reading' resonates with Philip E. Wegner's invocation of a hopeful or utopian kind of critique, which aims for 'the dialectical grasp at once of limitations and possibilities' (2020: 12). I do not, however, subscribe to his framing of postcritical or, as he puts it, 'dominant moralizing ethical criticism' (ibid.) and close reading as opposites. In fact, as I hope to have demonstrated, a postcritical or reparative readerly attitude requires close reading as methodology.

A criticism for the here and now: Queer temporality, new materialism, and the question of politics

At this point, it might be worth asking whether my argument in favour of a present-oriented, anti-paranoid understanding of hope and kinship as guiding theme and methodological practice might not be missing the point entirely: does not the privileging of anti-futuristic, anti-teleological modalities disable – as Edelman would have it – any real engagement of the political? Any discussion of such charged terms as hope and kinship seems to entail the necessity to disentangle empirical and political research interests. My investment in this book, however, lies in both of these areas. Mostly and primarily, my argument takes its cue from the observation that a certain (popular and influential) strand of contemporary narrative storytelling renders affective investments in temporality and community in a certain kind of way which, I contend, can most plausibly be framed as one possible configuration of hope as an individual and collective disposition, and of kinship as a form of emergent and negotiated belonging. As such, my point is not to make strong moral claims about these renderings of hope and kinship as they manifest themselves in the fictional imagination – a political project of this sort would have to be conducted on different terms. What I do hope to show, however, is that the cultural tendencies captured in my analyses are far from random: they emerge – perhaps counterintuitively – from the very political insight, explicated in different strands of contemporary critical theory, that both certain temporal investments often associated with hope, optimism, and futurity, as well as narrow (and historically recent) dynamics of in- and exclusion along the delineations of family or nation are, ultimately, unsustainable and detrimental to the political interest of even those emancipatory movements and schools of thinking that have often placed their bets (for good reasons) with paranoid politics.

Contemporary critical thinking of the explicitly engaged and political kind often acknowledges – sometimes against the grain of more hands-on activist beliefs – the need for conceptualizing ways of thinking, reading, and theorizing in and for the present in order to ultimately render more instead of less modes of belonging and care possible. The most striking cases in point are the ongoing negotiations of temporality and community in the fields of queer theory and, with a different emphasis, the new materialisms. Both combine an interest in the tension between the apparent need for political utopian vision and the necessity to sidestep a politics of 'no alternatives' with a pronounced interest in method and critical practice. While these debates are diverse and developing in different directions, I believe that we can gain valuable insights into the fictional (and cultural) contemporary imagination if we do not prematurely dismiss pessimistic and negative critical moods. If understood as reparative positions, these moods become tools that can enable a better understanding of the popularity both of certain fictional narratives, and of certain strands in the contemporary critical and political landscape. My own project inscribes itself into these lines of thinking by reading a body of contemporary fictional texts for their strategies of enabling modes of hope and kinship that are largely pessimistic in outlook, but also locate hope in moments of care and recognition which sidestep dominant notions of things getting better.

Queer theory and the new materialisms are, in many ways, quite different in agenda and outlook: where queer theory remains committed to questions of identity and representation, the new materialisms work towards a reconceptualization of how the world as such is made up. The former tends more towards the epistemological, while the latter is largely invested in questions of ontology. Both fields, however, also share a genealogy of feminist research and criticism, and both, to an extent, take their cue from an engagement with progressive politics and social movements – the ongoing fight for equal rights in the case of queer theory, and the fight against the climate emergency and for a less anthropocentric worldview in the case of the new materialisms. The two fields also overlap in a pronounced interest in the affects of temporality, and a search for a methodological toolkit appropriate for the urgencies of the contemporary moment. As such, queer theory and the new materialisms are paradigmatic examples of how a wider cultural concern with affective investments in temporality and belonging – what I frame as hope and kinship – has also become a paramount issue in contemporary criticism.

One of the dominant themes of the comparatively short history of queer theory is the tension – intimately tied to the question of how to relate to the political fight for queer emancipation – between committing to a positive and utopic vision of queer existence, and embracing the negativity inherent in both the history of queer suffering and exclusion, and the logic of representation itself. As such, the arguments moving back and forth between queer negativity and queer utopianism have been increasingly concerned with how best to relate to questions of history, the future, and temporality in general, and with whether to frame queerness as fundamentally antisocial, or as a concept that fosters creative and nurturing forms of belonging outside the mainstream of heteronormative existence. Heather Love, for instance, argues that, instead of buying into the ambiguous promises of a utopic future of tolerance for all queers, we should turn back to the losses of the past in order to understand how they still affect queer existence in the present. She speculates about what kind of reading might be most appropriate for her endeavour, and decides to bind her historical inquiry to a reparative methodology, proposing a mode of reading that does not try to ignore, qualify, or glorify the uncomfortable history of queer suffering, instead understanding the texts she engages with as teaching the meanings of 'living with injury – not fixing it' (2009: 4). Love proposes that criticism be wary of 'mere optimism', because 'hope that is achieved at the expense of the past cannot serve the future' (29). Her interest lies with the multiple (historical and present) tensions between queer community and queer isolation, and with queer kinship as 'emerging from a shared experience of social violence' (51). The task of the historian and critic then becomes to 'tak[e] care of the past without attempting to fix it … [and to] liv[e] with bad attachments, identifying through loss, allowing ourselves to be haunted' (43). Love's linking of anti-futuristic historical analysis (including a positive bias for the present) with reparative forms of reading and reception is instructive: while my own corpus of texts is from the much more recent past than Love's, and my interest lies with contemporary analysis rather than with historical understanding, I take my cue from her conviction that a critical acknowledgement of past and present pain, but also past and present possibility is best approached with the slow speed and patient lingering that characterizes close reading.

In a similar vein, Elizabeth Freeman associates her own queer take on temporality and artistic production with the queer insights and pleasures derived from reparative reading. Where Love focuses on the past's pain and trauma, Freeman argues for engaging the queer escapes, in narrative gaps and temporal detours, from what she calls 'chrononormativity'. Like Love, she favours 'trail[ing] behind actually existing social possibilities' (2010: xiii) over the optimism of political emancipation, foregrounding the insistent present-ness of her own material: 'the queerness of these artists consists in mining the present for signs of undetonated energy from past revolutions' (xvi). Freeman thus highlights the potentiality of the present as a site of queer possibility, and, similar to Love, identifies close reading as a reparative form of criticism and the most appropriate queer methodology: '[t]o close read is to linger, to dally, to take pleasure in tarrying, and to hold out that these activities can allow us to look both hard and askance at the norm' (xvi–xvii). With Freeman, I consider my decision in favour of lengthy close readings and individual analyses of only a few individual texts to be this book's 'queerest commitment' (xvii). While Freeman explicitly rejects the association of queerness with pure negativity, her understanding of queer temporality as emerging in 'textual moments of asynchrony, anachronism, anastrophe, belatedness, compression, delay, ellipsis, flashback, hysteron-proteron, pause, prolepsis, repetition, reversal, surprise' that become 'points of resistance' (xxii) to chrononormativity resonates strongly with my framing of hope and kinship as fictional modalities which open up possibilities beyond or in addition to dominant narratives of progression, betterment, and belonging. Like Freeman, I believe that writing itself (the act of fictional narration as much as that of critical writing) 'is only to hazard the possibility that there will be a future of some sort' (xxiv). One of this book's main concerns, however, is to show how contemporary fiction, in order to make different futures possible – or even just to make present existence sustainable – draws our attention away from the future horizon towards the here and now and its potential for agency and creative forms of making (or breaking) connection.

The move which animates both Love's and Freeman's arguments is thus twofold. First, they broaden the scope of queerness' semantic field so that it can accommodate both the historical and present cultural experience of queer identities *and* a mode of representation and narration that more generally eschews the logic of normative temporality and generation. This scope or lens of inquiry then, in turn, gets associated with a reparative methodology. In doing so, queerness – in the form of such framings as Castiglia's hopeful reading – becomes a category of analysis that will be, by definition, both analytical and self-reflexive in its attention to dynamics of temporality and community in both critical and fictional discourse. This methodological understanding of queerness is one of the main driving forces behind the close readings in the following chapters. It requires a critical commitment to ambivalence and nuance, and to epistemological and ontological possibilities that emerge in the vicinity of 'failed' worlds and identities. Jack Halberstam argues that favouring 'failing, losing, forgetting, unmaking, undoing, unbecoming, [and] not knowing … [as] more creative, more cooperative, more surprising ways of being in the world' (2011: 2–3) can bring about 'a new kind of optimism' (5), not one of grand utopian dimensions, but one that is provisional and aware of the mutual dependence of light and darkness. In this context, 'the queer art of failure' emerges as a methodological commitment to a reparative and open-ended epistemology which 'seeks not to explain but to involve' (15). Halberstam's engagement with his material highlights a multitude of different forms and degrees of anarchic cooperation, such that the relationship between knowledge and disciplinary culture gets realigned along lines of belonging, family, and generation. In his analysis, many of the early animated Pixar films, for example, provide the insight that 'children are not coupled, they are not romantic, they do not have a religious morality, they are not afraid of death or failure, they are collective creatures, they are in a constant state of rebellion against their parents, and they are not the masters of their own domain' (47). These children exist at a far remove from Edelman's Child that is the bearer of the political future. Where the Child represents an investment in normative futurity at the expense of any subjectivity that escapes its logic, the children in Halberstam's analysis are the ones who know that the present is full of possibility, and that the future is unknown. The critical and creative vision Halberstam presents thus invests in reparative versions of hope and kinship which acknowledge that 'the possibility of other forms of being, other forms of knowing, … a mode of being where the emphasis falls … on cooperation, trade and sharing animates all kinds of knowledge projects and should not be dismissed as irrelevant or naïve' (52).

My own project shares this commitment with Halberstam's engagement of his unlikely popular archive of failure. None of the texts I look at in this book is a story of success – most are set in failed, devastated, inhospitable, or individually unsustainable worlds. From these failures, however, and out of different reparative positions of pessimism (and varying degrees of realism and naiveté) emerge surprising and queer forms of agency which foreground the possibilities and impossibilities of existence under the conditions of the here and now.

In this respect, one of the lines of convergence that bring the texts I have selected for analysis in this book together is an affinity with a mode of fictional speculation that renders palpable the tensions between different temporal registers, and which is characterized by a certain strategic ignorance of historical pasts and positive political visions for the future. While this insistence on the present might be considered an annoyance in a cultural climate that regularly calls for a renewal of the utopic spirit in both politics and art, the popularity of such fiction deserves our attention. I argue that my material's hopeful spirit emerges precisely from its lingering in the here and now, which (counterintuitively) renders a speculative modality that fosters a radical openness necessitating reparative forms of reading for textual moments of connection and kinship.

Where queer theory's concern with turning the critical gaze towards the present and its dense texture of pain and potentiality stems primarily from experiences of marginalization and invisibility, recent new-materialist writing has voiced a similar interest in developing a set of critical tools aimed at theorizing the concerns of the here and now in the face of the global climate crisis and the political debates surrounding it. The vibrancy and effective agency of all matter, these critics argue, demand our attention, and require a reparative hermeneutics that strongly resembles similar propositions in queer theory. As opposed to the new-materialist concern with decentring the human in a turn towards an ontology which acknowledges 'the material agency or effectivity of nonhuman or not-quite-human things' (Bennett 2010: ix), my own focus, in this book, remains mostly within the confines of human world-making (and -unmaking). However, queer theory and the new materialisms' shared concern with reparative hermeneutics, and the latter's specific investment in understanding both human and non-human entities as assemblages of 'vibrant matter' (ibid.) are instructive for contextualizing the reconfigurations of temporal affects and structures of belonging at the heart of this project within a wider context of critical theory.

The new-materialist concern with collectives and connection emerges from a similar feeling of urgency as queer theory's recurrent turn towards questions of (un-)belonging under conditions of heterosexism and capitalism. As Jane Bennett puts it, her own interest lies in foregrounding 'a notion of publics as human-nonhuman collectives that are provoked into existence by a shared experience of harm' (2010: xix). Even more to the point of my own argument's thrust, she emphasizes that 'cultural forms are themselves powerful, material assemblages with *resistant force*' (1, emphasis in original). The investments in different iterations of temporality and belonging I will be tracing in the following chapters emerge, from this perspective, as fundamentally expressive of the kinship at the heart of human and non-human existence: 'all bodies are kin in the sense of inextricably enmeshed in a dense network of relations. And in a knotted world of vibrant matter, to harm one section of the web may very well be to harm oneself' (13). If we take fiction to be one form of expression of these networks of relations, the job of the critic becomes to trace these relations and the conditions of their making and unmaking. Hence, for Bennett, the concern with the networked nature of existence requires a methodology that eschews a hermeneutics of suspicion, 'because demystification presumes that at the heart of any event or process lies a *human* agency that has illicitly been projected into things' (xiv, emphasis in original). While the politics of this book remains far more anthropocentric and (sceptically) humanist than Bennett's, her explicitly *political* interest in disabling the exclusivity of ideology critique in favour of the tracing of material reverberances and connections resonates with my own interest in reading my corpus of texts for its many-faceted negotiations of (dis-)connection under conditions of global and local, natural, social, cultural, collective and individual devastation, and of a pervasive pessimist disposition.

As such, my interest in hope and kinship as both thematic and hermeneutic perspectives should not imply any easy notion of universal connection as a depoliticized alternative to more structure-oriented approaches to the social and cultural implications of fictional narrative. The point of origin of my considerations is the observation that a certain strand of contemporary fiction favours settings that are (more or less) detached from the grand narratives of history and the concrete concerns of social realism. Instead, these works render fictional worlds whose temporality is noticeably strange, in the sense of being either removed to some unspecified post-apocalyptic near-future that itself is emptied of any notion of progression, entangled in the circular temporal dynamics of the speculative imagination, or tied to some kind of stagnant present. My argument in favour, firstly, of considering these works as exemplary of a popular contemporary fictional and cultural mood, and, secondly, of approaching them with a critical mindset appropriate to their temporal and social negotiations thus aims less at making an ethical statement about the absolute value (or ultimate generalized usefulness) of the debate about reparative reading, or about the political desirability of orientations away from history and the future towards the present. Instead, my aim is to trace the different fictional and theoretical strands in contemporary discourse that, for different purposes and to different effects, come together in rendering hope and kinship as attitudes towards the world which favour queer ways of relating to time and belonging over the paranoid scripts of survivalism and happy endings.

It is in this sense that I see the texts under consideration in this book as participating in a conversation about the need for a shift of critical attention forcefully articulated by Donna Haraway. Like her call for a careful acknowledgement of the entanglement of all life under conditions of global environmental destruction, although with a stubborn fixation on human subjectivity – the awkwardness of which is precisely what motivates me to follow its implications – these texts are committed, in the act of narration, to '[s]ympoiesis – making with' and 'thinking-with: storytelling', and interested less in 'reconciliation or restoration' than in 'the more modest possibilities of partial recuperation and getting on together' (2016: 5, 39, 10). They are told in a mode that foregrounds the urgencies of '*[k]ainos*[, which] means now, a time of beginnings, a time for ongoing, for freshness' in 'thick, ongoing presence' (2, emphasis in original): '[c]all that utopia; call that inhabiting the despised places; call that touch; call that the rapidly mutating virus of hope, or the less rapidly changing commitment to staying with the trouble' (114).

Contemporary narrative fiction: Choice of texts

My corpus comprises four novels, two film adaptations, and two (web) television series, all published or released since 2004. I argue that they exemplify a tendency in fiction since the turn of the millennium to process and negotiate contemporary crisis discourse in terms of narrative renderings of temporality and belonging. This choice of material warrants a brief consideration of narratology. While my primary interest and analytical focus in the following chapters is largely thematic, privileging story over discourse, formal aspects will play a role where they have important implications for my reading of the respective text's internal dynamics – most obviously in the case of the metafictional elements in David Mitchell's *Cloud Atlas* and Hanya Yanagihara's *The People in the Trees*. To an extent, my thematic and cultural interest in fictional renderings of temporality prompts considerations of literary discourse for the project as a whole, not least because the temporal dynamics I highlight in my close readings unfold in the interplay between discourse-time and story-time, 'the time of the act of narrating and the time of the things narrated' (Ricoeur 1985: 5). With David Wittenberg, I take this distinction to be 'a dynamic process inherent in pragmatic acts of reading or viewing' (2018: 122), and a fundamental feature of narrative across the boundaries of genre. In the sense that one of the defining characteristics of narrative is a discrepancy between its implication of 'the possibility of a full or true "reconstruction" of events' – that is, its postulation of 'the "real" temporality of its story as regular, linear, true time, recoverable in principle if never fully in practice' – as 'the hypothetical telos or fantasy' of fiction, and the endless 'deviations undertaken by the text to communicate it' (123), this process describes, in formal terms, the dynamic tension between teleological and non-teleological temporalities I trace in this book. Narrative fiction lends itself so well to the concerns at hand because, like the cultural moods I consider as manifesting themselves in the texts under discussion, 'narratives must always vacillate between the ideal of chronological reconstitution and the continual perversion of time' (124).

As such, narrative temporality is, to an extent, structurally determined to produce the kinds of queer tensions that drive my analyses. Queerness and narrative, however, have a difficult conceptual relationship. While some of the proponents of queer negativity have posited queerness and narrative as fundamentally antithetical because of narrative's normalizing tendencies, more recent approaches attempt to map the nuances and ambivalences inherent in the interplay between queerness and form. Valerie Rohy, for example, points out that, while 'queer communities cultivate their own generic forms, seeing narrative not only as compatible with queerness but essential to it[,] … [t]he making of a popular narrative … may come at the cost of difference' (2018: 172). And although a 'dislocation of narrative chronology' (173) lies at the heart of many queer stories, it remains productively unclear 'to what degree nonnormative narrative is cognate with nonnormative sexuality and gender experience' (175). Where Rohy, however, still concludes that narrative representation inevitably sacrifices queerness' anti-normative potential, Tyler Bradway, in constructing what he calls a 'queer narrative theory', argues that, in fact, 'narrative affords important agencies for queerness' (2021: 712). His foregrounding of 'the multiple, braided, and often conflicting temporalities that compose narrative as well as potentially queer temporalities of plot, such as suspense, simultaneity, and surprise' (ibid.) is particularly productive for my own understanding of queerness as both denoting a reparative methodology and signifying the ambivalent potentiality of hope as expressed in the interplay between form and content in narrative fiction. Like Bradway's queer narrative theory, my own reading practice is concerned with 'shifting from teleology to trajectory' (721), and with a notion of kinship rendered in fictional discourse as 'a family that accumulates over time' (723). It is in this sense that my own project addresses the formal properties of narrative. In focusing on the ways the texts discussed in the following chapters produce tensions between teleology and non-teleology, between linearity and non-linearity through playing with theme, character, and narrative, I will be tracing hope as emerging not only in the shape of a cultural concern of these particular stories, but also as a queer property of narrative fiction as such, a property which, in turn, enables queer forms of kinship, in the sense that narrative becomes 'a condition of possibility for queerness' (712).

From this understanding of narrative fiction as lending itself particularly well to a project concerned with dynamics of hope and kinship follows another fundamental assumption underlying my approach to the texts under consideration. Any analysis of contemporary storytelling driven by more general cultural concerns and tendencies should, I believe, include narrative in different medial forms in order to properly appreciate the extent to which these forms share a cultural function as imaginative spaces in which fictional narration is realized – not least because, as Seymour Chatman points out, the 'transposability of the story' from one medium to another is a defining feature of narrative itself (1978: 20). Moreover, twenty-first-century narrative fiction, in particular, destabilizes any categorial separation of 'high' and 'low', 'serious' and 'popular' forms of storytelling, and requires a reparative engagement with undisciplined and anti-disciplinary 'knowledge from below' (Halberstam 2011: 11). While this separation has arguably always been much less pronounced in the Anglo-American cultural sphere and in Anglo-American academia than in some continental European contexts, in recent cultural production, more than ever, narrative storytelling emerges simultaneously across media: novels are adapted into films or series, while novelists, in turn, react to the adaptation in a literary sequel, or television series continue telling a story before their literary inspiration can catch up. More generally, film and literature have heavily influenced each other since the emergence of the former medium in the late nineteenth century, and analysts of fiction and narrative should take this into account (cf. Paech 1997).

This project, then, is rooted in a hermeneutics schooled in literary studies proper, but posits a definition of 'text' influenced by cultural studies[20] which allows for the inclusion of fictional narration in other media. In consequence, my readings will privilege the *narrative* and thus 'literary' aspects of the material at hand over its visual aesthetics (cf. Sarris 1971), although these will play a role when they contribute to an understanding of story and character. What all the texts under consideration have in common is a rendering of story in time, and their grounding in the imaginative development of story world and character calls for their shared place in a critical work on contemporary fiction and culture.

---

[20]Chris Barker and Emma A. Jane provide such a definition in arguing that '[t]he concept of text suggests not simply the written word, though this is one of its senses, but all practices that signify. This includes the generation of meaning through images, sounds, objects (such as clothes) and activities (like dance and sport). Since images, sounds, objects and practices are sign systems, which signify with the same mechanism as a language, we may refer to them as cultural texts' (2016: 13).

In my analyses, I focus on anglophone texts published after the turn of the millennium, which are all concerned with the negotiation of hope and kinship on the level of form and content, and, as such, contribute to a turn to reconstruction in contemporary fiction that aligns with recent theoretical investments in reparative and postcritical reading habits. I argue that these works all emerge from an early-twenty-first-century cultural mood of crisis and pessimism, while, at the same time, rendering a hopeful mode that engages urgent questions of human life under conditions of personal and global catastrophe and a shortened temporal horizon. I have deliberately chosen texts that are not explicit feminist/queer/emancipatory utopias, although I do include speculative fiction of the more mainstream kind. The logic of this work, in large parts, rests on engaging with the epicentre of popular texts in order to contribute to a theory of fiction that speaks to both academic discourse and popular culture.

A body of contemporary work is, by necessity, always largely idiosyncratic. It cannot rely on established dynamics of canon formation and lacks the benefit of later insights into what place a particular text will occupy within a culture at a much later point in time. I do not, however, see this as a disadvantage. Instead – and as part of this book's commitment to reparative thinking – I understand this point of departure as an opportunity to acknowledge individual reading habits and their impact on the formation of a critical corpus of material, in the sense of what Frederic Jameson calls a 'disposable canon' (2008: 222). In my case, this project and its theoretical outlook first emerged from a personal focus, in recent years, on reading a wide and eclectic range of very recently published, often prize-winning novels (many of them in the context of a book club), and on consuming a variety of equally recent television series now easily available on different streaming platforms. Over time, I discovered – at first more intuitively than systematically – affinities between several of these texts, and began to cluster them together in different combinations, until, slowly, a pattern emerged that I could – with the help of a background in queer theory – finally frame in more systematic terms. As such, while all my examples are, I would insist, paradigmatic both of the broader dynamics discussed in this book, and of their respective genres or 'minor cultural keys' in which I present them in the following chapters, the choice to settle for these *particular* texts is largely due to my own taste in fiction, and I hope that readers will discover similar dynamics in other texts, and find opportunities to continue the conversation started in these pages.

Another caveat might help readers understand my approach to the cultural 'sphere' under consideration. My selection of material – with five out of six texts emerging primarily out of US-American cultural contexts, and David Mitchell, as the only British author, seemingly the odd one out – deliberately disregards the institutionalized distinction between British and American Studies that is still very pronounced in some continental European English

Departments, and which is surely warranted in cases where the particularities of national culture are of primary interest. Although all of the texts I engage with are, to an extent, characteristic of their respective (mostly US-American) cultures of origin, I argue that both the global dissemination, reception, and success of all of these anglophone stories from the Global North through different media (facilitated by a globalized publication economy and the universal availability of films and series on streaming platforms), and – even more so – their pronounced lack of specificity in terms of history and geography justify their treatment as transatlantic or even global phenomena, as part of what Peter Boxall calls 'an emerging canon of international ... fiction' (2013: 6). The texts' embeddedness in western/northern, English-speaking traditions is instructive both because of the ongoing global influence (and privilege) of transatlantic British and US-American fiction, and because of their ambiguous position within seemingly globalized notions of a 'new humanism' – an issue I will address in detail later in the book – and the experience of globalized threats and crises.

Finally, another brief comment on my understanding of 'queer' as it applies to the texts under consideration. In terms of addressing questions of sexual identity, as it manifests itself in fictional setting, theme, and character development, these works are positioned on a fairly broad spectrum: where some are explicitly concerned with rendering forms of emancipatory and political queer identity (most obviously *Sense8*, but also, in its own way, *A Little Life*), others contain at least minor queer characters (*Cloud Atlas*, but also *The Walking Dead*) or, arguably, suggestions of a queer subplot (*The People in the Trees*), while at least one text (*The Road*) is, on the surface, not concerned with queerness at all. What unites all these texts, however, is a commitment to queerness as a critical cultural and narrative modality, as it emerges through the perspective of temporality and kinship. All the works I discuss in this book negotiate the (im)possibility and (un)desirability of reproductive futurity, the conditions of care and belonging under devastating social, environmental, and personal circumstances, and the queer hope that emerges from the temporalities of the present. As such, I understand 'queer' to bring together the thematic and the more abstract, epistemological concerns of contemporary theory and fiction addressed in this book. In this sense, 'queer' denotes the guiding methodological frame. Over the course of the last few decades (and in both academic and activist contexts), 'queer' has shifted away from working primarily as a non-category which sidesteps the categorical implications of emancipatory gay and lesbian politics to becoming (once again) an umbrella term for just these identity markers. One of my aims in this book is to return – in conversation with similar commitments in recent queer and cultural theory – to an understanding of 'queer' as an open signifier, one that allows for exactly the kind of reparative hermeneutics that guides my analysis of the texts at hand, and which, I believe, is the best analytical fit for the kind of cultural work my material does. Hence, my primary aim is not to do 'queer readings' of 'straight' texts (which would be nothing less than a repetition of the paranoid endeavour Sedgwick and others problematize), or to point towards the utopian realization of queer identities in the fictional space of stories (although these do, at times, occur). Instead, I want to explore the never quite realized, temporally suspended *possibilities* inherent in the stories and narrative built of the texts included in my corpus. Some of these possibilities, of course, gesture towards historically realized and actually possible queer identities: future-sceptic, anti-reproductive, and radically presentist notions of making kin, and of finding alternatives to political hope. In my development of a queer and reparative hermeneutics and my exploration of its performative rendering in fictional texts, however, I do not intend to do the (equally important) utopian work of emancipating queer identities, but to emancipate queer thinking from the politically driven reduction to this kind of archaeological recovery, and instead make it productive for a wider cultural debate about the temporality of hope and the performative making of kin.

The following close readings are ordered along three textual pairings in three chapters, each of which reflects this book's overall thematic interest from a different angle. The choice of different approaches to grouping the fictional material is deliberate. While I presuppose a strong affinity between different medial expressions of narrative – novels, films, series – in the present cultural climate, I also want to reflect the difficulty of selecting and privileging one overarching metanarrative for the grouping of texts under any category. As an intentionally contingent but productive answer to this problem, I have decided to discuss two complementary pieces of primary material per chapter. I will theorize the affinity and kinship of each of these textual couples according to a different meta-structural umbrella that will help bring the project's reparative hermeneutic programme to the fore along three different but mutually inspiring lines of thinking. All three chapters open with a theoretical introduction that engages (in deliberately anachronistic fashion) recent political and cultural developments (such as the Fridays-for-Future movement and the Covid-19 pandemic) in order to reflect on the relevance of post-apocalyptic narrative, modes of speculative storytelling, and cultural pessimism for an analysis of hope and kinship in contemporary fiction.

In the first analytical chapter, I discuss two recent examples from the growing body of contemporary post-apocalyptic storytelling, a particularly popular kind of genre fiction. Its influence reaches across different media, and it has often been argued to be intimately linked to more general cultural anxieties about the state of the world. Specifically, post-apocalyptic fiction sets a future-oriented notion of hope against the stark backdrop of an end time. A particular focus, in this chapter, lies on the question of who, under catastrophic circumstances, still counts as kin, and who as 'other' or monstrous. I engage with the scholarly debates about the growing quantity of post-apocalyptic narratives in the twenty-first century, and with the equally growing body of critical work on monsters and zombies. The chapter offers close readings of Cormac McCarthy's *The Road* (2006), already a contemporary classic of post-apocalyptic and dystopian fiction (along with a comparative analysis of the 2009 film adaptation), and of AMC's highly successful serial adaptation of the graphic novel *The Walking Dead* (2010–22). I am particularly interested in *The Road*'s contrasting visions of agency in the face of ultimate despair, located in the father-son dyad: while the father holds on to a conservative vision of hope in the (damaged) nuclear family and the preservation of his child for an impossible future, the son embraces a less futuristic and more radical vision of unconditional kinship with all those (human and otherwise) who are still alive in the present. *The Walking Dead*, while mostly invested in repeatedly referencing the heterosexual nuclear family as the telos of a society that needs rebuilding, also accommodates, over the course of its long and ongoing serial narrative, important questions about the limits of humanism, most obviously in its continual negotiation of the ambiguous position of the zombies as dead and alive, kin and ultimate 'other', but also through the introduction of characters that do not easily buy into the narrative of heroic progression represented by the protagonists, often children and queer characters.

The second analytical chapter approaches its material through the mode of speculative fiction, arguing that contemporary narrative of this kind often experiments with emerging notions of kin-making and solidarity on a global scale, reconfiguring kinship as transcending time and space, and hope as the will to change. The examples under consideration project a vision of transcultural connectedness which, on the one hand, strongly reverberates with certain kinds of contemporary activism and cultural theory, but also inadvertently gets caught in the unresolvable tension between futuristic idealism and a firm embeddedness of political action in the present. I consider David Mitchell's *Cloud Atlas* (2004) as a text that paradigmatically combines a metafictional approach with a sincere and affect-driven story of human interconnectedness. Mitchell makes use of a postmodern metafictional programme that creates an amount of distance to the text in the reader, while simultaneously constructing a tension between linear and circular notions of temporality, and working towards an ideologically charged message of humanism and universal human kinship. The chapter then moves on to an analysis of the 2012 film adaptation by the Wachowskis and Tom Tykwer, which adds an explicitly queer aesthetic register to the novel's original vision of human kinship, while also reducing the temporal complexities that characterize the novel. Only three years after *Cloud Atlas*, the Wachowskis and Tykwer collaborated again on the Netflix series *Sense8* (2015–18), which further develops the artistic and political programme – and the queerness – of their work on *Cloud Atlas*. Beyond these continuities in commitment, I am particularly interested in how the series portrays a vision of a global humanism and a celebration of diversity that overcomes divisions between the Global North and South. I ask how *Sense8*, on the one hand, positively asserts kinship as the common humanity and humanism that all protagonists share through a celebration of racial, sexual, and gender diversity, and, on the other hand, fails to free itself from a colonizing gaze which flattens nuanced possibilities and potentialities of the geographies and territorialities depicted.

In the last analytical chapter, I discuss a single author's work in order to trace recurring themes and concerns in her oeuvre, and their relation to historical moment and context. The works of Hawaiian-American novelist Hanya Yanagihara provide something of a very recent culmination point of fictional explorations of hope and kinship in the context of realist, melodramatic, and neo-gothic narration. They exemplify, I argue, a dominant mood in the contemporary cultural imagination which I call 'hysterical pessimism' in reference to James Wood's (2000) derogatory labelling of a certain strand of contemporary popular narrative fiction. Yanagihara's first two novels work through many of the concerns of the texts discussed in the two preceding chapters. Both novels vacillate between a queer re-imagining of kinship and a referring-back to patriarchal, male-homosocial, and transcendental narratives of both hope (for salvation) and kinship (as homogeneity and purity). *The People in the Trees* (2013) is a densely packed, neo-gothic exploration of the darker implications of humanist concerns. Written in the first-person voice of an arrogant, megalomaniac explorer-scientist, the convoluted confessional not only explores every cliché of the benevolent racist explorer of the colonial and exotic 'other', but also asks questions about the place of the human in a 'natural' world full of strange and fantastic life. The novel also forces the reader to take a moral stance in the face of a narrator who, in his scientific and personal hubris, strives to become god-like, and capable of extending life not only through his 'discovery' of a strange turtle, but also through his excessive adoption and ultimate abuse of more than forty children from the spatially and racially 'othered' island where most of his adventures take place. Yanagihara's second novel, *A Little Life* (2015), has its protagonists leave behind toxic masculinity and homophobia in favour of fluid notions of what it means to be there for each other. Even though the novel's central, traumatized, and Christ-like character eventually defies his friends' paranoid hope for him to get better and have a future, hope is repeatedly reframed in the story's incessant renegotiations of care and concern in the present. For some readers, the novel's reparative dissolution of narrow and potentially harmful notions of gender and sexuality opens up a different future, one not immediately reflected in its stagnant narrative temporality, but more in line with the notion of an emergent potentiality. At the same time, its insistence on positive affective bonds beyond the heterosexual family is problematically suspended between a sexist vision of purely male bonding and an idea of queer and reparative kin-making. The novel thus presents a kind of 'affective utopia', while, at the same time, returning to the fundamentally Christian idea of the suffering saviour. It complicates a notion of teleological hope and foregrounds a painful, but potentially reparative vision of the affective work of kinship, and the possibility that maybe things do not simply get better.

I conclude the book with a coda that both attempts to present a synthesis of my findings, and, in discussing two films – *Shoplifters* (2018) and *Parasite* (2019) – which fall outside the linguistic and cultural scope of this project, but received international popular acclaim, outlines possible points of departure for further explorations of the relationship between hope and kinship under the conditions of global capitalism and precarity. On the whole, this book aims to continue a critical dialogue on our understanding of the directions contemporary fiction has taken. I hope to explore possibilities for thinking about how we understand fictional texts in terms of their cultural implications about hope and kinship. What can it mean to turn sideways (to one another in the present) instead of looking behind or ahead (to the past or future)? How can we try to bridge the tension between hope and negativity in queer studies? And finally, what can hope and kinship come to mean for fiction and literary and cultural criticism in times of ongoing political, social, and cultural crises?

PART ONE

What comes after: Temporality and belonging in contemporary post-apocalyptic fiction

In the summer of 2019, Greta Thunberg, Swedish teenage climate activist and inadvertent founder of the Fridays-for-Future movement, crossed the Atlantic on a sailboat to attend the United Nations Climate Action Summit. One year earlier, Thunberg had stopped attending school on Fridays to demonstrate, in front of the Swedish parliament, against the devastating impact of human activity on the global climate. Since then, the emerging movement has gained a large following of young people around the world. In the context of the debates surrounding Greta Thunberg and 'her' movement, the current global climate crisis has not only become a matter of increased political interest and gained a new sense of urgency for political, economic, and social change on a global scale. It has also, more than ever, become a foil against which narratives of global destruction and apocalypse disseminate and are being made productive for different political and symbolic purposes.

In the context of this book's argument, I am most interested in Thunberg's (self- and external) positioning as a child activist in the movement's and its opponents' rhetoric. While some politicians have explicitly tried to discredit Thunberg for being 'just a child'[1], and thus not qualified to advocate for political, social, and economic change of the scale Fridays for Future keeps demanding, Thunberg herself has repeatedly used her own identification as a child for a self-conscious and affectively charged plea aimed at adult culture to help prevent imminent global ecological collapse. While some of this rhetoric employs rather conventional notions of a future that needs to be saved for the children, at the heart of several of Thunberg's early speeches and statements also lies a defiance against such futuristic co-optation. Thunberg and the Fridays-for-Future movement are most provocative in moments in which they foreground their cultural status as *unruly* children in a time of cultural crisis, figures that go off script and become prophets of that which adult culture falsely promises but fails to save in their name. What is at stake are different understandings of hope in the context of a vital threat to human (and non-human) life on this planet. In a statement published in March 2019, Thunberg and fellow activists Luisa Neubauer, Kyra Gantois, Anna Taylor, and Anuna De Wever explicitly reject a notion of hope which exclusively projects into the future, at the cost of action in the present: '[o]ther adults keep saying: "We owe it to the young people to give them hope." But we don't want your hope. We don't want you to be hopeful. We want you to panic and we want you to take action. We want you to join us' (Thunberg et al. 2019).

---

[1] Christian Lindner, leader of the German Free Democratic Party, for instance, criticized the Fridays-for-Future movement, arguing that 'you cannot expect children and young people to see all relevant global contexts, what makes sense technologically, and what is economically feasible. This is an issue for professionals' (qtd. in 'Eine Sache für Profis' 2019, my translation).

On the one hand, this plea for solidarity in what is being framed as a fight for survival is highly ambivalent because of its employment of a populist rhetoric of panic and lack of alternative.² It also, however, productively pits a notion of collective action in the present against a passivist and evasive hope for a future that will never come. In the current debates about the cultural implications of the climate catastrophe more generally, advocates of anti-futurism point out the necessity of thinking beyond naïve projections onto some never-to-be-reached horizon in the face of the climate crisis. Philipp Bovermann (2019), for example, implicitly evokes Sedgwick's notion of reparation in asking us to abandon hope in favour of the long-forgotten melancholic position, which would, he argues, enable us to accept that catastrophe is imminent, but also to see what, realistically, should matter in the here and now.³ Haraway's urgent call to 'Make Kin Not Babies!' (2016: 102) in the face of ecological devastation and the need to practice care for all those who live, suffer, and die on this planet in the here and now becomes another intriguing point to think from when discussing the cultural meanings of the child-eco-activist.

Considered from this angle, Greta Thunberg and her followers occupy an ambiguous symbolic position. Some of the cultural and symbolic work that they do invokes Edelman's figurative Child in need of protection, for whom a future must be built and preserved at all costs. At the same time, however, the fact that these children speak up for themselves and others, and claim their rights in the very present which always wants to put them off until some indefinite tomorrow, threatens to collapse a political economy that relies on the figure of the Child as a justification of harmful social and economic policies. It is a utopic possibility of the Fridays-for-Future movement that these children raise their voices and try to free themselves from a symbolic frame that attempts to render them harmless, and instead work towards a politics of radical solidarity that defies the temporal structures of futuristic hope and accepts that alternative ways of making kin might come at the cost of the sacrosanct Child itself.

Contemporary post-apocalyptic fiction negotiates many of these tensions around the cultural significance of the Child in the face of imminent disaster, a pitting of futuristic against anti-futuristic notions of hope, and

---

²In the same article, Thunberg and her fellow activists write three times that '[t]his movement had to happen. We didn't have a choice' (Thunberg et al. 2019).
³Strikingly, Bovermann closes his remarks with a call for a new utopia, which he locates, counter-intuitively, in the melancholic acceptance of imminent crisis: '[b]ut to lose hope is not just the story of a loss. It is also a new story ... An infernal realism spreads. Other things matter. What comes after hope? Melancholia ... In order to ignite itself politically, melancholia must not remain in contemplation of the coming loss, or else it is only a cynicism disguising itself as aestheticism. It must bring down the old thinking and make room: for utopia' (2019, my translation).

reconfigurations of kinship in the aftermath of a major cataclysm. I am especially interested in how this kind of fiction renders a model of time that problematizes an easy teleological progression from the past, through the present, and into the future – what Diletta De Cristofaro calls post-apocalyptic fiction's 'critical temporality' (2020: 1) – and speculates about human (and, sometimes, non-human) life and relationships under the conditions of the 'worst-case scenario': the dreaded future is already here, it is nothing to be feared or prevented any longer, but something to be dealt with. Like literature of the Anthropocene more generally, as Kate Marshall points out, contemporary post-apocalyptic fiction 'requires thinking proleptically, or registering a future point of view in which the material stratum of the human is no longer that which is the most recent' (2015: 533). More than just a feature of contemporary writing, this paradoxical idea of looking back from the future, as James Berger observes, is a core characteristic of the apocalyptic tradition's temporality more generally: '[t]emporal sequence becomes confused. Apocalyptic writing takes us after the end, shows us the signs prefiguring the end, the moment of obliteration, and the aftermath' (1999: 6). It is exactly this conflicted relationship between past, present, and future which interests me. In this chapter, I explore how contemporary stories falling under the category of the 'post-apocalyptic' negotiate the temporal confusion diagnosed by Berger, and make it productive for a fictional exploration of the dangers and chances of losing hope and of forgetting, the perks and pitfalls of sidestepping teleology, and of relating differently to what came before, what is, and what might be.

Most strikingly, in the texts I will be discussing – as in many other contemporary post-apocalyptic stories – the 'moment of obliteration' Berger invokes, the event itself that divides the 'before' from the 'after', remains unspoken and unspeakable. Readers cannot access it; they only get fragments of memories, as when the narrator in Cormac McCarthy's *The Road* vaguely refers to unspecific sight and sound impressions from the night that changed everything. The event itself remains absent from the text, and with it an explanation that would give meaning to the post-apocalyptic situation. As Berger puts it, '[t]he post-apocalyptic narrative is tautologous. What it cannot contain, what it circles around and can only exclude is, precisely, the apocalypse, the revelation that would explain the catastrophe' (1999: 12). Before discussing the fiction itself, then, we need to think about what exactly it is that 'post-apocalyptic' fiction is 'after'.

The label 'post-apocalyptic', denoting a particular kind of genre fiction – closely related to the broader notion of dystopian fiction, but with an additional drive towards cataclysms of a global scale[4] – immediately raises

---

[4] Jan Hollm sharply distinguishes between the post-apocalyptic and the dystopian traditions: '[w]hereas apocalyptic discourse has its origin in religious revelation, a literary dystopia presents a narrative in which current aspects in human society that are seen as negative are

two important questions. One relates to temporality and asks what 'post', in this context, means: how does a particular story position itself towards some event, major change, or catastrophe, and what kind of relationship does it construct between the time 'before', the time 'after', and the event. The other question relates to the nature of the event itself, and asks how we are to understand 'apocalyptic' in a certain context: does it merely denote a colloquial understanding of 'apocalypse' as a catastrophic event of a large scale, or does the story in fact perform something similar in kind to the biblical revelation of the future that is granted to St. John – is something, in fact, revealed or disclosed?[5]

It is probably no coincidence that post-apocalyptic fiction, as a genre, is thriving in a time full of ecological, social, and cultural anxiety. At the same time, it is not a recent phenomenon within modern fiction.[6] Heather J. Hicks even goes so far as to argue that, 'as an alternative to postmodern formal experimentation', contemporary post-apocalyptic fiction 'interrogate[s] the category of modernity' as such (2016: 2). Eva Horn observes that it is in the Anthropocene that humans tell more and more stories about worlds in which they cease to exist. The vision of imminent catastrophe on an apocalyptic scale, she argues, is, in contemporary western culture, both an anxious dream and the object of paradoxical desires (cf. 2014: 11–12). In fact, it has become common, in recent decades, to regularly diagnose 'contemporary' western culture as being obsessed with tales of the end. In a 1980 lecture, Jacques Derrida bemoans a 'Newly Arisen Apocalyptic Tone in Philosophy' and denounces it as an obsession of contemporary western society (cf. [1980] 1999: 145). At the same time, contemporary post-apocalyptic fiction also critically reflects on this cultural obsession with

---

extrapolated to a more or less frightening extreme in order to confront readers, as it were, with the writing on the wall' (2015: 379). I would argue, however, that the distinction cannot be drawn as strictly as this model implies. Instead, I believe it is more productive to think of dystopian and post-apocalyptic fiction as a continuum, with more or less religious or eschatological implications, and a more or less explicit concern with being read as a warning. Hollm himself, in fact, acknowledges this continuum in contemporary fiction by discussing it as 'post-apocalyptic dystopia'.

[5]The *Oxford English Dictionary* gives exactly these two interpretations of the usage of the word 'apocalypse', although the examples given there also demonstrate that the former, more colloquial usage of the term is a much more recent phenomenon.

[6]James Lovegrove (2012) traces the history of apocalyptic and post-apocalyptic fiction throughout the nineteenth and twentieth centuries, starting from the publication of Mary Shelley's *The Last Man*, which Jan Hollm, too, identifies as 'the first relevant text in English that described the world after a global epidemic and the ensuing post-apocalyptic struggle for survival' (2015: 380). Strikingly, and in contrast to Berger's observations about more recent post-apocalyptic fiction, Shelley's novel is all about the representation of the cataclysmic event itself, which suggests that the unspeakablility and unrepresentability of the 'moment of obliteration' might be a specifically modern phenomenon.

apocalyptic temporality and shifts its emphasis 'from apocalypse as utopian revelation to apocalypse as dystopian catastrophe', enabling stories beyond the scripts of teleology, and insisting on 'the power of agency' (De Cristofaro 2020: 6, 15).

Historically speaking, several recent periods have been argued to have produced a particular cultural proclivity for post-apocalyptic narration, such as the Holocaust and the horrors of the Nazi regime (cf. Berger 1999), or the development of nuclear and hydrogen bombs in the Second World War and the Cold War (cf. Hollm 2015: 382). In 1999 – two years before 9/11 – Berger diagnosed 'a pervasive post-apocalyptic sensibility in recent American culture' (1999: xiii)[7], and Eckart Voigts, sixteen years after Berger, observes more generally that 'narratives of a future societal collapse or crisis have responded to a set of urgent challenges that, if anything, have increased at the beginning of the 21st century' (2015: 2). At the heart of this fascination with stories of a great disaster lies, according to Horn, a vexed relation to the future, which becomes a radical break with what is now, an end to continuity, the idea that if the status quo continues, catastrophe is inevitable. The present is perceived as a tipping point, the culmination of a crisis that is about to fulfil itself in the total destruction of life (cf. Horn 2014: 15–20).

Fiction about the post-apocalypse, then, says more about the present condition of a culture that produces it than about any possible futures that are being projected in these stories. In this sense, we can understand post-apocalyptic fiction as, in fact, aspiring towards the revelatory: it claims that it unearths something that lies hidden underneath the structures of current society and culture (cf. Horn 2014: 25). This claim, of course, is highly controversial because it can make post-apocalyptic fiction, like any prophetic sort of text, tend towards the ideological: the structures that are laid bare in a fictional account of a possible future can come to seem almost inevitable, while, in fact, they always remain narrative decisions and projections of their time. Berger outright rejects the idea that, in postmodern post-apocalypse, anything is revealed at all. In reference to Baudrillard, he denounces the post-apocalyptic rhetoric of contemporary commodity culture as pure surface: '[t]here can be no unveiling because there is nothing under the surface: there is only surface; the map has replaced the terrain' (1999: 9).

Reading post-apocalyptic fiction, then, is an ambiguous task, because fiction of this kind always presents itself as both a warning, as 'haunting admonishments about the legacy we risk leaving generations to come'

---

[7]Hollm also argues that '[p]olitics and apocalyptic vision … create a unique blend in American culture' (2015: 389).

(Hicks 2016: 9), calling us to action in the present if we want to prevent *this* future, and as an elegy: it is, within the fictional world, too late anyway, and we can do no more than mourn what has been lost (cf. Horn 2014: 24–9). Post-apocalyptic fiction performs a crisis of meaning, grappling to come to terms with the realization that neither history nor stories of linear progress and process can help explain the loss at hand. In this chapter, however, I argue that some contemporary post-apocalyptic texts do more than just adhere to this double-bind. Instead, rather than just projecting either naïve and ideologically charged warnings about the end to come, or an eloquent sadness about loss, the ambiguous and complex narratives that this fiction unfolds become spaces which dodge the apparent inevitability of events, the teleological necessity of a certain set of actions, and the general notion of a lack of alternatives. As such, my argument follows Hicks' claim that stories of the post-apocalypse 'also imagine new ways in which life might take shape after the destruction of contemporary modernity' (2016: 9).

The settings of post-apocalyptic fiction often host manifold conservative reiterations of the nuclear family as a last beacon of hope for the survival of the human race. They also, however, make room for thinking kinship afresh, and present their audience with fictional 'practice[s] of learning to live and die well with each other in a thick present' (Haraway 2016: 1). In this context, queerness emerges as an unruly, anti-futuristic drive, which ultimately becomes an impulse to act differently. Post-apocalyptic fiction, on this level, too, creatively negotiates the possibilities of thinking and living not just either backwards or forwards, but also sideways, and thus unfolds a 'powerful critical mechanism' (Hicks 2016: 14). The place of hope, in post-apocalyptic fiction, I argue, stems not so much, as Hicks claims, from the residual utopic impulse inherent in the pleasurable generic conventions of this kind of storytelling (cf. 21). Instead, hope lies in the possibility to do things differently in the present, to deviate from the futuristic, teleological script, which often becomes manifest in a paranoid fixation on the figure of the Child. It lies in embracing reparation in the form of what Bovermann (2019) would diagnose – and prescribe – as a melancholic disposition, an acceptance of the possibility that things really are as bad as they seem. From this reparative position, hope emerges not on some future horizon, but in the potential for acts of solidarity and for the formation of kinship in the shared experience of loss in the here and now.

The anti-futurism practised in the texts at hand also problematizes any straightforward – or rather straightbackward – relation to the past. History and memory, in the post-apocalyptic situation, can become paranoid points of reference that keep characters from relating in new and caring ways to their post-disaster environment, while some of those who do not share in the memories of 'before' – like many of the child characters – manage to practise forms of belonging and care that go beyond the generational scripts passed on and preserved by those who want to re-establish the status quo. This ambiguous relation to the past bears a lot of potential for moral conflict. What, after all, is a society without memory or history? Both a strategic denial of historical facts, a re-writing of history, and, importantly, a certain obsession with imminent disaster have long been part of the anti-democratic and discriminatory practices and mindsets of right-wing politics and propaganda.[8] This discomfort is something worth observing in and of itself in the context of contemporary fiction's partial a-historicism.

In this chapter, I analyse how the texts under discussion use the conflicted relationship with memory and history under the conditions of the post-apocalypse to make room for the emergence of reparative notions of kinship, and for a hope that enables care and action in the present. As such, what I am looking for in these texts reverberates with Derrida's critique of memory as always reconstructive: 'the memory of a past that has not been present, the memory of the future – the movement of memory as tied to the future and not only the past, memory turned toward the promise, toward what is coming, what is arriving, what is happening tomorrow' (1995: 383). With Derrida, and with some of the characters in the texts discussed below, I want to turn away from a memory which, in a continual teleological movement, keeps constructing a past and a future which are liveable only for some, and instead observe that the fictional experience – like, for Derrida, the philosophical experience – 'is not just a matter of remembering but also of something altogether other' (ibid.). This 'something altogether other', in my explorations of Cormac McCarthy's *The Road* and AMC's *The Walking Dead*, are the reparative relations to temporality and belonging that emerge in-between and aside from dominant paranoid logics of teleology and futurism. The focus thus shifts from a question of survival or salvation to a pragmatic concern for care in the devastated present.

---

[8]Theodor W. Adorno, for example, in a recently published 1967 lecture he gave in Vienna, points out these apocalyptic tendencies in right-wing cultures, 'that, in some sense, they crave for catastrophe, that they feed on fantasies of the end of the world' ([1967] 2019: 19–20, my translation).

1

Radical solidarity: The (anti-) futuristic politics of Cormac McCarthy's *The Road*

Considering the fairly recent publication of Cormac McCarthy's 2006 Pulitzer Prize–winning novel *The Road*, it has attracted an astounding amount of critical attention, not least because it reverberates both with fundamental questions concerning the limits of humanity, and with its immediate cultural and historical context in the early twenty-first century. Alan Warner (2006), in his review for the *Guardian*, accordingly calls it 'a very great novel, but one that needs a context in both the past and in so-called post-9/11 America'. *The Road* tells the story of an unnamed father and son who travel through a dead and devastated North American landscape towards the sea in the south to escape the cold of winter. With a few exceptions, everything, from the ever-present ash to the few surviving people themselves, is described as grey; colour exists mostly in the context of the father's dreams and memories of a lost pre-apocalyptic past. The novel's language is both reduced to a minimum of dialogue and description, and loaded with archaic and biblical terminology, rendering an elegiac register that imbues the text with a claim to ancient and timeless authority. On the one hand, this claim is seductively convincing (and probably part of the reason for the novel's critical success), but also begs the question as to who the guarantors of this narrative authority are.

That this is a text fundamentally concerned with questions of hope and kinship (in terms of both the nuclear family and its dissolution, and the 'community of men') has been repeatedly established by critics. Eva Horn includes the novel as a paradigmatic example of a narrative breakdown of the future in her study of the future as catastrophe (cf. 2014: 240), and several critics have read the text alongside Edelman's polemic against reproductive futurism.¹ Despite this rare instance of queer theory becoming safely embedded in mainstream discussions of a novel by a less-than-queer author, none of these critics attempt to contextualize the text's dynamics of hope and futurity within a wider debate on negativity of a specifically queer strand.

In this chapter, I explore the consequences of the fact that, as Inger-Anne Søfting puts it, the novel 'play[s] with opposites as its discourse contains elements of utopia as well as dystopia' (2013: 705). In order to offer a new perspective on the story's rather sober take on a future-oriented notion of hope, I will attempt to synthesize different approaches to the novel's ambiguous rendering of temporality and belonging, and make them productive for thinking about a reparative decoupling of hope and futurity. My reading thus contrasts with and complements those by critics who, like Matthew Ryan (2008), foreground the text's more conventionally utopian impulses.² At the heart of the narrative in *The Road* lies, I argue, a concern with paranoid and reparative notions of temporality. My aim is to make Sedgwick's framing of contemporary *critical* modalities productive for an analysis of the dynamics of fictional discourse. The father's investment in futurity and generation finds expression in his religiously justified will to save his child and, ultimately, his belief in God. This investment grinds against a blatant lack of narrative progress and a general sense of timelessness, and the child's at times radical opposition to his father's futurism, to which he offers an alternative stance of passivity and unconditional solidarity beyond the heteronormative nuclear family. While the father insists on a clear-cut opposition between 'the good guys' and 'the bad guys', and gives this dichotomy an additional moral charge by claiming himself and his son to be 'carrying the fire', the son's own position oscillates between an orientation by his father's ethics of kin and futurity, and an independent drive to action in the here and now, which makes him, in the bleak and brutal context

---

[1] Naomi Morgenstern, for example, describes the novel as 'a fantasy of escape from the Traumatic Real, a phantasmatic escape that Edelman designates "The Child"' (2014: 42). Adeline Johns-Putra extends the metaphor even further, arguing that the novel, read as a contemporary comment on climate change, aligns the figure of the Child with 'Nature' as such: '[i]t is ... children who serve as shorthand for the future and therefore as a particularly emotive marker of the problem of climate change' (2016: 520). Julian Caradec, finally, reads the novel in the context of the wider sociological history of the value of children in the United States, arguing that, in the context of the novel's post-apocalyptic world, '[n]ot only have children reverted from a sentimental value (which the father desperately attempts to uphold) to an economic one, they have reverted even further to a status of consumption goods, as have all remaining humans' (2020: 117).

[2] Ryan discusses McCarthy's unique combination of formal registers – pragmatic description, Beckettian dialogue, and elegiac nature poetry – arguing that '[t]his formal dissonance in the novel alludes to the desire for the eventual reconciliation of these elements, beyond the boundary of the novel, in the utopian remaking of the world itself' (2008: 162).

of the story, the more radically humanist and the more radically Christian character.

In order to arrive at a useful complication of the intersection between hope and kinship as they feature in *The Road*, I proceed from a consideration of the broader implications of temporality and gendered/(non-)reproductive structures of belonging in the text, through a more detailed analysis of the two male protagonists and their entanglement in paranoid/reparative dynamics, and conclude with a reading of the novel's 2009 film adaptation and its recent appropriation in an installation by Swiss multimedia artist Christoph Draeger. I am aiming for a reading of the text that acknowledges the implications of a fictional journey which turns out to be 'not a linear progress, ... [but] a turning back' (Gray 2010: 119), for an affective notion of hope which 'turns its back' on futurity, and instead gestures towards a radical politics of solidarity in the present. That this understanding of *The Road* comes at the cost of any safely articulated notion of social or political community and settles for the 'mere' prospect of immediate continuance – 'the chance not of being saved but of surviving' (Gray 2010: 123) – makes this novel sit uncomfortably within a recent archive that addresses the question of what remains of hope in disillusioned times. The translation into film and its artistic reception, especially, show that the text's own journey through different media has been running the risk of reducing its multiple ambiguities and uncertainties to the story's ultimately conservative, paranoid surface narrative of a damaged heterosexual family's struggle to be fixed and made whole again. And while I agree with Arielle Zibrak that *The Road* is 'situated in the paranoia of its contemporary moment ... [and] establishes hope where we always hope to find it: within the structure of familial relationships' (2012: 104), I will show how we can read this particular contemporary text for more than just its paranoid surface structure, and find that it also evokes a reparative notion of hope which sidesteps the logic of paranoid futurity.

'The clocks stopped at 1:17': Temporality and teleology

Temporality, in the general narrative setup of *The Road*, emerges as a constant tension between a pervasive sense of timelessness and stagnation, and the implicitly teleological drive of the journey trope. Like many contemporary post-apocalyptic narratives, the novel is concerned with the idea of a before and after, while the event that divides the two remains curiously vague: we do not learn what it was exactly that brought about the ecological and social devastation the aftermath of which is the story's setting. There is only one explicit reference to the event itself: '[t]he clocks stopped at 1:17. A long shear of light and then a series of low concussions' (McCarthy 2007: 52). The image of the stopping clock reinforces the sense that the division of time into a before and after is also a cut between a world in which time had meaning and provided structure, and one in which time itself has been lost and characters move through a space of eternal nowness. In this space, the external world has not simply stopped. It is both the same as before, but also fundamentally changed: '[e]verything as it once had been save faded and weathered' (8). This particular moment also demarcates the beginning of the end of meaning: those – like the father – who can still remember things and their names survive alongside those – like the son – who lack experience of the vanished world, and for whom the objects and ideas from that world are nothing but empty signifiers: '[t]he names of things slowly following those things into oblivion. Colors. The names of birds. Things to eat. Finally the names of things one believed to be true. More fragile than he would have thought' (88–9). It is important to note that it is the father's voice which evokes this elegiac register. A crucial difference in temporal experience divides his own from the boy's experience of the current reality: the child cannot access meaning and memory of a past he cannot make to signify in his own present. Within the specific context of the novel's fictional setup, this lack of historical embeddedness becomes a liberating condition: the work of mourning the past is all the father's, while the boy's language and meaning rely on his experiences in the present. For him, language can become 'the stuff of social bonding' (Temko 2014: 174) in the here and now. Significantly, McCarthy sets the stopping of the clocks alongside the birth of the boy, an 'improbable appearance' (2007: 59), which charges the child with a twofold meaning: on the one hand, he very obviously represents that which goes on despite the end of the world, a canvas on which a futuristic fantasy of continuance can be inscribed; on the other hand, however, he is also the one born into the timeless present, not charged with the task of memory or tradition. The lost world simply is not his world.

Where the ability (or burden) to remember the pre-apocalyptic past represents a crucial dividing line between the father and his son, this temporal break is also reflected in the novel's overall rendering of the past. Traces of history, which pull the story back into the temporal specificities of a particularized geography – the United States – only feature in two ways in the novel. As a more general theme, the remnants of contemporary consumer culture emerge both as that which enables survival in the present – the man and the boy keep finding things – and as signifiers that have lost their meaning in a post-capitalist world, 'advertisements for goods which no longer existed' (128). The Coca-Cola the man finds, for example, means nothing to the boy (cf. 23). At the same time, in a world in which nothing grows or lives any more, survival crucially depends on finding stocks of consumer goods, as the man and the boy do when they miraculously happen upon a bunker filled with everything they need just when they are about to starve to death: '[c]rate upon crate of canned goods. Tomatoes, peaches, beans, apricots. Canned hams. Corned beef. Hundreds of gallons of water in ten gallon plastic jerry jugs. Paper towels, toiletpaper, paper plates. Plastic trashbags stuffed with blankets' (138).

It is quite striking that McCarthy's novel, as Simon Schleusener puts it, 'conceives of a version of the end of capitalism, which indeed – in keeping with the neoliberal imagination – coincides with the end of history, and eventually, the end of the world' (2017: 8) – a common theme of many post-apocalyptic narratives. In contrast to Schleusener, however, I see something reparative in the novel's unlikely series of discoveries of leftover 'stuff': for the boy, in particular, these residual traces of consumerism are neither charged with nostalgia, nor do they give him a critical perspective on a dehumanizing system. Instead, they are vital goods which can be found and shared. While it is certainly plausible to put forward a reading of the novel which 'postulates that a world devoid of capitalism just as quickly becomes a world devoid of any human collective' (Miller 2014: 39), I argue that the remnants of goods scattered throughout this fictional landscape serve to highlight the contrast between the father's sense of competition and his logic of scarcity, and the boy's drive to share whatever they have and find.

Apart from its emergence through the debris of consumer culture, history, understood as a specific, supra-individual, and recognizable past, materializes in the text in only two other instances, both of which evoke histories of violence that have left their painful mark on contemporary cultural consciousness. The first is an observation the father makes about his son: '[h]e looked like something out of a deathcamp. Starved, exhausted, sick with fear' (McCarthy 2007: 117). This unusually concrete reference to the Holocaust on one level serves to foreground the absurdity of the situation in which the novel places its characters. Bringing the story world's global and all-embracing devastation, the cause of which remains unknown, into conversation with the racist and politically motivated extermination of millions of people evokes the ongoing difficulty to process historical trauma of this scale. It also foregrounds the protagonists' struggle to deal with a situation which, to an extent, denies them agency: because it 'has no clear cause there is no one and nothing to blame for it, and also nothing to be done about it' (Søfting 2013: 708). At the same time, this offhand invocation of the historical horror and trauma of the Holocaust is provocative, to say the least, if not downright inappropriate. The narrative, in this instance, does not distinguish between historically specific violence done by one group of people to another (in the actual deathcamps of history), and the de-historicized hopelessness of a universal cataclysm, which places the text uncomfortably in-between the more general implications of its otherwise minimally referential plot, and a kind of social criticism that seems oddly out of place.

Even more striking in this respect is a moment in the novel which marks the beginning of a climactic scene towards the end of its first half, and which foreshadows its horrific conclusion. Entering 'a once grand house … tall and stately with white doric columns across the front', the narrator remarks that '[c]hattel slaves had once trod those boards bearing food and drink on silver trays' (McCarthy 2007: 105–6). While, throughout the rest of the novel, localizing its fictional geography rests on contextual knowledge about McCarthy's general preference for certain US-American geographies as settings for his stories, this remark suddenly makes explicit the intuition that this house indeed represents the violence done by plantation owners to Black slaves. In a curious move that is at once historically specific and de-specifying, the violent open secret of the history of the actual United States becomes the literalized uncovered secret of this fictional space: opening a locked door in the floor, the father and son discover 'naked people, male and female, all trying to hide, shielding their faces with their hands. On the mattress lay a man with his legs gone to the hip and the stumps of them blackened and burnt' (110). While this scene more generally figures as part of the novel's questioning of the boundaries of those that still count as human, it is curious in terms of the novel's relation to history: it uncomfortably parallelizes a clearly raced history of violence with a scene of brutality in which the humans-turned-chattel-turned-food are still gendered ('male and female'), but, like all other characters in the novel, not racially marked. One question that arises, then, is what to make of a text which, despite a clear and, in fact, unique historical reference, seems to relegate race to a pre-apocalyptic social past, while binary gender relations are both highlighted and done away with: the fight for survival on the road, it seems, is a white man's fight. In this sense, the novel stages a rupture with the pre-apocalyptic past which is partially bridged by fitful hauntings of histories of violent social relations and social stratification. These hauntings appear all the more ghostly for their lack of cultural context in a fictional world in which the experience of social and cultural continuity in historical time has been broken off.

Aside from negotiating different relations to hope and futurity through its human characters, the novel grounds a wider idea of a future *beyond* human survival in the material world: just as the physical remains of consumer culture voicelessly harken back to what was before, the material artefacts of human making in the present are the only clues about what *will* remain. Coming upon a train in the woods, the father and son reflect on its existence across the imaginable past and future: '[h]as it been here for a long time? Yes. I think so. A pretty long time … If they saw different worlds what they knew was the same. That the train would sit there slowly decomposing for all eternity and that no train would ever run again' (180). This temporal contrast between the disinterested transition of material remains from one stage of existence and one point in time to another, and the human survivors' struggle in the present is even more blatant when, towards the end of the novel, the father and son finally arrive at the sea, where a ship has stranded on the coast: '[t]he steel was gray and saltscoured but he could make out the worn gilt lettering. Pajaro de Esperanza' (223). In this fictional world, hope clearly needs to be reconfigured to mean something more (or something less) than the failed technical, social, and geographical progress the rusting ship's name announces. In a novel which, aside from its heavily symbolic materiality, employs a striking amount of Christian imagery and language, the question of hope must be considered alongside the question of redemption.

This already brings us close to thinking more concretely about the place of reparation in the novel. Shelly L. Rambo rightly points towards the crux McCarthy confronts his readers with in *The Road*, presenting us with 'a schizophrenic, and distinctly American post-apocalyptic crisis of meaning; between the craving for a happy ending (for resolution, for redemption) and the recognition of its impossibility (there is, in Christian terms, no resurrection ahead)' (2008: 101). I want to follow some of the lines of thought in Rambo's exemplary reading of the novel. Like myself, she locates the possibility of the text's ambiguous suspension between hope and its impossibility in the novel's rendering of the temporal: '[t]emporal categories of past, present, and future shatter in experiences of trauma. The past does not remain the past; a future is not imaginable' (108). This idea of witnessing in the present gestures towards the attempt, in my own analysis, to locate reparation in an acknowledgement of a traumatic rupture from the past, and a turning-away from a futuristic narrative of redemption which, as it manifests itself in the character of the father, is as harmful as it must remain unfulfilled.

Whereas the father can only fully embrace the narrative's anti-futuristic drive when he is about to die ('What time of year? What age the child?' (McCarthy 2007: 261)), for the boy, the acceptance of a loss that is not his own – of a past and a future – can become an enabling stance that leads him to acts of radical solidarity. As such, for the son, redemption, understood as reparation, does not – or at least not mainly – lie, as Stefan Skrimshire would have it, in 'the persistence and memory of that which refuses to be forgotten ... the persistence of beings who can remember' (2011: 12), but rather in the boy's ability to succumb neither to the pull of a traumatic past, nor to the harmful figuration of a future at all cost. That this perspective sits awkwardly with the novel's few references to actual, harmful, and traumatic historical pasts is a contradiction the text itself does not resolve, just as it does not resolve its symbolic and heavily loaded conflation of mothers, 'catamites', and anthropophagy. Before exploring the paranoid and reparative dynamics represented by the father and son in more detail, I would like to turn precisely to the novel's politics of gender and sexuality, and the manner in which they become associated with cannibalism.

Mothers, catamites, and cannibals: Gender, sexuality, and family

In *The Road*, female characters are conspicuously absent from the narrative. Nell Sullivan convincingly explains this absence by categorizing the text as a male sentimental novel, 'a sentimental form that is only possible in the absence of the mother and indeed the nation ... *The Road*'s fictional apocalypse is a crisis point, allowing McCarthy to imagine a manhood unconstrained by domesticity, capitalism, and nation' (2013: 81, 84). Women are mentioned only a few times as part of the groups of 'bad guys' the father and son encounter, and only four women are singled out from the crowd to appear as individual characters: the boy's mother; a pregnant woman whose child gets killed and eaten right after birth; a woman whose male companion the father kills; and the woman whose family take in the boy at the end of the novel. All but one of these women are mothers, and the novel's treatment of reproduction and motherhood deserves some consideration in the context of my wider interest in the relationship between temporality and kinship.

The boy's mother is the text's most prominent female character. She is absent from the beginning, and only occasionally features in the father's memories and dreams, which often reduce her to an object of his desiring male gaze, while also confirming the reader's suspicion concerning her probable death: '[i]n dreams his pale bride came to him out of a green and leafy canopy. Her nipples pipeclayed and her rib bones painted white' (McCarthy 2007: 18). A later dream explicitly refers to the question of responsibility, which is one of the novel's central concerns: '[i]n his dream she was sick and he cared for her. The dream bore the look of sacrifice but he thought differently. He did not care for her and she died alone somewhere in the dark and there is no other dream nor other waking world and there is no other tale to tell' (32). The father's doubts, in this passage, about whether he has cared enough for a person he deems his charge mirror his sense of responsibility for the child, his self-declared mission of saving his own (already damaged) family from succumbing to the end of the world. On the one hand, this ties in well with the general impression that this is a novel about questions of care – for each other, or, in a more abstract sense, for the world (cf. Johns-Putra 2016) – but this sense of responsibility is also put into stark perspective by the mother's own refusal to care for others. As opposed to the father, the mother (only ever referred to as 'she' in the narrative) fully embraces negativity, and fundamentally questions not only the father's futuristic logic, but also the continuance of the gendered meaning of ethical and social frameworks, and the meaning of humanity as such: '[w]e're not survivors. We're the walking dead in a horror film ... I don't care. I don't care if you cry. It doesn't mean anything to me ... They say that women dream of danger to those in their care and men of danger to themselves. But I don't dream at all' (McCarthy 2007: 55, 57). Even more explicitly, she rejects the father's wish to charge their child with the burden of signifying a futuristic hope, and points to the limits and the absurdity of the father's quest:

> You cant protect us. You say you would die for us but what good is that? I'd take him with me if it weren't for you. You know I would. It's the right thing to do ... The one thing I can tell you is that you wont survive for yourself. A person who had no one would be well advised to cobble together some passable ghost. Breathe it into being and coax it along with words of love. Offer it each phantom crumb and shield it from harm with your body. As for me my only hope is for eternal nothingness and I hope it with all my heart. (56)

The mother thus frames the father's hope for a future as he finds it in the child as an empty fantasy, a mere ghost, a projection dependent on an externalization of the will to go on into an object of love. The mother's radical refusal of motherly love and care as opportunistic fictions in a world which renders these categories meaningless makes her a striking figure among other literary child killers. Her alternative vision of nihilistic hope for nothingness is a provocation in a cultural context in which a mother's murder of her own children is still considered the ultimate transgression. In the end, the mother in *The Road* simply leaves, vacating the narrative to be forgotten, and to let others fight for survival: '[s]he was gone and the coldness of it was her final gift' (58).

The novel's equation of 'woman' with 'bad mother' is further enforced by the fact that the story does not offer a single example of a female character who is not implicated in reproduction, a narrative choice which reinforces the contrast between hope invested in the continuation of family – which 'is made into an institution of paranoid defence' (Ryan 2008: 156) – and the impossibility of such reproductive hope in the life-denying world that is the novel's setting. In fact, the mother's threat to kill the child is actualized at a later point in the novel. In one of the text's goriest episodes, the father and son observe a group of people, '[t]hree men and a woman. The woman walked with a waddling gait and as she approached he could see that she was pregnant' (McCarthy 2007: 195). There is no further description or personification of this rare female character – she is reduced to representing 'the pregnant woman' as such in this post-apocalyptic world. A few pages later, the father and son discover 'a charred human infant headless and gutted and blackening on the spit' (198). Even within the novel's brutalized fictional landscape, this scene stands out for its shock value, and the horror goes two ways: the image of the cannibalized infant – in a gory literalization of Freud's child who is afraid of being devoured by its own mother (cf. [1931] 1963: 531) – in effect directly transferred from womb to mouth, as witnessed first by the boy, evokes the scandalizing accusation that seems to follow from the logic of reproductive futurism: if the child is *not* the future, the bad guys will eat it! As Arielle Zibrak puts it, '[t]he most horrific act of violence is the act of violence against the baby – not the adult – and the most debased human is the one who commits this act ... Humanity becomes divided between those who would do anything to protect their children ... and everyone else' (2012: 111). I would add that, in *The Road*, this division seems to run along gendered lines: throughout most of the novel (with the exception of the ending), those who do not care enough and expose their children to the double threat of being killed and cannibalized are the women and mothers. Men, in particular the boy's father, must protect the children from this female threat: 'Papa is all that stands between the boy and death, the only thing that protects the boy from his lethal mother' (Sullivan 2013: 90–1). In this scene, the mother's transgressive act – be it the killing itself or the lack of care for the child – is not shown, but it is present as the dark, unspoken implication of the image of the dead infant. And like the boy's mother, this transgressive female vacates the scene, without outrage, and without explanation.

Where the novel thus equates reproductive femininity with negativity and antisociality, the association of motherhood and cannibalism also becomes curiously combined with 'deviant' masculinity and sexuality, reinforcing the story's underlying masculinist drive. Just before the father, for the first time, designates a group of people they encounter on their journey as 'the bad guys', the narrative characterizes this group's otherness through a striking amalgamation of differently connoted signifiers:

> They passed two hundred feet away, the ground shuddering lightly. Tramping. Behind them came wagons drawn by slaves in harness and piled with goods of war and after that the women, perhaps a dozen in number, some of them pregnant, and lastly a supplementary consort of catamites, illclothed against the cold and fitted in dogcollars and yoked each to each. (McCarthy 2007: 92)

Within the space of these few lines, the text establishes a complicated grid of associations that designates the wandering hordes the father and the boy encounter as morally defunct. Women are – this time collectively – relegated to an existence as machines for producing more human meat. Since the narrative – or rather the father who serves as the narrative's main focalizer – clearly places the group the women are travelling in with the fearful cannibals, reproduction here fully becomes production for an anthropophagic meat market. Motherhood and cannibalism again go hand in hand as negative foils for the moral quest of the 'good guys'. In addition, however, this is the only instance in which the novel also explicitly links the moral deprivation of 'the bad guys' with sexual perversion. Apart from the sado-masochistic connotations of the slaves' harnesses and the dog collars, the most curious single word is the mentioning of 'catamites'. This archaic term for the passive partner in male-male anal intercourse fully unfolds, in this context, its negative connotations of effeminacy and sexual perversion. Arielle Zibrak even argues that, '[w]ere the gaze reversed, the relationship between the man and the boy might also appear catamitic. The death of the boy's mother has disturbed the proper heteronormative order' (2012: 114). While I do not find Zibrak's reading of the relationship between father and son as potentially transgressive fully convincing, I agree that both the text's designation of its mothers as quitters and/or monstrous child eaters, and its evocation of 'perverse' male-male sexuality produces a heterosexist aesthetics and politics which structures much of the dynamic of the story's drive towards a programme of futuristic hope, evoking Edelman's '*sintho*mosexuals who figure the death drive of the social' (2004: 153, emphasis in original).

Cannibalism itself appears in the narrative only in the two instances discussed above, both of which leave a lasting impression on the reader because of their crass interruptions of the otherwise less graphic violence that regularly features throughout the novel. David Huebert differentiates between two readings of cannibalism in *The Road*. One, 'traditional' cannibalism or anthropophagy, he argues, implies another, a more abstract ecological criticism implicit in the text:

> [T]hese humans eating other humans serve as monstrous emissaries of a possible future, demonstrating what may become of a species already engaged in the act of eating itself. *The Road* suggests that insofar as the planet is the 'body' of humanity, human history, at least since the Industrial Revolution, has been a spectacle of the particular kind of self-cannibalisation I call 'ecological cannibalism'. (2017: 67)

I find Huebert's reading of cannibalism as both a failed past and an undesirable future very productive: like the uncaring mothers and the un(re)productive catamites, cannibalism – which here serves as a scandalizing 'umbrella deviation' from proper morality – seems to place the father and his quest to save the child and reach the coast on the right side of a history which, although it has ended, must be saved by those who 'carry the fire' and hold on to a telos which claims to preserve the moral 'community of men' itself. That this community literally ends up being a community of *men* is a tension which not only offers opportunity for criticism, but also becomes the space in which a potentially reparative counter-programme, as acted out by the boy, may emerge. The associative chain cannibals-mothers-catamites, then, works to establish, for the father's authoritative narrative – and, to an extent, for the novel as a whole – the realm of moral deprivation the father's futuristic hope aims to save his child from. And the phantasmic telos of this hope must be the (vanilla-) heterosexual, reproductive, caring nuclear family.

Just before the novel's conclusion, when the father has died and the boy is on his own, the narrative actualizes this hope in the form of a family that adopts the boy, reintegrating him into the structures of the nuclear family, including substitute father, caring mother, and siblings. Once the boy has ascertained that the man is 'one of the good guys', 'carrying the fire', and not a cannibal (McCarthy 2007: 282, 283), thus re-establishing the boundaries of the father's moral community, his new mother, whose 'presence quite simply reestablishes the proper heteronormative order ruptured when the boy's mother died' (Zibrak 2012: 123), finally inscribes the boy into a seemingly inevitable logic of familial continuity and Christian redemption: '[t]he woman when she saw him put her arms around him and held him. Oh, she said, I am so glad to see you. She would talk to him sometimes about God ... She said that the breath of God was his breath yet though it pass from man to man through all of time' (McCarthy 2007: 286). By invoking the temporal structure of Christian eschatology, and by embodying the very logic of reproductive futurism that underlies much of the story's narrative drive, the woman relegates the nightmare of cannibalism, transgressive sexuality, and bad motherhood to the boy's past, and provides him with a sequel and conclusion to the father's quest for salvation.

Of course, this 'happy ending' is more than ambiguous: the context of the story world provides enough evidence to assume that, ultimately, a continued existence of human beings in this world cannot be sustained. Although it might seem 'hopeful that there are other good people left in the world, ... there are no promises of regeneration in or through nature' (Søfting 2013: 712). As such, I am not convinced by the apparent promise of biological continuity some critics see in this reconstruction of the nuclear family (cf. e.g. Sullivan 2013: 97), and rather agree with critics who, like Arielle Zibrak, are suspicious of the redemptive connotations of the novel's ending: 'the new family is not a convincing vision of redemption; they are instead just another oasis amid a wasteland without hope or future' (2012: 123).[3] The question then remains whether the novel affords room for a reading towards reparation and hope that does not either buy into the flawed logic of reproductive futurism, or succumb to an unambiguous stance of desperate negativity. In the following, I argue that it is in the figure of the boy and in his actions that a reparative notion of hope beyond futurity becomes tangible. While the father's ideology and actions coincide with the more directly obvious programme of masculinist, heterosexist survivalism, a careful analysis of the child protagonist opens up a perspective on the story's more subtle undertones of radical passivity and solidarity.

---

[3] Jacob M. Powning even reads the novel's happy ending as 'the boy's wishful dream' (2020: 26).

Paranoia: The father

As we have seen, on one level, hope, in *The Road*, is closely tied to heteronormative generation and a teleological and theological narrative of redemption, and the text marks this kind of hope as paranoid. In terms of characterization, this paranoia is most obviously condensed in the ideological dispositions and actions of the father. Most of the novel is told from his perspective, and he thus also becomes the hegemonic voice of meaning making in this world devoid of meaning. In fact, it often remains unclear whether the more generally reflexive episodes in the book are meant to originate in the father's thoughts, or to be read as comments from the heterodiegetic narrator. The text is scattered with paragraphs like the following, which present more general considerations concerning the state of the story world, but also seem to be imbued with the father's relation to memory and temporality:

> In those first years the roads were peopled with refugees shrouded up in their clothing ... Creedless shells of men tottering down the causeways like migrants in a feverland. The frailty of everything revealed at last ... Look around you. Ever is a long time. But the boy knew what he knew. That ever is no time at all. (McCarthy 2007: 28)

Curiously, this passage ends with an insight into the boy's thoughts, which the reader generally does not get to share. While this detail might be an argument for assigning the passage to a more abstract narrator figure, its general tone corresponds with the father's elegiac disposition. This stylistic peculiarity makes the question of the text's dominant ideology especially pertinent, since most of the religiously charged and eschatological episodes in the book sit in this ambiguous space between the father's thoughts and a potentially more abstract and diffuse narrative voice.[4]

How, then, can we characterize the father's position in the novel's rendering of different relations towards time and temporality? I argue that the father both remains traumatically tied to his memories of a pre-apocalyptic past, and clings to a paranoid narrative of futurity in which he can save his child – and *the* Child, which produces meaning for him. In consequence, he must remain suspicious of anything in the present that renders either his memories or his futuristic quest obsolete. As such, I would qualify Naomi Morgenstern's reading of the father as 'torn between the

---

[4] Tore Rye Andersen, in this context, makes a convincing argument about the relationship between the father's insistence on finding meaning in a post-apocalyptic world and his role as narrator and storyteller: the father 'insists on staying alive and on creating meaning for himself and his son as meaning has been created through millennia: by telling stories' (2021: 68).

appeal to an eternal present, the utopian space of idealized relation between father and son ... and the appeal of a future for his son (hence a future per se)' (2014: 51). While I agree that *The Road* presents the reader with the notion of 'a kind of radical present' which can very well be called 'the utopian dimension of McCarthy's novel' (48), I would hesitate to assign this utopian, radical present to the father. Instead, I would contend that the father's paranoid entanglement with teleology in fact keeps him from seeing beyond the 'appeal of a future', and that it is only the son whose radical solidarity and refusal of the father's ideology enable him to realize a hope that materializes in the here and now.

On one level, the father's entanglement with a teleological temporality of past, (suspicious) present, and future finds expression in his repeatedly remembering things, both from the time when his wife was still alive (and the nuclear family thus intact), and from his own childhood. At an early point in the story, the father uses the defunct remnants of technology to conjure up an illusion of not only traversing space, but also time: 'he picked up the phone and dialed the number of his father's house in that long ago. The boy watched him. What are you doing? he said' (McCarthy 2007: 7). This nostalgic performance is only the first instance in a series of strategies through which the father, while continuing on the road towards his fantasy of a future, also continuously moves back into the past. In several flashbacks, which appear in the text as either memories or dreams, the father links the landscape he is moving through with his son to his own past in an all-male familial pastoral idyll. Remembering a day spent by 'a lake a mile from his uncle's farm where he and his uncle used to go in the fall for firewood', he observes: '[t]his was the perfect day of his childhood. This the day to shape the days upon' (12, 13). The father thus constructs an all-male, pre-apocalyptic past in which nature was still accessible as the scenic backdrop of male-sentimental outdoor activity, and which serves as the bygone standard for happiness. Similarly, his dreams of the past draw him ever further back into a reality that no longer exists. And although he acknowledges early in the narrative that these escapes into memory are dangerous ('He said the right dreams for a man in peril were dreams of peril and all else was the call of languor and death' (18)), he keeps returning to this space, the bygone world of his dreams, throughout their journey.

Crucially, the father also inscribes the religiously sanctioned task of saving his child (for the future) into a mystical past:

This is my child, he said. I wash a dead man's brains out of his hair. That is my job ... [H]e sat holding him while he tousled his hair before the fire to dry it. All of it like some ancient anointing. So be it. Evoke the forms. Where you've nothing else construct ceremonies out of the air and breathe upon them. (74)

Here, the text very explicitly acknowledges the fictional nature of the father's narrative of progression from a past which legitimizes his current task – his 'job' – into a future which is meant to be the result of this task: a phantasmic time and space in which his son will be safe, the journey over, and the job done. The father repeatedly sanctions the legitimacy of this logic through theological reasoning, and simultaneously constructs his task and its implied teleology as a vindication for his violently defensive attitude towards all others outside the father-son dyad: '[m]y job is to take care of you. I was appointed to do that by God. I will kill anyone who touches you. Do you understand?' (77). The father's 'excessive unwillingness to allow the boy to form relationships outside their own' (Zibrak 2012: 107), in fact, comes to stand in stark contrast to the boy's instinct to reach out to others despite the potential threat they might pose. More generally, the father regularly expresses his investment in saving his child and a fantasy of futurity *for* the child and complements the *figure* of the Child with the figure of God as the Father who vouches for this fantasy of reproductive futurism: '[h]e only knew that the child was his warrant. He said: If he is not the word of God God never spoke' (McCarthy 2007: 5). This religious grounding of the father's investment in saving the child is, as Alan Noble argues, what makes his hope both possible and absurd, an absurdity also constitutive of the fantasy of reproductive futurism as such:

> [T]he man in *The Road* believes himself to be appointed by God to care for his son, which also entails a promise with a moral obligation: it must be right and good to keep his son alive even in a world which appears to offer no future … [T]he man's appointment to care for the boy leads him to an absurd hope: that it would be better to keep his boy alive despite the apparent hopelessness of the world. (2011: 97)

We can, however, also read the father's logic of making sense in this world as crucially dependent on a linear movement from traumatic past into redemptive future, and the child and the journey south as the only available signs this logic can inscribe itself onto. Then the father's hope appears less absurd or 'blatantly irrational' (101), but rather profoundly paranoid, in the sense of an investment in teleology at the cost of agency in the present. As Justin T. Noetzel puts it, '[t]he father's driving force in his endless march along the fractured and disintegrating landscape is hope for the discovery of a true homeland for his son, something the boy has never experienced' (2014: 126). While this 'true homeland' most probably does not exist, the march itself and the child with and for whom the father marches take on existential meaning for him. The integrity of the character of the father, then, crucially depends on a religiously sanctioned teleology that needs to preserve a fantasy of leaving behind a destructive past and a devastating present to move linearly on to a better future, however unlikely this might be.

The father's claim to creating a future for his son, which is meant to escape the destruction that surrounds the two characters, finds an apt image in his fixing things. McCarthy's father is a veritable *homo faber*, constantly engaged in activities that aim to transform the broken material world into something that resembles wholeness. For example, when the father fixes a broken wheel on the shopping cart they use to carry their belongings, the text provides detailed evidence of his technical skills:

> [H]e found some tools and emptied out the cart and sat working on the wheel. He pulled the bolt and bored out the collet with a hand drill and resleeved it with a section of pipe he'd cut to length with a hacksaw. Then he bolted it all back together and stood the cart upright and wheeled it around the floor. It ran fairly true. (McCarthy 2007: 16–17)

Throughout the novel, the father's urge to repair broken objects mirrors his more abstract desire to make things right in a world in which the possibility of reparation in the sense of a full reversal to a former state of wholeness has become all but impossible. This dilemma becomes particularly apparent when the violence the father keeps trying to shield his son from finds them nevertheless. After their discovery of the murdered infant, the father keeps insisting, in a prayer-like speech act, that 'everything's okay. I promise' (135). Immediately afterwards, however, the narrator/father acknowledges what the story as a whole keeps pointing to, that maybe there are things in this world that cannot be fixed: 'when he bent to see into the boy's face under the hood of the blanket he very much feared that something was gone that could not be put right again' (136). Hence, the father continuously has to negotiate between re-establishing his credo of futurity, and acknowledging the damage already inflicted, holding himself in denial for the benefit of keeping alive a narrative of teleology that is supposed to keep his son (and himself) going: '[t]his is what the good guys do. They keep trying. They don't give up' (137). The question this character's ethics raises, however, is whether to keep trying and to give up are the only two available options. The son, as we will see later, manages to escape this binary logic.

In *The Road*, the question repeatedly arises as to what the father will do if he can no longer keep his promise that he will never leave his son, and this question involves the father's pondering whether he could – and should – kill his son if he can no longer protect him: '[c]an you do it? When the time comes? When the time comes there will be no time. Now is the time. Curse God and die ... Could you crush that beloved skull with a rock?' (114).[5] On

---

[5] It is striking that McCarthy has the father use this direct quote from the Book of Job in this context. In the Bible, it is Job's wife who exclaims 'Curse God and die' in her exasperation at her stubbornly faithful husband. While the quote appropriately expresses the father's struggle with his own faith, it also ironically evokes an external (female) perspective that questions the man's religious justification of their quest.

the one hand, this spectre of paternal infanticide mirrors the mother's earlier resolution to kill her own child to protect him from a supposedly worse fate ('They'll rape him. They are going to rape us and kill us and you wont face it' (56)); on the other hand – and on a more abstract level – the father's conviction that he must be the one deciding over the life or death of his child also emphasizes both the man's paranoid fear of the present ('Now is the time.'), and his fixation on the idea that *he* is the one who, following God's will, must create a future for this child.

When he is about to die, the father, in a belated move towards a more reparative perspective on his son, both releases the boy from his tie to his own fate and meaning, and ceases to project his existence into an unpredictable future, instead binding him to a moral obligation which, albeit still finding its source in the past, emphasizes the child's social function in the present: 'I cant hold my son dead in my arms. I thought I could but I cant ... You have my whole heart. You always did. You're the best guy. You always were' (279). Not: you always *will be*. The father, however, does not completely surrender his claim to being the author of his son's future: '[b]ut you'll be okay. You're going to be lucky. I know you are' (ibid.). Just before his death, then, the father once more links his paranoid vision of 'fixing things' ('[Y]ou'll be okay.') to an impossible epistemological privilege ('I know you are.'), but this time qualified by the absolute contingency and potentially random nature of luck.

His last words, however, bring the father's ideology fully back to his paranoid belief in the survival of the child as the emblem of goodness in the past and the future, disavowing a present in which nothing is certain but the possibility of sheer dumb luck: '[g]oodness will find the little boy. It always has. It will again' (281). This passage not only negates the possibility of the child being an acting subject, but also projects a phantasmic image of a purely good child which has no potential for actuality in the present. On the other hand, these dying words are absolutely in line with the father's (and the novel's) religious framing of futurity. As Alan Noble puts it, 'to kill his son and commit suicide would be for the man to attest to the belief that God is not good and that there is no better tomorrow waiting' (2011: 104). I do not, however, agree with Noble that the ultimate message of *The Road* is to suggest 'that regardless of how horrific our situation might be, we can act in faith and resist the siren call of nihilistic suicide or cannibalism; we can choose to have hope in a good God, in goodness itself, although this hope is irrational by "human calculation"' (108). I think the text opens up a possibility that lies beyond either of these two options: the boy, as I will demonstrate below, fully accepts the possibility of both individual death and the death of God, sidestepping teleological hope, and instead positions himself with such strategies as improvisation, spontaneous solidarity, and sharing. He weaves a counter-narrative and a counter-ideology into the text which provide it with openings onto more reparative and less futuristic positions. This, it seems to me, is not necessarily 'irrational', but a version of hope that rethinks what being hopeful might mean in a world in which there very well might be no better tomorrow.

Reparation: The boy

The boy repeatedly opposes the father's paranoid focus on teleological hope and heteronormative generation. At several points in the story, he both questions the father's promise of a better future and actively accepts and embraces the fact that he might die. While, for example, the boy openly addresses the very realistic possibility of death, the father displaces this thought out of the present into a vague future: '[a]re we going to die? / Sometime. Not now' (McCarthy 2007: 10). On a more abstract level, the way the boy expresses his wish for death can also stand for an escape from the narrative thrust of the story as such: 'I wish I was with my mom … / You mean you wish you were dead. / Yes. / You musnt say that. / But I do' (55). Within the logic of the novel, we can assume that the mother really did take her own life, and, as such, the boy's desire to be with her really amounts to a death wish. At the same time, however, neither the father and son nor the reader actually witnesses the mother's alleged suicide. She simply leaves, opening the boy's renitent wish to be with his mother up to a reading as a refusal of the text's more general futuristic narrative logic, and of the all-male context he has been forced into by the father and the story of the quest. Leaving this story and its attendant ideological baggage might seem the more attractive option.

This tendency, on the boy's part, to escape the father's (and the novel's) dominant narrative is also reflected in his relation to temporality. He exists purely in the present. To him, the father's memories and stories from the pre-apocalyptic past do not have any meaning: '[s]ometimes the child would ask him questions about the world that for him was not even a memory. He thought hard how to answer. There is no past' (53–4). At the same time, the boy's unusual perspective on temporality gets tied into an emerging framework of kinship which also sharply differs from the father's familial fixations: he not only actively questions the father's futuristic logic, but also extends and partly reverses familial dynamics of care. Throughout the story, the boy keeps insisting on sharing all resources equally with his father, not allowing the latter to sacrifice his own wellbeing for the son's sake: '[y]ou have some [of the Coca Cola], Papa. / I want you to drink it. / You have some' (23). He also bypasses the father's logic of 'good guys' versus 'bad guys' by repeatedly reaching out to strangers, both human and non-human, a strategy the father stubbornly opposes: '[t]hey came upon [a man] shuffling along the road before them ... / Cant we help him? Papa? / No. We cant help him' (49, 50).

This care, which the boy generally extends to all individuals they encounter on the road, is the one most reparative aspect the story has to offer, and several critics have pointed it out as remarkably and productively at odds with the novel's generally paranoid register.[6] I would like to extend these discussions by reading the boy's ethics as a reparative alternative to the father's (and the novel's) paranoid register. Despite his actual dependence on his father for immediate physical protection from the marauders and cannibals they run into on their journey, the boy is quite aware that the father's construction of 'the good guys' versus 'the bad guys' rests on an unstable logic that legitimizes one kind of violence while condemning another. Having witnessed his father killing someone – a man who threatened them – for the first time, the boy asks: '[a]re we still the good guys?' (77).

The only point, in fact, at which the father's and the boy's ideologies continuously merge, and which enables them to always re-establish an ethical line that neither of them would cross, is their shared dissociation from the possibility of ever resorting to cannibalism: '[w]e wouldnt ever eat anybody, would we? / No. Of course not ... / No matter what. / No. No matter what ... / Because we're the good guys. / Yes. / And we're carrying the fire. / And we're carrying the fire. Yes' (128, 129). Where the man-eating zombies in *The Walking Dead*, as I will discuss in the following chapter, function as an ambiguous no-longer-human 'other' against which the series' uninfected protagonists define and organize their networks of care and protection, cannibalism here, too, takes on the narrative function of an ultimate transgression that divides those who are meant to be identified as still human (in a moral sense) from those who have basically regressed to the status of amoral animals. However, although the man and the boy share this concern, the foundations of their respective convictions differ slightly but crucially: whereas the man generally constructs everybody except himself and his son as 'the bad guys' and thus cannibalistic, the boy bases his fear of moral disintegration on specific encounters, while staying open to the option of reaching out to strangers.

The boy's radical solidarity with all surviving creatures manifests itself, for the first time, not in an encounter with another human, but when he hears a dog bark – the first (and last) sign in the novel that there is also some non-human life left in this world: '[i]t's a dog, [the man] said. / A dog?

---

[6]Christine Temko, for instance, characterizes the boy's ethics as 'a spontaneous faith in the goodness of strangers' (2014: 168); and Christopher T. White even calls 'the boy's irrepressible inclination to feel with other people in spite of the extreme vulnerability and threatened state of his and his father's existence' the 'central miracle of the novel' (2015: 132).

/ Yes. / Where did it come from? / I dont know. / We're not going to kill it, are we Papa? / No. We're not going to kill it' (82). Shortly after, in one of the novel's most curious scenes, the reader gets a rare insight into the boy's perspective. Escaping the father's narrative authority for a short moment, the child claims to have seen another boy, his mirror image. This is the first instance in which the novel suggests the possibility that there might be other children out there: '[a] face was looking at him. A boy, about his age, wrapped in an outsized wool coat with the sleeves turned back ... There's a little boy, Papa. There's a little boy' (84). The man, however, denies this little boy's existence, thus questioning his son's truth – thereby affirming his own narrative authority – and making it impossible for the reader to know whether this boy is real: '[t]here is no little boy. What are you doing? ... There's no one to see. Do you want to die. Is that what you want?' (84, 85). Arielle Zibrak argues, in this context, that the boy's desire to 'keep' those other individuals they encounter on the road is an expression of his 'need for existential nourishment ... [: e]ffectively, the boy needs a boy' (2012: 114), thus replicating the father's investment in the child as the emblem of futurity. I would, however, suggest that this scene is much more telling as an example of the willingness, on the boy's part, to look into the world and see others *as like him*, accepting responsibility for them regardless of biological kinship or even species, in effect extending his notion of kin to embrace all living beings, while the man must insist on the impossibility of such an encounter outside the (bio-)familial sphere. The father relegates responsibility for the little boy to unspecific other 'good guys' who, however, within his logic, cannot actually exist: '[w]hat if that little boy doesnt have anybody to take care of him? he said. What if he doesnt have a papa? / There are other people there. They were just hiding' (McCarthy 2007: 85).

In contrast to the father, the son also bases his sense of sharing resources on an uncompromising politics of care. In the bunker, while the father takes what is there as a welcome help in his quest (keeping himself and his son alive as long as possible), the boy insists on considering the possibility that somebody else might need the goods more than they do: '[i]s it okay for us to take it? / Yes. It is. They would want us to. Just like we would want them to. / They were the good guys? / Yes. They were. / Like us. / Like us. Yes. / So it's okay. / Yes. It's okay' (139–40). This little dialogue is particularly telling as an example of how the two characters negotiate their respective politics of community and responsibility. The boy needs confirmation that the goods they have found are, in fact, at their disposal, while the father reverses his usual line of argument: framing the assumedly dead creators of the bunker as the 'good guys' makes it possible for him to re-contextualize their usual (ultimately selfish) scavenging as a voluntary donation from other people *like them*. For a moment, then, the father makes use of the boy's general tendency to think less in terms of a competition for survival than in terms of a solidary notion of sharing.

The most extended negotiation of this sort takes place in the encounter with Ely, the only character in the novel who is given a name, even though he himself acknowledges that this name itself might be a lie (cf. 171). Again, the boy wants to share food with the old, almost blind man, while the father remains suspicious. Ely, within the text's overall logic, acts as a blind fool and prophet of the apocalypse. Whereas, throughout the novel, the man keeps confirming his grasp on his paranoid narrative by insisting that he 'just knows', Ely, literally not seeing the world and its truths, answers most questions concerning his past, his age, and his situation either with a claim to ignorance, or ambiguously: '[w]hen did you last eat? ... / I dont know. / ... Do you want to eat with us? / I dont know ... / How old are you? / I'm ninety. / No you're not. / Okay' (166, 167). Significantly for the text's negotiation of the relationship between temporality and knowledge, Ely offers a non-futuristic attitude more in line with the boy's concern for the present than with the father's paranoid futurism: 'I knew this was coming ... This or something like it. I always believed in it ... People were always getting ready for tomorrow, I didnt believe in that. Tomorrow wasnt getting ready for them. It didnt even know they were there' (168). Ely's rejection of tomorrow, however, is also different from the boy's: where, in the child, hope manifests itself in his drive to reach out to help strangers, Ely's anti-futuristic stance embraces the absurdity of the situation as a call to inaction, a mere waiting for death: '[d]o you wish you would die? / No. But I might wish I had died. When you're alive you've always got that ahead of you' (169).

Speaking in terms of the novel's theological framing, the father saves God for himself by constructing his quest to save the child as God's will for a future. The boy himself, in contrast, substitutes a grand narrative of redemption for a radical ethics of care in the here and now. Ely, however, gets stuck between these two positions, announcing the death of God and the resulting uncertainties in a paradox: '[t]here is no God and we are his prophets' (170). In fact, the father and Ely explicitly voice their different takes on the symbolic meaning and religious reading of the child in a dying world: 'I never thought to see a child again ... / What if I said that he's a god? ... / I'm past all that now. Have been for years. Where men cant live gods fare not better. You'll see. It's better to be alone' (172). Neither the father nor Ely, then, can escape their religiously charged logic of either/or: either God must be alive (located in the child through the father's speech act) and provide hope for a future against all odds, or God is dead, and with him all meaning and sociality: '[w]hen we're all gone at last then there'll be nobody here but death and his days will be numbered too' (173).

Again, it is the boy who offers a way out of this ideological impasse. His actions sidestep the either/or of futurity versus fatalism, and neither the father nor Ely can make sense of his insistence on sharing, because he does not act within the confines of either of their ethical frameworks: '[m]aybe he believes in God. / I dont know what he believes in' (174). The two men's theological framing of the situation acts as a stark foil to clarify that, for the boy, the crisis is neither religious nor historical. Survival, for him, depends less on a narrative of hope or its absence, but on the existential ability to reach out to others in the present. As Christine Temko very aptly puts it, 'the boy appears to realize at a deeper level than the father ... that a world where sociability has been eradicated by the primacy of violence and paranoia and life reduced to pure physical survival is a dead one' (2014: 169).

The life the boy thus affirms is life as it comes into existence in an encounter with another, that is in true experiences of kinship. In a (fictional) world in which a future is more than uncertain, the individualized reproductive logic underlying the father's actions must ultimately appear as a dead end. On the other hand, it is openness and the will to cooperation, as they manifest themselves in the boy, that make life possible, despite the implied risks for the individual. As Andy Du Mont points out, 'the boy marks the potential existence for any form of life because of his ability to relinquish the security of his self to the current of possibilities that defines the unimaginable futures of life' (2012: 70). Future*s*, here, in the plural, lose some of the paranoid closure that any narrative of *the* future necessarily implies. It is precisely because of the precariousness and contingency of the possibility of *any* future in this fictional setting that I remain suspicious of religious readings of the boy's goodness towards all beings as a manifestation of 'New Testament love and forgiveness' (Pudney 2015: 301), or as an 'embodiment of the Christian virtue of love [which] offers hope for the restoration of the human community' (DeCoste 2012: 82). The reparation that becomes manifest in the boy is much more provisional, and rests on improvisation and the very real possibility that 'restoration' will remain unattainable.

Throughout the novel, then, both the child's refusal of linear temporality, and his capacity for spontaneous solidarity become a reparative foil to the father's paranoia. In the end, reparation in *The Road* lies in the text's potential for non-teleological, non-redemptive, and non-futuristic readings. Although the boy is integrated into a kind of substitute nuclear family after the death of his father, his repeated insistence on the possibility of death and his openness for spontaneous solidarity are not lost to the reader. As Shelly L. Rambo puts it, 'the impossibility of ... forward movement ... could place its readers in the aftermath of death without the promise of a new life ahead ... The question is not who will save the world but, instead, who will witness its shattering' (2008: 113, 115).

The technicolour couple: John Hillcoat's *The Road* (2009)

Before moving on, I want to briefly sketch out the dynamics of John Hillcoat's 2009 film adaptation of McCarthy's novel, and its later appropriation in an art installation. The tracing of this process can provide some interesting insights into how, in this case, the translation from one medium into another, and then into a third, in tandem with certain narrative and aesthetic choices, crucially changes the story's politics of hope and kinship. The film sticks very closely to its literary inspiration in terms of plot and atmosphere: several lines of dialogue are exact quotations from the book, and the set design is a faithful rendering of the material landscape described in the novel. Apart from some minor changes to the structure of the narrative, however, there are also certain aesthetic choices the film makes that, on the one hand, heighten the novel's idealization of the heterosexual couple and sanitize some of the visceral brutality with which the novel confronts its readers, but, on the other hand, also undermine the text's heavy reliance on the imagery of reproduction.

The film's very first scene introduces the audience to its use of contrasting colour schemes. Unlike the book, the film starts with a flashback: in three steps, we move from a collage of the man and his wife in a pre-apocalyptic world with green trees, colourful flowers, and a horse, via a short scene set during the night of the unnamed cataclysm, with the man and the woman hearing screams and shouting outside, and the light of what must be fires shining on their faces, to the man waking up in the all-grey world of the road. The film takes its cue for this colour scheme from the novel, but its visual rendering on screen heightens the effect: the glowing colours of the flashbacks – often in combination with a calming underlying score – appear like a visual Garden of Eden that contrasts sharply with the exclusively grey and dark palate of the man and the boy's journey. In this grey present, the only colour stems from the yellow and orange of fires, which figure ambiguously as either the mortal threat of forest fire, or as the improvised relative domestic safety of the man and the child's campfires.

The colourful flashbacks serve as the exclusive backdrop of sensual encounters between the man and his wife: here, the two of them regularly appear as an idealization of heterosexual romantic bliss. Strikingly, these scenes not only pre-date the journey on the road, but also the wife's pregnancy: the film – more explicitly than the novel – uncouples the arrival of the boy from an idealization of past pastoral bliss (in the garden, by the sea) for the man and his wife. More than the novel, the film's use of colour presents the *couple* as the man's object of nostalgia, rather than the reproductive family as such. Similarly, the wife's unwillingness to bring new life into this world becomes explicit in the scene of birth: sitting more or less composedly by her piano – which, in the film, becomes a symbol of the love between the woman and the man, and later of the woman herself – despair shows on her face when her waters break, and the necessity of giving birth becomes imminent: '[o]h no. Oh no … We don't have to … What kind of life is this … I can't'. Her stubborn denial of the fact of birth emphasizes her refusal to buy into a logic of reproductive futurism in the context of the current state of the world.

As opposed to the book, the wife's pregnancy is the only one shown in the film. Neither the woman whose new-born child gets murdered for food, nor the group of pregnant women travelling with the cannibals and 'catamites' appear here. In the film, the role of female characters shifts: while, in the book, women mostly appear as bad mothers and potential child eaters, the film also introduces one woman who is obviously an active and quite verbal member of a group of cannibals, and one 'good mother' who is chased and caught trying to protect a/her child. The film, then, is more ambiguous than the novel in its gendered rendering of morality: although it preserves the transgression of the mother who leaves as a crucial plot element, the tuning-down of an imagery of reproduction and the diversification of female roles as quitters *and* carers *and* aggressors lessen, to an extent, the novel's extremely gendered characterization of the conflict over care, and its heavy reproductive symbolism.

At the same time, the film also loses some of the subtleties and ambiguities the novel offers in terms of its Christian allusions and its handling of the figure of the Child. Where the novel produces its religious subtext exclusively through evocative, pseudo-biblical language, the film announces the death of God through fairly unambiguous images: defunct and falling transmission towers against a glowing sky evoke the site of the crucifixion (minus resurrection), and a partly destroyed church in which the father and son find shelter for a night announces not redemption, but the approaching death of the (F)father by illness. And where the novel never (unambiguously) produces any child characters apart from the boy, the film actually shows us the 'little boy' who the child claims to have seen, and, at the end, presents us with an actual encounter between the boy and his whole substitute family, son, daughter, and dog included.

Overall, the film enables more potential for agency beyond the father's hegemonic narrative on the level of character by giving minor female and child characters active roles, gesturing towards the possibility of multiple narratives where the novel remains entangled in the paranoid reality of the father/narrator – the voice of whom, in the film, fittingly becomes a first-person voice-over.

In 2013, Swiss multimedia artist Christoph Draeger created the video installation *The Rd.*, which was first shown as part of a solo exhibition at Kunst(zeug)haus Rapperswill, and then, in 2018, as part of the exhibition *Nature Unleashed: The Image of Catastrophe since 1600* at Hamburger Kunsthalle. The piece is a split-screen installation showing, on the left, excerpts from the 2009 film in which the man and the boy silently travel through the open country, and, on the right, a 'remake' of these travels in which the artist himself walks through a snowy landscape with his three-year-old son. The video is accompanied by some lines from the father's first-person monologue from the dubbed German version of the film.

What is striking about the work is both its extreme reduction of the film's narrative, and its contextualization in the curatorial process. By placing himself and his own son – who is obviously much younger than the boy in the novel and film – in a position that mirrors and imitates the movement of the fictional father and child, Draeger both conflates a fictional post-apocalyptic future with the actual landscape of the here and now, and reduces the story to one element: a man and a small child, the only people left in the world, travelling through an inhospitable landscape. The curators at Hamburger Kunsthalle placed the piece close to the exit of their exhibition on natural catastrophes. Without the element of agency for the boy himself that we find in the novel, and without any further material to contextualize this image of the journey, this piece really brings *The Road* back to just the one question: how, in the context of complete ecological and social devastation, can one man maintain hope and create a future for his child? The installation thus serves as a very unambiguous warning, and the child remains the voiceless image that must inspire pity and compassion, and a paranoid rendering of futurity. Draeger's work foregrounds a reading of *The Road* that can only either insist on the futurity the figure of the Child can be made to represent, or render the repetitive nature of the couple's mundane activities absurd. Matthew Fledderjohann accordingly reads the man and the boy's actions in the novel in the context of Beckettian ritual and concludes that 'the repetitions themselves provide rationale for continuance ... [D]oing them allows them to do them again which may provide more immediate motivation than any grand vision of familial love or societal value' (2013: 55). On one level, *The Road* certainly provides a foundation for this kind of reading. However, the novel itself – and, to an extent, the film – also renders a more complex negotiation of paranoid and reparative ideologies of hope and kinship. I would argue that the text indeed resists, as Fledderjohann rightly points out, 'any grand vision', but I locate this resistance less in the ritualistic absurdity of the protagonists' mundane activities, but rather in the boy's insistence on disregarding his father's paranoid protocol. By giving the boy a voice and independent agency, *The Road* enables a figure that repeatedly has to stand in for the future to also embody something else: a radical stance of solidarity and action in the here and now, and a drive towards repeated and improvised encounters and strategies of sharing. The novel's very last sentences offer an ambiguous image of life, loss, and the persistence of damage done, and insist on the impossibility of any easy path to restorative futurity: '[o]nce there were brook trout in the streams in the mountains ... On their backs were vermiculate patterns that were maps of the world in its becoming. Maps and mazes. Of a thing which could not be put back. Not be made right again' (McCarthy 2007: 287).

2

'No more kid stuff': Monstrous kinship in AMC's *The Walking Dead*

In the context of the rising popularity of complex serial narration in television since, roughly, the turn of the millennium, and, more recently, on online streaming platforms, post-apocalyptic fiction has found a new home and another context in which to proliferate. Starting in 2011, the Channel 4 and Netflix anthology series *Black Mirror* has been exploring the possible negative consequences of unrestrained technological development for human society; in 2016, HBO launched its own take on the 1973 film *Westworld*, a vision of a future in which cyborgs question the 'humanity' of humans; and 2018 saw Netflix's first original Danish production, *The Rain*, in which almost the whole of the population of Scandinavia is wiped out by a virus in the water, and those who survive have to build a new world against the odds of social chaos and human conflict. What all these narratives have in common is some configuration of two related questions: what kind of hope remains in a situation that fundamentally points towards things getting worse rather than better; and what impact does radical change on a global scale – technological, moral, epidemic – have on the structure of human society and personal belonging? One of the most prominent and successful instances of this kind of television series has been AMC's *The Walking Dead*, based on Robert Kirkman's graphic novels of the same name. The series ran for eleven seasons from 2010 until 2022 and has continued to keep its audience captivated by the adventures of Rick Grimes and the other survivors of a mysterious epidemic that has turned most people into mindless, man-eating zombies or 'walkers'. Following others before me, I want to discuss *The Walking Dead* as a popular dystopic narrative that can 'offer a space where society can safely represent and address anxieties of its time' (Levina and Bui 2013: 1), and which can help us explicate and conceptualize more general questions about the place of hope and kinship in the contemporary social and cultural imagination.

A post-apocalyptic setting like the one of a world run over by zombies stands in a peculiar relation to the question of hope: if we take hope as an (emotional, cognitive, affective) investment in a better future, then the world of *The Walking Dead* seems both an appropriate – in the sense of a drastic foil to a hope that is finally not completely lost – and a deeply inappropriate setting – in that the premise of the story as such makes hope, in its futuristic rendering, appear fundamentally meaningless. As James Berger puts it, '[t]he zombie fantasy … is an incarnation of anxiety about the future as such' (2015: 151). At the same time, the 'zombie apocalypse' lends itself particularly well to a consideration of how kinship structures are being reconfigured in the context of both the violent disintegration of familial and societal ties, and the confrontation with a monstrous 'other', the zombie, whose otherness, however, always bears the trace of the humanity it originated in. In this chapter, I want to explore how *The Walking Dead* negotiates this tension between hope's futurism and the urgent present-ness of the post-apocalypse, focusing on the series' first eight seasons, with some occasional references to the graphic novel.

The zombie, as a figure in popular culture, has an unusual history. In contrast to its 'monster relatives' – the ghost, the vampire, and the werewolf – who all have long *literary* histories, the zombie found its way, via Haitian folklore myth among slave communities, and colonial and neo-colonial contact with the United States, straight into the emerging art of cinema. The zombie 'comes directly out of a history of colonialism, enslavement, exploitation, and appropriation' (Lauro 2017: ix), a lineage which still partly determines the undead's figurative potential for thinking about 'self' and 'other'. Zombie narratives lend themselves particularly well to a speculation about what happens to hope and kinship under extreme conditions. As Jeanne Cortiel observes, zombie fiction 'compromises both space and time and disrupts virtually all key life events, including birth, childhood, initiation to adulthood (sexual maturity), marriage, parenting, and, finally, even death' (2015: 188). More specifically, *The Walking Dead* is deeply invested in a narrative 'focus on an American family reinvented through an apocalyptic narrative' (ibid.). I will discuss how the series explicitly and repeatedly threatens, destroys, reinstates, and glorifies the heterosexual nuclear family against admittedly more subtle, but nevertheless pronounced reconfigurations of family and belonging. Over the course of the series' long narrative, who is kin repeatedly and unstably gets tied to whether, when, and where there is hope; and hope itself is, once again, repeatedly tied to the figure of the Child. Moving beyond this rather conventional framework, however, I want to demonstrate how *The Walking Dead* also – especially in later seasons – begins to experiment with what could happen when those subject positions that paranoid teleology and reproductive futurism either marginalize or turn into a mere symbol – actual child and queer characters – speak up and have a voice of their own. With Lorenzo Bernini, I am suggesting that zombie narratives like *The Walking Dead* do not simply reiterate figurations of (queer) negativity in which marginalized subjects (and herds of the undead) come to represent the end of the social and of meaning as such; instead, both those who are called upon to signify the future of the social (children), and those who do not embody the future of the social in terms of reproduction (queers and – to an extent – the zombies themselves) emerge as figures who know 'that the present can, for them, be a time of political queer action' (2017: 97). I am particularly interested in how a fictional text like *The Walking Dead* can simultaneously be invested in a teleology of hope – not least, as a narrative, through its long-running serialized format – *and* challenge future-oriented notions of hope through the introduction of characters, mindsets, and specific kinds of fictional setting that sidestep such a logic. It is these challenges which make this story productive for a reparative configuration of hope, and its narrative sustainable for season after season. The future, in the post-apocalypse, is always precarious. At the same time, as the success of *The Walking Dead* demonstrates, the suspension of the end has great potential for popularity. Instead of a 'mere' future – in the sense of species reproduction, and of a rebuilding of established social, cultural, and political structures – these stories offer a continual reinvention of the present, based on improvisation and negotiations of relationality and survival.

'Us' and 'them': Humans vs. zombies/ humans vs. humans

The Walking Dead speculates about what might happen when a major biomedical catastrophe leads to a breakdown of society and the arrival of a monstrous 'other' that keeps those who struggle to survive as individuals and groups stuck in a state of constant insecurity. In the series, monstrosity emerges in a twofold manner: while the zombies are the more obvious monster that everyone is in danger of turning into, the increasing violence between groups of survivors makes it clear that monstrosity might be the fate of all those who buy into a survivalist logic of 'us' against 'them'. It is also, however, precisely because the series' post-apocalyptic setting questions established notions of morality and even ontology that the monstrous, in *The Walking Dead*, becomes tied to a counterintuitive potential for becoming that lies beyond hope. As Amit S. Rai observes, '[m]onstrosity problematises becoming, understood as the changeless process of change itself … [A] monstrous emergence is that for which we have no name (no cultural code), and simultaneously an emergent form (a contravention of majoritarian forms) ... [M]onstrosity is a universal revolutionary becoming' (2013: 15, 22, 28). I understand monstrosity in *The Walking Dead* as a condition which forces subjects and groups to continually reinvent and improvise practices of morality and belonging, and in which reparation manifests itself in fleeting and transitory moments of collectivity. Monstrosity and hope emerge, in the series, as an ambiguous choice between survival and (un)death, violence and peace, revenge and forgiveness, and the reparative capacity to improvise community. Zombies, in his context, become powerful symbols of ambiguous temporality: 'surviving but not really alive, they persist in a future without hope, a paradoxical future without a future' (Vint 2013: 134).

The zombie, in contemporary popular culture, is an ambiguous signifier, a metaphor capable of embracing a multitude of cultural anxieties and shifting meanings. As Lorenzo Bernini maintains, the zombie's ambiguous positioning vis-à-vis the social and signification as such makes it fundamentally queer: the zombie and the queer share a 'semantic mobility'; 'both can easily be used with irony, ... [in the sense of] the possibility to plurivocally and even ambiguously signify and thus to fluidize signification', and both share a social minority status (2017: 106). The zombies in *The Walking Dead*, too, I argue, emerge as ambiguously queer signifiers whose 'hunger for human flesh threatens our lives, ... [and whose] almost-life threatens our imaginary' (107). At the same time, apart from thus signifying a threat to the future of the social as such, the undead also, however, become the foil against which post-apocalyptic social relations come into existence and are continuously renegotiated. In the encounter with this particular monster, the limits of the human are delineated: the zombie walks the uncanny valley, '[i]t cannot be understood as either "alive" or "dead"; it is in transition and it is this which has the powerful and disturbing effect upon us' (Hubner, Leaning and Manning 2015: 6). It is in this space of transition that the series positions its most interesting explorations of boundaries and belonging. In *The Walking Dead*, the zombies always feature as both the mindless masses of 'classic' zombie horror, the paradigmatic harbingers of 'no future', *and* as individualized beings that keep serving the series as reminders of and comments on the precarious negotiations of who is friend and who is enemy, who counts as kin, and who deserves protection and inclusion. Not only are the zombies undead humans – and, as such, prototypically uncanny in their integration of the strange and the familiar – but they are often the recognizable bodies of previously living characters, the remainder of friend and kin. In this sense, a good deal of narrative energy in the series is spent on negotiating this tension between viewing the 'walkers', as the characters call them, as a grey mass of de-individualized moving corpses, and struggling with recognizing the individuals and subjects they used to be in the moving, disintegrating, and flesh-eating bodies.

Over the course of the series, characters must learn to see their zombified friends and family members as a threat to their own safety, and it is established – albeit never quite without reservations – that ending the existence of those who have been turned into walkers by destroying their brain is not only a life-saving necessity, but also an act of mercy. As such, the walkers – whose name evokes their fundamentally nomadic and unhomed nature – not only signify an existential threat to human existence, but also gesture towards fascistic ideologies of 'unworthy lives' and towards the cutthroat connotations of racist, ableist, and homophobic discourse in contemporary society. One of the first conflicts over the question whether the life of a zombified relative should still be respected – and whether or not a relative thus changed can still count as kin – occurs early in the first season after an attack on a camp of survivors outside of Atlanta. After Andrea's sister Amy has been killed, Andrea refuses to let the group stab the dead girl in the head to prevent reanimation, and sits with her until, when she does 'wake up' as a walker, she shoots her in the head herself with the words 'I'm here now, Amy. I love you' (season one, episode five, 'Wildfire'). Like other characters in many later instances in the series, Andrea continues to address her zombified sister *as* her sister, even though, at the same time, her status as a subject who deserves care and protection is unquestioningly revoked once she becomes, as one of the undead, a threat to the group.

Michonne, a sword-wielding female protagonist introduced at the end of season two, displays a similarly ambiguous attitude towards zombified kin. Long after her introduction, in which she encounters Andrea in the woods and is accompanied by two walkers she leads on a chain as protective 'pets', she reveals to Rick's son Carl that the two walkers used to be her husband and his best friend, who 'turned' after a zombie attack in which Michonne's only child was killed. Blaming them and herself, Michonne lets the two men become walkers, and keeps them as both a practical protection, and as a reminder of their and her own guilt (season four, episode sixteen, 'A'). The ambiguous tension between treating the walkers either as a dehumanized mass or as diminished versions of human subjects that still deserve respect and ethical treatment – or, at the very least, individualized attention – runs as a theme through the series.

As Kyle William Bishop points out, one of the central questions of contemporary zombie narratives in general is who gets to choose when and how to end someone's existence to prevent them from becoming a threat to others:

> Those bitten or otherwise infected by a zombie now have to be killed immediately to protect the rest of the human survivors, or, more often than not, at least given a choice as to when and how to die … Part of the 'ethics of infection' includes respecting a victim's choice: a violent, if permanent death, or hope at a new existence as one of the zombie horde. (2015: 27)

Bishop's assertion highlights an uncomfortable question raised in a world in which humans can plausibly lose their status as subjects: do the uninfected have the right, or perhaps even the obligation, to decide – almost in the manner of an ethnic cleansing – whether those whose presence is framed as the queer, uncanny other, and as a threat to the continuation of the social order should be allowed to go on existing? As the series progresses, it increasingly raises doubts about the validity of the pseudo-fascist self-defence logic and the prevalent 'post-apocalyptic zombie necropolitics' (O'Mahony, Merchant, and Order 2021: 93) propagated by most of its characters. Early in season one, Jim, one of the survivors from the Atlanta camp, chooses to be left behind after having been bitten by a walker, and refuses to commit suicide, opting instead for a 'life' as a walker in the hope of being reunited with his already zombified family: 'I want to be with my family … I know what I'm asking. I want this' (season one, episode five, 'Wildfire'). This is one of the very rare instances in which the survivors accept a character's wish to become a zombie in the hope for a different, but continued existence, a wish that is usually regarded as transgressive and dangerous.

Within the post-apocalyptic logic of *The Walking Dead*, going zombie always remains both a horrific fear and a dangerous temptation. In a world in which human violence always threatens to outweigh human solidarity, the queer prospect of merging with the ultimate mindless collective surfaces as a strange attraction which, as Kyle William Bishop speculates, fits our times, and contemporary culture's suspicion of the future:

> Zombies don't have to worry about their future … It should come as no surprise that this most recent decade, one defined by both the fears associated with the war on terror and the hopelessness stemming from an expansive economical collapse, has catered to the desires of an angst-ridden generation largely defined by malaise, boredom and perceived isolationism. (2015: 36–7, cf. Greely)

Where monstrosity thus emerges as a viable escape from the predictable scripts of the existing social order, the 'evil guys' – and they really are mostly guys – are very much human and still alive. Throughout seasons three and four, the Governor serves as a despotic antagonist who claims to care for his community in Woodbury, while his real motives are fundamentally selfish. From season six to season eight, Negan and his 'Saviors' represent a stance of violent dictatorship that keeps people alive primarily as a resource. In fact, while the 'zombie apocalypse' determines the series' setting, it is the violent conflicts between the different human groups and communities that structure much of its action. As several critics have observed, the audiences – and even more so the readers of the often more violent and more explicit graphic novel – have to keep asking themselves whose acts are more monstrous, those of the zombies – who, in a way, do not know any better and 'have no autonomy or freedom to choose (they're an existentialist's worst nightmare!)' (Round 2012: 163) – or those of the humans: 'some recent zombie narratives have flipped the original allegory: humans are truly monstrous ... [B]y using markedly coded differences from humans, monsters function as revealing and didactic critics of the very humanity from which they ostensibly appear to be distanced ... [T]hat which we should most fear is not the monstrous Other but the monstrous *selves*' (Bishop 2013: 74, 75, 77, emphasis in original).

In *The Walking Dead*, the systemic violence perpetuated against *both* the zombies *and* other human collectives thus evokes, as indicated above, the monstrosity of processes of human othering along artificially constructed but historically powerful lines of demarcation. In this context, Gerry Canavan reads the series as a text that both questions and perpetuates the dependence of colonial and capitalist temporalities on racist violence. The zombie apocalypse, he contends, 'interrogat[es] ... the "future" of late capitalist hegemony, and its concordant state racism, through fantastic depiction[s] of its breakdown and collapse ... [Zombies are] completely realised colonial objects ... [Z]ombies flatten time, they obliterate the present alongside the past and the future, only against "us", not for "us"' (2017: 414, 418, 422). Many contemporary zombie narratives, Canavan goes on to argue, parallelize the racist othering of the zombie as the ultimate threat with the legitimization of violence against other humans, and the establishment of symbolic means of delineation and physical fortifications to mark the borders between 'us' and the heterogeneous human/zombie 'other':

> The telos of the fortress, like the telos of empire, is always, in the end, to fall ... This is what we do whenever zombies strike: we build fortifications, we hoard supplies, we 'circle the wagons' and point our guns outward. And we do this even, and most tragically, when the zombies don't exist, when outside the walls there are only other people like us. (426, 428)

In *The Walking Dead*, the idea of a fortified 'safe haven' that keeps out those that the ones within define as standing outside of their community again and again structures the different story arcs, beginning with the Greene family farm in season two, and moving on through the prison in seasons three and four, to Alexandria, the Kingdom, and the Hilltop in later seasons. Other enclosed spaces either function as deceptive traps for those seeking refuge – like the Terminus in season four, which houses a community of cannibals[1] – or remain ambiguous, non-democratic spaces in which only

---

[1] Nicholas Lawrence convincingly argues that, via the trope of cannibalism, the series inscribes itself into a tradition of US frontier narratives in which cannibalism 'provides moral cover for and interrogates atrocities committed by "civilised" actors on the frontier' (2020: 116, emphasis in original). Cannibalism thus serves to further separate the good from the bad, the 'civilized' from the 'uncivilized'.

those who abide by the rules of a violent leader can buy themselves their livelihood – like Woodbury in season three, or the Sanctuary in seasons seven and eight. While all of these spaces have the function to keep the 'walkers' out, their more significant meanings emerge through a human politics of defining in- and outgroups, and through contrasting modes of collaboration and sharing: as enclosed spaces, they determine who counts as kin and thus deserving of care and protection; as relatively insular microcosms, they also, however, differ in the ways in which they are organized and (more or less) stratified, and how resources, responsibilities, and privileges are allocated. The series thus, to a significant extent, uses its post-apocalyptic setting to stage contrasting experiments in *human* sociality, while pushing the obvious monsters to the background, 'diminish[ing] their role within their own narratives in order to better illustrate the existential plight of humanity: the real walking dead' (Round 2012: 166).

There is, then, in *The Walking Dead*, no straightforward way of delineating man from monster, of establishing a safe boundary between the community of humans and those who must be ostracized, killed, extinguished, and fought. This is in great part due to the continuous re-establishment of in- and outgroups, of those that are kin and merit the protagonists' protection, and those that are either expendable or deemed dangerous. It is also due, however, to the fundamentally ambiguous nature of the zombie as queer and colonized 'other', and as a silenced member of a faceless crowd, 'never wholly terrifying but also pitiable, in between agent and object, master and subject' (Lauro 2017: xi). As I will outline below, *The Walking Dead* concentrates the zombie's potential to be pitied and its ambiguous position between human and not-human in some of its child characters, releasing a potential for subversion which, albeit subtly, disturbs the series' dominant narrative of false humanism, heterosexual reproductive futurism, and teleological hope. Before addressing this dynamic, however, I want to elaborate on how *The Walking Dead* imagines kin-making in the context of the formation of communities of care and protection.

Making kin – building communities

The Walking Dead is an experiment in social formation under extreme circumstances. The series contrasts the dissolution of the established social and political order under the conditions of the zombie apocalypse with the characters' efforts to recreate structures of community and belonging. These efforts mostly go in two directions: either to re-establish and preserve familiar, pre-apocalyptic notions of family and society, or to creatively imagine and improvise unlikely structures of kin and solidarity. In this context, Darren Reed and Ruth Penfold-Mounce foreground the series' potential to further an understanding of social dynamics:

Relationships are played out on the move. No longer are they purely a matter of static position in relation to material constraints, each interaction contains numerous possibilities: family units fragment and break apart and then reforge in different constellations, friendships are no longer taken for granted. All are imbued with the dynamic movement of the road; the only defining qualities are contingent enactments of emotional needs and their responses. (2015: 134–5)

I find this analysis very helpful because it emphasizes both the potential (and necessity) to create new kinds of social relation under fundamentally changed circumstances, and the improvised and contingent nature of kinship as it emerges in *The Walking Dead*. Strikingly, even though the series – especially in its earlier seasons – remains nostalgically invested in the preservation of pre-apocalyptic notions of kinship, it increasingly constructs as more sustainable those structures that do *not* merely try to recall and re-establish bygone ideals under the changed conditions of the present. The series repeatedly demonstrates that those communities that hide behind walls to try and lead their lives as if the world outside had not changed are doomed to ultimate failure. For instance, the Alexandria safe zone, introduced midway through season five, consists, before the arrival of Rick and his group, mainly of people who have lived behind walls since the beginning of the outbreak. Significantly, the community's leader Deanna Monroe still defines herself by her former job as an Ohio congresswoman and derives her authority from this position. After the arrival of Rick's group in the community, Deanna realizes that the newcomers are much better adapted to surviving in this new world and agrees to restructuring the community according to Rick's militant survival plans (season six, episode one, 'First Time Again'). A nostalgic preservation of bygone social structures no longer appropriate to the current circumstances thus gets pitted against the logic of violently pragmatic survivalism.

Based on this observation, several critics have problematized the tendency, in *The Walking Dead*, to do away with pacifist approaches to community building in favour of the seemingly 'natural' adaptation to a violent defence of one's own people. Angela Tenga and Jonathan Basset, for example, observe that the series inscribes itself into an American myth of the necessity of violence for the survival of society, 'suggesting that violence may again play a central role in Americans' response to the challenges of an uncertain future' (2016: 1281). They also, however, rightly point out that the series takes its violent context as an opportunity to balance its militant survivalism with abundant opportunities for positive audience identification through characters' acts of solidarity and altruism: '[c]onfrontations with existential anxiety can also lead to prosocial behaviour if death terror is managed through enhancement of self-worth based on cultural standards of meaningful behaviour. In cultures that value helping others, threat can lead to altruism' (1284). In the case of Alexandria, this kind of altruism develops when dynamics shift from a predominant suspicion between Rick's group and the 'native' Alexandrians towards a shared interest in collaboration, mutual trust, and friendship, which is later extended to an emerging network of communities consisting of Alexandria, the Hilltop, and the Kingdom.

Throughout the series, who belongs to a group and thus deserves protection and who does not is, on several occasions, explicitly framed in the vocabulary of kinship. Maggie, a series regular since season two, who later becomes an important protagonist, is one of the characters most outspoken about how in- and outgroups are made and defended. In the final episode of season five, in which the hierarchies in Alexandria are being re-negotiated, Maggie both explicitly refers to her own group as family, and affirms the affective attraction and potentially inclusive nature of their bond: '[n]o matter when we found each other, we're family now. Rick started that, and you won't stop it. You can't and you don't want to. This community, you people, that family – you want to be a part of it too' (season five, episode sixteen, 'Conquer'). At the same time, after the death of her husband Glenn, Maggie becomes increasingly defensive of the boundaries of her improvised family. During season eight, having taken prisoners from the 'Saviors', some of whom show an interest in joining Maggie's group at the Hilltop, she is initially adamant not only on keeping them separate from the inhabitants of the Hilltop, but also insists that they are expendable as bargaining goods because and as long as they are not family: '[t]hey're alive because we might need them … If we don't, we can't let them live' (season eight, episode six, 'The King, the Widow, and Rick'). Within the series' logic, and for most characters in it, in order to be part of a moral community, being human and a survivor is not enough. Instead, a performative notion of kinship takes precedence over a generalized ideal of humanism: who deserves care and protection is negotiated in active and often verbalized processes of (dis-)identification, and contingent upon gaining or losing a particular group's trust.

The series thus proposes a notion of family and belonging that is based less on blood lineage than on shared experience, mutual trust, and such contingent factors as luck and chance. At the same time, the biological family unit remains an integral part of the story, both as a remnant of pre-apocalyptic social structures, and as the conservative telos of part of the series' narrative drive. From the start, *The Walking Dead* makes its audience familiar with the idea that the zombie apocalypse disintegrates the heterosexual, nuclear family, both through the immediate threat of the zombies themselves and, more significantly, through conflicts among the human groups which the new situation makes more pronounced. In the series' very first episode, after Rick Grimes has woken up from a coma that has made him miss the onset of the catastrophe[2], he meets Morgan Jones, whose wife has already been taken by the walkers, and who struggles to survive with his son Duane (season one, episode one, 'Days Gone Bye'). Later in the series, we learn that Duane gets bitten and turned into a zombie by his own undead mother – evoking the cannibalism and child-killing mothers of McCarthy's *The Road*. The zombified mother is subsequently killed by Morgan, who goes increasingly mad (season three, episode twelve, 'Clear'). For Morgan, the zombies – or, more accurately, the virus – are the external force that destroys his familial happiness and his hope for a future as embodied by his son, while the nature of the disease also temporally locates the threat in the mother as monster.

A parallel, but crucially different fate is told of Carol Peletier, whose storyline in the television series departs significantly from the one in the graphic novels. In the series, Carol starts off as the mother of a young girl, Sophia, and as stuck in an abusive relationship with her husband Ed. While for Morgan, the zombie threat first turns his wife into a monster and then takes both wife and son tragically away from him, Ed's death means liberation and the development of a strong and independent character for Carol. Bitten by zombies just after a potentially incestuous and violent suggestion towards his own daughter, Ed is not only about to become a zombie himself, but Carol, in a grossly symbolic move, smashes his head in herself to prevent reanimation (season one, episode four, 'Vatos'; season one, episode five, 'Wildfire'). In this case, it is not the father who has to protect his offspring from the child-killing and future-defying mother, but the mother whose violent emancipation from an abusive marriage – and later, in fact, from being a mother at all – liberates her, and makes possible the series' most unusual and complex character development.

Rick's own storyline is crucially marked both by social threats to his heterosexual and reproductive family unit, and by the external threat of the zombies. His friend Shane starts an affair with his wife Lori, which leads to conflict and violence unrelated to the zombies. And Shane, appropriately, gets killed by both Rick and his son Carl, first being stabbed in the heart by Rick after threatening to kill him, and then shot in the head by Carl to prevent reanimation (season two, episode twelve, 'Better Angels'). Over the course of the series, the will to protect his offspring and those he considers 'family' becomes Rick's main driving force: 'Rick has proven himself willing to do anything, to anyone, in the name of survival for himself and his surviving prepubescent son, Carl' (Canavan 2017: 416, cf. Bishop 2013: 80).

---

[2]Like in *The Road*, and in many other examples of contemporary post-apocalyptic fiction, the 'event' itself (in this case the onset of the pandemic that has turned large parts of the population into undead predators) happens outside and beyond the narrative, although here, as opposed to in McCarthy's novel, it is more or less clear what has happened.

Overall, *The Walking Dead*'s use of its post-apocalyptic setting, which affords the series something of a 'clean slate' to experiment with different approaches to the recreation of social structure, keeps oscillating between a conservative, backward-looking affirmation of familiar patriarchal structures of family and society, and a more creative take on what family and kin might mean in a situation in which solidarity and mutual trust are continually being tested by a very real fear of a monstrous 'other' that lurks both in the zombie and in other survivors. In many ways, this is a conservative story: the breakdown of society through a viral pandemic serves to legitimize both the macho-masculine survivalism 'necessary' to make it through this fictional situation, and the quasi-pastoral return to the 'roots' of direct human interaction, immediate relationality, and improvised cooperation. While the latter bears reparative potential as a contrastive foil to the violent paranoia prevalent throughout much of the story, it can also be read as an ultimately conservative longing for a return to a human 'essence' which has been lost in contemporary, technologized society.[3] Read this way, the series provides its audience with an uncomfortable version of reparation, one which caters to the need to counter the paranoia of the contemporary moment by providing a violent but processable outlet for our cultural fears and anxieties. Hope, then, must lie in the continual deferral of the re-establishment of a stable order. Stuck in a perpetual present, it is enough to face the zombie horde and forge an alliance that affords one more day of safety.

Violent fathers, rogue mothers: Masculinity and femininity

In order to better understand the series' ambiguous take on generational familial bonds outlined above, it is worth considering in some more detail the role of fatherhood and motherhood in *The Walking Dead*. As a rule, natalism abounds throughout the series: almost all protagonists, both male and female, have been, are, or will be parents, and, for the most part, parenthood serves as an easily decipherable symbol of the possibility of human survival, and of hope for a sustainable future. At the same time, however, the series also makes use of its extensive narrative space to play out

---

[3]At the heart of *The Walking Dead*, as Alicia Kozma rightly observes, lies 'the renunciation of technology, or, indeed, the renunciation of human dependence on technology as the foundation for the re-creation of society ... [and] a call to renounce constructions of humanity created through technology as an attempt at reestablishing human agency and mastery over the world as a way to combat the intrinsic fears of modernity' (2013: 63).

different versions of fatherhood and motherhood that do not easily fit into a futuristic pattern of hope. Motherhood, especially, emerges as an often less than harmonious encounter with the brutal realities of the post-apocalypse.

One of the central relationships throughout the first eight seasons of *The Walking Dead* is that between Rick and his teenage son Carl, which, in many ways, runs parallel to that between the father and son in *The Road*. In both cases, the wife and mother is absent – Rick's wife Lori dies early in season three – and, like the unnamed father in McCarthy's novel, much of Rick's motivation stems from wanting to protect his son and his baby daughter Judith. In both cases, too, the new, post-apocalyptic order is thus framed as primarily emerging out of a homosocial order of patriarchal generational bonds at the expense of women. Rick quite explicitly justifies his commitment to building a new society with his futuristic investment in his son: when Carl gets shot in the eye, and Rick cannot be sure if he will survive, he ties his quasi-religious vision of a new society to his son's survival: 'I want to show you the new world, Carl. I want to make it a reality for you. Please Carl, let me show you. Please, please, son, don't die' (season six, episode nine, 'No Way Out'). One of the series' main driving forces is the commitment of some of its characters to returning to a lost familial idyll, best embodied in Rick's attempt to protect his son and find him a 'foster mother'. As such, Jeanne Cortiel is right in stating that *The Walking Dead* is a story about endings in an endlessly deferred seriality, but there is ultimately a clear goal and a destination that is validated through the continued survival of the father-son pair: a new society grounded in the heterosexual family as central unit of reproduction, supported by a pre-industrial village economy (cf. 2015: 201). I would argue, however, that the series also problematizes this vision of a return to familial safety, not just through the continual deferral of its realization, but also through its depiction of the failure of the father-child pair. Halfway through season eight, Carl dies, and with it the series' long-standing reliance on the patriarchal couple and its focus on the son's survival.

Patriarchy as such, however, quite literally thrives in the series. Apart from Rick, many of the other male group leaders are or have been biological fathers, and the different ideologies of leadership itself that the series produces and propagates are patriarchal throughout. At best, as Geoffrey A. Wright (2017) points out, during the first few seasons, *The Walking Dead* differentiates between tyrannical and democratic kinds of male group governance. Rick, for example, is the continually reluctant, but mostly consensus-oriented leader. A sheriff by pre-apocalyptic profession, he carries much of his assumed structural authority into the new reality of the zombie apocalypse. Throughout the series' first eight seasons, he oscillates between a nostalgic commitment to both his past role and habitus as an officer and to his biological family, and his potential to construct a collective identity through charismatic leadership. These tendencies manifest themselves most obviously in Rick's frequent speeches to his group. Halfway through season five, one of his monologues stands out because, for the first time in the series, its title is explicitly addressed:

> When I was a kid I asked my grandpa once if he ever killed any Germans in the war. He wouldn't answer. He said that was grown-up stuff, so I asked if the Germans ever tried to kill him. But he got real quiet. He said he was dead the minute he stepped into enemy territory. Every day he woke up and told himself, 'Rest in peace. Now get up and go to war'. And then after a few years of pretending he was dead he made it out alive. That's the trick of it, I think. We do what we need to do and then we get to live. But no matter what we find in DC, I know we'll be okay. Because this is how we survive. We tell ourselves that we are the walking dead. (Season five, episode ten, 'Them')

Here, Rick both reinforces the series' tendency to legitimize a violent soldier masculinity by binding its fictional post-apocalyptic setting to the historical realities of the Second World War and the mystification of the male veteran, and propagates an identification with the monstrous other – and an associated loss of subjectivity – by asking the survivors to think of themselves, and not of the zombies, as 'the walking dead'. This rhetorical strategy, however, remains firmly embedded in a paranoid knowledge of good and evil, and in a fundamentally conservative commitment to soldierly strategy and state warfare which might be completely out of place in a speculative scenario like that of a zombie apocalypse.

On the other hand, on several occasions, Rick's speeches enable a glimpse of the reparative potential of group building and solidarity. In the finale of season six, Rick once again addresses his group and appeals to their strength as a group *not* in terms of their potential success in violently fighting down the threat posed by the 'Saviors', but in terms of their structural and emotional commitment to one another: '[e]verything we've done we've done together. We got here together, and we're still here. Things have happened, but it's always worked out for us, 'cause it's always been all of us. That's how I know. 'Cause as long as it's all of us, we can do anything' (season six, episode sixteen, 'Last Day on Earth'). As opposed to, for example, the Governor or Negan, who also work towards mobilizing their respective groups for their aims, but by means of deceit and intimidation, Rick repeatedly establishes the importance of democratic collaboration as opposed to tyrannically led mass action. The kind of power Rick thus appeals to, as Geoffrey A. Wright points out, 'is power that individuals wield for the sake of others, for the sake of the community as a whole. The group follows Rick because they see in him a leader who is fair and who … pursues the good of the group over his own personal gains' (161). In the end, however, although Rick's leadership style does bear traces of a more reparative approach to community and collaboration, and despite the repeated nods in his speeches towards the emergent potential for reparative community building that has been present but never quite realized in the series, he remains invested in a backward-gazing belief in patriarchal authority, and the legitimacy of violence in the context of what is framed, again and again, as a war between opposing parties.

Even though much of the violence in *The Walking Dead* – both against the walkers and against other survivors – is implicitly legitimized as a necessity to protect the family – both in a nuclear and in a wider sense – there is surprisingly little criticism of the series that explicitly engages with the relationship between patriarchal masculinity and violence. Many critics seem to simply accept the premise that, under the given fictional circumstances, a man needs to protect his loved ones. Notable exceptions are Nadine Dannenberg (2017), who criticizes the series for its lack of imagination in producing a dystopian re-institutionalization of pre-apocalyptic patriarchal relations, and Stephen Olbrys Gencarella (2016), who reads *The Walking Dead* alongside Klaus Theweleit's analysis of early-twentieth-century Freikorps literature. Within a psychoanalytical framework, Theweleit argues throughout his two-volume study that those types of masculinity that thrived under fascism and in the world wars are best understood as psychotic and as characterized by a fundamentally antisocial and violent relationship with the world. Taking his cue from Theweleit, Gencarella critiques *The Walking Dead*'s glorification of fascist masculinities:

> *TWD* relies upon representation of the leader and the heroic male who subjugate the masses, living and undead ... [T]he cascading glorification of soldier male mentality makes it difficult to accept the series as an admonitory tale against violence and a fractured republic, just as the murderous seriousness of its distinction between friends and enemies makes it difficult not to question its homage to fascism. (2016: 131, 132)

I find Gencarella's argument extremely useful for linking the series' dynamics of violence with its politics of kinship. *The Walking Dead*'s construction of self and other not only enables the formation of social structure in the first place, but the primacy of biological kinship and its unquestioned need of protection and propagation further legitimize paranoid violence against all those that stand on the other side, wherever this may be. At the same time, as Gencarella further argues, male-male generational kinship becomes increasingly defined *less* through biological heritage than through the social practice of warfare: '*TWD* reeks of the soldier male. ... [W]ar in *TWD* serves as the ultimate opportunity for affirmation of self-control and membership in a brotherhood ... Biological fathers and sons are not unified, then, through mutual relations as parents and children, but through their bond as brothers-in-arms and their shared obedience to their leader and their group' (133, 135). This, of course, complicates any easy dichotomization of biological and social kinship as either paranoid or reparative in nature. Not all forms of improvised kinship based on social practice and shared experience are, within and beyond the fictional world of *The Walking Dead*, necessarily constructive, or even inclusive. The brothers-in-arms logic that characterizes large parts of the story defines as kin those who are united in the fight against a common enemy. And biological kinship relations only serve to legitimize and dramatize the boundaries between friend and kin on the one hand, and enemy and monster on the other, eclipsing – at least during the first few seasons – a viable alternative to paranoid patriarchal violence. As Gencarella concludes, '*TWD* knows friends and enemies but not neighbours' (129). It is only in later seasons that this dominant narrative gets convincingly challenged by calls for trans-group cooperation that promise to be, even within the series' survivalist logic, more sustainable than the prevalent model of violence.

While fatherhood, in *The Walking Dead*, then, to a large extent serves as a familial base for patriarchal forms of masculine violence and leadership, motherhood takes us further towards more nuanced renderings of gendered temporality. It would certainly be difficult to construct and read *The Walking Dead* as a feminist text. Its gender politics mostly relies on conservative binary codes, and, especially in its earlier seasons, 'the successful fulfilment of stereotypical gender roles appears to represent the survivors' desire to cling to some semblance of the society that is crumbling around them' (Vinney and Wiley-Rapoport 2016: 208). Nevertheless, the series' handling of gender and sexuality becomes a crucial site on which it negotiates paranoid and reparative forms of social life. Unfortunately, its more creative undercurrents of handling kinship and gender do not, until the end of season eight, become dominant enough to eclipse the series' prevalent logic of paranoid patriarchal survivalism. As Gerry Canavan rightly points out, the series' 'uncritical relationship to a particular prefeminist narrative about the need to "protect" women and children cannot be glossed over. "Proper" control over wombs, and anxiety that they will somehow be captured, polluted, or compromised is a kind of Ur-myth for the apocalyptic genre in general and the zombie subgenre in particular' (2017: 424). In fact, the series' early seasons place even its stronger female characters firmly within the series' logic of fascist masculinity, as Gencarella observes: '[i]t is striking how few mothers populate *TWD* ... [B]oth Carol and Michonne were mothers, but lost their children to the ghouls and thereafter embraced the attitude of soldier males' (2016: 136).

However, *The Walking Dead* has learned to make use of its potential for more creative post-apocalyptic renderings of femininity and motherhood, many of which point towards an escape from the paranoid logic of the dominant patriarchal structure of warfare. The most interesting character development in this sense is that of Carol Peletier. Starting out as an unsure and abused wife and mother, she grows into one of the strongest and most multifaceted characters in the whole series. While adopting some of the ideology of the soldier male, Carol's actions and ethics also question and complicate the series' dominant logic of reproductive futurism and teleological hope, and gesture towards a never easy compromise between individuality and collectivity, and between parental care and care for the community.

In one of the series' most controversial episodes, Carol chooses to kill a young girl to protect others from her. In another, she kills two ill members of her group to prevent them from becoming a threat to the rest of them. While the moral legitimacy of her actions is certainly debatable, Carol's shifting position between a caring mother figure to many of the series' child characters, and a ruthless utilitarian willing to inflict deadly violence on those she deems a threat to her own group raises important questions about the role of filial relations and more improvised forms of kinship. On the one hand, Carol's development confirms one of the series' underlying fears – and a dominant theme in many post-apocalyptic narratives: that mothers might become a lethal threat to their own and other children. *The Walking Dead* conjures up this fear repeatedly when mothers turn into walkers, most prominently when, in season three, Lori dies in childbirth, and her own son Carl shoots her to prevent her from turning (season three, episode four, 'Killer Within'). On the other hand, Carol is one of the few characters who is neither stuck in a nostalgic relation to the pre-apocalyptic past, nor in any kind of naively futuristic hope. Instead, she tackles her immediate realities in the here and now, opting for improvisation and the potential pain of compromise. To an extent, she thus embodies a radical turn to the present that sharply contrasts with the simultaneously nostalgic and futuristic ideologies many of the other characters advocate. As Melissa Vosen Callens observes, '[u]nlike other characters, Carol recognises that the laws of the pre-apocalypse no longer apply in this world. For Carol, protecting the group is more important than protecting the lives of the individuals, a perspective not supported in the pre-apocalypse' (2016: 156). Carol's transformation is reparative in the sense that she is willing to adapt to the current situation without remaining invested in a paranoid logic of good versus bad, or any teleological sense of redemption. At the same time, of course, this version of reparation is starkly at odds with an understanding of reparation as radical solidarity, as, for example, embodied by the boy in *The Road*. From a different angle, her individual commitment to her own utilitarian ethics could even be read as just a different form of paranoid epistemology.[4]

---

[4] As Robert A. Delfino and Lea R. Lesinski argue in this regard, 'Carol is not only capable of acting on her own, but also ... feels justified in making decisions that will affect others without consulting anyone' (2016: 179).

Parenthood and gender, then, play an ambiguous role in *The Walking Dead*. On the one hand, the series uses its post-apocalyptic setting to revert to a conservative narrative of masculinist warfare, a division of gender, and reproductive heterosexuality as a legitimizing base for patriarchal authority. At the same time, its handling of character development, especially towards later seasons, points towards a self-conscious questioning of the legitimacy and sustainability of the paranoid logic of the soldier male's commitment to warfare and the teleology of victory. The ambiguous role of motherhood, especially, turns out to be a promising site for thinking about the place of reproduction and community, although reparation here comes at a painful cost. While fatherhood and motherhood are certainly productive categories for a differentiated reading of *The Walking Dead*, the series' rendering of child characters really brings its future-sceptic potential to the fore.

Children against the future

In the very first scene of *The Walking Dead*, officer Rick Grimes scavenges for petrol in the abandoned streets of rural Georgia. Among a few broken-down cars that used to belong to a camp, he comes across the paraphernalia of childhood – a tricycle, dolls, other toys – before seeing a girl picking up a teddy bear and walking away from him. He approaches her hesitantly: '[l]ittle girl? I'm a policeman. Little girl. Don't be afraid, ok? Little girl?' (season, one, episode one, 'Days Gone Bye'). In his first ever line in the series, Rick sets the stage for one of the series' most uncanny 'others': the child who might or might not submit to a dominant narrative laid out by patriarchal authority, and who might, in fact, not be a child at all: '[i]s she a monster? A little girl? Both?' (Pye and O'Sullivan 2012: 108). Fittingly, Rick's first appellation is a question, as if, already, he cannot be sure of the nature of the being he has encountered; and despite his supposedly reassuring assertion of state-sanctioned authority, the scene's climax puts an early end to the idea of the Child as receiver of paranoid protection and bearer of the future. As the girl turns around, we look at the face of the series' first undead, still grasping the teddy bear, and charging forward towards Rick, who, by an intuition which will become the survivor's second nature, shoots the zombie-child in the head.

Children occupy a central yet ambiguous position in the world of *The Walking Dead*. While they are, within the story's prevalent logic, the carriers of hope and futurity, they also serve as disturbances in this normative narrative and remind the audience of the inconsistencies in any easy solution to negotiations of kin, and of the vexed question of hope in a profoundly devastated world. The zombie and the child also, as James Berger points out, share epistemological ground as the symbolic extremes of the sustainability of futuristic hope: zombies 'reproduce. The zombie apocalypse is a story of procreation. It condenses the problem of the future to an opposition between the zombie and the child' (2015: 153). The series' fictional premise thus rests on a fundamental struggle over who the future belongs to in the eternal present of the post-apocalypse: '[a]s long as human biological and social reproduction can take place, the apocalypse is incomplete. Something of the old world remains as it is passed on, biologically and culturally, to the child. And the death or absence of the child signifies the end of the human project, the end of this world' (154). The zombie-child that introduces us to the world of *The Walking Dead* is the perfect image to encapsulate the series' negotiation of reproductive and monstrous takes on temporality and hope. However, even though the series' first undead is a little girl, children hardly ever feature visibly as part of the zombie horde. In a strangely conspicuous kind of way, the anonymous masses of the walkers mostly appear to be more or less middle-aged. The series' creators, it seems, are well aware of the representative power of the figure of the Child, and of the stakes in showing the child as the dead-but-alive, no-longer-human monster – hence the symbolic power of the series' opening scene.

When children do figure as the undead, they mostly do so as zombies that we recognize as former human characters with a name and a history. Strikingly, the series thus associates the monster child more with the past (of the story) and with bygone structures of family and society than with the symbolic power to signify the future. One of the first and most striking instances of this is Carol's daughter Sophia. While Carol, over the course of the series sheds her role as a meek and submissive victim of domestic violence to become a capable fighter, she is also cast as an anxiously caring and warm-hearted mother. This is a role she retains throughout the series, despite her development into a strong, able, and at times violent female lead. After Sophia's disappearance at the very beginning of season two (episode one, 'What Lies Ahead'), and after a frantic search for her by the whole group, she is rediscovered among a horde of walkers in a barn on Hershel's farm, herself now one of the undead. This scene clearly plays with the audience's (via the characters') affects: the zombified body of the child stuns the whole group into disbelief and inaction. Carol, the devastated mother, tries to run to what she still perceives as her child, and Rick, in shooting Sophia-as-zombie in the head, commits a seemingly necessary, but symbolically transgressive act. In this act, he also mirrors and repeats the series' very first scene, which is thereby framed as only the first of many violent acts against the zombies and other humans increasingly excused as 'necessary' for survival (season two, episode seven, 'Pretty Much Dead Already'). The affective identification of children especially, then, as those characters that do not easily move from being regarded as kin – in the double-sense of family and the human community – to being 'othered', feared, and killed affirms the heavy charge of the figure of the Child with projections of hope and futurity, but also questions the validity of such a charge, and its use in the post-apocalyptic narrative of *The Walking Dead*. Perhaps, Sophia-as-zombie seems to provocatively ask, it is not the Child that is the future of humanity, but the zombie who is the only possible future for all.

The divide between human and zombie, and the validity of the survivors' changing set of morals about who deserves protection as kin and who does not, finds its most explicit challenge in Lizzie Samuels. Introduced in the first episode of season four, Lizzie and her sister Mika are orphaned survivors living with the protagonists in the relative safety of the prison ('30 Days without an Accident'). From the beginning, Lizzie's relationship with the walkers is portrayed as unusual: she identifies with them, shows pity and affection towards them, gives them names, and even secretly feeds them. As opposed to most of the other characters, Lizzie will not easily perform the move of seeing the walkers as fundamentally 'other' from living humans: '[t]hey're not dead, they're just ... different' (ibid.). To an extent, this behaviour is framed in terms of a potential mental pathology, and Carol, who – true to her role as mother-figure – 'adopts' the two girls, struggles to convince Lizzie to see the zombies as dangerous and no-longer-human. When, however, Lizzie goes so far as to kill her sister Mika, arguing that once Mika has become a zombie herself, the walkers will not be a threat to her anymore, Carol decides that she has to kill Lizzie to protect other humans from the child's logic of seeing the undead as everybody's hope and future instead of as fundamentally monstrous (season four, episode fourteen, 'The Grove'). Carol, the 'mother', kills her adopted offspring – and, as such, one of the bearers of post-apocalyptic, humanist hope – once it is clear that the child stubbornly defies the survivalist logic of 'humans' versus 'monsters', and 'good' versus 'bad'. She thus ignores the child's not altogether absurd alternative ethics. As Heather L. Castro and Dave Beisecker point out, '[f]or Carol, walkers are solely active threats, as they have been and ever will be; but for Lizzie, they are an alternate consciousness, a viable option for not-death/life before a person's final death and the onset of survivor grief' (2016: 169). Lizzie poses a challenge not only to the immediate safety of her group, but to their overall moral framework, thus questioning the survivor's paranoid epistemology of 'us' versus 'them'. As such, this child character is, from a certain point of view, more creative in dealing with the new environment of the post-apocalypse than most of the series' adult protagonists. Her transgressive acts can be read as symbolic negations of the sustainability of her group's dominant narrative: 'she refuses to surrender to moral nihilism by crafting post-apocalyptic values. Those values happen to include what appears to be an emerging or incipient concern for the non-dead' (170, cf. Yuen 2016). Lizzie's version of the future is not hopeful in the sense of a redemptive return to the pre-apocalyptic boundaries of patriarchal, middle-class existence – and, of course, it blatantly runs counter to a very understandable wish for self-preservation on the part of the human survivors of the zombie apocalypse. However, her vision is nothing less than pragmatic in the given context, and a provocative foil to the series' prevalent instrumentalization of children as cute and pitiable objects in need of the soldier male's protection.

The most reparative reversal of and, at the same time, one of the most problematic uses of reproductive futurism in *The Walking Dead* is the development of Carl Grimes during season eight. For long stretches of the series' early seasons, Carl more or less serves as a pubescent extension of his father's cowboy masculinity, including predictable conflicts between the two, thus confirming Jeanne Cortiel's conclusion that Rick and Carl, as 'father and ... son[,] are the core of the imagined heavenly order that completes the apocalypse' (2015: 198). On the other hand, Carl's position as a *child* in the story, and his symbolic relation to both past and future social orders is complicated early on when he participates in the murder of Rick's rival lover Shane. In the penultimate episode of season two, Carl only vicariously participates in Shane's murder, shooting the reanimated man in the head after Rick has already stabbed him to death. In the graphic novel, however, Carl first shoots Shane through the neck in an attempt to defend his father, and then Rick deals out the coup de grace much later in a supposed act of mercy (issue six; issue fifteen; season two, episode twelve, 'Better Angels'). As Brandon Kempner puts it, '[a]ny illusions we might have that these zombie survivors will return to society, and the values and conformity civilization represents, are blasted away when Carl pulls that trigger. This is an entirely new world where children are now killers ... [O]ur concepts of "child" and "innocent" don't mean anything in Kirkman's zombie world' (2012: 150–1). In this sense, Carl is as much part of the series' disillusionment of idealized childhood narratives as Sophia and Lizzie, but, for the larger part of the following seasons, remains an extension of his father's militant survivalist logic. Over the course of season eight, however, and in the context of the final stages of the conflict between the protagonists' group and Negan's 'Saviors', Carl takes on the role of prophetic child critic of his father's and Negan's increasingly fanatic warfare strategy and militant rhetoric, propagating instead, like the boy in *The Road*, a stance of trans-group solidarity and future-sceptic hope.

Over the whole course of the eighth season, flashbacks and flashforwards frame the preparation for the final battle between Rick's group and the 'Saviors'. Strewn-in blurry sequences show a much older Rick in a potential future which develops in two ways, one each for Rick's and Carl's version of how events should turn out. In Rick's variety, his family is reunited in the domestic bliss of the Alexandria community, with Carl still alive, an older Judith, and Michonne as wife and adoptive mother. For Rick, a nostalgic return to the scripts of a stable middle-class existence within the confines of the domestic and the nuclear family is still the telos of his struggles. In Carl's version, however, Negan plays with Judith, indicating that for Carl, the goal must be to find a peace that unites the opposing groups in solidarity, and that permanently shatters the boundaries of the family, even if this comes at the cost of Carl's own death: he does not appear in this version of the future, foreshadowing his potential demise.

In the season's first episode, Carl's politics of reparative solidarity manifests itself in two ways. While Rick gives another rousing speech to his group which reinforces the boundaries between 'us' and 'them' as a prerequisite for the group's survival in what many of them now consider to be an outright war, Carl, in a flashback scene, contradicts his father's version of hope which, like that of the father in *The Road*, is based on paranoid assumptions about friends and enemies. When Rick drives away a stranger they encounter by a gas station, arguing that he could be a 'Savior', but hopes he will survive if he is not, Carl frustratedly contradicts his father's logic of paranoid, self-centred hope: '[i]t's not going to be enough, Dad. / Enough what? / Hope' (season eight, episode one, 'Mercy'). Carl insists that an abstract hope, coupled with paranoid, anti-communal behaviour in the present, will not solve the problem at hand. Instead, he opts for action in the here and now, and goes off in search of the stranger to bring him food and invite him to join their group. Later in the season, in another flashback to the same situation, Carl again confirms his preference for action in the present over futuristic hope: '[i]f you care, you do something. You don't just hope. It takes more than that' (season eight, episode eight, 'How It's Gonna Be'). Like the boy in *The Road*, Carl is prepared to take a risk if it means exploring the reparative potential of solidarity in the present. Unlike McCarthy's boy, however, Carl's self-exposure leads to his getting bit by a 'walker'. He spends the rest of the season working towards a productive martyrdom, reaching out directly to Negan to convince him to stop fighting, and making his father promise, just before he dies, that he will abstain from violence in favour of solidarity: '[e]verybody's living, helping everybody else … That's how it could be' (season eight, episode nine, 'Honor'). At the same time, Carl presents an alternative to Rick's perspective on children as mere objects of the soldier male's and father's paranoid protection:

> [Carl:] Sometimes, kids have to show their parents the way … [Rick:] You were just a boy … [Carl:] You put away your gun … How you stopped fighting. It was right. It still is … There's gotta be something after. For you. For them … [Rick:] I'm sorry I couldn't protect you. A father's job is to protect his son. [Carl:] Love. It's just love. (Season eight, episode nine, 'Honor')

Carl, the series' eternal boy character, here becomes the reparative voice that teaches his father to stop fighting a fight in the name of the children, pointing out the flaws in Rick's ideology of hope and futurity, and offering instead an alternative stance of radical love and pacifism. It seems almost a bit cheap that the series chooses to frame this act of reparation in a heavily cheesy religious register: Rick carries his son to die in the chapel of the burning Alexandria, thus finally turning him back into a symbol, a child martyr, whose legacy and meaning Rick and Negan subsequently begin to fight over: '[Negan:] I had plans ... That kid ... That kid was the future ... [Rick:] Carl is dead because of you' (season eight, episode ten, 'The Lost and the Plunderers'). Carl's moral development, however, is part of a productive narrative current, in the later seasons of *The Walking Dead*, which questions and complicates the series' dominant logic of reproductive futurism and militant masculinity, giving a voice to the child that no longer wants to simply represent a future which produces ever more monsters.

Some of the child characters in *The Walking Dead*, then, problematize the series' investment in a teleology of hope as mere human survival, and in the logic of reproductive futurism. The child who becomes a zombie and the child who sees the zombies as kin dangerously blur the line between 'we' and 'them' that the survivors repeatedly have to re-establish, and confirm that, in *The Walking Dead*, 'the zombies aren't metaphors for human failings; they are the catalyst that reveals the monstrous potential that has been exposed within us all' (Bishop 2013: 83). So, although I agree with Jeanne Cortiel that, in both the graphic novel and the series, 'the repetition of individual story arcs pointing towards the utopia of a family-based society and economy helps reinstate it' (2015: 195), there are also points in the narrative where those that are invested with this hope do not necessarily buy into the unstable survivalist, humanist, hetero-productive logic most prominently represented by Rick Grimes. These characters, like Sophia-as-Zombie, Lizzie, and even Carl, ask uncomfortable questions about who, in a zombie-apocalypse, is still considered kin, and what it means to hope for a future when the future seems to have already come – and it has come in the form of the walking, disintegrating, de-humanized, but extremely motivated zombie.

Queer outlooks

So far, I have argued that queerness, in *The Walking Dead*, mainly emerges in the form of the ambiguous meanings of social (dis-)integration that the metaphor of the zombie encapsulates, and which enables productive negotiations of family and social reproduction. Queerness in the sense of an emancipatory programme of non-heterosexual representation, however, arrives fairly late in the series' fictional world. Despite the potential for new and creative approaches to family and belonging that the post-apocalyptic setting of *The Walking Dead* offers, the series remains, for the most part, firmly within the boundaries of seemingly naturalized notions of heterosexual relationships and reproduction. At the same time, however, it does produce emergent counter-narratives which not only challenge the sustainability of these hegemonic patterns, but also fundamentally question their authority. Despite the series' continuous reiteration of normative assumptions about family, and its affirmation of the ideology of reproductive futurism, it has also managed to use the figure of the zombie and many of its child characters to gesture towards less paranoid and more reparative, albeit at times disturbing, iterations of community, and a rejection of futuristic impulses. The question remains, however, whether this is enough to read *The Walking Dead* as 'queer'.

John R. Ziegler has advanced the most detailed exploration of the relationship between queerness and the family in *The Walking Dead* to date. Contrasting the series' easy legitimization of extreme violence and a fundamentally new set of morals under the changed circumstances of the zombie apocalypse with its characters' paranoid reluctance to change their view of specifically *sexual* morals as they pertain to relationships, family, and reproduction, Ziegler writes:

> In *The Walking Dead*, … the traditional family persists even in the absence of any state apparatus, its support and defence carried out through ingrained ideology … The conceptualization of the family … seems to escape [any] profound reimagining. The sweeping changes in other areas of postapocalyptic behaviour and social organization only highlight more strikingly by contrast the persistent dominance in *The Walking Dead* of the monogamous, heterosexual, nuclear family. (2018: 7)

Those relationships that the series introduces that are not monogamous mostly serve to further foreground a character's villainy. Negan, for example, keeps several 'wives', whose relationship with the despotic leader is not based on mutual choice, and instead adds a layer of sexual and misogynistic violence that differentiates Negan and his 'Saviors' from the supposedly morally superior survivors in Rick's group. For the most part, non-monogamy and extra-marital 'cheating' are condemned throughout the series.

Over the course of its several seasons, *The Walking Dead* has, however, developed a certain tolerance for non-heterosexual desire, but only if this desire remains abstract and does not become manifest in actual sexual acts, or if this desire is framed in the terms of monogamy and thus contributes to the ideology of reproductive futurism and paranoid futurity. The two most visible queer relationships in the series' first eight seasons are those of Tara and Denise, and of Aaron and Eric, and neither of them gets the chance to develop a narrative depth comparable to that of the relationships of characters of opposite sexes. Both Denise and Eric die soon after their introduction, confirming the impression that, in the fictional world of *The Walking Dead*, the queer must stay on the side of the monstrous, and end up dead or written out of the script. The series' dominant narrative of futuristic hope that so heavily relies on reiterations of the heterosexual, nuclear family and its concomitant ideology of reproduction leaves no room for exploring the potential of more creative and more reparative versions of care for the community. Those queer characters that do survive put themselves, after the death of their short-lived partners, in the service of the soldier male's paranoid eye-for-an-eye logic – as in the case of Tara – or become integrated into quasi-straight familial structures that stabilize the ever-damaged family unit: at the beginning of season three, and right after the zombification (and absorbance into the monstrous collective) of Eric, Aaron 'adopts' a baby – tellingly named Gracie – who has lost her biological father at the hands of Rick's premature, paranoid, defensive violence.

In the end, then, it turns out that *The Walking Dead*'s most subversive potential lies not – at least not within the space of its first eight seasons – in its regrettably underdeveloped queer characters and storylines, but instead in the interruption of narrative and reproductive teleology located both in the zombies themselves, and in the child characters' potential for going against the grain of their culturally prescribed role as carriers of futuristic hope. In a strangely self-conscious way, the series seems to know – as it confirms again and again in its diverging storylines – that the zombie apocalypse requires more than a mere paranoid holding-on to past notions of family and sociability. In its first eight seasons, it uses the excitement around the question of care and belonging in the timeless space of the post-apocalypse to play out fears about the danger of an inner breakdown of heterosexual norms and patriarchal structures. At the same time, the monsters and the children in *The Walking Dead* know that tomorrow is not coming, that the paranoid knowledge of who is kin and who is not has been destabilized. They know that the only way out is to give up looking back or forward, and to make all the raging soldier males understand that neither the zombies nor the children will continue to make themselves available as easy metaphors for a future that is based on violence and exclusion. Rick begins to grasp this when, in several flashforwards throughout season eight, he repeats the same sentence that his dead son Carl has learned from the stranger in the woods, and which this man – Siddiq – paraphrased from the Qu'ran: '[m]y mercy prevails over my wrath.'

In a sense, then, queerness does lie at the heart of *The Walking Dead* and its rendering of anxieties over hope and kinship. And it might be for this very reason that it can never be fully allowed to become manifest in the characters' relationship structures. Instead, queerness remains the foil that balances the series' paranoid commitment to patriarchal, heterosexual, and reproductive structures. In the space between iterations of reproductive futurism and the ultimate threat of a complete loss of meaning, reparation can emerge in the form of uncomfortably renitent child characters and their monstrous associates – not always as a stabilizing force, but always as a voice that questions, contradicts, and offers ways out of a dominant paranoid paradigm of teleological warfare.

PART TWO

Beyond time and space: Queering hope and globalizing kinship in contemporary speculative fiction

So far, I have argued that post-apocalyptic fiction provides a good starting point for considering emerging discursive patterns in contemporary cultural production which imaginatively privilege affective investments in the present moment and improvised forms of belonging and care over the symbolic perpetuation of the nuclear family as the bearer of the promise of a better future. While the fictional examples under consideration never fully abandon the foil of the family as a spectre that haunts their severely damaged social settings, both McCarthy's novel and the serial narrative of *The Walking Dead* make room for imagining hope and kinship otherwise, in the form of local and often fleeting dynamics of solidarity and belonging that refrain from looking far ahead. While post-apocalyptic fiction is an obvious entry into an investigation of fictional discourses which are sceptical of optimistic and exclusionary renderings of temporality and structures of care, contemporary speculative fiction more generally provides a multitude of examples that negotiate the relationship between the contemporary imagination and questions of community and hope on a global scale.

Beyond the realm of fiction, the ongoing relevance, urgency, and limitations of thinking kinship globally, and of narratives that imagine hope beyond the merely perpetuated promise of an overcoming of crisis in a world increasingly framed in terms of the catastrophic have recently become strikingly apparent in the context of the Covid-19 pandemic. In the early months of its spread, the pandemic mutated, in the western imagination, from being safely compartmentalized within the exoticizing and racist frameworks of anti-Asian cultural stereotypes[1] into a universalized threat that appeared to make all people akin in their universally shared vulnerability. The pandemic also uniquely challenged optimistic accounts of a global future in which humanity's survival as such – and that of all other species whose habitat is threatened by human actions and their far-reaching consequences – seems increasingly at stake. As if in answer to this challenge, political rhetoric at the time focused on tying hope to an emphasis on a globally networked, mutually dependent human community. In a declaration published in 2020 on the occasion of their seventy-fifth anniversary, the General Assembly of the United Nations frame the UN themselves as a unique carrier of hope for human survival – where 'humanity' is imagined as an entity abstracted from nation, society, and history. At the same time, the Covid-19 pandemic is taken as evidence that such global 'natural' disasters require a response from the human community imagined and endowed with agency *as* a global community:

---

[1] For an on-point analysis of the racist entitlement of early intellectual discourse surrounding the pandemic, and the need for decolonial knowledge practices see Xiang Zairong's comment 'On the Epistemic Condition' (2020).

No other global organisation gives hope to so many people for a better world and can deliver the future we want. The urgency for all countries to come together, to fulfil the promise of the nations united, has rarely been greater ... Our challenges are interconnected and can only be addressed through reinvigorating multilateralism ... The COVID-19 pandemic has reminded us in the most powerful way that we are closely interconnected and only as strong as our weakest link. Only by working together and in solidarity can we end the pandemic and effectively tackle its consequences. Only together can we build resilience against future pandemics and other global challenges ... The time to act is now ... We will be prepared. (2020)

Humanity's only hope for a better future is thus framed as contingent upon all humans becoming aware of each other as kin. Reading this declaration against the grain of its urgent call for action and its unabashed commitment to humanism and optimism might seem cynical. Nevertheless, I would like to take the UN statement as paradigmatic of a rhetoric, popular during the pandemic, that frames the virus as an externalized threat which necessitates and *produces* a networked human community. Using the language and imagery of a universal humanism that arrives at its own self-consciousness through a shared existential crisis – 'We are all in this together!'[2] – this discourse necessarily grinds against both the reality of a starkly differential impact of the pandemic on individuals into whose bodies the effects of social and economic inequality, racism, and sexism are inscribed, and the vastly different presents and futures enabled and disabled as a result of this unequal distribution of catastrophic effects. A rhetoric of universal human kinship and comprehensive teleological hope thus reduces and simplifies the complexities and non-synchronicity of a globalized world to a single narrative.

At the same time, the imagery of an intricately connected web of human nodes, vulnerable to the reproductive and migratory strategies of a virus, seems a particularly fitting narrative for a global culture still suffering under the hung-over awakening from late-twentieth-century digital utopianism, which celebrated the internet as a space of present and future individual and collective liberation. In an algorithmic age that experiences technical innovation in the field of AI and big data as both an economic promise and a potential threat to individual and collective rights and freedoms, the

---

[2] Another UN publication, a statement by secretary-general António Guterres which forms part of the UN Covid-19 response, prominently employs this basic call to communal self-identification in its title: 'We are all in this Together: Human Rights and COVID-19 Response and Recovery' (2020). In it, Guterres also acknowledges that 'the virus does not discriminate, but its impacts do'.

realization that we are all connected and collectively vulnerable in more ways than we feel comfortable acknowledging raises questions about the nature (communal, fragmented, empowered, vulnerable) of a globally connected human species.[3] At the same time, the urgencies and social realities of life in pandemic times heighten the collective impression that the future is unknown, and that the only temporal variable accessible to epistemological inquiry is the present.[4]

In many ways, the combination of metaphors of the digital age and the language of viral disease in accounts of the Covid-19 pandemic are reminiscent of the narrative conventions and popular themes of speculative fiction: not only have certain kinds of science fiction or dystopian writing already told stories that, in hindsight, seem to eerily predict later real-world developments like the current global health crisis[5], but the narratives *about* the spread of the virus themselves could often be regarded as the stuff of the most outrageous fiction. Or, to put it differently, it seems that we tend to fabulate the realities of the pandemic in ways similar to those in which contemporary speculative fiction fabulates the presents and possible futures of humanity in the shadow of technical innovation and under the conditions of the digital age.

'Speculative fiction' is a contested term. In most contexts, it is used as an umbrella category for genre fiction that lies outside the conventions of strictly realist narration, such as science fiction, fantasy, horror, and various forms of utopian and dystopian storytelling – works, that is, which 'conjecture about matters that in the normal course of things could not be[,] … presenting modes of being that contrast with their audiences' understanding of ordinary reality' (Gill 2013: 72, 73). Speculative fiction asks us to consider what we know, and to think it with a difference: it 'invites its audiences to consider different *what-if* scenarios to encourage them to see the world from a new angle' (Kraatila 2019: 419, emphasis in original). At the same time, it is precisely speculative fiction's relationship with reality and 'the world' that is most often debated: how far removed from 'the normal course of things' does a work have to be to classify as

---

[3]There is a host of research and journalism that aligns the development of the pandemic with algorithmic models of networked relations. One article on the popular-science website *Futurity*, for example, states that 'COVID-19 transmission "webs" show how we're all connected … Visualisations of COVID-19 outbreaks and transmission networks around the world reveal how interconnected we truly are, across all borders and oceans' (Varela 2020).
[4]In an article for the German newspaper *Süddeutsche Zeitung*, Friederike Zoe Grasshoff aptly observes 'the discovery of the present' under pandemic conditions (2020, my translation).
[5]One instance of this sort of realization is the renewed popularity Steven Soderbergh's 2011 thriller *Contagion* received during the Covid-19 crisis. The film explores the medical, social, and political consequences of the pandemic spread of a virus that causes a lethal respiratory disease in humans.

speculative? While many critics agree that speculative fiction almost always comments on the world we live in (cf. Gill 2013: 80–1), the exact nature of this dialogue (satirical, prophetic, allegorical) varies drastically between individual texts. Some degree of removal from the current state of the world and humanity seems to be an uncontroversial prerequisite. In practice, however, the kinds of removal that different genres regularly classified as 'speculative' perform differ vastly in terms of their being either temporal (back to some fantastic past, or forward to some scientifically advanced future) or spatial (to a fantastic land not quite our own, or to some distant planet), or both at the same time.[6]

This diversity in content and imaginative strategy accounts, to an extent, for the contested definitional ground between speculative fiction and science fiction – both regularly and ambiguously abbreviated as 'SF'.[7] This definitional debate, in turn, is instructive for an understanding of speculative fiction's relation to temporality. In her book on *SF and the Human Imagination* (2011), Margaret Atwood recounts her own history as a writer with the terms 'science fiction' and 'speculative fiction'. Having, on repeated occasions, publicly voiced her scepticism about her novels being called 'science fiction', it was a review of *The Year of the Flood*, written by fellow SF writer Ursula K. Le Guin for the *Guardian* (2009), which prompted Atwood to consider the question of science versus speculative fiction more seriously. In the review, Le Guin expresses her consternation at Atwood's supposedly strategic avoidance of the 'science fiction' label. She posits that, to her, most of the novels in Atwood's oeuvre 'exemplify one of the things science fiction does, which is to extrapolate imaginatively from current trends and events to a near-future that's half prediction, half satire'. In response, Atwood puts forth her own definitions of SF, foregrounding SF's relationship with reality and temporality:

> What I mean by 'science fiction' is books that descend from H. G. Wells's *The War of the Worlds*, which treats of an invasion by tentacled, bloodsucking Martians shot to Earth in metal canisters – things that could not

---

[6] Some critics, like Carolin Gebauer, argue that works of speculative fiction necessarily 'anticipate possible *future* scenarios, evoking storyworlds that are set in a future not too remote from our present' (2020: 20, emphasis mine). I would argue that such a narrow definition excludes a host of works that often (legitimately) fall into the category. Gebauer's definition, however, is a good example of the critical tendency to associate speculative fiction exclusively with speculation about the *future*, disavowing fictional fabulation about the past, the present, or a time in uncertain relation to our own.

[7] Like other writers, I find this ambiguity productive, and will, in this chapter, use 'SF' to designate the blurry definitional space between 'science fiction' and 'speculative fiction', while privileging the pairing 'SF/speculative fiction' as denoting the kind of work the texts under consideration in this book do.

possibly happen – whereas, for me, 'speculative fiction' means plots that descend from Jules Verne's books about submarines and balloon travel and such – things that really could happen but just hadn't completely happened when the author wrote the books. I would place my own books in this second category. (2011: 6)

Strikingly, Atwood thus distinguishes science fiction from speculative fiction not primarily according to their differential relation to temporality (both, for her, speculate about a future yet to come), but mostly according to their different degrees of realist possibility. Speculative fiction, for Atwood, thus always takes the historical past and present as a starting point, and then goes on to fabulate about different further, possible developments: SF, that is, takes its cue from the possibilities and potentialities of the here and now.

For the purpose of my own project, I understand 'speculative fiction' to loosely denote works that put at their centre the 'what if' question, and that do so in relation to historical and sociological, present and past reality, but not necessarily in a fixed temporal relation to the same: while they might speculate about possible futures, they are often equally invested in circular, nostalgic, or indeterminate temporalities. Like Alexis Lothian, I appreciate the term 'speculative fiction' for its concrete semantic value: my concern here is with 'the act of *speculation*: of imagining things otherwise than they are, and of creating stories from that impulse' (2018: 15, emphasis in original). As such, my usage of the term is probably most closely related to Donna Haraway's iterative understanding of SF: in *Staying with the Trouble*, she repeatedly evokes the urgent need for and reparative potential of 'SF: science fiction, speculative fabulation, string figures, speculative feminism, science fact, so far' (2016: 2, cf. also 10, 14, 81, 105) for making kin in a troubled present. Her own book of contemporary critical analysis accordingly contains the fictional 'Camille Stories', an 'invitation to a collective speculative fabulation' (8, cf. also 134–68) about the possibilities of community and healing in an age of ecological devastation. This kind of fictional speculation, Haraway insists, is neither optimistic nor pessimistic; instead, it acknowledges the importance of imaginative storytelling for 'comforting, inspiring, remembering, warming, nurturing compassion, mourning, and becoming-with each other in [our] differences, hopes, and terrors' (150). In this way, speculative storytelling becomes a crucial tool for a politics of reparation which rejects both the blindly optimistic trust in techno-fixes and hyper-individualism, and the nihilism of those who assume that it is too late anyway: '[b]locking the foreclosures of utopias, SF kept politics alive' (150). It is in this sense of SF/speculative fiction – as storytelling which takes the present seriously, which fabulates about and across possible pasts, presents, and futures, and which foregrounds the importance of making kin for discovering a new kind of hope – that I read the material in this chapter.

This framing of SF/speculative fiction as firmly anchored in and starting from the conditions of the present, and as invested in a politics of hope that is at least as much about telling stories of survival in damaged times as it is about optimistic projections of the future warrants some elaboration. While speculative fiction is by design committed to fabulations about worlds at a certain temporal or spatial remove from our own – in this sense, it is truly utopic – its projections are not *necessarily* futuristic, and they are certainly not always optimistic. Instead, SF speculates about worlds related to but different from our own, sometimes in possible futures, but also in alternative presents and past, sometimes with an optimistic approach to its 'what if' scenarios, but as frequently in ambivalent or dystopian registers. SF's temporal displacements can reach towards both the future and the past – or be situated in an undefined temporal 'elsewhen' (Gilarek 2015: 35). The point of reference, however, remains the historical present of production and reception: works of utopic and dystopic SF are most often read as comments on the present state of affairs, as thought experiments that present themselves either as meditations on a better alternative or as warning texts in a mode of anticipation (cf. 36, 43).

Contemporary SF, in particular, resonates with the narrative strategies employed in non-fictional discourse to capture the state of the world under the influence of recent technological developments, globalization, and ecological devastation. As Lisa Garforth puts it, 'environmental crisis can productively be read as a science-fictional object – that is, as an epistemic entity composed of orientations to planetary futures that are at once descriptive and speculative, scientific and fictional' (2019: 240). Drawing attention to the possible *future* implications and consequences of past and current developments, both scientific and fictional SF speculation, Garforth goes on to argue, draw collective critical attention to the present: the SF imagination can prompt 'a pause in which the critical imagination is mobilized to interrogate what is plausible, and to consider what is ethical or desirable' (242). Discourses on environmental crisis emerging over the last few decades, coupled with scientific developments and new methods of representation and, crucially, an SF imagination which produced its own knowledge about planetary pasts, presents, and futures, have enabled a new kind of imaginary. This imaginary looks at planet Earth from the outside and foregrounds the vital webs of connection and modes of kinship between all humans, and between humans and the system as a whole in times of looming catastrophe (cf. 243–9).

How, then, should we read contemporary works of speculative fiction, works that have emerged in the context of contemporary, present-oriented crisis narratives, and under the impression of an escalating global connectivity that creates new temporal regimes of knowledge for some, new exclusions for others, and increased vulnerability for all? Within the wider context of this book's framework, and bearing in mind the recent shifts in the speculative imagination laid out above, I want to engage with the works under consideration in this section with the assumption that '[t]he expansive, emergent language of the speculative fosters ... radical openness' (Lothian 2018: 17). Like Alexis Lothian, in her investigation of the bearings of 'old futures' – speculative renderings of the future from the historical past – on the present, I am interested in 'the process by which cultural producers reconfigure their historical present in order to speculate about what a possible future might be like' (18); and, like her, I acknowledge that my material, in speculating across real and imaginary pasts, presents, and futures, ultimately does not fully escape the logic of linear and colonial temporality (cf. 19). Lothian goes on to search for '[t]he lingering presences and possibilities of past futures [that] open possibilities for thinking and living the present in different, deviant ways' (20) in speculative fabulations from earlier times. In contrast, my own selection of very recent works of speculative fiction is meant to enable new perspectives on how contemporary cultural production speculates with, against, and across current spatial and temporal imaginaries that contribute to an understanding of fictional (and wider cultural) framings of hope and kinship in the ever receding historical now.

Before moving on to discussing the fictional examples at hand, however, I want to briefly address the complex relationship between SF and coloniality. SF/speculative and science fiction, in their evocations of global (and intergalactic) imaginaries that push against and beyond the frontiers of known space, have always also been about confrontations with the human and non-human 'other', and about interrogating, de- and re-stabilizing the ideological regimes that guarantee the privileged position of the enlightened human (often white, often male) subject. As such, as Nancy Batty and Robert Markley observe, 'science fiction and utopian writing, in particular, have historically invoked and interrogated visions of colonisation on earth as well as in outer space' (2002: 6). Recent decades have, however, seen the rise, in fictional as well as critical discourse, of voices that think and write with and in SF to engage 'issues of race and class, and social justice; issues of authority and freedom; and issues of a "universal", inclusive human destiny' (9). Post- and decolonial thinking and critique have long begun to reconfigure the ideological range and political impetus of speculative cultures in order to claim the future for those regularly excluded from it, and to reparatively reclaim the past for those left traumatized by it. One of the most prominent cases in point is the writing subsumed under the label 'Afrofuturism', writing which 'redefine[s] culture and notions of blackness for today and the future', and which enables modes of creative, politically engaged fabulation across different temporal and spatial positions in order to open up the potentials of both 'a total reeinvisioning of the past and speculation about the future rife with cultural critiques' (Womack 2013: 11). In this section – and in this book as a whole – I do not directly engage with the utopic and imaginative energies of Afrofuturism and other influential and continually emerging emancipatory subfields of SF. My focus here is on a very particular instance of white, western, transatlantic, and global cultural production across different media. The examples discussed are works of speculative fiction that have received a great amount of public attention, and have come to be considered milestones of the popular imagination. As instances of global speculative storytelling emerging from two particular but historically intimately related contexts – the English literary scene and US media production – they are productive for my investigation of hope and kinship because they exemplify the tension, within the contemporary cultural imagination (of 'the west'), between the resurrection of the liberal human subject (and the idea of a globally shared humanism as such) and the awareness of histories of colonization, global inequalities, and contemporary identity politics.

Both David Mitchell's 2004 novel *Cloud Atlas* and Netflix's *Sense8* (2015–18) are concerned with foregrounding universal human connection across space and time, and with reconfiguring notions of narrative temporality and their attendant affective investments in fictional pasts, presents, and futures. Both also centrally locate hope in the potentialities of human connection and understanding across boundaries of nation, race, gender, and sexuality, and abstain from inscribing themselves fully into either a utopian or a dystopian mode. While the connections between the two texts thus arise, to a large extent, from shared thematic commitments, they are also linked through processes of adaptation and cooperative cultural production. Lily and Lana Wachowski, together with Tom Tykwer, wrote the screenplay for, co-produced, and co-directed the 2012 adaptation of Mitchell's novel. Only a few years later, the Wachowski siblings picked up many of the themes, ideas, and aesthetics from their work on Mitchell's novel and created, together with science-fiction legend J. Michael Straczynski, the web television series *Sense8*, for the final episode of which Mitchell, in turn, served as co-writer. Both the novel and the series thus share a common artistic vision and can be legitimately regarded as results of one ongoing process of creation, which, over the course of roughly a decade, fabulated, in a speculative mode, about ideas of universal human kinship and the place of hope in the contemporary imagination.

Critics regularly emphasize David Mitchell's formative influence on contemporary storytelling.[8] His oeuvre as a whole is a complex network of interrelated stories, 'a fictional universe of which one mere four- or five-hundred page novel is just a fractional part' (Dillon 2011: 5): characters,

---

[8] Pico Iyer even goes so far as to credit Mitchell with '[h]aving created the 21st century novel' (2007); and Peter Childs and James Green argue that Mitchell regularly produces topical fiction that 'articulate[s] a complex response to the current material conditions of the world, … [and] the fluidity and multiplicity of contemporary relations and subjectivities' (2011: 25, 26).

artefacts, themes, and ideas appear and reappear across his novels, with each individual book 'constituting a room in the house of fiction that he is constructing' (6). For my own argument, Mitchell's ongoing concern with 'a sense of apocalypse and the end of the world[,] hope that the actions of individuals can quell the tide of human predacity[,] and the role of memory and story in creating identity' (13) is particularly productive, as is the fact that ideas of 'interconnectedness and interdependency ... [and t]he possibility of sympathetic reciprocity, which acknowledges co-dependency' (Childs and Green 2011: 31, 34) are at the heart of his fiction. *Cloud Atlas*, in particular, is concerned with thinking about and with the consequences and the potential of universal human connection and kinship, and both this novel and *Sense8* are invested in finding hope in the moments of realization, on the part of the characters and the audience, that humanity (and humanism) can only rediscover itself in processes of connection, even and especially when there is no brighter future on the horizon.

3

'What is an ocean but a multitude of drops': Metafiction and universal kinship in David Mitchell's *Cloud Atlas*

Two themes which run as a common thread through David Mitchell's work are temporality and human connection. Several of his novels share an episodic structure and contain stories that travel the globe, while themes and even characters reappear across the different publications. Dirk Wiemann poignantly summarizes the defining feature of Mitchell's accumulated work as 'the engagement of literary storytelling with the complexities and ambiguities of time in an intensely (and more often than not mysteriously) interconnected and at the same time threatened and precarious world' (2017: 499). This combined interest of Mitchell's in time as an affective dimension and the web of connections that bring subjects together make his novels ideal case studies for my investigation of the dynamic relationship between hope and kinship in contemporary fiction. While his 1999 debut novel *Ghostwritten* already features an episodic narrative spanning the globe, with individual characters inadvertently becoming connected through a series of events, it is in his 'unexpected crossover hit' (Ng 2015: 107) *Cloud Atlas* (2004) that Mitchell most fully engages with the possibilities of embedded narratives, metafictional play, and metaleptic[1] connection. *Cloud Atlas* consists of six separate storylines – all rendering different literary

---

[1] Throughout this chapter, I use the term 'metalepsis' exclusively in the narratological sense of the transgression of boundaries between different narrative levels, not in the sense of a specific trope or figure of speech.

genres – which span a period from the mid-nineteenth century to a faraway post-apocalyptic future, and which are dispersed across different regions of the world. Set in the nineteenth century, lawyer Adam Ewing writes a journal about his adventures travelling the South Pacific from the Chatham Islands to Hawaii. In 1930s Belgium, young composer Robert Frobisher writes letters to his lover Rufus Sixsmith. A raunchy spy novel tells the story of journalist Luisa Rey's fight against a large atomic power corporation in the 1970s Bay Area. Set vaguely in the novel's contemporary time, vanity publisher Timothy Cavendish narrates his misadventures in an old-people's home in England in a picaresque memoire. In a dystopic futuristic Korea ruled by corporate powers, the clone Sonmi 451 is interviewed by an archivist before her execution. And in an even farther post-apocalyptic future presented in the form of oral storytelling, the reader encounters Zachry and Meronym, two of only a few humans left in the world who, on the Big Island of Hawaii, fight for the survival of humanity and its collected knowledge. The book presents the first half of each story in chronological order, with Zachry's tale the only uninterrupted one in the middle, and reverts, in the book's second half, back to Adam's story, with which the novel concludes. The first five stories metaleptically become texts (in the widest sense) to be read and consumed by the chronologically following protagonist, with Zachry's story – as a counterintuitive frame – containing all others.

Many critics (and Mitchell himself) have pointed out the novel's indebtedness to Italo Calvino's *If on a Winter's Night a Traveller* (1979)[2], which consists of several unfinished 'beginnings of novels' and foregrounds the act of reading as the sustained attempt of a fictional subject to make sense of a fragmented narrative without closure. Mitchell's own rendering of fictional subjects that literally read each other across sometimes vast temporal and geographical distances combines this interest in the epistemological function of reading with the conscious manipulation of narrative pace and linearity to ask questions about the workings of both story and history, and about the place of the individual acting and reading subject in a web of global connections. Accordingly, Mitchell's work regularly features as exemplary in discussions about a recently emerging type of fiction that has been described as 'the world novel', 'the global novel', 'the planetary novel', or 'the cosmopolitan novel' (Wiemann 2017: 500). Wendy Knepper even reaches back to one of the oldest literary forms to frame *Cloud Atlas* as an 'experimental world epic[which] encourages

---

[2]For a sustained discussion of both novels' employment of postmodern techniques, see McMorran (2011).

readers to expand and exercise their global literacies as capabilities for challenging inequalities and rethinking developmental freedoms' (2016: 95). Such labels and framings attempt to grasp the tendency of novels such as Mitchell's to combine the inheritance of postmodernism with a renewed interest in a global humanism and a 'new sincerity' (cf. Kelly 2010). For my own purpose, Berthold Schoene's characterization of *Cloud Atlas* as 'pioneer[ing] a new cosmopolitan modus operandi for twenty-first-century British fiction' is particularly productive, since he foregrounds the connective drive of the novel, and characterizes Mitchell's writing as 'chart[ing] human existence both transterritorially and as always determined by locally specific conditions' (2010: 97). My analysis of the novel explores the stakes of such a fictional rendering of global connection through localized story and character. It interrogates the text's potential normalization of a temporal and communal universalism which, on the one hand, locates hope in the possibility of individual choice and agency, but, on the other hand, reproduces an apocalyptic logic that posits a rigid dichotomy between humanity's inevitable drive towards global destruction, and the evocation of a generalized and thus potentially politically defunct humanism. While, as Diletta De Cristofaro argues, the novel does produce, through its formal features, 'anti-apocalyptic critical temporalities' (2018: 243) in a conscious turn away from any easy access to utopian alternatives, in the process 'defy[ing] chronology, linearity, continuity, foreshadowing, cause and effect, and the sense of an ending itself' (246), *Cloud Atlas*, at the same time, finally achieves its powerful effect and sincere message by locating hope in the residual possibility of a brighter tomorrow.

In this chapter, I will first examine the novel's complicated structure and its commitment, on the one hand, to the legacy of postmodernism and, on the other, to a 'new sincerity' and humanism. I will then turn to its rendering of time and temporality as ambiguously suspended between linear and circular notions of time, and the implications of this ambiguity for the novel's politics of hope. My examination of metafiction and the role of reading as a concrete and metaphorical device for creating community will lead to a consideration of Mitchell's generalization of kinship as embracing the 'human family'. Finally, I will critically examine how the novel inscribes itself into an ultimately conservative notion of humanism in order to counter-balance its pessimistic take on human progress and history. The chapter concludes with a reading of the Wachowskis and Tom Tykwer's 2012 film adaptation of *Cloud Atlas*, arguing that, while creatively using the means and techniques of filmmaking to translate the novel's investment in temporality and global connection into a different medium, the film also rids the story of its ambiguous suspension between optimism and pessimism, and relocates hope in a narrative of heterosexual romance and reproductive survival.

Towards a new sincerity:
Postmodernism and humanism

In *Cloud Atlas*, Mitchell combines postmodern formal features with an ethical commitment to a sincerely humanist message, locating hope in a renewed trust in human connection. As such, his novel is paradigmatic of recent tendencies, in contemporary fiction, towards what Irmtraud Huber describes as a literature of reconstruction, which is characterized by 'a tentative but pervasive optimism concerning the impossible possibility of communication' (2014: 36). Mitchell consciously plays with postmodern deconstructive technique on the level of discourse to foreground his novel's overall reconstructive thrust and commitment to connection. *Cloud Atlas* features many of those elements most readily associated with a postmodern literary style, most obviously its metafictional play with genre and its fragmented narrative, but also intertextual references and self-conscious discourse. The novel's very first sentence ('Beyond the Indian hamlet, upon a forlorn strand, I happened on a trail of recent footprints' (Mitchell 2004: 3)) evokes Daniel Defoe's *Robinson Crusoe*, and numerous other direct and indirect references to works of literature and popular culture (such as, repeatedly, Richard Fleischer's 1973 dystopian film *Soylent Green* (cf. e.g. 179)) are scattered across the different episodes. Structurally, the novel foregrounds fragmentation and readerly self-consciousness, for example by breaking off each episode apart from Zachry's halfway through – mid-sentence in Adam Ewing's case; integrated within the logic of the story; or constructed as an obvious cliff-hanger at a moment of high suspense (cf. 39, 183, 245). In an ironic twist, Timothy Cavendish, whose memoir features the greatest density of metafictional commentary, explicitly dismisses the very postmodern techniques the novel as a whole remains indebted to: '[a]s an experienced editor I disapprove of backflashes, foreshadowing and tricksy devices, they belong in the 1980s with MAs in Postmodernism and Chaos Theory' (152). This kind of self-deprecating commentary from within the story world is typical of Mitchell, who holds just such a degree himself. Cavendish is not the only character he uses to comment apologetically on the playfully constructed nature of his novel. While this self-deprecating gesture would still locate the text in a postmodern tradition, *Cloud Atlas* does not subscribe to the wholesale rejection, often associated with postmodernism, of grand narratives and Enlightenment ideals.[3] It is

---

[3] Although Gerd Bayer rightly characterizes the novel as 'a carefully orchestrated catalogue of anti-Enlightenment vignettes', in the sense that '[m]any of the major achievements, or what have been presented as such, are carefully dissected and thereby revealed to be corrupted' (2015: 351–2), this thematic rejection of the Enlightenment notion of progress does not prevent the novel from remaining committed to an enlightened vision of a common human essence and goodness.

certainly debatable whether Mitchell's particular amalgam of metafictional technique and a politics of sincerity is a mere variety and development of postmodern writing (but would still count as such), or, indeed, an altogether new kind of fictional attitude that contributes to the emergence of a new literary style or movement. I find Nick Bentley's argument convincing, who discovers, in Mitchell's writing (and in that of Zadie Smith), a kind of post-postmodernism he defines as 'metamodernism'. This post-postmodernism, Bentley asserts – echoing Huber – 'starts at a point of fragmentation and explores possible ways of (re-)forming connections. If postmodernism is a movement of deconstruction, post-postmodernism is about the possibility of reconstruction' (2018: 740). I, too, would argue that, in *Cloud Atlas*, Mitchell uses established elements of postmodern writing, but only in order to reinforce an ultimately humanist and sincere message of a 'quest for human connectivity across diverse times, locations and cultures' (Bentley 2018: 734).[4] He thus suspends his novel between deconstruction and reconstruction, framing his particular vision of humanist hope as emerging from, rather than contradicting metafictional experimentation and irony.

Beyond a narrative commitment to the idea of a generalized human kinship, the novel's particular mode of sincerity emerges most obviously in its thematic engagement with metaphysical 'truth', and with its mostly positive framing of belief as enabling (teleological) hope. Although the book refrains from presenting a unified vision of what 'the truth' is, several of its protagonists base their decisions as agents of change for the better on their commitment to some kind of higher, metaphysically removed ethical certainty. Adam Ewing, faced with different attitudes towards slavery and racism maintains that '[o]ccasionally, I glimpse a truer truth' (Mitchell 2004: 17), which ultimately helps him become an abolitionist. In her journalistic research, Luisa Rey, with almost comic emphasis, remains stubbornly committed to finding out the 'truth' (cf. e.g. 99). Sonmi begins her interview with the archivist by confirming that '[n]o other version of the truth [but my own] has ever mattered to me' (187). And Zachry painfully begins to understand that '*the true true is diff'rent to the seemin' true*' (287, emphasis in original). While all these 'truths' play out on different levels of the religious, the (seemingly) factual, the personal, and the existential, in combination, they create an abstract idea of a transcendent 'truth' that becomes a driving force for human action. Similarly, the novel evokes metaphysical belief as a generally positive influence. On the one hand, *religious* faith emerges, on several occasions, as a mere path to personal salvation for the unenlightened – as Robert Frobisher sees it (cf. 75) – or as a delusion which is followed by

---

[4]Hélène Machinal makes a similar point in arguing that 'David Mitchell's novel is rooted in postmodernity but ... also transcends it by introducing a philosophical dimension that goes beyond the individual level to a more collective one' (2011: 127).

painful but necessary disillusionment – as for Sonmi when she begins to understand that her beloved Logoman is no god (cf. 198), and for Zachry when he is similarly confronted with the fact that his goddess Sonmi was herself only human (cf. 291). The narrative, however, gives pride of place to Adam Ewing's passionate plea for the *humanist* belief in the potential for moral goodness and betterment:

> If we *believe* that humanity may transcend tooth & claw, if we *believe* divers races & creeds can share this world as peaceably as the orphans share their candlenut tree, if we *believe* leaders must be just, violence muzzled, power accountable & the riches of the Earth & its Oceans shared equitably, such a world will come to pass. (528, emphasis in original)

Cloud Atlas thus suspends its ethical investments between a dominant theme of human predacity and progression towards apocalyptic destruction, and an emphasis on the importance of individual acts of resistance and bravery based on the belief in the fundamental human capacity for goodness. Crucially, it is the latter dynamic that helps bring together the novel's fragmented narrative. In doing so, the text, although never completely leaving the ironic mode, opens up the possibility of hope in the form of a sincere commitment to a humanist message of common understanding and moral universalism that Luke Hortle identifies as 'a neohumanist return to tropes of Enlightenment humanism and a revitalisation of the liberal humanist subject' (2016: 254). Similarly, Hélène Machinal argues that *Cloud Atlas* scatters protagonists across time and space to arrive at 'the essence of humanity. What connects the characters is their aspiration or ability to resist politico-ideological systems trying to impose their "truth" as an immutable model' (2011: 143–4). Fragmentation and the structural interwovenness of the novel's individual episodes thus come to serve as a contrastive foil to highlight a metaphysical human essence that transcends time and space, and that arguably becomes the central grand narrative to which the novel subscribes. As Berthold Schoene puts it, in *Cloud Atlas*, '[a]ll individuality amounts to is the production of different variations on one and the same theme of contemporary human existence' (2010: 99). Both *Cloud Atlas*' ambiguous position between postmodern fragmentation and a new humanism and sincerity, and its structural suspension in-between different modes of temporality highlight the novel's differential investment in what I have been framing as hope and kinship in terms of a temporal and affective structuring of narrative and relationality. While the text's rendering of temporality remains ambiguous, the novel ultimately favours a non-linear and non-circular notion of simultaneity, and the present as the space where hope emerges in openness and potentiality.

Arrows and circles: Temporality and the ambiguity of hope

Cloud Atlas replicates the tension between its shared commitment to both postmodern detachment and a humanist and sincere message on a structural level by combining contradictory modes of temporality. Critics struggle to adequately describe the way the six episodes contained in the book relate to each other. The novel itself provides the reader with several images that self-consciously refer to its counterintuitively nested structure. In Luisa Rey's episode, Isaac Sachs speculates about a model of time as '*an infinite matryoshka doll of painted moments*' (Mitchell 2004: 409, emphasis in original). This, however, is a misleading image. While Adam Ewing's story begins and ends the book, and thus intuitively serves as a frame which, in the end, contains the reading experience of all other fragments, within the temporal logic of the story itself, it is Zachry's section in the middle of the book which, in fact, contains all others that historically precede it.[5] A more adequate image reflecting this structure is suggested by Timothy Cavendish. After waking up from an induced stroke – and, structurally, at the beginning of the second half of his interrupted narrative – he speculates about his experience of time, characterizing it as 'no arrow, no boomerang, but a concertina' (370). Projected onto the novel's structure at large, Cavendish's observation aptly dismisses both the story's linear and teleological drive towards conclusion and destruction, and its implications of history as eternally recurring. Instead, he finds, in the image of the concertina's smooth and bending back-and-forth movement, the ambiguous 'both-and' of time as it becomes manifest in human affective investments and actions which the novel reflects in its structure. The concertina image implies that the novel 'moves both forward and backwards, and, in doing so, premises not only that past events can affect the future but also that future events can affect the past' (Parker 2010: 206). As Diletta De Cristofaro puts it,

> instead of looking for chains of causality and for clues that may foreshadow the conclusion(s), the repetitive patterns of the bellows signal that we must pay attention to the interconnections between the six narratives … [W]e should consider [the stories] as if they were running in parallel, each influencing our understanding of the other and, in turn, of the present world. (2018: 249)

---

[5] As Will McMorran puts it, '[e]ach segment enjoys an extradiegetic relationship to the *preceding* one, commenting upon it, questioning it, and so seeming to master and contain it' (2011:163, emphasis in original).

Through its particular rendering of a nested narrative, and by means of thematic emphasis, *Cloud Atlas* constructs a tension between linear and circular notions of time which ultimately remains unresolved (cf. Wiemann 2017: 506). It is through this tension that the novel imbues the present moment and the potential for individual agency with significance. In the context of the different individual storylines, time itself is repeatedly foregrounded, contemplated, and complicated: either through an explicit narrative juxtaposition of linearity and circularity, as in the case of Cavendish's first-person account;[6] in apocalyptic terms ('Time itself shall come to an end' (Mitchell 2004: 82)); as a rare commodity (cf. e.g. 120, 188); as contextually determined and subjective ('Questions of "when" are problematic in a world with no calendar or windows' (191, cf. also 295)); or as a generalized structuring principle ('Time is what stops history happening at once; time is the speed at which the past disappears' (244)). The most complex theory of time the novel contains is put forth by Isaac Sachs moments before his own death: he speculates, somewhat crudely, that there must be both 'actual' and 'virtual' versions of the past and the future – what has 'in fact' happened and will 'in fact' happen versus what we remember and hope for. Both 'virtual' versions of past and future time are, he maintains, potentially more significant than their factual counterparts because, in the case of the past, '*[t]he present presses the virtual past into its own service[ ] to lend credence to its mythologies + legitimacy to the imposition of will. Power seeks + is the right to "landscape" the virtual past*' (408–9, emphasis in original). The 'virtual' future is constructed by '*wishes, prophecies + daydreams. This virtual future may influence the actual future, as in a self-fulfilling prophecy, but the actual future will eclipse our virtual one as surely as tomorrow eclipses today*' (409, emphasis in original). To an extent, this passage metonymically expresses the novel's overall temporal logic. Taken individually, each protagonist (and, by extension, their particular environments) 'misconstrues' the 'actual' past – as when Zachry and his people assume that Sonmi is a goddess – and epiphanic memory takes precedence over factual history. At the same time, each character's hopeful investment in the possibility of a better future – without slavery and destructive predatory behaviour – although clearly running counter to the way events actually unfold over the course of the novel's fictionalized past, present, and dystopian future, appears as a prerequisite for individual action and feasible localized change. The potentiality of the present thus rests on its affective investments in 'virtual' pasts and futures, which productively run counter to their 'actual' or factual counterparts. In this sense, *Cloud Atlas*' rendering of

---

[6]Cavendish makes the reference to time as an arrow or boomerang twice, once in the instance discussed above, but also once before, much earlier in his section, and with additional reference to the *Cloud Atlas Sextet*: '[t]ime's Arrow became Time's Boomerang and I lost count of all my majors. A jazz sextet kicked off a rumba' (Mitchell 2004: 149).

temporality is arguably utopian, in that it ties hope to the characters' ability to speculate about times different from their own, and to evoke possible worlds that are not necessarily congruent with the real course of events. On the other hand, the fact that the novel never resolves the tension between linear and circular temporalities, between the necessity of history repeating itself and the possibility of real change qualifies its characters' commitment to a teleological notion of hope.

Critics disagree over whether circular or linear notions of time ultimately take precedence in *Cloud Atlas*. On the one hand, a thematic concern with return and repetition lies at the heart of the story: its central theme is the recurrence of human predacity and the will to power. On several occasions, the narrative suggests that the six protagonists might be (actual or symbolic) reincarnations of the same soul or spirit, symbolized by the comet-shaped birthmark they all share. The idea of individual and human history and lives repeating themselves comes up again and again (cf. 86, 165, 173, 255, 345, 360–1, 488). Intertextually, too, the novel repeatedly picks up the idea of a cyclical notion of history. Nietzsche's concept of the 'eternal recurrence' of all events in history features several times across the different episodes, most explicitly in Vyvyan Ayrs' composition 'to be named *Eternal Recurrence* in honour of his beloved Nietzsche' (84). Robert Frobisher cynically refers to this composition again right before his suicide when he, too, characterizes history as an endless cycle of rebirth and repetition: 'Nietzsche's gramophone record. When it ends, the Old One plays it again, for an eternity of eternities' (490). While this Nietzschean notion of history indeed seems to prevail in *Cloud Atlas* in the form of the fight of individuals against a prevailing human tendency to destroy each other and the world at large (cf. Kucała 2018), it is contrasted and complemented with both a tendency towards linearity and teleology, and the affective foregrounding of the local power of individual choice and action. In consequence, hope, too, emerges simultaneously as a teleological investment in a better future, *and* as a non-linear commitment to the possibility of agency in the present moment. Teleological temporality, however, turns out to be fundamentally ambiguous: the novel's dominant telos is the self-inflicted human drive towards cataclysmic self-destruction, which thus qualifies the character's investment in hopes for a better future. This tension is most cruelly actualized in Sonmi's storyline: the cloned 'servers' of her dystopian society work towards a promised liberation after twelve years, and their transformation into full citizens or 'consumers' (Mitchell 2004: 190). This teleological hope is, in the end, turned on its head when Sonmi finds out that the servers are, in fact, murdered and transformed into food to be consumed by their kind (cf. 357–60).[7] On a different level, Robert Frobisher stands out as the

---

[7] As Diletta De Cristofaro puts it, '[t]he simulacrum of Xultation engenders a virtual future telos that affects the clones' actual future by keeping them submissive and depriving them of their agency' (2018: 251).

only character who rejects the circle of eternal repetition and fully subscribes to the novel's association of teleology with negativity by committing suicide. His philosophy is strongly characterized by a fatalistic belief both in the 'eternal recurrence' of history's violence, and in humanity's collective death drive: '[t]he End is what we want, so I'm afraid the End is what we're damn well going to get' (471). In this sense, the novel's teleological tendencies, and, if read in chronological order, the story's linear progression towards ever greater precarity and destruction only seem to complement the idea of a recurring human thirst for power and violence.

On the other hand, the novel's particular rendering of 'eternal recurrence' also emerges as the novel's most reparative impulse, guaranteeing the reappearance of individual acts of resistance, of choices against the grain of the overwhelming dominant tendency towards doom. In this sense, *Cloud Atlas* posits the radical openness of the present as the place of an enabling, if provisional kind of hope. I agree with those who, like Diletta De Cristofaro, find, in the book, a simultaneity of both linear and circular temporal drives, but also a tendency towards 'repetition with difference' (2018: 250). Heather J. Hicks provides the most detailed analysis of this kind, arguing that 'while the novel's obsession with temporality is largely expressed as a critique of both linear and cyclical ontologies, it also explores the potential benefits of each' (2016: 66). I would argue that, by not fully subscribing to either model of time, and by presenting the reader *both* with real historical injustice and a bleak story of a seemingly inevitable future cataclysm, *and* with the unexpected workings of memory and investments in open-ended futures, *Cloud Atlas* foregrounds individual responsibility and the potentiality of the present moment.[8] Temporality, in the novel, thus folds in upon itself in what Berthold Schoene calls 'the global synchronicity of all human time', a 'refocusing [of] attention onto the here and now, on you and me and y/our other/s' (2010: 114, 120).[9] Read in apocalyptic terms, the novel, as Gerd Bayer points out, refuses to commit to the futuristic logic of apocalyptic teleology, with its continual deferral both of an ever-to-come catastrophic or cathartic event, and of responsible action in the present. Instead, he argues, *Cloud Atlas* acknowledges that 'human experience has been catastrophic for quite some centuries', and invites its readers to focus their energies on the potentialities of 'the eternal present' (2015: 346, 347).

Like much contemporary post-apocalyptic fiction, *Cloud Atlas* repeatedly refers to an unspoken major cataclysm which separates the first four

---

[8] As such, I disagree with Dirk Wiemann's diagnosis of the novel's characters' 'impoverishing imprisonment in the here-now', and as stuck in 'a constricting present from which there appears to be no escape' (2017: 511).

[9] Jo Alyson Parker, in a similar line of argument, emphasizes the novel's commitment to 'a Long Now, providing a vision of the future linked to the past and present, which is intended to make clear the importance, the necessity, of acting responsibly' (2010: 210).

episodes from the last two, which are set in the future. In Luisa Rey's story, Rufus Sixsmith speculates about the imminent dangers of nuclear disaster, '[w]hen prevailing winds shower radiation over California' (Mitchell 2004: 108). The characters in Sonmi's testimony keep alluding to the 'deadlanding' and flooding of large parts of the planet (215, 236), to 'the Californian Boat-people solution' (224), and 'the abortive European democracy' (243), suggesting not only that the world has been heavily altered by climate change, but also that, in consequence, the centre of political and cultural influence has shifted away from the old colonial powers towards the East. Zachry's account, finally, implies that, by this point, only few humans survive 'since the Flotilla what bringed our ancestors got to Big I to 'scape the Fall' (255). At the same time, the novel also frames each temporal level as already catastrophic, and the decline of human civilization not so much as the result of some individual cataclysmic event, but of the accumulated exploitation of natural resources by the selfishness of a powerful few. As Meronym explains to Zachry, '*Old'uns tripped their own Fall. … [Their Smart] didn't master one thing, nay, a hunger in the hearts o' humans, yay, a hunger for more*' (286, emphasis in original). In this sense, *Cloud Atlas* is a warning text (cf. Rickel 2015) about the failure to read the signs of the present as already indicative of an ongoing change for the worse. On one level, the novel frames this failure in terms of a morality that argues for a positive investment in the future, and against the gratification of needs and desires in the present. Meronym serves as the most outspoken proponent of this view: '*[t]he savage sat'fies his needs now … Now the Civ'lized got the same needs too, but he sees further. He'll eat half his food now, yay, but plant half so he won't go hungry 'morrow*' (Mitchell 2004: 318). It is tempting to project this model of futuristic responsibility onto the novel as a whole, which, indeed, repeatedly pits villainous figures only pursuing their own agenda against the protagonists who (with the exception, perhaps, of Robert Frobisher) begin to act on behalf of and together with others in the interest of a common good (cf. Parker 2010: 203, 214). Meronym's employment of the colonial logic of the progress of civilization ('savages' versus 'the civilized') should, however, prompt readers to ask in how far her statement is fundamentally different from the racist worldview voiced by Adam Ewing's contemporaries (cf. Mitchell 2004: 506–7). I would argue that the simple juxtaposition of present/evil versus future/good as voiced by Meronym, but also contained within other parts of the novel, does not, in fact, adequately capture the dynamic produced by the book as a whole, not least because, as Aaron Francis Schneeberger points out, 'many of *Cloud Atlas*'s most villainous characters are often some of its most "forward-thinking"' (2019: 560). Instead of believably projecting a vision of futuristic hope, what differentiates the novel's protagonists from its 'villains' is a conscious turn towards solidarity and selfless thinking and acting. They do not make their decisions according to some grand utopian vision or revelation, but in response to the immediate concerns of their respective surroundings – and very much with their minds on the present.[10]

While the novel, then, as De Cristofaro points out, is emphatically anti-utopian and anti-apocalyptic in that it 'critically effac[es] the etymological sense of a revelation of a better world to come and the sense-making function of the end' (2018: 247), it prominently locates the possibility of hope in the present, in the local actions of individuals who resist the dominant power structures of their respective circumstances. Caroline Edwards identifies this minor hopeful mode, which is constitutive of Mitchell's politics in *Cloud Atlas*, as 'a processual, scaled-down utopian imaginary that is expressed through the networking of variously disjunct temporalities all acting within the "present"' (2011: 196). Even though the novel tells a dystopic story of unrelenting human predacity, exploitation, and destruction, it also uses this dystopian imaginary as a foil against which the protagonists' local dissenting actions acquire particular force. By metonymically connecting the different stories through various thematic and metafictional links, Mitchell foregrounds the value of seeing the here and now as imbued with the possibility to act otherwise.

What is more, by having the novel end with Adam Ewing's humanist plea for individual action in the face of seemingly overwhelming structures of injustice, Mitchell gives this kind of hopeful mode pride of place, and at least as much narrative plausibility as the chronological, post-apocalyptic ending of Zachry's episode in the book's middle section. Both stories, at the farthest ends of the novel's historical trajectory, converge in important ways. Adam's name recalls the biblical first man on Earth, while Zachry both sees his own brother Adam die, and contains, within his own name, the alphabet's last character, thus reinforcing the sense of an ending his story more generally implies for human civilization. And not only does Zachry's 'Bony Shore' (Mitchell 2004: 254) on Hawaii, where his people bury their ancestors, recall Adam's encounter with Henry Goose on the 'forlorn strand' (3) of the Chatham Islands, where Goose collects human teeth, but Adam's journey from San Francisco the Chatham Islands, and from there to Hawaii on the *Prophetess* also mirrors, on a small scale, the novel's journey across the Pacific region, ending on a post-apocalyptic Hawaii. As such, Adam's story progresses, within its own temporal confines, towards the novel's future ending. Although Zachry's storyline is 'granted the highest ontological authority' (Hopf 2011: 118), because it contains, within the logic of the

---

[10]Courtney Hopf, in this context, plausibly identifies Robert Frobisher as the odd one out in terms of his motivations, and frames his peculiarity in temporal terms: '[h]e ... lives squarely in the present, with little sense that the "I" he was in the distant past brings much to bear on the "I" he is during his narration. He makes decisions based on his immediate needs and desires, living quite gleefully from moment to moment' (2011: 114).

nested narrative, all other stories that chronologically precede it, Adam's perspective is the one which finally contains the reader's experience of all the stories that actually come before it in the book, thus leaving it up to the reader to decide which temporal impulse to follow. As Will McMorran puts it, 'how we map the novel in our minds will ultimately rest upon whether we privilege Ewing's fragile optimism or the bleak post-apocalyptic world of "Sloosha's Crossin" as the ultimate message of the novel' (2011: 165). I believe, however, that the ambiguity the novel present its readers with is not primarily about pitting hope against despair. Instead, it foregrounds a provisional hopeful mode that accepts the possible inevitability of a dystopian grand narrative, but nevertheless finds meaning and value in the work of connection, the unpredictable repercussions of small-scale actions and ideas, and in an openness to reverberations across time and space that the novel's protagonists all display. As Sonmi puts it, when the archivist asks her about her motivation for playing along with a resistance movement which ultimately turns out to have been orchestrated by the ruling 'corpocracy' to further delegitimize this very resistance, '[m]y ideas have been reproduced a billionfold' (365). In *Cloud Atlas*, then, hope emerges as the belief in the potential if unpredictable efficacy of individual legacies, as they acquire a life of their own and are appropriated by others. The novel achieves this by using metafictional strategies to weave webs of kinship which connect the protagonists to each other and to the reader through acts of reading and remembering.

A community of readers: Kinship and metafiction

In *Cloud Atlas*, kinship becomes manifest as the mythologically charged connection of individuals across time and space. The novel employs themes, symbols, and metafictional play to create connections between the six different sections. It evokes a shared substance which draws the protagonists together in a way resembling Marshall Sahlins' understanding of kinship as a 'mutuality of being' (2013: ix). Sahlins' focus on kinship as emerging over time, and as closely associated with memory and 'the recall of acts of compassion' (8) is also productive for understanding how Mitchell anchors his idea of human connection and the collective repercussions of individual acts of kindness and selflessness less in notions of family or friendship (although these do keep emerging as residual discourses of belonging in the individual sections) than in a generalized sense of a shared human potential for moral goodness in the face of overwhelming adversity and pain. Caroline Edwards captures this notion in the idea of 'transmigration': 'a utopianized literary strategy in which a post-individual mode of community and political agency can be posited at a symbolic level' (2011: 191). I argue that this idea of a humanist moral community, which emerges from the temporal tensions discussed above, enables the novel's politics of hope.

The dominant theme in *Cloud Atlas*, which runs as a common thread through all six sections and foregrounds the novel's apocalyptic drive, is the recurrence of human predacity and the will to power across the ages, 'support[ing] a sense of history repeating itself' (Wiemann 2017: 504). In Adam Ewing's storyline, a racist society defends the enslavement of people (cf. Mitchell 2004: 508–9), and one indigenous community oppresses another. Robert Frobisher's letters repeatedly allude to the antisemitism in interwar Germany (cf. 71), and reflect upon war as humanity's favourite pastime that will ultimately lead to their own destruction (cf. 462). Luisa Rey's narrative features the ruthless crimes of powerful individuals in the interest of corporate profit, and the enslavement of underprivileged workers in an 'underworld sweatshop' (443); it thus already announces the rule of powerful corporations (cf. 420) that will characterize Sonmi's story. In his memoir, Timothy Cavendish similarly foreshadows the enslavement and murder of clones in Sonmi's dystopian Korea (cf. 170, 179), while himself becoming the victim of a society that locks away the elderly. Sonmi denounces the dehumanization and enslavement of her kind, and finds out about the creation of a social stratum that is considered '*untermensch*' (332, emphasis in original). And Zachry and Meronym face both the imminent extinction of humankind as a result of environmental catastrophe, and the more direct threat of the war-waging Kona tribe, a conflict which mirrors and indirectly reverts back to that between the Maori and Moriori in Adam Ewing's account. Significantly, minor characters repeatedly frame these states of inequality and violence as an inevitable Hobbesian condition of nature. As Alberto Grimaldi reflects in Luisa Rey's story, '[t]here is no "Why". This is our nature' (132). Even more to the point, Henry Goose's 'first law of survival' in Adam's storyline is: '[t]he Weak are Meat the Strong do Eat' (508, cf. also 523–4).

A supposedly natural law of the strong who may prey on the weak thus motivates the actions of the novel's antagonists and becomes a dominant driving force feeding into the story's chronological progression towards social and environmental collapse. What unites the novel's protagonists, however, is the fact that they become mouthpieces of a humanism that propagates universal human rights. Their actions provide a reparative contrast to the bleak outlook of the prevalent theme, embodying 'the promise of a transhistorical and transmigratory community that resists the will-to-power' (Shoop and Ryan 2015: 94). Taken together, the struggles of each of the six protagonists in the face of overwhelming adversity across the ages thus evoke what Gautama Polanki calls 'the iterable messiah' (2018: 1), a saviour figure who sacrifices themselves for humanity again and again. While all protagonists take great risks to act in the interest of others and on what they believe is right – with the exception of Robert Frobisher, who, however, also believes that his musical legacy is a quasi-religious gift to mankind – not all of them become Christ-like martyrs. What they do share is the fact that they all become unwitting agents of revelation. None of them announces the Kingdom of Heaven – although Sonmi gets closest to this in the recording and distribution of her declarations (cf. Mitchell 2004: 362–3) – but they all leave behind their stories to be found and consumed by the protagonists that chronologically succeed them. In passing on their stories, which are then appropriated to a new context, the protagonists literally – if indirectly – participate in each other's existence.

Before turning to the act of reading as a means of creating kinship in *Cloud Atlas*, however, I would like to address the novel's use of symbolism and metalepsis, which both imbue the story's generalized sense of a moral community with metaphysical and mythological depth. The most obvious symbol Mitchell introduces to evoke a sense of connection between his protagonists is the comet-shaped birthmark that Robert Frobisher, Luisa Rey, Timothy Cavendish, Sonmi, and Meronym (not Zachry) all bear (cf. 85, 124, 204–5, 319, 373).[11] Significantly, in keeping with the novel's general tendency to oscillate between an ironic mode and a sincere humanist message, Cavendish explicitly deconstructs the mythological implications of the birthmark in reference to Luisa Rey's story in *Half-Lives*, which he is considering for its sales value: '[o]ne of two things will have to go: the insinuation that Luisa Rey is this Robert Frobisher chap reincarnated, for example. Far too hippie-druggy-new age' (373). At the same time, however, Cavendish immediately confesses to also having 'a birthmark, below my left armpit, but no lover ever compared it to a comet' (ibid.). By introducing the birthmark as a prominent symbol which connects the individual episodes, and simultaneously questioning the validity of such a fanciful image of reincarnation, the novel thus remains ambiguous about the symbol's meaning. On the one hand, thanks to its prominent position in the story as a potential indicator of transhistorical kinship, it cannot go unnoticed. At the same time, its simultaneous deconstruction ensures that the birthmark can also not be unambiguously understood to verify the 'reality' of reincarnation within the fictional universe. The 'conceptual awkwardness of the device' (Schoene 2010: 115) guarantees that it will, in effect, draw the separate episodes together for the reader, while the novel itself never fully buys into the symbol's metaphysical implications.

---

[11]Adam Ewing's diary is the only section in the novel in which neither the protagonist nor another character is mentioned to bear the birthmark. One explanation for this omission could be that if the birthmark refers to the idea of a reincarnated soul, Adam 'originates' this soul. His not bearing the mark would then also reflect the fact that he is the only character who, as the oldest of the six, does not 'read' any of the others.

The eponymous *Cloud Atlas Sextet*, which Robert Frobisher composes and considers his greatest legacy (cf. Mitchell 2004: 489), serves a similar function. Mitchell places its origin in the realm of dreams: the composition is inspired by 'the "dream music" piece' (84) Vyvyan Ayrs dictates to Robert one night in a moment of epiphany. Mitchell has Robert describe his work in such a way that it metonymically renders, in the language of classical music, a faithful description of the book's structure as a hole. Like Cavendish in reference to the birthmark, however, Robert also provides his own self-deprecating deconstruction of this second metafictional device: 'a "sextet for overlapping soloists": piano, clarinet, 'cello, flute, oboe and violin, each in its own language of key, scale, and colour. In the 1st set, each solo is interrupted by its successor: in the 2nd, each interruption is recontinued, in order. Revolutionary or gimmicky?' (463). Robert's music and the number six reverberate throughout the other sections, but its most explicit mentioning outside of Robert's letters once again strongly reinforces the idea of a mythological connection and kinship between the protagonists. Luisa Rey, whose close affinity with Robert is repeatedly foregrounded when she reads his letters and meets his aged lover Rufus, hears the *Cloud Atlas Sextet* for the first time in a music store, and it triggers an epiphany: '[t]he sound is pristine, riverlike, spectral, hypnotic ... *intimately familiar*. Luisa stands, entranced, as if living in a stream of time. "I know this music"' (425, emphasis in original). Where the birthmark implies the never quite actualized possibility of kinship through rebirth, the fictional musical composition, which evokes the travelling clouds (that themselves are a recurring image in the novel), suggests an epiphanic sort of memory that the protagonists can access. It also always, however, allows for readings of the individual instances as mere coincidences, turning the novel's reader, in Sedgwick's sense, into a paranoid subject who has to decide whether to follow the recurring symbols' mythological implications, or to agree with the characters themselves, who, like Luisa Rey, '*just don't believe in this crap*' (122, emphasis in original).

More generally, as indicated above, the novel's six different narratives metaleptically 'intrude' upon one another, most obviously in that one story appears as a textual artefact in the chronologically following one, but also in the form of visions, dreams, epiphanies, and instances of déjà vu that grind against the otherwise realist framework of each individual section. These intrusions are not restricted to the protagonists, which further complicates any smooth reading of these six characters as reincarnations of one soul, or as connected through privileged access to a shared mind and memory. Rather, these instances of metalepsis create a diffuse sense of transhistorical and transnational kinship which defies any unified metaphysical explanation. As Courtney Hopf puts it, 'the influence of each text is felt tangentially, through a nagging sense of recognition, a dream, a moment brushed off as déjà vu' (2011: 111). Moreover, the 'memories' that emerge in these instances do not follow a chronological order. For instance, Vyvyan Ayrs dreams of a 'nightmarish café, brilliantly lit, but underground, with no way out. I'd been dead a long, long time ... The music in the café was ... this' (Mitchell 2004: 80). Ayrs dreams of Sonmi's future world, the sounds of which then come to serve as an inspiration for Robert's *Cloud Atlas Sextet*, which, in turn, travels through the ages, and across the different storylines. This moment mirrors, on a small scale, the novel's larger structural parallelization of circular and linear temporal modes discussed above. Similar moments are repeated throughout the novel. Luisa Rey is haunted by a 'swarm of *déjà vu*' (142) when her own flight from Swannekke Island reminds her of Robert's escape from a hotel room (which, however, she has also actually read about in one of his letters (cf. 43)); and on her encounter with the *Prophetess*, the ship which carried Adam across the Pacific, 'Luisa's birthmark throbs' (448). In a much vaguer fashion, the drunk Zachry has a vision of 'years passin' an' ev'ry drumbeat one more life shredded off of me, yay, I glimpsed all the lifes my soul ever was till far-far back b'fore the Fall' (302). Sonmi's experience of sitting in a car which drives off the road shakes free 'an earlier memory of blackness, inertia, gravity, of being trapped in another ford' (330), clearly recalling Luisa's fall from Swannekke bridge. Referring to the same moment in Luisa's narrative (and possibly also to Sonmi's own experience of being chased), Timothy Cavendish 'flung away the sensation of having lived through this very moment many times before' (396). And Robert aptly gives expression to the non-linear nature of these metaleptic 'memories'; when he is tempted to cut Ayrs' throat, the reader recognizes the parallel to a scene in Zachry's account, and Robert observes: '[n]ot quite *déjà vu*, more *jamais vu*' (476). The use of metalepsis in the form of dreams and visions in *Cloud Atlas*, then, serves both to further implement the novel's deliberately ambiguous rendering of temporality, and as another structural element which implies intimate kinship between the characters in the separate sections.

Beyond the use of recurring themes and symbols, and the metaleptic interlocking of the different episodes through dreams and visions, the activity of reading itself serves to create kinship between the novel's protagonists. By extension, the book's reader is implicated as a participant in a transhistorical act of fictional worldmaking (cf. Hopf 2011: 116, Machinal 2011: 134). While Kevin Brown rightly points out Mitchell's particular use of metafiction 'as a way of forcing the reader to consider the importance of narrative in one's life and in the world, in general' (2016: 78), I argue that, where *Cloud Atlas*, in terms of its rendering of temporality and the semantics of symbols, tends to produce productive ambiguities, reading, too, gets suspended between effecting ironic distancing and affective identification, between deconstruction and reconstruction. As several critics observe, the way the novel's protagonists consume each other's stories metafictionally reproduces the theme of cannibalism in the novel, which emerges most prominently in the narratives of Adam Ewing, Sonmi, and Zachry (cf. Hopf 2011: 119,

McMorran 2011: 165, Ng 2015: 118, Wiemann 2017: 509). To an extent, then, the act of reading is linked to the novel's apocalyptic drive, aligning the hungry 'gobbling ... down' (Mitchell 2004: 479) of stories and ideas with the hyper-capitalized consumption of resources which, within the narrative's dystopian logic, brings human society and the world at large to the brink of collapse (and beyond). On the other hand, it is also as receivers and creators of stories that the six protagonists become agents of change and members of a community of readers and storytellers who locate hope in the inspirational potential of narrative artefacts.

Like any and all of the novel's tendencies, this process is far from straightforward. It would be too easy (and outright wrong) to claim that the metaleptic introduction of each story in the next in the form of a textual or visual artefact inspires the receiving protagonist in a sort of direct transmission of revolutionary ideas. Instead, the characters who find and consume the stories ironize, sentimentalize, capitalize on, misread, and appropriate the fragmented stories they encounter, while often questioning the authenticity of the material, thus foregrounding its potential fictionality.[12] Finding and reading Adam Ewing's journal, for example, Robert Frobisher comments on '[s]omething shifty about the journal's authenticity – seems too structured for a genuine diary, and its language doesn't ring quite true' (64). Robert's letters are repeatedly foregrounded in their material existence as unique artefacts being conserved and handed down over time: 'their texture, rustle and his friend's faded handwriting calm [Rufus Sixsmith's] nerves' (112). For Louisa, the letters trigger visceral feelings of memories that are not her own (cf. 121), and her experience of reading them turns into a fantasy of physical symbiosis which reflects the novel's implication of reincarnation: '[a]re molecules of Zedelghem Chateau, of Robert Frobisher's hand, dormant in this paper for forty-four years, swirling in my lungs, now, in my blood?' (453, emphasis in original). Timothy Cavendish decries the quality of *Half-Lives* – the spy novel, authored by 'Hilary V. Hush' (158), that questions the non-fictional existence of Luisa Rey – only to be inspired by its potential to become 'a publishable thriller' (373), and to follow in her investigative steps in his own attempt to escape the old people's home (cf. 379). Sonmi learns the importance of being able to read to acquire knowledge (cf. 216), but is inspired by Timothy Cavendish's heroic escape not by reading his memoir, but by watching fragments of a film adaptation (cf. 243). And Zachry finds an 'orison' that shows him Sonmi as 'a ghost-girl' (276) sharing her *Declarations*, leading him, in turn, to question his own

---

[12]As Heather J. Hicks observes in this regard, 'the constructedness of the stories complicates a historicist understanding of the novel as a whole. The events that are taking place in the various narratives are not "real" events – they are stories, encountered by characters in other stories' (2016: 74).

worldview. While the novel thus makes sure that the metaleptic appearance of one story in another in the form of a textual or visual artefact does not reduce itself to a mere repetitive act of reading-as-inspiration, the different instances of mediation and remediation, of appropriation, misreading, and distancing ultimately serve to foreground that, as Jason Howard Mezey observes, 'for Mitchell's characters, the textual artefacts they encounter help them to answer central questions as they attempt to make meaning to their lives and histories' (2011: 16). At the same time, the readers in the book share an investment in narrative closure, performatively mirroring the novel's teleological tendencies (cf. Hopf 2011: 115, Parker 2010: 205). As Robert Frobisher puts it, '[a] half-read book is a half-finished love affair' (Mitchell 2004: 65). Significantly, this readerly investment within the fictional world gets projected onto the extradiegetic level in the way the novel tempts its readers to identify with its several reading subjects (cf. Hopf 2011: 110, 120), and to actively participate in turning the fragmented narrative into a coherent whole. As Will McMorran argues, 'we continue to look for a unity that entails completion, for reassurance that the text we are reading is not going to be "just" a collection of stories ... [W]e want to read in the knowledge that the pieces of the puzzle will fit together, that there is still a link between the artist and the artisan' (2011: 169).

In this sense, *Cloud Atlas*, through its play with literary genre and archetypical character, uses the act of reading as a symbolic and metafictional means to foreground the fragmented, incoherent, and 'fictional' nature of both history and subjectivity.[13] The book thus ultimately tells a story that, as Hicks points out, 'is less about how individuals can become historical agents in order to derail our momentum toward the apocalypse than about how literary genres provide us archetypes to resist the "terror of history"' (2016: 75). In the same vein, the novel foregrounds the power of literature to create community:[14] it suggests the potential of creative and appropriative reading as a source of hope, and as an activity that can connect, in uncertain and unpredictable ways, disparate stories and subjectivities that share in each other's existence across time and space. In this way, as Mezey puts it, the novel's 'bleakness is repeatedly punctured by the desire to connect on individual and communal levels through the acts of imagination implicit in narrative creation and consumption' (2011: 31). The story's

---

[13]As Courtney Hopf puts it, 'the novel encourages the reader ... to imagine the self as a discursive construction as well' (Hopf 2011: 111). Hélène Machinal similarly argues that the novel's 'rhetoric of illusion ... leads to the blurring of the sense of identity both within diegesis and without. Implicitly, the reader is also submitted to the fictionalizing process as he shares the position of reader with each new narrator' (2011: 133).
[14]Along these lines, Kevin Brown observes that 'Mitchell believes that stories contain power and beauty, that they are a means for how to live one's life' (2016: 80).

rendering of transhistorical and global kinship via the creation of an all-embracing community of readers as a catalyst of hope that emerges from the potentiality of the present moment, however, comes at an ideological price. Before turning to the 2012 film adaptation of *Cloud Atlas*, which further lays bare some of the pitfalls of the story's collective politics, I want to briefly address some of the challenges that have been brought to the novel's potential reproduction of normative and colonial discourses around ideas concerning globality and cosmopolitanism.

Where hope lies: Normativity and cosmopolitanism

Cloud Atlas goes to great lengths to tease out, by means of a variety of narrative techniques, a sincerely humanist message of global kinship and the infinite possibilities of a creative understanding of the present moment, while never losing sight of the historical and ongoing violence and destruction that make hope such a difficult topic for contemporary fiction and criticism alike. At the same time, both the novel's very global and transhistorical scope, and its partial commitment to hope understood in terms of reproductive futures reiterate a set of normative logics that grind against the novel's otherwise creative suspension and inherent criticism of apocalyptic temporality, hyper-capitalist exploitation, anthropocentrism, and imperial oppression. My concern here, however, is not primarily to offer an ideological critique of Mitchell's fiction. Instead, I am interested in how *Cloud Atlas'* particular rendering of temporality and belonging comes at the price of buying into some of the very exclusionary logics the novel, on another level, appears to deconstruct.

As discussed above, *Cloud Atlas* foregrounds the ambiguous relationship between linear and circular notions of time, framing hope as suspended between futurist projection and the possibilities of the present moment. It also, however, evokes the potentiality of queer and posthuman takes on temporality and belonging – by introducing, for instance, a bisexual artist-genius who ends his own life, and a clone who discovers the joys of nonreproductive sex in the process of attempting to liberate her own kind. The novel's philosophy, however, is fundamentally dependent on the preservation of heteroreproductive imagery. Mitchell scatters references to threatened children and society's reliance on the heterosexual family across the different storylines. For example, Bill Smoke's status as a villain in *Half-Lives* is confirmed in a curious little episode right before he pushes Luisa Rey's car off Swannekke bridge: having blackmailed the guard on duty into compliance, Smoke states that 'your young family's future is secure, son' (Mitchell 2004: 144). Similarly, Luisa's employer at Spyglass fires her after receiving anonymous threats to his own and his family's safety, admitting that 'I won't be ashamed for putting my family ahead of the truth' (433). In Sonmi's storyline, sexual (albeit genetically refined) reproduction and having a family are framed as a privilege rightfully denied the 'servers', and children as potentially threatened by the clones (cf. 192, 203, 237). Sonmi's section also features the killing of a cloned 'doll' that is clearly attributed human status and dignity in Sonmi's account ('her miniature scream was wordless but imploring' (351)), further demonstrating this society's cruelty and inhumanity. Most prominently, however, it is Adam Ewing, the novel's most outspoken humanist, whose message of hope the reader is left with at the end of the book, who embeds his humanist agenda within the logic of reproductive futurism. Thinking that he is about to die, Adam directly addresses his son: 'Jackson, when you are a grown man do not permit your profession to sunder you from loved ones' (521). Read within the logic of Adam's storyline, this sentence clearly refers to the ideologically charged safety and bliss of the (Victorian) family. On the novel's very last pages, Adam's belief in human goodness also explicitly gets aligned with the belief in a better tomorrow for his child: '[a] life spent shaping a world I want Jackson to inherit, not one I fear Jackson to inherit, this strikes me as a life worth the living' (528). In the end, then, despite structurally going into a different direction, *Cloud Atlas* prominently associates its optimistic and life-affirming tendencies with the figure of the Child – in Edelman's sense – and its symbolic weight as the bearer of a better future. Taking his cue from a similar observation, Luke Hortle identifies the novel's commitment to reproductive futures as decisive for the tension between humanist and posthumanist fantasies that emerge throughout the book. While inviting the reader to imaginatively transcend conventional human boundaries of time, space, and matter, Hortle argues, *Cloud Atlas* ultimately 'stabilizes itself upon a conservative human scale organized by heterosexual romance' (2016: 258). Although, for example, Sonmi's sexual encounter with Hae-Joo, and the cloned 'doll' whose killing the two of them witness suggest the possibility of non-reproductive desire and queer futures, the novel, by framing the clones as expendable, forecloses this desire in favour of the human family (cf. Mitchell 2004: 262–3, 266–7). Hortle concludes that from the novel's symbolism of transhistorical and global connection emerges, on the one hand, 'a hopeful future of political inclusivity to counteract liberal humanism's violent exclusions. But in this fantasy of a "multitude" of lives welcomed into the human's ambit, the novel submits to the very erasure of difference that concepts like the human and its geological epoch rely upon' (2016: 271).

I agree with Hortle's criticism of the novel's tendency to stifle its own posthuman potential in the service of a conservative vision of human connection, and of its heavy reliance on an imagery of reproductive futures to carry this vision. However, I give the book some more credit in terms of its rendering of queer temporalities. In light of its general tendency to produce ambiguous tensions between irony and sincerity, linearity and circularity, and pessimism and optimism, it makes sense to contextualize the novel's blatant politics of reproductive futurity in a similar manner. On the one hand, the two storylines at the far ends of the plot's chronology prominently cater to the idea of a redemptive ending on reproductive terms: Adam Ewing, as humanist optimism's sincerest proponent, couples this optimism with the hope to reunite with his family; and Zachry, in many ways Adam's double, fathers a new generation of human survivors who pray to their goddess Sonmi whose 'murmurin's babybye our babbits' (Mitchell 2004: 325). On the other hand, it remains productively unclear what we are to make of the fate of the other protagonists. The queerest of them die by choice or violence: bisexual aesthete Robert Frobisher kills himself in the cynical expectation of eternal recurrence (cf. 487–90), while his former lover Rufus Sixsmith, too, is shot after getting caught up in the turmoil of corporate conspiracy (cf. 113–14); and Sonmi dies at the hands of a system that cannot tolerate posthuman insurrection. Their deaths certainly foreclose queer possibility. At the same time, they also serve to decry the very systems and philosophies that survive. Other equally queer fish escape death, but also manage to eschew integration into heterosexual or reproductive 'happy endings'. Picaresque hero Timothy Cavendish forms a bumbling, queer alliance/foursome with three other elderly residents of the home they escape from together, two of whom are something of a couple out of necessity, and another is a confused Scot, who only learns to say more than 'I know' when revealing his nationalist passion at a critical moment in their escape; Cavendish cheekily plans, in his own epilogue, a very much non-reproductive and non-romantic ascension to fame and fortune (cf. 402–4). And Luisa Rey, after having to let go off the 'foster child' she took care of to protect him from his violent stepfather, ends her narrative as a successful journalist, engaging, in her final paragraph, in a queerly romantic, visceral encounter with Robert Frobisher's final letters (cf. 453). At closer inspection, then, *Cloud Atlas* not only always checks its own impulses towards sincerity and towards either apocalyptic or circular temporality, but it also opens up alternatives to both the celebratory and the survivalist repro-futuristic logics foregrounded in the novel's inner- and outermost sections.

Similar tensions serve as starting points for controversies around *Cloud Atlas*' relation to postcoloniality. On the one hand, as Nicholas Dunlop argues, it is the novel's very commitment to humanism which enables a particular kind of postcolonial critique in the form of 'a persuasively subversive reading of the history, present and projected future of colonialism and its associated ideologies' (2011: 205). Focusing on Sonmi as the character who most prominently signals 'the return of the repressed colonial Other' (217), and 'the omnipresent yet repressed possibility of disruption and inversion' (219), Dunlop foregrounds the novel's emphasis on the potential for change in the direction of a more humane society, which he frames as a fundamentally anticolonial move. On the other hand, as Philip Tsang points out, *Cloud Atlas*' premise of global connection and understanding inevitably takes for granted 'the English language's hegemony as a global lingua franca[,] … transfer[ring] the idea of a geographic homeland to the sense of a linguistic community' (2018: 400). Tsang argues that the novel's implicit privileging of the English text as a medium of global connection does not create a convincing vision of humanist universalism; instead, in relying on the historical reality of the global dominance of English-language culture and literature, it 'must render its cultural other unrepresentable in order to maintain a coherent, powerful representational system that extends across the globe' (408). I believe that both Dunlop and Tsang have a point: the novel's universalizing humanist tendencies clearly mean to inscribe themselves into an anti-imperialist discourse; but the very fact that the novel writes this universalism from a particular linguistic centre (and from the centre of the historically colonizing world), and works with a very particular vision of Enlightenment humanism inevitably produces ideological exclusions. *Cloud Atlas*' politics of hope as located in the potentiality of the present moment, for instance, appears in the shape of the liberal subject's freedom of choice (cf. Dunlop 2011: 219, Mezey 2011: 18), as Sonmi observes when faced with the option of entering the world beyond her confinement in the Papa Song's dinery: '[i]t was the first choice of my life' (Mitchell 2004: 208). The novel's rendering of kinship as the sharing of one individual's life in another, although ambitious in scope, remains ideologically attached to ideas of undifferentiated universalism and reproductive human survival. I would argue, however, that what makes Mitchell's novel truly interesting in this respect is the simultaneity of potentially contradictory ideological commitments contained within the fragmented narrative. In the end, neither hope nor kinship emerges, in the novel, as a clearly delineated concepts. Instead, the ambiguous temporal dynamic, in tandem with the text's playful proliferation of metaleptic connections between the individual sections, produces a kaleidoscope of positions that leaves the reader, in the best sense possible, with many loose ends. This unresolved ambiguity also produces a sense of the future's truly 'radical openness' (De Cristofaro 2018: 252), making *Cloud Atlas*, as Will McMorran aptly puts it, 'the ultimate philosophical litmus test for its readers, a means of separating the optimists from the pessimists' (2011: 172).

'Everything is connected': The Wachowskis and Tom Tykwer's *Cloud Atlas* (2012)

Despite David Mitchell's own conviction that his structurally unwieldy novel could never be turned into a film (cf. Jeffries 2013), an adaptation, directed by Lana and Lilly Wachowski and Tom Tykwer, was released in

2012. Instead of trying to replicate the book's complex metafictional mode of narration, the directors translate the novel's central idea of transhistorical connection into another medium, using specifically cinematic strategies, and thus making the film a piece of art in its own right. To conclude this chapter, I will have a look at how the film crucially alters the novel's own ambiguous politics of hope and kinship, and how – although at times following the plot of the different sections in a lot of detail – it inadvertently rids the story of ambiguity. The film pushes the book's complicated temporal dynamics in the direction of linearity, reducing its nuanced evocations of hope as located in the possibility of interpersonal recognition and kinship that cross space and time almost completely to the teleological logic of happy endings in (mostly) heterosexual romance.

As opposed to the novel, the film tells all six individual stories more or less simultaneously, 'play[ing] havoc with conventional chronology' (Parker 2015: 126), and it employs a reappearing ensemble cast and various cinematic techniques to foreground the idea of connection. In doing so, the film necessarily sacrifices the tension produced in the novel between linear and circular notions of time in favour of aligning the different sections into one story, which is given coherence through narrative and visual parallelization and the use of music. Where the novel has no clearly delineated frame narrative, instead positioning Zachry's story, which historically contains all others, in the book's middle, and Adam's fragments as first and last, thus producing, for the reader, the experience of an impossible frame, the film goes with a more conventional strategy, and explicitly embeds the whole story in a frame told by the old Zachry (cf. Parker 2015: 130, Krause 2017: 104). After Zachry's prologue, a first scene, connected by the score's title sequence, quickly introduces all protagonists, after which each of them, in chronological order, is given a longer sequence. The rest of the film proceeds to cut back and forth between the individual storylines, using visual clues, suspenseful moments, and music as means of connection, creating an effect Jo Alyson Parker calls 'omnitemporality': we get the impression 'of all six stories taking place at once and impacting upon one another, rather than of each embedded artifact influencing its reader/viewer' (2015: 127).

The directors' most striking aesthetic choice is the employment of a fairly small cast in various roles in the different storylines, picking up on the novel's theme of rebirth. All actors appear in up to six roles, crossing ethnic, gender, and age boundaries, often suggesting that not only individual souls reincarnate, but also particular dynamics or constellations. For instance, Jim Sturgess plays both Adam Ewing and Hae-Joo Chang, with Doona Bae appearing both as Ewing's wife Tilda and as Sonmi 451, contrasting the tragic short love affair between Sonmi and Hae-Joo with Adam and Tilda's stable bond. Similarly – and inspired by the close affinity between the two characters in the book – Ben Wishaw, who plays Robert Frobisher opposite Halle Berry as Jocasta Ayrs, reappears in the 1970s as a record store clerk who sells Luisa Rey (Berry) a recording of the *Cloud Atlas Sextet*. And Tom Hanks as Isaac Sachs forms a trusting relationship with Berry as Luisa Rey, which is later mirrored in their friendship-turned-romance as Zachry and Meronym. The film thus makes use of the audience's investment in looking for reappearing actors in order to evoke an idea of reincarnation and connection, often focusing on the rebirth of romantic couples (cf. Krause 2017: 111). Some of the novel's symbolism is also taken up in the film, but relegated to a secondary position. In the film, the birthmark, for instance, only appears on Robert's hip and Luisa's shoulder, and Rufus Sixsmith recognizes his dead lover's unusual feature when trapped in an elevator with Luisa. On the other hand, where the novel only vaguely hints at the crossing and recrossing of actual geographical locations by having Adam travel from San Francisco to the Chatham Islands, and from there to Hawaii, ending up where Zachry's story will take place, the film works with the idea that the different protagonists literally end up in the same places. The most obvious case in point is the satellite link that Meronym has Zachry guide her to: while, in the book, it is located in an observatory on Hawaii, in the film, it appears to be the same building as the one in which Sonmi broadcasts her declarations. And, more subtly, instead of going to Belgium, Robert Frobisher, in the film, goes to Scotland, and Vyvyan Ayrs' mansion turns out to also be Aurora House, the old people's home where Timothy Cavendish is held against his will – with an additional effect achieved by Jim Broadbent playing both Ayrs and Cavendish.

Much more than the novel, then, the film constructs a coherent story of resistance enacted by the same 'souls' across history, with a unified drive towards conclusion. Strikingly, although the book itself already displays a bias towards heterosexual and reproductive futures, the film even hedges in those narrative strands which, in the novel, prove resistant to being incorporated within this logic. With the exception of Luisa, who, in the film, remains her teenage neighbour's substitute mother figure, all other protagonists, even dead Robert Frobisher, end their stories in romantic pairs of two. Coupledom thus becomes the film's ultimate telos, reducing its professed vision of universal connection to an individualized politics of romantic love. Adam and Tilda reunite to join the abolitionist movement together. Rufus Sixsmith finds and embraces Robert, who has only just shot himself after confessing his version of an afterlife as containing the possibility of romantic reunion: 'I believe there is another world waiting for us, Sixsmith, a better world. And I'll be waiting for you there'. Timothy Cavendish is, unlike in the novel, reunited with Ursula, the love of his youth, and his last reference, in the novel, to Russian writer Aleksandr Solzhenitsyn is extended in the film to reflect this conclusion in coupledom: '[l]ike Solzhenitsyn, labouring in Vermont, I shall beaver away in exile. Unlike Solzhenitsyn, I shan't be alone'. Sonmi's relationship with Hae-Joo, the authenticity of which is questioned in the novel when the reader finds out that the whole Union rebellion was a staged act, is unambiguously romantic in the film, and the rebellion real and heroic. And Zachry and Meronym turn into an old couple surrounded by grandchildren on a faraway planet. This archaic idyll leaves the audience much more lulled than both the ambiguous ending of lost knowledge and language in Zachry's section in the book, and Adam's final passionate message of the ocean as 'a multitude of drops', which features in the film, but does not constitute its ending.

While the film thus creatively reworks *Cloud Atlas*' concern with kinship with cinematic means, using visual and aural cues to send the audience on a conscious and unconscious quest of recognition over the course of all of the film's fast-paced edits and parallelizations, it disables the hope that emerges in the novel out of the potentiality of the present moment. As Jo Alyson Parker observes, 'through its restructuring, the film shifts its emphasis from a future in flux to a future that is fixed[,] ... entailing a conclusion that is both less and more hopeful than Mitchell's and that shifts the emphasis from global to local concerns' (2015: 123, 124). At the same time, the directors' choice of having actors cross boundaries not only of time and space, but also of race and gender, coupled with the film's exoticizing portrayal of cultural (particularly Asian) otherness, arguably reinforces the potential depoliticization of the story's global outlook which is, to an extent, already inherent in the novel, creating, as Haerin Shin argues, a 'disjuncture between the film's intended message of cultural, ethnic, and racial transcendence and its mimetic delivery' (2017: 132). Where the novel balances fragmentation and metafictional irony on the one hand, and a sincere message of universal human responsibility on the other, the film reduces this ambiguity to the vague insight that, as Warner Brothers put it in their marketing campaign for the film, 'everything is connected' (qtd. in Krause 2017: 103); or as Sonmi declares in her prophetic message, which, in the film as opposed to in the book, we get to hear multiple times, '[o]ur lives are not our own. From womb to tomb, we are bound to others, past and present. And by each crime and every kindness, we birth our future'. In the end, this kindness and these mutual bonds emerge, in the film, primarily in the shape of the romantic couple, and the hope of the present moment dissolves, once again, in the fulfilment of romantic love. This is testament to the difficulty of popular narratives to find a language of kinship which does not resort to the romantic plot of coupledom, and which locates hope in the possibilities of a present that does not yet know its future.

4

'I am also a we': Affect, simultaneity, and the global imagination in Netflix's *Sense8*

Following their 2012 film adaptation of David Mitchell's *Cloud Atlas*, Lilly and Lana Wachowski wrote, produced, and directed the space opera *Jupiter Ascending* (2015). After this (critically unsuccessful) detour into science-fiction 'proper', the siblings returned to working on some of the themes and concerns from *Cloud Atlas*, creating, together with J. Michael Straczynski, the web television series *Sense8*, which was released on Netflix between 2015 and 2018. Featuring an ensemble cast of eight that includes three people of colour and a trans woman in leading roles, the series immediately gained a considerable international following, and was celebrated as 'one of the most diverse programmes in television history' (Parsemain 2019: 216). In many ways, the series presents a continuation of its creators' interest in the idea of intersubjective connections that transcend time and space. Like *Cloud Atlas*, *Sense8* portrays a vision of a global humanism and a celebration of diversity that overcome geographical, social, and political divisions. Its speculative science-fiction premise playfully invokes the insight that all humans are, in fact, genetically related. The series also, however, reproduces boundaries between those who are and those who are not kin. In *Sense8*, kinship is imagined as a genetically determined *and* queerly initiated empathetic affinity that grinds against, substitutes, or complements more conventional notions of familial blood relations and forms of chosen family. Hope, once again, emerges as suspended between, on the one hand, a future-oriented fight for emancipation along the lines of contemporary identity politics, and, on the other hand, the pleasures and uncertainties of a temporality which collapses past and future into the present.

Sense8 follows eight protagonists from eight different countries: Sun Bak, a Seoul businesswomen and night-time martial arts fighter, whose sense of duty lands her in prison when she takes the blame for her brother's crimes; Wolfgang Bogdanow, a Berlin gangster haunted by his past with an abusive father and struggling to find his place within the Berlin underworld; Kala Dandekar, a pharmacist in Mumbai who navigates family expectations and her own desire; Will Gorski, a Chicago cop negotiating a difficult relationship with his father; Riley Gunnarsdóttir, an Icelandic DJ living in London and trying to come to terms with the tragic death of her husband and infant daughter; Nomi Marks, a trans hacktivist based in San Francisco with a supportive girlfriend and a transphobic mother; Capheus Onyango, a Nairobi matatu-driver-turning-politician who takes care of his HIV-positive mother; and Lito Rodriguez, a gay actor in Mexico City living with his boyfriend and their self-proclaimed female 'beard'. While all eight protagonists, in their individual storylines, struggle with difficult family situations and with finding, claiming, and owning their (social, political, sexual) identity, they discover that they belong to a newly evolved human species called 'homo sensorium', whose members are able to share experiences, emotions, memories, and abilities through a kind of genetically coded telepathy. Eight sensates form a 'cluster', an alternative family of sorts, whose members were all born on the same day, and which a more senior sensate can 'birth' in a decidedly queer take on generation and reproduction: sensate filiation establishes empathetic kinship ties between living adults. The series' eight protagonists gradually get to experience and share more and more of their mental and emotional commonalities, while facing the threat of an evil organization that is hunting them and all of their species down. All protagonists have their own local plotlines, but the narrative focus lies on their shared experiences. The series makes a strong claim for diversity and a positive acknowledgement of a common humanism across gender, sexual, racial, and geographical boundaries. As such, it also, like *Cloud Atlas*, universalizes kinship to the level of the human community, and propagates 'a new globalism built on solidarity, empathy and progressive gender and sexual politics' (Shaw 2017).

In this chapter, I will first discuss how *Sense8* engages sex and sexuality thematically and visually to present its vision of universal connection. I contend that the series successfully generalizes the idea of transness, but also evades a problematization of the racialized and aestheticized body. Taking my cue from the criticism the series has received, I further argue that its utopic vision only becomes possible at the expense of a deliberately naïve take on globalization and postcoloniality. Abstracting from these controversies, I want to sketch out how *Sense8*, more generally, uses its science-fiction premise to queer notions of kinship, foregrounding the human capacity for empathy and love as a radical necessity in the face of global and social divisions. The series presents the sensates' affective family as a hopeful fantasy of human evolvement beyond selfish individualism, catering to 'a deep need among audiences all over the world to find transnational connections and community in times of national isolationism, sexual conservatism, homophobia and transphobia' (Shaw 2017). Finally, I propose that the series' utopic energies unfold from a place of naiveté which manages to mobilize an affective vision of hopeful kinship, but also remains strategically forgetful of its own position within the logic of progressive neoliberal appropriation.

Amor vincit omnia: Bodies, sex, and representation

To a large extent, *Sense8*'s hopeful impetus emerges from its investment in the representation of culturally and sexually diverse characters, and the erotic charge of their telepathic connection. The series thus shifts the logic of determining who is kin and who is not from a focus on the demarcations of the heterosexual nuclear family, of nation, race, and culture towards a fantasy of kinship which, on the one hand, reproduces exclusions along genetically determined lines, but which also actively transcends the boundaries of race, culture, gender, and sexuality. At the same time, the series' positing of sex as a force that can create kinship between diverse individuals cannot outweigh the fact that it also reiterates colonial structures of seeing and showing that seem to be an almost inevitable result of the creators' attempt to render a unified vision of global connection and understanding. Both the series' ultimately US-centric take on global representation, and its preservation of the physical and mental boundaries of the liberal subject despite its speculative science-fiction premise of trans-subjective connection and experience structure *Sense8*'s projection of hope and kinship as rooted both in a fantasy of equality, in the sense of an erasure of difference in ecstatic communion, and in a narrative of individual heroism and progress that disregards histories of colonialism and racist representation. Several voices in US media have commented positively on the show's racial and sexual diversity. Out of eight actors and characters, four are women, and four are people of colour from non-US and non-European contexts. One character is trans, played by a trans woman.[1] However, the series' very positioning *as* a diverse show with an inclusive message also drew a lot of scrutiny from critical voices that pointed out the producers' failure to

---

[1] The widespread positive reception of the series' inclusive casting choices became most explicit in the reactions to Netflix's announcement that it would cancel the show along with several others. Maureen Ryan (2017) and Daniel Holloway (2017), in this context, decry a general trend in the cancelling of shows with racially and sexually diverse casts and creative teams.

translate what the series posits on the level of fictional representation to the level of the production itself: two of *Sense8*'s creators are trans, but the team was mostly white and US-American. Here, too, as Claire Light remarks, the series inevitably remains within the constraints of a US-American perspective: '[t]he great irony of this show is that it failed to do what the show itself depicts: allow people from disparate cultures to work together, influence each other, clash with each other, and to live moments of each other's lives' (2015). Due to these creative restrictions, and also due in part to the series' setup *as* explicitly diverse in its selection of protagonists, the gaze the show establishes for its viewers inadvertently constructs the non-white characters as 'other'.

One of *Sense8*'s most striking features, which exemplifies this tension, is its use of sex as a means of connection and community building. Several times throughout the series, the characters inadvertently 'visit' each other while one or several of them are having sex: the ecstasy of the sexual encounter, like other extreme emotions, calls them to each other. These scenes are worth contemplating both for their message and for their aesthetics. When a character 'shares' a sexual encounter with another sensate through their mental connection, from the audience's point of view, and thanks to the series' choice of representing the sensates' telepathic connection physically, they actually partake in the sexual act themselves, which enables all kinds of bodily encounters. The series features several 'virtual orgies' which pleasurably queer the sexual identities of those involved, and which deconstruct conventional notions of sexual fidelity and coupledom. The most elaborate of these scenes occurs at the beginning of the second season, when all eight sensates – plus some of their respective partners – share an almost three-minute-long sex scene across different locations. The experience is 'triggered' by Lito and Hernando, Nomi and Amanita, and Will and Riley 'actually', physically having sex with each other, and Kala worrying about having sex with Rajan for the first time. Sun, who Kala 'visits' and discusses her worries with, appropriately frames, like the series as a whole, sex as a fundamental element of the human experience: '[w]e exist because of sex. It's not something to be afraid of. It's something to honour, to enjoy' (season two, episode one, 'Happy Fucking New Year'). The sex scene itself is shown in slow motion. It focuses both on the expressions of ecstasy, joy, and happiness on the characters' faces, and on the dynamics of touch involved. The series' very last scene, too, is a sex scene that starts with the couples (and two threesomes) retreating to their hotel rooms in Paris, and evolves into a telepathic orgy involving all eight protagonists and their non-sensate partners (season two, episode twelve, 'Amor Vincit Omnia'). These 'virtual orgies' 'highlight the beauty and human connectedness inherent to sex' (Parsemain 2019: 225), and they are a strong element in the series' overall narrative and aesthetic politics of kinship and diversity. All bodies touch all other bodies, the 'straight' characters are queered – as are the 'gay' characters – and the resulting images are an obvious plea for tolerance, and for the power of touch – in a concrete and abstract sense – across races, genders, and sexualities. As Stephanie L. Young and Art Herbig put it, '[t]he sexual/sensual orgies become a liberating power that simultaneously binds and frees the sensates and their partners as well as queering larger social structures and institutions fundamentally premised on (hetero)normativities' (2020: 85).

At the same time, however, the aesthetics of the sex scenes in *Sense8* is not without pitfalls. The sex shown here is excessively beautiful, which potentially disables its queer, norm-exploding effect. As Vassilis Gerasopoulos argues, celebrations of *Sense8*'s take on queer sexuality and sex itself are misplaced if they do not also acknowledge 'the normalizing imagery of non-heternormative identity, the persistent essentialisms and boundaries of beauty and attractiveness, and the stereotyping of sexual relations and expressions' (2018). The sex scenes are clean and easy to consume, an idealized fantasy of sexual liberation, while also referencing different uneasy attitudes towards the naked and sexualized body. For instance, Max Riemelt, the German actor playing Wolfgang, is the only actor who has a scene involving full-frontal nudity: on seeing (together with the audience) Wolfgang's exposed penis at her own wedding, Kala faints (season one, episode five, 'Art Is Like Religion'). It seems almost comically significant that this happens in the context of the Indian storyline: mainstream Indian cinema is notorious for its avoidance of explicitly physical demonstrations of affection, let alone full-on sex. As such, *Sense8*'s visual and narrative style references and, to an extent, caters to different cultural attitudes towards sex, sexuality, and the naked body, inadvertently qualifying its own message of universalized equality. What is more, as Godfried Asante, Noorie Baig, and Shuzhen Huang point out, 'desires for pleasure with the non-white, non-western others are always entangled with racialized histories and geopolitics. In *Sense8*, the desiring of the non-white, non-western other's body through corporeal intimacy reproduces the whiteness of liberal humanism that refuses to practically engage with the colonial histories and imperialist gaze that continually produce the non-western other' (2019: 321). *Because* the series chooses to make use of the visual representation of sex to make a statement about equal agency, desirability, and beauty, these visual claims inevitably also evoke histories of the (sexual) othering of the racialized body. The utopic energy the series evokes through its employment of sex as a connecting force is thus inevitably a '(white) queer utopia' (322), whose hopeful message of global sexual kinship comes at the cost of a form of postcolonial amnesia.

Where, however, *Sense8* arguably fails to live up to its own claim to inclusivity, it succeeds in its creative integration of transness. One of the show's most nuanced revaluations of physical representation is its depiction of trans protagonist Nomi. The positive representation of a trans protagonist (played by a trans actress) in a mainstream serial format must itself still be considered a revolutionary move at the time of the series' making. Trans, however, also emerges as a leitmotif for the series. As Rye Gentleman argues, Nomi, as trans hacktivist, becomes 'an avatar of the algorithmic age' (2019: 149), metonymically embodying the potentially transformative power of the virtual space of the internet and its utopic possibilities as a space of individual evolvement and collective energy.² And, as Cáel M. Keegan points out, we can read *Sense8*'s take on trans as the recuperating version of its otherwise problematic take on globality: '*Sense8* offers different routes into trans as an aesthetic practice or as a set of narrative strategies for simultaneously representing and replicating hypermodern globality … [It] seeks to aesthetically *translate transgender* as a form of consciousness – a way of perceiving or knowing that occurs between and across bodies, cultures, and geographies' (2016: 606, emphasis in original).³ According to Keegan, the cultural clichés the series employs only serve as a foil to emphasize the trans movement of overcoming these narrative and cultural conventions: '*Sense8* comments metanarratively on the manner in which ethnic and racial differences are transformed into generic forms of personhood from which it asks its characters and its audience to "wake up"' (609). While I certainly agree that *Sense8*'s take on trans both unfolds emancipatory energies in terms of representation, and successfully universalizes the trans experience in relation to technology and globality, I remain more critical of the series' depiction of different cultures in the service of an affirmative and hopeful message of global kinship. In the final analysis, the cultural and racial tensions outlined above do not dissolve in the notion of transness: crucially, Nomi is US-American and white. *Sense8*'s hopeful framing of an experience of belonging that transcends racial, cultural, and sexual difference through ecstatic and immediate connection and understanding remains embedded in aesthetic and narrative conventions that inevitably reproduce certain colonial clichés and dynamics.

---

²This positive reading of the internet and the 'algorithmic age' seems, in a way, to nostalgically hark back to the liberatory hopes invested in the internet in late-twentieth-century discourse, and quite deliberately grinds against the current dominance of more critical perspectives on recent developments in the fields of big data, algorithms, and digital security. Its emphasis on the power of virtual communities also stands in contrast to those who, like Judith Butler (2015), insist on the importance of actual, physical gatherings for the emergence of collective action.

³Deborah Shaw makes a similar point in arguing that '"trans" is the key word in any attempt to summarize the series – interactions are characterized by the crossing of national, gender and sexual borders' (2017).

Glocal vision – colonizing gaze: Territoriality and the global imagination

Where *Sense8*'s strategy of attaching its hopeful message of global connection and individual emancipation to the representation of sexualized bodies raises questions about the relationship of this message to postcolonial critique, this is even more true for the series' depiction of its different settings across the globe. On the one hand, it positively asserts a common humanism that all protagonists share through a celebration of racial, sexual, and gender diversity. It also, however, fails to free itself from a colonizing gaze[4] which flattens nuanced possibilities and potentialities of the geographies and territorialities depicted. This tension calls for a careful contextualization of the series' message of universal kinship and the hope inherent in affective communities. *Sense8* complicates gendered and racialized economies of vision through its narrative questioning of both patriarchal and imperialist oppression and, as such, explicitly resists imperialist structures of representation. However, the series' aesthetic and authorial choices also imply a re-affirmation of hierarchies of vision that cater mainly to a white, western, English-speaking audience, and confirm visual and narrative colonial clichés in the depiction of the geographies and cultures involved.

Set and filmed on location in Berlin, Chicago, London, Mexico City, Mumbai, Nairobi, San Francisco, and Seoul, *Sense8* uses the backdrop of the megacity to establish a vision of the 'glocal'[5] that blurs the differences and local particularities of each into one 'megacity of the world'. The sensates' experiences are glocal in the sense that they both navigate the conflicts and relationships of their own local storylines in their respective countries and communities, and get drawn into being in all other seven places at the same time. As such, the series' science-fiction premise allows its protagonists to embody the experience of glocality more literally than any real-life setting could. Strikingly, the sensates navigate easily across geographical,

---

[4]The notion of a 'colonizing gaze' I employ here re-contextualizes E. Ann Kaplan's concept of the 'imperial gaze', which she theorizes as fundamentally entangled with the 'male gaze', the gendered power asymmetry in economies of vision, especially as determined by the camera in film (cf. Mulvey 1975). Kaplan posits that 'the "male gaze" and the "imperial gaze" cannot be separated in western patriarchal cultures ... The gaze ... connotes an active subject versus a passive object' (1997: xi, xviii).

[5]Wincharles Coker defines the glocal as 'a sense of how individuals are increasingly becoming products of both the ways of thinking and doing in their immediate micro-social environments and the macro-structures of the international community ... [G]localisation is experienced when a global phenomenon is re-appropriated into a local context and then undergoes a transformation through specific socio-cultural practices' (2014: 54).

linguistic, cultural, and contextual difference in the environment of the global megacity – both mentally and physically. Here lies one of the series' potential structural difficulties: it clearly favours certain easy assumptions of similarity over the difficult negotiations of difference in a way discourses of globalization also 'tend[] to ignore the subtleties and uniqueness of social beings as having peculiar identities and cultures' (Coker 2014: 54). I would argue that it is precisely the ways in which *Sense8* favours narrating the *liberating* potential of globalized technologies (such as the internet) and transnational understanding over a nuanced differentiation between different cultural contexts that obscure, for the sake of the series' emancipatory message, the ways power is differently inscribed in post-colonial territories. As Fernando Coronil argues,

> postcolonial nations ... are traversed through and through by the tension between their formal sovereignty and their effective subjection ... [They] are torn by the increasing internationalisation of markets and communications that characterizes the contemporary period ... If on some postcolonial terrains practices of conviviality mark the daily life and link rulers and ruled, the meaning and uses of these practices must be found in the larger play of power taking shape on these terrains, not in essentialized attributes of abstract peoples. (1992: 104, 106)

Some of the discomfort that *Sense8* creates despite (or rather for the sake of) its 'glocal vision' is due to its displacement of territorial sites of (post-)colonial power relations onto an abstract struggle against a mysterious, white, western antagonist, set against the background of a mostly abstracted transnational geography.

In the series, all four cities not located in either Europe or North America are depicted as tourist or colonial clichés. For instance, we are shown colourful Hindu temples in Mumbai, and the Seoul plotline revolves around the philosophies and aesthetic qualities of martial arts. The characters from these cities, too, act within heavily stereotypical plotlines. Capheus' world consists of gangsters and drug lords, and he cares for his mother who has AIDS. Sun is a martial arts genius and struggles with her society's sexism. And Lito is a shimmering pastiche of Mexican macho and Spanish lover. As Asante, Baig, and Huang contend, '[t]he representation of the sexually liberated queer western subject in *Sense8* is made possible against the backdrop of a backward other, who is sexually repressed, poor, needs saving ... and ... strongly desires whiteness' (2019: 327). The series' non-white, non-western characters thus become trapped within an exoticizing fantasy of their respective 'cultures', and its emancipatory narrative and hopeful impetus awkwardly hinge upon the extent to which the characters manage to move from their supposedly repressive original cultural contexts towards an ideal of universal liberalism. As Laura Fernández puts it in her critique of *Sense8*'s portrayal of Mexico, 'Lito is "free" to be whoever he wants, so long as it is not in a Mexican setting' (2018: 222). The series' narrative employment of its ensemble of characters, too, tends towards privileging the white and western storylines, while the non-white, non-western characters often serve as sidekicks or aids (cf. Gentleman 2019: 144). For instance, throughout the series, saving one of the protagonists from the mysterious Biologic Preservation Organization (BPO) becomes a central driving force for the plot on three occasions; and all three times, it is one of the white characters who needs to be saved with the help of the skills of the others: first Nomi, then Riley, and then Wolfgang.

On the other hand, *Sense8* actively and self-consciously engages with its employment of cultural clichés. Metafictional play with its own investment in stereotypes runs as a common thread through the series. In the final episode, for example, the protagonists pose as stereotypical tourists in order to gain access to a heavily guarded Naples palazzo (season two, episode twelve, 'Amor Vincit Omnia'). And while the Indian and Korean storylines do reproduce cultural clichés, they also reverently reference Bollywood aesthetics and Korean martial arts cinema as local cinematic traditions that imply histories of success and positive cultural identification. Moreover, the European and North American cities also, to an extent, appear as their own cliché in *Sense8*: Berlin features as a no-nonsense, gritty, crime-ridden city of the night, and San Francisco is reduced to its hippie queerness. As Claire Light puts it, one of the series' redeeming virtues is that 'it commits totally to its clichés and rides them out to their conclusions' (2015). I would argue, however, that this self-consciousness fails to undo the fact that *Sense8*'s ambitious rendering of a global imagination almost inevitably produces postcolonial discomfort. The series' vision of the Global South, in particular, remains problematically entangled with a colonizing gaze onto the territories depicted, despite the series' very strong visual claim for a physical and affective overcoming of the boundaries of nation, race, gender, and sexuality. *Sense8*'s opening titles already announce its geographical vision of a global community. The sequence is a fast succession of shots of the busy, colourful, and diverse lives in the eight cities the series is set in. Many of these shots work with time-lapse technique, which, combined with the underlying epic orchestral score, expresses a feeling of rush and an overflow of impressions. Snippets of scenes show people of many ages, skin colours, genders, and apparent sexual orientations. Through the editing techniques employed, the scenes from the different actual cities – all shot on location – get blurred into one 'megacity of the world'. This effect is achieved by juxtaposing images of those elements that do, at first glance, appear in all of the different actual places. The sequence begins with high-angle shots onto the rivers, bridges, and traffic in the different cities at dawn, followed by snapshots of iconic buildings and sights, which, despite being clearly anchored in their cultural context, here mutate into generalized dots on a global itinerary. The viewer becomes a highly mobile tourist, jumping from one iconic place to the next, but only ever getting polished glimpses of each. The camera capturing the people and city scenes sees and is seen: some of the people smile directly at it and return its gaze. This gaze, however, does not allow itself to linger, and it stays on the surface. What it captures is a hurried impression, a deliberately overwhelming cascade of images that expresses both the camera's interest in engaging with what it sees, but also in never ceasing to rush on, to stay with the perspective of the ever-moving traveller. In a way, the opening titles thus capture both the series' utopic vision and its limits and shortcomings. As Johanna Isaacson puts it, the sequence articulates 'the instagramming of social life, but also the occlusion of processes of circulation, production, and distribution ... [and] demonstrates the invisibilization of capitalist infrastructure' (Isaacson, Lane-McKinley and Sharpe 2015).[6] Anna McFarlane similarly argues that, over large stretches, the series as a whole 'give[s] the impression of a whistle-stop world tour' (2017: 150). *Sense8*'s ambitious global scope, then, shortens the distance between disparate places and cultures, but, in doing so, also blurs these places and cultures into a vague idea of an aestheticized and anaestheticized global community. The positing of universal human kinship here comes at the price of a nuanced rendering of historically determined difference.

In the emerging scholarly debate about *Sense8* in journals and online blogs, commentators are predictably torn between celebrating the series for its commitment to a global imagination and criticizing it for its approach to its diverse territorialities. Deborah Shaw, for instance, points out that *Sense8*'s 'seemingly disparate characters transcend their national and social identity labels and come together to form a new family ... [T]hey present a challenge to individualism, self-interest and narrow tribalism' (2017). On the other hand, as Clare Light argues, *Sense8* remains, in many ways, stuck in its creators' US-American perspective: the show 'attaches itself to Americans' perceptions of how things are in other idioms, as much as, or more than, it attaches itself to how things *actually* are' (2015, emphasis in original). Like many other critics, Light comments negatively on the show's employment of national and cultural clichés, especially in its depictions of countries of the Global South, and its seemingly lazy choice of having all actors speak English, while, within the logic of the series' premise, they actually all continue to speak in their own languages and dialects – at least as long as they move within their own national and cultural settings. For example, halfway through the first season, Sun and Lito, Capheus and

---

[6] Using a similar image, Madeline Lane-McKinley describes the series' opening credits as capturing the 'total google-mappification of the world' (Isaacson, Lane-McKinley and Sharpe 2015).

Riley, and Kala and Wolfgang 'visit' each other respectively for the first time. On the diegetic level, they switch from speaking their own languages to speaking English, suggesting to the audience that their sensate abilities enable them to seamlessly understand each other across linguistic divides. The scenes are also, to a degree, framed as comic. Kala and Wolfgang, for example, are both in a bathroom in their respective cities. At the beginning of the scene, in a moment of misunderstanding as to why someone else – and someone else of a different gender at that – is in the bathroom with them, both actors speak in their own language, although the characters obviously still understand each other. Wolfgang even briefly speaks Hindi when his friend Felix comes in and asks him – now, once again, in English – what language that was. As soon as other characters enter the scene, the dialogues all go back to being spoken in English (season one, episode five, 'Art Is Like Religion'). These scenes are a few of only a handful of instances where the audience actually gets to *hear* that the series really does rest on the premise that all characters usually speak their own language. Strikingly, once the characters begin to meet each other physically, and travel to different places, the assumption seems to be that they all use English as the most natural means of communication. This, however, is never explicitly addressed over the course of the series, and the status of English as a globally available lingua franca is never questioned or creatively complicated.

The general aesthetics of the series, too, can easily be read as a form of cultural imperialism in the name of a global humanistic vision: 'the universality promoted here is a universality of *American* ideas, *American* popular culture, *American* world views' (Light 2015, emphasis in original). Locations and incidents that form part of the individual characters' plot lines mostly remain vague and general. The audience is presented with *some* unspecific neighbourhood in Nairobi, *some* general idea of an upper-middle-class Hindu family in Mumbai, while, for instance, Nomi's San Francisco is 'intimate, layered, nuanced, and above all, specific' (Light 2015), and it abounds with recognizable places, landmarks, and events, such as the Dykes on Bikes parade Nomi and Amanita take part in (season one, episode two, 'I Am Also a We'). Much of what happens in the countries and cities outside the United States remains detached both from the specificity of actual city geography, and from the more particular social, political, and cultural structures in each context. As such, the hopeful global imagination that *Sense8* conjures up comes – maybe unavoidably – at the expense of giving diversity an actual, believable locality outside the boundaries of the United States, its language, and its cultural imagination.

Speaking more generally, *Sense8*'s investment in hope as the speculative realization of global human kinship and the emancipation of the liberal subject through affective and sexual connection necessarily remains attached to the ideological baggage that comes along with these investments. The series' utopic imagination inscribes itself into a seemingly outdated strand of optimistic takes on globalization, and 'pair[s] problematically with the flattening effects of cosmopolitanism and a global imaginary[,] ... reducing its characters to stereotypes and mouthpieces of a liberalist, universalist, and cosmopolitan fantasy' (Elrod 2019: 52, 53). Against a divided world, *Sense8* – like *Cloud Atlas* – posits the fantasy of universal human kinship, resurrecting, as it were, humanist beliefs in unity in diversity. Hope thus emerges from the individual and collective potential for action and change, but this hope is contingent both upon an all-out war for survival – which both the series' protagonists and its antagonists declare repeatedly – and upon a simplistic division of in- and out-groups along dodgy moral lines which ignore the embeddedness of the political status quo in histories of colonialism and economic imperialism.

So far, I have outlined and discussed the tensions that arise from *Sense8*'s ambitious attempt at telling a story of global kinship and hope for transcultural connection. The series' own premise, and its narrative and aesthetic choices make this sort of criticism – and this sort of paranoid reading – almost inevitable, and suggest engaging with these debates as a point of departure for a discussion of hope and kinship in the series. In the remainder of this chapter, however, I would like to move beyond these critiques, and address *Sense8*'s reparative rendering of belonging and temporality in more nuanced detail.

What family actually means: Kinship, affect, and empathy

Sense8 decidedly queers notions of kinship and family, most obviously through its introduction of the idea of non-reproductive filiation, and of empathetically linked clusters of individuals that grow into incorporating many of the fundamental functions commonly associated with family. The series foregrounds this queering of kinship as an open-ended process by interweaving three iterations of affective belonging: the protagonists' families of origin; their chosen families, ties of friendship, and romantic involvement within their individual geographical and social contexts; and, most importantly, their sensate cluster. Generally speaking, the series holds on to the importance of biological families of origin for its protagonists' sense of self, but mostly portrays these families as fragmented, conflicted, and a source of both pain and violence. Nomi's mother's transphobia, for instance, is a recurring point of conflict; and Wolfgang, it turns out, killed his alcoholic father in an attempt to protect his mother, before, in the course of the series, also killing his cousin and uncle (season one, episode ten, 'What Is Human?'; season one, episode twelve, 'I Can't Leave Her'). Except for Nomi and Kala, none of the other protagonists have more than one parent left, and while Kala's relationship with her parents is good, she struggles with their expectations.

Sense8 complements this ambiguous portrayal of family relations and biological kinship networks with an array of chosen families based on queer reproductive commitments, love, or friendship. For example, Nomi's girlfriend Amanita grew up with one mother and three fathers. This queer family unit positively contrasts Nomi's own heteronormal family, and becomes a literal refuge when she and Amanita are on the run (season 1, episode 6, 'Demons'). It is Nomi, too, who most explicitly claims her right to choose her own family despite and against assumed biological commitments to immediate relatives. When she wakes up in hospital after fainting at the San Francisco Dykes on Bikes parade and is confronted by her mother – who keeps insisting on misnaming her by her male birth name – Nomi desperately insists, in reference to Amanita, who has been denied visits, that '[s]he is my family'; and, in answer to her mother's claim that '[y]ou're going to need us, you're going to need your family', she defiantly replies that '[y]ou are not my family' (season one, episode two, 'I Am Also a We'). Accordingly, in the series' final episode, at her wedding, although reconciled with her parents, it is Nomi's good friend Bug who leads her to the front: '[t]hank you for being my family' (season two, episode twelve, 'Amor Vincit Omnia').

Apart from foregrounding the vital importance of chosen families for some of its protagonists, *Sense8* also complicates the cultural dominance and normativity of romantic dyads. Over the course of the series, two threesomes emerge that deliberately explode conventional notions of romantic coupledom. Lito and his boyfriend Hernando begin to live with Lito's co-star Daniela, a relationship that evolves from Daniela's being sexually aroused by the gay couple to a full-on sexual threesome in the series' finale (season two, episode twelve, 'Amor Vincit Omnia'). This relationship arguably 'destabilizes the heteronormative model of domesticity … Lito, Hernando and Daniela form a profoundly queer family where labels, sexual orientation, monogamy and genetics are irrelevant' (Parsemain 2019: 219). Kala, in turn, stumbles into a polyamorous commitment to two men: torn between her love of her non-sensate fiancé/husband and her desire for fellow cluster member Wolfgang, she arrives at the conclusion that she does not have to decide between the two. While the introduction of romantic triangles is arguably a rather conservative narrative choice that has a long and not necessarily progressive literary and cultural history, oscillating between pornographic trope and a strategy for male-homosocial bonding (cf. Sedgwick 1985), the series' take on the idea forms an organic part of its emancipatory programme. The threesomes, as well as an array of bisexual and pansexual minor characters exemplify *Sense8*'s commitment to liberal and emancipatory notions of family and love, 'creating a space for a diversity of desires, sexualities, and relationalities beyond heterosexual mononormativity' (Young and Herbig 2020: 83). At the same time, however, the couple remains an important point of reference for most of the series' characters. This dual commitment both to a queer expansion of possible kin makings, and to the traditional narrative trope of the dyadic romance runs as a common theme through the series.

Where *Sense8*'s contrasting of 'traditional' and 'progressive' notions of family and romance thus remains oddly entangled with cliché, it is the series' speculative premise and its queering of kinship through the employment of elements of science fiction and fantasy that enable a truly creative take on relationality and belonging (cf. Parsemain 2019: 230). *Sense8* uses its positing of the existence of 'homo sensorium' and the attendant possibilities of queer kin making to expand and reappropriate conventional kinship metaphors: 'kinship is extended beyond blood ties. The sensates provide audiences with an alternate form of relatedness and connection, a type of family that is defined by empathy' (Young and Herbig 2020: 81).[7] The sensate cluster emerges both as a different kind of family still rooted in genetic determinism, and as a collective based on solidarity and mutual dependence. It represents 'a non-coercive form of connection governed by empathetic bonds rather than rational consensus' (Mincheva 2018: 36) which posits a utopic alternative to tribalistic and divisive notions of kinship, and to capitalist individualism. Within the logic of the series, a cluster forms in a conscious, non-reproductive act of creation by a senior sensate, who calls together eight people who, until this point, have been unaware of either their evolved abilities or their potential connection. The act of 'giving birth' itself is thus queered and given new meaning. In the series' opening scene, a woman we later learn is called Angelica lies on a dirty mattress in an abandoned church and is obviously in pain. Her gestures and body language imply that she is having contractions, while the pain seems to be mainly located in her head. When Angelica exclaims 'I see them', the audience is presented with short sequences of all eight future protagonists, Angelica's 'children', who have just been 'reborn' as empathically evolved sensates. The fact that this is indeed a scene of birth is confirmed both by Whispers, the series' main antagonist ('You're giving birth'), and, throughout the series, by several references to Angelica as the cluster's 'mother' (season one, episode one, 'Limbic Resonance'). While this scene thus evokes female reproductive labour, it queers the act of giving birth by disentangling it from the creation of *new* life, instead associating the event of birth with the intensification of ties of kinship between already existing, adult subjects.

---

[7] Deborah Shaw makes a similar point: '[t]he sensates are a better version of us – they present a challenge to individualism, self-interest and narrow tribalism. The eight care deeply about each other with an empathy born of the fact that they can literally inhabit their co-sensates' spaces, walk in each other's shoes and even become them when need arises' (2017).

Sense8 is aware of the stakes of framing the cluster as family and kin, and it playfully invokes the tension between supposedly atavistic notions of totemic kinship beyond blood ties and the incest taboo. The series repeatedly frames the sensates of one cluster as telepathic siblings, not only by providing them with a scene of collective rebirth, but also by revealing that they have all biologically been born at the exact same time, taking their first breath together (season one, episode nine, 'Death Doesn't Let You Say Goodbye'). From within the cluster of sensate siblings, two romantic couples emerge, a development foreshadowed early on in the narrative by having both future couples be the first of the protagonists who inadvertently 'visit' each other. At the end of the series' first episode, Riley 'visits' Will in the church that Angelica killed herself in, and the two see each other and talk. This is the first instance of a telepathic encounter between two cluster members beyond the earlier fragmented sense impressions (season one, episode one, 'Limbic Resonance'). Similarly, Kala and Wolfgang begin to see each other in the second episode of the first season ('I Am Also a We'). Strikingly, Yrsa, a senior Icelandic sensate who builds a connection with Riley, warns her that '[l]ove inside a cluster is the worst kind of narcissism' (season one, episode nine, 'Death Doesn't Let You Say Goodbye'), referring to the blurring of boundaries between individual and collective, 'I' and 'you', and between love of the other and love of the self. This speculative combination of romantic love and familial kinship thus evokes the spectre, inscribed into western modernity via Freud and others, of collective kinship and the tendency towards incest as regressive (cf. Freud [1913] 1961: 5–25). It also, however, productively complicates conventional understandings of the taboo-sanctioned differentiation between blood relations and potential romantic and sexual partners. As Young and Herbig observe, the series 'blurs the[] boundaries of the familial and romantic, queering the sibling relationship … By viewing these relationships as symbolically incestuous, Sense8 points to the limitations of the familial metaphor that is fundamentally premised on the hegemonic heteronormativity of the institution of family' (2020: 82).

Strikingly, what sets the sensate cluster apart from both narrow biologistic understandings of family and 'mere' cultural convention is its combination of genetic predetermination, the queer agency inherent in the act of giving birth to a cluster, and, most of all, the fact that affect is the foundation of this form of kinship. The cluster is an affective 'community of virtual intimacy, learning, and support' (Elrod 2019: 54), tied together by shared thoughts, feelings, memories, and abilities. In the series' first episode, right after their 'rebirth', the eight protagonists inadvertently receive aural and visual impressions from the others' reality, a narrative device by which the series also introduces its aesthetics of simultaneous storytelling: Will hears Riley's disco music; Kala hears the rain at a funeral Wolfgang is attending in Berlin; and Riley suddenly sees through Nomi's eyes (season one, episode one, 'Limbic Resonance'). Over the course of the series, the protagonists learn to consciously control their connective abilities, to 'visit' one another and to 'share' their skills. Affect is thus central to the sensates' connection. It is 'one attempt to imagine alternative and more sensual forms that solidarity could take in a moment of informational speed-up and globalisation' (Isaacson, Lane-McKinley and Sharpe 2015). The series frames affect as a community-creating force, and as closely connected to the positioning of bodies. Certain extreme affects call the members of a cluster together. When one of them is in danger, and thus afraid or under stress, the others also feel these emotions, and regularly come to each other's aid, sharing their different abilities through their telepathic one-ness. As Jonas, a senior sensate and ambiguous mentor to the protagonists, puts it towards the end of the series, '[p]ain, Will, pain connects us. Pain binds us better to one another than anything else' (season two, episode twelve, 'Amor Vincit Omnia'). In a similar fashion, however, moments of extreme joy also bring the sensates together. On their birthday in the second season, we first see them celebrate in their individual contexts, but soon they all 'visit' and dance together on Riley's cue: '[w]e shared our first breath. Now it's time we celebrate that breath, together'. In the same episode, the group 'share' their emotions and 'visit' each other on Christmas and New Year's Eve, while the association of the cluster as a family is emphasized by their 'mother' Angelica's watching them (season two, episode one, 'Happy Fucking New Year').

Affect, in *Sense8*, then, is not primarily evoked as an individual psychological process, but as thoroughly social and relational. As such, the series' rendering of affect and its relation to the sensates' (actual and virtual) bodies is in line with what Sara Ahmed calls 'affective economies':

> Emotions shape the very surfaces of bodies, which take shape through the repetition of actions over time, as well as through orientations towards and away from others. ... [In] affective economies, ... feelings do not reside in subjects or objects, but are produced as effects of circulation .... The circulation of objects allows us to think about the 'sociality' of emotions. ([2004] 2014: 4, 8)

Within the series' logic, the characters do not actually physically join each other when experiencing extreme affective states together. However, the filmmakers' decision to always *show* the characters as if they were actually all in one place while still being somewhere else is an effective visual and narrative take on the way affect and embodiment intersect. While the sensates' connection is largely virtual, the emotions they share take on physical reality for them. The fact that the series shows the protagonists together also reinforces the impression of a tight-knit community, especially when they come together in shared celebration. Such scenes occur repeatedly throughout the series, and serve to highlight the collective power of shared positive affect, which also becomes a potential point of identification for the audience. For example, halfway through the second season, Lito comes out publicly at São Paulo pride parade, where the other sensates join him for the party. Here, several layers of affective community building merge: the cluster is brought together by Lito's joyful act of public self-identification; since the actors and filmmakers actually shot this scene at São Paulo Pride, we see the people present at the parade watch and share the protagonists' joy; the series' audience, in turn, gets drawn into this avalanche of uplifting audio-visual cues (season two, episode six, 'Isolated Above, Connected Below'). Generally speaking, as James M. Elrod argues, '*Sense8* invites the process of identification with a group counter-intimacy and kinship in unison – man, woman, gay, straight, cis, trans – and to disrupt queerly the very labels that delineate their differences' (2019: 56). This invitation to identify queerly with a process of kinship in the making is also, in the series as a whole, closely associated with the collective experience of activism and queer emancipation. When Nomi, vlogging prior to her appearance at the San Francisco Pride parade, proclaims that '[t]oday, I march to remember that I am not just an I, but I am also a we. And we march with pride' (season one, episode two, 'I Am Also a We'), she publicly inscribes herself into the emancipatory energy of collective action and the affective community of her queer kin. She also, however, inadvertently premeditates the process of becoming part of a sensate cluster, a new kind of kinship group based on shared affect and empathy. The sensates' unique sensibilities, then, enable a mode of kinship that is characterized by 'a continuous being/becoming with/through self/other that resists regimes of normativity' (Young and Herbig 2020: 73).

In *Sense8*, however, affect not only creates connection, but also boundaries, in accordance with Ahmed's observation that 'the "I" and the "we" are shaped by, and even take the shape of, contact with others' ([2004] 2014: 10). On the one hand, the affectively charged connections between the eight protagonists cross the boundaries of race, gender, and sexuality. At the same time, however, the cluster's sense of identity also depends on its sometimes violent demarcation from its persecutors, and from other sensates who have gone 'evil'. The series' antagonist, Whispers, a sensate who hunts his own kind down for his own benefit, works together with BPO, whose original goal was to foster exchange and cooperation between 'homo sensorium' and 'homo sapiens', but which has been taken over by forces that seek to turn sensates into warrior drones. Strikingly, the racist demarcation between the two kinds of humans is explained, in the series, as a result of 9/11 and the War on Terror, and this racist othering goes both ways: where the series suggests that many non-sensate humans fear and hate those who are 'homo sensorium', some of the sensates also cultivate an arrogance and contempt vis-à-vis homo sapiens. To an extent, too, this demarcation is tied to different notions of kinship, with 'traditional' ideas of family being associated with the supposedly 'less evolved' homo sapiens.

As Jonas puts it to Will about Whispers: '[f]ancies himself quite the family man. Likes to consider himself one of them' (season two, episode one, 'Who Am I?'). At the same time, while certainly emulating a 'normal' family ideal and only using his sensate abilities to persecute his own kind, Whispers retains an arrogant disdain for non-sensates, and decries 'the smallness of the sapien mind' (season two, episode twelve, 'Amor Vincit Omnia'). By employing different uncommon and sometimes fantastic notions of group formation, care networks, and in- and outgroup dynamics along various identity markers (such as cluster member versus non-cluster-member, or 'homo sensorium' versus 'homo sapiens'), *Sense8* thus does not simply do away with the potentially detrimental effects of discriminatory group formation. Instead – and alongside its upbeat emancipatory agenda – the series' politics of kinship highlights the contingent nature of in- and exclusions along certain categories of difference, but also their ongoing efficacy and power.

The sensates, as genetic 'freaks' and hunted individuals, represent the 'queer other' that can no longer just 'fit in', but has to fight to survive. This queer other, in *Sense8*, intersects with the subaltern other, the southern subject, and an affective coalition becomes possible through the shared experience of being 'other' from the point of view of what, in the series, is constructed as a 'normal human being', that is, not a genetically evolved 'homo sensorium'. Here, too, then, the series' overall plea for accepting and embracing difference becomes apparent. However, we might ask who gets to participate in the affective solidarity the series conjures up, and who does not. In other words, '[w]ho can and cannot embody the queer ideal?' (Ahmed [2004] 2014: 151). Although the series' choice of a diverse cast was certainly exceptional, at the time of its making, in the context of the general landscape of US-American television, and, as Ava Laure Parsemain observes, its 'depiction of queer relationships is groundbreaking because it emphasizes happiness rather than punishment and death' (2019: 218), its aesthetics relies on the fact that the beautiful, young, able bodies of the actors involved lend themselves easily to a pleasing visual tale of affective-bodily connection. The series also, despite its grand gestures at the utopic expansion of notions of kinship and belonging, holds on to rather conservative ideas about love and relationships. Especially its portrayal of Nomi and Amanita's love story, which culminates in their wedding on top of the Eiffel Tower, has been criticized for its taming of queerness' potential within the confines of 'homodomesticity'.[8] I would argue, however, that

---

[8] As Ava Laure Parsemain argues, the series' overall portrayal of Nomi and Amanita's relationship de-radicalizes queerness: '[t]he text often emphasises their domesticity by showing them at home and doing mundane tasks like folding the laundry or reading in bed. Situating same-sex couples in such domestic spaces normalises queer relationships. This 'homodomesticity' depoliticises queer sexuality and renders it non-threatening to mainstream

it is exactly the series' combination of 'traditional' love story and family drama both with more obvious and clichéd queerings of kinship and relationships, and with speculative fabulations of transcontinental empathy and connection that makes *Sense8* so alluring to many audiences, but also hard to digest for others. Its politics of kinship is both realistic/conservative *and* fantastic/utopic, trying to save the liberal subject's personal love story, while also doing away with the individual altogether.

Just turn the wheel and the future changes: Queer temporality and the crowded present

While *Sense8*'s most obvious queer intervention is its complication, expansion, and explosion of conventional notions of family and belonging, it also commits to a notion of temporality which complicates common assumptions about linear and teleological (narrative) progression. By endowing its sensate protagonists – and, through them, the series' audience – with the ability to experience past and present as a thick simultaneity, the series locates its utopic energies in the present moment. Its science-fiction premise enables a mode of queer temporality which foregrounds the crowded present, and which resonates with Elizabeth Freeman's theorization of queer time. Freeman finds, in her analysis of several works of visual art, that 'the queerness of these artists consists in mining the present for signs of undetonated energy from past revolutions … [in] moments when an established temporal order gets interrupted and new encounters consequently take place[,] … moments of asynchrony, anachronism, anastrophe, belatedness, compression, delay, ellipsis, flashback, hysteron-proteron, pause, prolepsis, repetition, reversal, surprise' (2010: xvi, xxii). Freeman's observations refer to the ways queerness emerges from a structural break with or turning away from the conventions of linearity and teleology. In part, *Sense8*'s queerness, too, lies in its approach to the temporality of storytelling. The narrative jumps back and forth between the different protagonists and locations, often producing an effect of simulated simultaneity, where fast cuts between scenes in different storylines imply that events are happening at the same time. The series' complex and multilinear setup borrows from a cinematic style which Alissa Quart (2005) describes as 'hyperlink cinema', a narrative technique that relies heavily on multiple narrative strands, simultaneous

---

heteronormative culture' (2019: 217); in a similar vein, Vassilis Gerasopoulos comments on the series' 'moments of normalized imagery', and argues that '*Sense8* potentially initiates a new chapter of capitalist commodification, where not only gay identities but, more saliently, fluid, malleable, carnivalesque, queer sexualities are consumed and commercialized' (2018).

narration, and non-linear storytelling. As Ava Laure Parsemain observes, '[l]ike hyperlink movies, [*Sense8*] uses a "network narrative" that jumps between multiple timelines to reveal a hidden connection' (2019: 223). I argue that *Sense8*'s narrative setup is not only paradigmatic for fiction of the internet age, but that it also draws the series' energies and its audience's affective investments firmly into the present moment. As such, the hope invoked through its emancipatory politics of utopian connection and individual freedom emerges – despite the protagonists' repeated claim that they are fighting for a 'better future' – less as a linear story of social and political emancipation, and more as an overflowing audio-visual immediacy, in which individuals in networked relations fight over who best navigates the urgencies of the intensely connected story world.

In this regard, *Sense8*'s narrative temporality is queer: it locates its emancipatory potential in the utopian narrative possibility that past, present, and future merge and can be shaped best (and only) in the here and now of global simultaneity. As Young and Herbig put it, in the series, '[t]ime and space are queered – the dualities of here/there and present/past are collapsed into now … [It] question[s] the existence of time as chronological (consisting of a beginning, middle, and end) as well as to actively challenge linear narrative' (2020: 79, 80). This focus on the present has important implications for the series' relationship with identity politics. Although its positing of identity categories as 'bodily limitations to achieving empathy and global connectivity' (Asante, Baig and Huang 2019: 320) that need to be overcome in the name of a global humanism has invited harsh criticism, this anti-identitarian stance is also what enables, together with the series' temporal mode and its science-fiction anti-realism, *Sense8*'s hopeful register. As Dilyana Mincheva contends, 'true *presence* … is conceptualized as an exodus from the normative brutality of the available physical world. Utopia as autonomy, then, functions not as a desperate attempt to hold onto a particular racial, gender, economic, or national identity, but rather as an ecstatic, erotic, and pleasurable exit from these identities' (2018: 37, emphasis in original).

As such, the queer narrative mode that the series enables can also be read as a way out of the impasse of identity politics in modern, liberal, capitalist societies which Wendy Brown provocatively problematizes in 'Wounded Attachments'. Brown points out the irresolvable tension between the individualist and collective egalitarian promises of liberal democracy, and the unfortunate dependency of identity politics on a 'wounded attachment' to 'its reviled subject – in this case, bourgeois male privileges – as objects of desire' (1993: 394). Contemporary politicized identities (queer and otherwise), Brown argues, 'are premised on exclusion from a universal ideal' (398), and focus obsessively on their 'historical and present pain rather than conjur[ing] an imagined future of power to make itself' (400). As a reparative alternative to continually investing in 'suffering as the measure of social virtue' (403), Brown points out the potential 'virtues of "forgetting"' (406), and suggests a moving away from a politics of 'being' towards one of '"wanting to be" or "wanting to have"' (407), that is, a shift from a perpetual self-inscription into an ontological status of hurt and pain towards a political dynamic of movement, surprise, and agency. While, to an extent, *Sense8* remains committed – in an almost celebratory form of wounded attachment – to the oppositional rhetoric of emancipation and inclusion, the series also, through its speculative complication of temporality and narration, uses its protagonists' exceptionality to evoke a utopic modality which sidesteps identity politics and opens up potentialities that run alongside the series' more conventional celebration of a fight for equal recognition.

Where, structurally speaking, queer temporality, in *Sense8*, thus enables a hopeful mode which emphasizes the crowded present and the potentiality inherent in simultaneity, the queerness of the series' protagonists, in similar fashion, lies not only in their positioning vis-à-vis different modalities of kinship, but also in their relationship with time: '[f]or the sensates, the present is something that is happening *simultaneously to them all* ... [They] can experience time as woven together, transcending the constraints of experiential time and place. They do not "remember" the past. They invoke it and experience it in the present' (Young and Herbig 2020: 78, 79, emphasis in original). Their sensate nature and potential for empathy enable them to experience a simultaneity of affect across the boundaries of individual experience, and to directly access their own and other sensates' memories as if they were experiencing them in the present moment. Individual cluster members not only relive their own past experiences, but also see and speak to sensates long dead, and share moments from their own past that they could not have a conscious memory of. 'Memory', for the sensates, thus gets queerly drawn into the present, sometimes in the shape of the involuntary intrusions of trauma, but more often as indicators of a positive expansion of individual experience. The individual and shared experience of the now, in turn, gets crowded with the thoughts, feelings, sense impressions, and experiences of both the simultaneity of each cluster member's present, and the collective affective history of those whose experience gets passed on through the sensates' telepathic and empathetic bond. As such, *Sense8* privileges the affective sharing of experience and the workings of collective memory over the potential authority and rationality of history.

Individually, the sensates have unmediated access to their own past: they can 'revisit' experiences from earlier in life as if they were living through them once more in the present. Like their cluster bond, this process is intimately associated with their heightened affective sensibilities: the memories individual cluster members keep re-experiencing are all, in a sense, traumatic, and they cannot actively control their occurrence, often living through them when they are unconscious. Out of the eight protagonists, however, only three – Riley, Wolfgang, and Will – regularly experience such an invasion of the past into their present. When Riley lies in a coma in a hospital after fainting at her father's concert, she first sees her dead husband, who speaks to her, and later vividly experiences the car crash in which her husband and baby daughter died. These memories are clearly distinct from 'normal' traumatic flashbacks: part of her evolved sensate nature becomes apparent when Riley's doctors notice her unusual brain activity during the experience (season one, episode eleven, 'What Is Human?'). This idea is further developed when Riley 'remembers' going into labour during the accident, and she apparently feels the same pain again in the present moment. When she has woken up and been rescued by Will, and they return to the site of the accident, past and present further blur even while Riley is awake. She has difficulties distinguishing between present and past realities, almost giving up on their escape because she does not want to abandon her dying child, an acute wish induced by her vivid memory of the past: (season one, episode twelve, 'I Can't Leave Her'). Similarly, Wolfgang, having been captured and sedated by BPO, relives memories from his childhood, in which he was bullied by his alcoholic father, and tried to protect his mother from him (season two, episode twelve, 'Amor Vincit Omnia'). Traumatic memory here literally forces itself into the present, and is given equal ontological status through Riley and Wolfgang's sensate perception. For the sensates, events from the past become part of their present reality, and directly influence their feelings, actions, and decisions.

In one sense, the sharing of (traumatic) memory through affect thus becomes, for the members of a cluster, a substitute for the creation of a shared identity through the telling and sharing of a linear and rational account of a common history, crowding the present with experiences from the past. The sensates' unique ability also enables them to access the experiences of individuals who are dead, thus effectively rendering them literal 'data clouds' for the memories, experiences, 'ghosts', or 'souls' of (potentially) all of their kind. The most interesting case in point is Will. As a young boy, he had 'visions' of a young girl, Sara Patrell, who was asking for his help, and who, as we later find out, was herself a sensate, and got experimented on and ultimately killed by Whispers. It is implied that her presence is so vivid that the young Will has trouble lying to his therapist about seeing her (season one, episode twelve, 'I Can't Leave Her'). Although the audience could easily read Sara as a Gothic element, an actual ghost, the series is explicit about embedding her presence within the logic of the sensates' empathetic abilities and privileged relation to the past: when, still as a boy, Will goes to see Sara's mother to help her communicate with her dead daughter, he insists that she is not a ghost, but a memory (season two, episode two, 'Who Am I?'). This implies that the empathetic connection between the sensates works to leave a trace of their mental existence which can then, at any given moment, become the present reality of the sensate who 'remembers'. Most strikingly, the protagonists can even interact with these 'hauntings' from the past. At several points throughout the series, Will and Riley – who seem to be particularly sensitive to these trans-temporal encounters – see and talk to their 'mother' Angelica. For example, at the beginning of the second season, when Will regularly drugs himself to prevent Whispers from invading his thoughts, he 'meets' Angelica at the scene of her suicide. They have an extended conversation, towards the end of which both Angelica and Will shoot themselves. The implication is that Will's interaction with her is a memory shaped by his present reality, which, in turn, actively shapes his present (season two, episode one, 'Happy Fucking New Year'). The sensates' ongoing connection to others who have already died thus serves to further complicate their relation to time and collectivity: the memories, feelings, and even intentions of, for example, Sara Patrell and Angelica have a concrete impact on the actions and decisions the protagonists make in the present and become part of a shared affective identity.

To a large extent, then, *Sense8* uses its protagonists' privileged relation to their shared past and present to foreground a temporal mode which locates collective agency in the present moment. These speculative elements also, however, serve to further highlight the series' humanist vision. Where it repeatedly uses the idea of shared moments of joyful communion at parties and on special occasions to enforce the cluster's sense of affective kinship with one another, the series also foregrounds their ability to recall and share past moments of ecstatic joy, a process which contributes to their collective experience, and which also foregrounds the series' humanist politics. The most striking scene in this respect is Riley's visit to her father's concert towards the end of the first season. The music's (Beethoven's fifth piano concerto) celebratory mood visibly moves Riley, and the intense emotional experience calls the other seven members of her cluster to 'share' the experience with her. In a further enhancement of this moment of collective affective experience, all eight then 'remember' or rather recall the moment of their own birth. The series' speculative premise suggests that what the sensates, in fact, recall is the extreme pain, joy, and confusion experienced by all those present at the scene of birth – that is, they 'remember' as much their own confusion coming into the world as their families' joy. For Riley, this scene then triggers a complete collapse of different levels of past and present: she not only remembers her own birth, but also, once again, the birth of her daughter and the accident (season one, episode ten, 'What Is Human?').

For the sensates, then, the past intrudes upon the present via the force of extreme emotions, and it takes on ontological reality. They encounter the here and now as a crowded present which complements the simultaneity of their shared realities. Rather than experiencing temporality as a linear investment in memory, information transfer, rational processing, and history, the sensates' empathetically enhanced reality enables and forces them to live through both the past and their shared present as one ongoing process. At the same time, the emancipatory energies of their fight against BPO, and for equal recognition as deviations from the (genetic, sexual, social) norm emerge from a narrative focus on simultaneity and transcontinental connection that locates hope in the potentiality of the present. This utopic focus on the present finds one of its most striking expressions in *Sense8*'s use of sexual ecstasy, but also comes at the price of eliding a nuanced negotiation of global histories of colonialism and racism.

For our fans: Hope, kinship, and progressive neoliberalism

In the end, then, it seems that *Sense8*'s aesthetics of an affective, physical, and geographical simultaneity and globalized kinship is, for better or worse, the show's main allure *and* what makes it so easy to criticize. Viewed from within the context of US-American – and thus also, inevitably, international – media production, the show is both ambitious in terms of its inclusivity, and innovative in terms of its foregrounding of transcultural affective relationships. However, the world represented in the series also heavily relies on the neoliberal structures of global capitalism, structures that have a significant impact on social realities. *Sense8*'s second season did promise to dive more into questions of corruption and global inequality, in particular between countries of the Global North and South. For instance, it seemed that narrative entanglements between the Indian plotline centred around illegal activities uncovered by Kala in her husband's pharmaceutical company, the organized crime scene of Wolfang's Berlin, and the traffic of HIV drugs in Capheus' Nairobi storyline might somehow connect, asking questions about international and postcolonial dependences and responsibilities. The series' early cancellation, however, made it impossible to develop this potential, and react to the widespread criticism.

A particularly interesting aspect of the discourse surrounding the show's creation, cancellation, and Netflix's decision to renew the series for a final, two-hour special is the way *Sense8*'s exploration of affective community building expanded beyond the context of the series itself and into a transnational community of fans. In an open letter to the audience, Lana Wachowski explicitly compares the fans' help in getting *Sense8* a proper narrative ending to the protagonists' fight for a shared community against the pressures of a mysterious international corporation[9] – while the decisions surrounding the series' cancellation and continuation are themselves,

---

[9]In acknowledgement of their indebtedness to their fans, the series' creators have its finale end with a dedication: 'For our fans' (season two, episode twelve, 'Amor Vincit Omnia').

ironically, a process ultimately driven by the marketing considerations of a big, US-American company:

> By myself, there was nothing I could do. But just as the characters in our show discover that they are not alone, I too have learned that I am not just a me. I am also a we. The passionate letters, the petitions, the collective voice that rose up like the fist of Sun to fight for this show was beyond what anyone was expecting. In this world it is easy to believe that you cannot make a difference; that when a government or an institution or corporation makes a decision, there is something irrevocable about the decision; that love is always less important than the bottom line … Improbably, unforeseeably, your love has brought *Sense8* back to life. (qtd. in Miller 2017)

In the case of *Sense8*, then, the trouble seems to be that its hopeful message of a global humanism and kinship based on radical love, empathy, and sex, in tandem with its elaborate aesthetics, plotlines, and likable characters, has great allure. We *want* to believe it. If anything, a critical/paranoid viewer might wonder what it means to buy into the series' feel-good message, and its narrative and aesthetic appeals to our affects. It might be cruel to call a series as ambitious as *Sense8* naïve – after all, why should a commercially produced series with a clearly positive message about human bonds *not* be naïve – but one of the series' most striking characteristics is that its very premise invites postcolonial critique. Despite the fact that *Sense8*'s speculative setup enables unusual insights into the dynamics of belonging and temporality in the contemporary cultural imagination, its dominant pop-cultural take on globality and connection deflects from its more nuanced undertones. It is impossible not to remark on how easily the series' rendering of hope and kinship fits into a US-American vision of globalization: 'the dominant discourse in the United States regards accelerating global flows as a surfer's paradise rather than as a tidal wave eroding territorial sovereignty or swamping traditional self-conceptions with a flood of images produced elsewhere' (Livingston 2001: 147).

Although *Sense8*'s protagonists themselves represent the fictional realization of a hope for adequate representation of racial, gendered, and sexual diversity, they are also hyper-mobile, capable characters with access to a wide range of means of communication and resources (not least of all their telepathic talents), and as such remain strangely detached from the local social and cultural realities around them. And although, arguably, by successfully lobbying for the series' 'resurrection' through concerted action, 'the fans of *Sense8* essentially outmanoeuvred, albeit in fairly temporary and limited ways, the logics of neoliberal capitalism' (Elrod 2019: 56), this success is more akin to the limited and localized hope that characterizes the series' plot than to any kind of actual cultural or anti-capitalist revolution.

Read in a wider context, the series' claim to diversity and transculturality thus appears as potentially complicit in, or at least forgetful of the pitfalls of what Nancy Fraser calls 'progressive neoliberalism':

> In its US form, progressive neoliberalism is an alliance of mainstream currents of new social movements (feminism, anti-racism, multiculturalism and LGBTQ rights) on the one side, and high-end 'symbolic' and service-based sectors of business (Wall Street, Silicon Valley and Hollywood) on the other. In this alliance, progressive forces are effectively joined with the forces of cognitive capitalism, especially financialisation ... [This process historically came] at the expense of ... emancipation, in so far as the whole edifice rested on the ongoing (neo-)imperial predation of the Global South, on the institutionalisation of women's dependency through the family wage, and on the racially motivated exclusion of agricultural and domestic workers from social security. (2017: 41, 43)

In many ways, a deeply ingrained awareness of these processes seems to lie at the heart of the ambiguous rendering of temporality and affective community in *Sense8*. Perhaps this discomfort, and the fact that a debate has evolved in response to the series, is what makes it worthwhile watching and contemplating. In the specific context of this book, *Sense8* serves as a reminder that the contemporary fictional imagination – especially as it emerges in web television narration[10] – is, more often than not, equally committed to the (in this case liberal and progressive) politics of its projected target audience, and to the commercial and cultural logic of its context of origin. While the series' vision of an overcoming of identity politics through kinship that emerges from ecstatic networks of affect has escapist allure, it also buys into fantasies of post-identity that make the series – because its impetus *is* political – sit uncomfortably within contemporary global realities. And while its crowding of the present as the locus of hope is

---

[10] As Anna McFarlane observes, 'Netflix does not carry advertisements, but rather runs on subscriptions. This means that it has no need to provide viewing figures as a means of selling advertising space; rather, in order to make its business model more successful, it has to give the impression of cultural hegemony. If Netflix is seen at the forefront of the cultural conversation, that is the biggest incentive to subscribe for people who do not want to be left out of the zeitgeist. It is perhaps this business incentive that has encouraged Netflix to make its name with shows that are culturally daring' (2017: 153). Rye Gentleman similarly points out Netflix's particular relationship with culture and identity politics: 'Netflix has no use for the conventional demographic categories through which subjects are traditionally constructed. Netflix is not nearly as interested in the gender, class, or race of its viewers as it is in factors such as their past viewing history, the times during which they tend to watch television, and whether they binge watch or jump from series to series' (2019: 148).

characteristic of a more general trend in contemporary fiction, other, less speculative works react in a decidedly different manner to the challenges of a prevailing cultural pessimism, and position themselves more strategically outside the sphere of globalist – or even, strictly speaking, social – utopia. These works represent a current tendency, which I explore in the following chapter, towards an almost complete rejection of history and politics in favour of fleeting moments of reparative belonging and care.

PART THREE

Hysterical pessimism: Contingent hope and the proliferation of the present in the novels of Hanya Yanagihara

I introduced the last two sections of this book by making reference to recent protests raising awareness of climate change in apocalyptic times, and to the global coronavirus pandemic that swept across the globe starting in 2019 in order to point out a tendency in contemporary political and cultural discourse to propagate positions which carry feelings of anxiety, suspicion, and ambiguity towards futurity, and which struggle to identify a frame of reference that would create a viable mode of kinship. I have also shown that recent fiction has produced responses to this age of anxiety which, on the one hand, reflect and confirm contemporary culture's general lack of optimism, but also enable modes of hope and kinship that sidestep normative expectations, and rely on improvisation, spontaneity, and speculative experimentation in the present. What looks bleak on the surface thus proves to hold its own promises of local and fleeting, but often vital potential for reparative visions of belonging and care.

In this last chapter, I want to continue this investigation by considering two recent pieces of fiction in which many of the concerns discussed so far culminate, and which open up further perspectives onto what hope and kinship might come to mean in pessimistic times. In a recent issue of *The Comparatist* dedicated specifically to the dominance of pessimism in current cultural discourse, Zahi Zalloua frames pessimism both as a diagnosis of our times, and as an analytical perspective:

> Suspicion of the status quo, discontent with the now discredited rhetoric of progress, and a lingering dissatisfaction with bland hope or optimism … have settled in. It seems that pessimism characterizes more and more today's political horizon … But pessimism can also embody a more active disposition. It can, for example, take the form of a hermeneutics. A pessimistic interpretive mode entails an unconditional refusal to accept that 'things will get better'. (2019: 1)

It is this potential inherent in a pessimistic perspective, understood as a specific iteration of the reparative positions traced in this book as a whole, that I want to explore in this chapter. Reading and analysing Hanya Yanagihara's first two novels, I suggest that these texts paradigmatically perform a politics of pessimism which acknowledges disillusionment, pain, trauma, and the violence of political realities and enduring structural power imbalances, while also opening up spaces of narrative resistance, of care and concern against all odds. These fictional spaces and strategies of reparation, I argue, only become possible from a pessimistic stance which first admits that perhaps – most likely even – things will not get better. Considered from this angle, Yanagihara's relentless exploration of violence and trauma, which has irritated and fascinated readers and critics of her novels, works as the stark but necessary foil to her equally pronounced interest in the possibility of connection and kinship, both between human individuals and across species.

In interviews, Yanagihara regularly confesses to her interest in the bleakest realities of human interaction and psychology,[1] but also in the importance of friendship and love,[2] and she has expressed her conviction that one of the important concerns of her second novel, *A Little Life*, is 'that the idea of a blood family is, if not irrelevant, then certainly too narrow for our world' (FP Staff 2017). Strikingly, Yanagihara also frames her – literary and biographical – preference for friendship over romantic relationships as a queer position in relation to mainstream (US) culture, 'a different kind of adulthood, one that isn't often celebrated in fiction, but which is adulthood nonetheless. An adulthood in which there is a primacy of friendship' (Adams 2015). I want to take these authorial confessions as a cue to argue that it is precisely the twin fascination with the dark realities of human existence and with non-normative forms of belonging and care that make Yanagihara's fiction speak to a contemporary audience and context. While she herself frames her interest in non-romantic relationships almost exclusively in the language of friendship, the forms of mutual recognition, care, and concern – and their attendant flipsides: violence and abuse – that emerge in the two novels at hand stretch across different dimensions of friendship, love, romance, adoption, desire, and momentary recognition which can all be subsumed under what I have been defining as kinship. Reading Yanagihara's fiction in a pessimistic tradition enables crucial insights into the dynamics of temporality and (un-)belonging in her novels, especially considering the specific relevance of philosophical pessimism for US-American cultural production.

Philosophical pessimism, briefly put, is an ethical position which maintains that it is, firstly, necessary to acknowledge the terrible realities of our existence, and, secondly, to abstain from investing in false hopes that do

---

[1] In an interview with Alexis Cheung for *The Believer*, for example, Yanagihara proposes that 'we need to be reminded of violence at its most visceral and explicit: it exists, after all, and there should be no sense that its detailing is not a subject for serious literature' (Cheung 2017); and in conversation with poet and writer Meghan O'Rourke, she explicates her understanding of the relationship between trauma and temporality: '[w]e prefer to think of things on some sort of continuum, and that they always end in a result. One of the things I did want to do in [*A Little Life*] was talk about this idea that for people who have experienced trauma, there is no such thing as past tense. It's always encroaching upon the present' (FP Staff 2017).

[2] In the same conversation with O'Rourke, Yanagihara summarizes her philosophy of love as fundamentally non-teleological: '[n]o one person can save another person. But that's the beauty and the pain of love itself – when so much in life is results-oriented, when we expect a hard finish line on so many relationships we have in life, and we do so many things because we expect something from it. The love for a friend, or for a parent, or a child, or for anybody is one of the things that makes us human because there is no result from it. Except for the pleasure, and the wonder, and the horror, sometimes, of loving someone. That's it' (FP Staff 2017).

not take the implications of these realities seriously. Hope, in this account, can become a threat, because it potentially endangers those who buy into its illusions, and those who suffer the consequences of the actions of those who do (cf. Scruton 2010: 1). At the same time, pessimism can emerge as a particularly strong humanism, because it maintains that, since nothing is certain apart from our own mortality, and since it is precisely this mortality which makes us human, pessimism also enables us, as 'dying creatures[,] … to cherish one another, to sacrifice ourselves, to make sublime and heroic gestures' (11).[3] While I am not concerned with putting a new humanism at the centre of my argument, it is worth noting that, in pessimism, a distrust of narratives of betterment merges with a concern for relationality, and that pessimism does not necessarily take negativity as a cue for resignation or fatalism. As Joshua Foa Dienstag argues, '[i]n the right hands, pessimism can be – and has been – an energizing and even a liberating philosophy. While it does indeed ask us to limit and eliminate some of our hopes and expectations, it can also provide us with the means to better navigate the bounded universe it describes' (2006: ix). Pessimism, according to Dienstag, accepts the challenge which arises when we accept that things might not get better. It considers human existence as trapped in the consciousness of temporal existence, and proposes that we expect nothing (cf. xi, 5). As such, while pessimism generally maintains an underlying modern understanding of time as linear, its rejection of any affective investment in the future – in the form of concrete expectations or politics – strongly resonates with the presentism at the heart of the works analysed in this book. And while most pessimistic philosophy is more strictly humanist in outlook than this project, it usefully captures the essential dilemma outlined in these chapters. It understands conscious existence in time as fundamentally defined by loss and trauma, and futuristic, teleological hope as flawed, 'since most of our hopes are bound to be disappointed, and those that are fulfilled are disfulfilled in the next moment as the objects of our hopes slip into the past' (23). Pessimism thus understands the acting subject as bound to the present. This, however, does not necessarily entail recourse to nihilism or despair. On the contrary, as Dienstag argues, pessimism sets the future free by turning it into a truly unpredictable open plain: '[p]essimism embodies a free relation to the future. In refraining from hope and prediction we make possible a concern that is not self-abasing and self-pitying. By not holding every moment hostage to its future import, we also make possible a genuinely

---

[3]It is worth noting here that philosophical pessimism easily lends itself to a general political conservativism. Roger Scruton, for instance, who I quote here for his valuable insights into the limits of hope, uses pessimism to draw wide-ranging conclusions about the dangers of technological developments, and propagates a traditionalist and conservative agenda that lies far outside the concerns and politics of this book.

friendly responsibility to ourselves and to others' (245). Pessimism, understood as an acceptance of the limitations of human subjectivity and agency in the world, thus opens up creative potential for care and concern in the present. What interests me most for the purpose of my own argument is that Dienstag and others foreground pessimism's potential to make accessible the possibilities and potentialities of the present in a 'democracy of moments' (248); its essential openness to surprises and spontaneity; its fundamentally relational, communal, and responsible nature; and its affinity with friendship as the pessimist's ideal form of kinship (cf. 40, 248, 263; Scruton 2010: 14, 16, 18, 224). Pessimism thus becomes a useful framework to continue the argument proposed in this book, and to understand the politics of the two novels discussed in this chapter.

While I am not primarily interested in the cultural specificities of the US-American context these two novels emerge from, it is worth noting that several critics have pointed out pessimism's curious position within the cultural history and landscape of a country whose national character has long been assumed to be emphatically or even fanatically optimistic and bright. The 'American Dream' of individual betterment and success, and the still powerful belief in America's inherent greatness grind against an undercurrent of not only contrary political and social realities, but also a darker narrative current which John Stroup and Glenn W. Shuck diagnose as a particular kind of 'cultural pessimism' (2007: xvi), a pessimism that has informed, they argue, many popular forms of storytelling in the United States since the second half of the twentieth century.[4] In fact, a renegade interest in pessimistic philosophy and thinking has long been central to American culture. As Christa Buschendorf demonstrates, although the narrative of an unbroken national ethos of optimism ultimately prevailed, a specifically Anglo-American variant of pessimistic thinking, strongly influenced by a reception of Arthur Schopenhauer's writing, has been a prominent intellectual and popular presence since the late nineteenth century (cf. 2008: 3, 5). It is in this context of a generalized tension between a culturally prescribed optimism and an ever-present crosscurrent of pessimistic thinking that I want to place my readings of Yanagihara's novels. This necessitates another disclaimer. Recent political developments, in particular, have triggered a renewed interest in thinking the dynamics of racism and potential political and philosophical answers in terms of the radical logics of Afro-Pessimism. While the powerful negativity of this philosophy certainly deserves

---

[4]Curiously, like Roger Scruton (2010), Stroup and Shuck ultimately take their analysis of contemporary US-American cultural pessimism as a cue to propagate a conservative political agenda, and to blame liberal 'doctrines' like political correctness for depressing the social psyche, instead of following the thread of potentiality inherent in their own diagnosis. I believe this is an unnecessary and unfortunate move.

further and continued consideration – and productive criticism (cf. e.g. Radhakrishnan 2019) – it is not, I would maintain, the kind of pessimism to which the texts discussed here subscribe. While race and racism do play a role in them, their politics do not necessarily align with the specific thrust of Black politics and philosophy.

While pessimism is the most important context for my analysis of Yanagihara's fiction, I want to further emphasize the particular value of her writing for my argument by proposing that her novels not only perform a pessimistic register, but that they do so in a 'hysterical' fashion. Two decades ago, James Wood (2000), in an article for *The New Republic*, coined the term 'hysterical realism' to capture – mainly in derogative terms – what he considers the essential characteristics of the 'big, ambitious novel'. According to Wood, a prominent selection of novels published at the end of the millennium – by Zadie Smith (Wood's main object of attack), Salman Rushdie, Don DeLillo, David Foster Wallace, and others – inappropriately (in moral terms) explode the conventions of realism by driving them all to extremes: too much plot, unlikely arrays of accidents and occurrences, and overflowing bonds of connectedness. What interests me most is Wood's criticism of these (without exception very long) novels' alleged excess of human connection. Charging 'hysterical' novels with a lack of humanity, he complains that '[l]ife is never experienced with such a fervid intensity of connectedness. After all, hell is other people, actually: real humans disaggregate more often than they congregate. So these novels find themselves in the paradoxical position of enforcing connections that are finally conceptual rather than human'.

I find Wood's generalized criticism based on a genre definition which remains rather vague problematic, to say the least, and would not go along with his all-out dismissal of the fiction he attacks as somehow deficient or morally defunct. I do, however, share his impression (even more so twenty-four years after the publication of his essay) that there is something 'too much' in the contemporary 'big ambitious novel'. Yanagihara's works are prominent examples of texts that both fascinate and exasperate their readership. Their sheer length, emotional intensity, exuberant prose, and scandalizing choice of topic (child abuse, sexual violence), while not strictly confirming all characteristics Wood originally ascribed to 'hysterical realism', would most likely strike a chord with those who share Wood's impression that a certain kind of ambitious contemporary novel deliberately walks the fine line between sincerity and wild exaggeration, and between realist human conflict and emotionally exploitative melodrama. Yanagihara herself confesses to her intention of working against an intellectually detached style of writing and reading that she bemoans as a contemporary malaise, and to risk a 'too much' of emotion: '[w]e're living in a literary age (at least in America) that is marked by a sense of distance, a coolness, in all senses of that word. To be too obviously, unapologetically emotional is to risk being considered foolish, or at the very least not serious' (Cheung 2017). Specifically in reference to the intensity of *A Little Life*, she explains that

> I wanted there to be something too much about the violence in the book, but I also wanted there to be an exaggeration of everything, an exaggeration of love, of empathy, of pity, of horror. I wanted everything turned up a little too high. I wanted it to feel a little vulgar in places. Or to be always walking that line between out and out sentimentality and the boundaries of good taste. (Adams 2015)

Going 'hysterical', then, in the case of Yanagihara, is a conscious choice, one that is founded in considerations of aesthetics and potential reader response. I argue that it is precisely this tendency to exaggerate in terms of affective and emotional register which enables, in Yanagihara's fiction, a literary mode that pits a pessimistic ethics against the possibilities and potentialities of connection and belonging. Where these novels lack an optimistic outlook and a narrative of progress, they fill their worlds with an abundance of connection – abusive, loving, destructive, and reparative. *The People in the Trees* uses elements of metafiction to foreground the power of narrative in the making of temporal realities, and problematizes the ambiguous place of morality in the vibrant material world. *A Little Life* contrasts the debilitating physical and psychological consequences of sexual violence and trauma with the reparative power of love and friendship. Both novels are intimately concerned with complicating the dominant logic of progressive temporality and (individual, social, and ecological) betterment, and both place the individual subject in a context in which different kinds of kinship – chosen families, friendships, intimacies, abusive adoptions, and affective encounters with the non-human – are improvised, adjusted, shift over time, and emerge both as the origin of relentless suffering, and as the only source of reparative hope in pessimistic times.

Crucially for my purpose, introducing pessimistic thinking as a frame for continuing a discussing of paranoid and reparative temporalities and subjectivities also has further implications for criticism as such. Reparative and postcritical hermeneutics are essentially pessimistic in that they complicate the liberal belief in criticism's power to unveil hidden violence, and to unambiguously contribute to an emancipatory project. Critics of postcritical thinking, like Jeffrey R. Di Leo, have come to the same conclusion. Di Leo, however, goes on to argue that postcritique's affinity with pessimism makes it a 'life-denying approach' (2019: 8), against which critique proper must be redeemed as the only form of reading and thinking that 'holds the pedagogical promise of not only self-change, autonomy, and freedom, but also of social hope and reform' (18). Di Leo's outrage is telling in its paranoid framing of hope as exclusively bound to the optimism of resistance inherent in the belief that criticisms job is to unveil, again and again, violent power structures. While my concern in this book is not to negate the importance of critique to continue to do its paranoid work, I suggest that reparative and postcritical hermeneutics are the best fit for the kind of fictional material I analyse. My point is that reparative and postcritical reading are, like philosophical pessimism, committed to the possibilities afforded by openness, to the challenge of surprises, and to the multiplication of perspectives. Fiction like Yanagihara's novels calls for a methodology and mindset which can account for their simultaneous commitment to a pessimist outlook, and to structures of belonging as the ambiguous locus of hope.

If we were to put a label on the kind of fiction I am framing here, it would be tempting to subscribe to Annika Gonnermann's analysis, who, in her reading of two contemporary dystopian novels, defines 'post-pessimism' as 'a contemporary literary movement that presents readers a world void of alternatives besides neoliberal capitalism', and as 'the understanding that neither an optimistic nor pessimistic attitude is justified due to the lack of alternatives' (2019: 27). While both of Yanagihara's novels – and several of the other texts discussed in previous chapters in this book – certainly do present such a world immersed in the inescapable logic of capital, I believe that their particular import stems from something other than 'shock[ing readers] into political activism', and they certainly do not unambiguously 'teach us to continue to look for a more optimistic future *despite and because of* capitalist realism' (38, emphasis in original). Instead, I think it is more accurate to think of these novels' politics as a form of 'hopeful pessimism'. I am borrowing this term from Rebecca Coleman's analysis of recent British austerity politics. She proposes it as a concept that can grasp a political, social, or aesthetic mood

> where pessimism about the future involves attention to the present, … where expectation refers to a linear model of time …, and hope to vaguer aspirations to and imaginations of the future that emerge through … non-linear affective temporality … Hope in this sense might not be a deferral to the future, … but rather might involve a focus on the 'day to day'. One of the implications of the mood of pessimism about the future, then, might be the creation of a politics of the present, focussing attention on how the day to day requires change, now. (2016: 85, 99–100)

It is this kind of pessimism (and this kind of hope) that Yanagihara's fiction performs in an aesthetic register. Her novels' 'hysterical' mode is as much about rendering the impossibility of escaping the violent realities of structural and individual oppression and violence, as it is about 'the courage of hopelessness' (Zalloua 2019: 2).

5

Moral matters: Power, coloniality, and narrative in *The People in the Trees*

Hanya Yanagihara's 2013 debut novel *The People in the Trees* offers the fictional memoir of Nobel Prize–winning biologist Dr Norton Perina, edited and annotated by his friend Ronald Kubodera. Beginning with memories from his early childhood, the confessional account's main focus is on Norton's travels to a fictional Micronesian archipelago, his encounter with a mysterious turtle which seems to be the key to eternal life, and his successive adoption and abuse of several dozens of the islands' children. The novel is a rich and complex neo-gothic exploration of scientific megalomania, colonial exploitation, the human/nonhuman divide, and the physical and epistemological abuse of power. It also foregrounds the devastating consequences of the imposition of a dominant (colonial/paranoid/ teleological) narrative, and the potential perversions of improvised kin making. Early reviews put a lot of emphasis on a feeling of unsettlement and hopelessness, describing the novel as 'almost defiant in its refusal to offer redemption or solace' (Ciuraru 2013), pointing out its 'mood of almost glacial uncertainty, … [which] beguiles and unnerves' (Kidd 2013), and warning that 'some sensitive readers … might be disturbed by the content' (Kimzey 2013). Yanagihara's debut both fascinates and repels readers thanks to its dense rendering of a scandalizing yet intriguing story, the deployment of an ambiguous narrative voice, and the self-conscious play with metafictional elements. The novel thus emerges as a disturbing inconvenience, an unsettling reading experience which prompts important questions about the relationship between morality, materiality, and historically situated power relations. As such, the text also addresses the darker side of kinship, and the (im)possibility of hope in pessimistic times and in a material world imbued with the violence of power imbalances.

In this chapter, I want to explore how, in *The People in the Trees*, plot and narrative structure interact in a way that both foregrounds complex questions of materiality and affect, and complicates any easily available solution to the conflicted relationship between temporality, social and biological generation, and morality. The novel puts in motion a dynamic interplay between elements of plot and elements of narrative. It brings together a protagonist obsessed with discovering immortality – by means of the colonial-scientific exploitation of native fauna, the compulsive, non-biological creation of 'family', and the self-righteous restoration and preservation of his fame and reputation – and a narrative setup that lays bare the power structures inherent in the authorial and authoritative creation of pasts and the violent destruction of possible futures. The text thus considers the contingency of hope and the moral ambiguity of processes of non-reproductive kin-making.

In my discussion of the dynamic relationship between hope and kinship in *The People in the Trees,* I want to address three different, but interrelated dimensions. Firstly, the novel's metafictional structure, with its introduction, comments, scholarly footnotes, and climactic revelation of a left-out piece of the story, refers back to a long tradition of 'fictional editions' – most prominently Vladimir Nabokov's *Pale Fire*. It draws attention to the ambiguous nature of both the confessional narrative in general, and to the power inequalities and material processes of imperial knowledge production inherent in the logic of western science more specifically. The logics of selecting, ordering, and referencing foregrounded here prompt questions about the power hierarchies produced and cemented in curating an archive of material and immaterial artefacts, and a teleological narrative of personal exculpation.

On the level of story, the novel produces an abundance of detail in the fictional construction of the island of U'ivu. The text's narrative evocation of material richness, the density of 'natural' fabric and human and non-human agency the protagonist observes and remembers, creates a fictional space which reproduces an exoticizing dichotomy of western rationality and foreign/tropical materiality, and which evokes 'the construction of the tropics as a space of difference' (Nayar 2012: 47).[1] This dichotomy is problematized in Norton's encounter with the mysterious life-extending turtle – the opa'ivu'eke – and through his fascination with the 'dreamers'. These zombie-like humans, having eaten the turtle's flesh, grow unusually old physically, while their minds and brains decay. Both the opa'ivu'eke and

---

[1] On the ongoing effects of such dichotomous thinking in contemporary scholarship see, for example, Mohanty (1984).

the dreamers point towards the fragility of the material and epistemological boundaries between the human and non-human, and of western dualistic thinking in general.

Finally, by choosing two narrative voices completely caught up in their scientific/imperial/masculinist perspective, the novel both provokes immediate affective reactions – disgust, outrage, irritation – and begs the question as to the moral positioning of the reader towards the narrative. Perina, the novel's protagonist and main point of identification for the reader, clearly lacks a moral compass compatible with humanist ideals. His unabashed physical/material and colonial/abusive penetration of the island and the ultimate sexual abuse of the many children he adopts and brings to Europe to serve as substitutes for his unfulfilled dream of immortality raise questions both about the material damage inflicted through colonial and sexual violence, and about the relationship between knowledge production, inequality, and violence.

In my analysis of the novel, I will thus be moving back and forth between questions of plot and questions of structure. I will begin with a discussion of how, in *The People in the Trees*, fixed boundaries between the scientific/colonial subject and the studied/colonized objects, and between the human and the non-human become undone in Norton's encounter with Ivu'ivu's natural elements and the island's human population. The chapter will then move on to an exploration of the novel's narrative voice, its employment of metafictional elements, and its rendering of time and temporality, which all contribute to a problematization of how a white/male/colonial/western voice imposes a linear narrative of progression and decline onto 'othered' spaces and bodies. I will conclude by looking at one of the novel's child characters and his function as both the object of colonial/sexual violence, and the agent of anti-colonial narrative resistance against Norton's dominant account of past, present, and future.

Porous boundaries: Kinship, disgust, and colonial affect

One of the defining features of *The People in the Trees* is its exuberant evocation of a fictional environment almost ready to be touched, felt, and experienced. The novel produces an abundance of detail in the creation of the island group of U'ivu. Norton's account provides thick descriptions of exotic and unknown/unknowable flora and fauna, which are dominated by a pervasive feeling of disgust. Winfried Menninghaus points out the role of disgust as a fundamentally differentiating affect: 'disgust brings eminent affective powers to bear: it processes elementary civilizing taboos and social distinctions between what is foreign and one's own. At the same time, it is a medium for the intercourse with strong libidinal impulses' (2003: 2). In this sense, disgust, as an affective process on the border between conscious and unconscious, nature and culture, can come to play an important role in the formation of social structure, allowing 'for ever new demarcations of the boundaries of acceptability, group membership, and ever finer gradations of ever increasing and ever smaller "subcultures"' (5). Torn between violent repulsion and ambiguous attraction, disgust negotiates one's attitudes towards the proximity of something or someone else. In the context of narratives of colonial exploration and imperial encounter, disgust can emerge as an affective nodal point determining distance and proximity – and thus, in this book's vocabulary, degrees of kinship – between scientist/colonizer and the environment he encounters.

In *The People in the Trees*, Norton's reactions to the unfamiliar environment of U'ivu, its flora, fauna, and native population, and to female reproductive sexuality can be understood in terms of the ambiguous repulsion/fascination characteristic of disgust. And Norton's disgust at the island's overflowing sensuality and animacy, in turn, emerges as intimately related to the dynamics of historical colonial encounters. As Pramod K. Nayar observes, in the early stages of the European imperial project in Asia, the local environment and its population, while at first perceived as overwhelmingly strange, were turned into objects of scientific inquiry to be 'examined, categorized, studied, and judged by European writings about them' (2012: 3). In the long run, this process helped naturalize colonial power relations, and paved the way for military and colonial conquest. Narrative organization of the colonized territories was thus an integral part of the imperial project as a whole: the colonized territory was constructed, through what Nayar calls 'the scientific exotic' as fundamentally different from British identity, 'preserv[ing] the boundaries of us/them' (9). In *The People in the Trees*, Norton, as neo-colonial explorer-scientist, evokes the historical mode of imperialist discovery, 'performing a narrative ordering' (16) of the island he explores, trying to turn it 'into a *knowable, manageable entity* in and through narrative forms' (18, emphasis in original). At the same time, Norton's memoir oscillates between sentimental and scientific modalities of colonial discourse, constructing the living environment on U'ivu both as 'an object to be admired or hated or to repel', and as something to be 'particularize[d] and ... itemize[d]' (60). His account is dominated by the desire to overcome, by narrative means, the confusion of difference/sameness implied by the workings of colonial disgust.

Disgust, in *The People in the Trees*, links Norton's sense of power and (self-)possession as white, male colonizer/scientist-subject to his generalized misogyny and fear of a loss of clear-cut boundaries between the known and the unknown, the human and the non-human, and that which he can control through scientific means and that which keeps escaping his scientific gaze.² In its emphasis on the entanglement of affect, ontology, and epistemology in narrative encounters with the colonized natural environment, the novel also exemplifies elements of what Heather Houser calls 'ecosickness fiction': '[i]n ecosickness fiction, humans and the more-than-human world do not only interact, but more importantly, are co-constitutive ... [It] attests that an array of stories and narrative affects is necessary for apprehending the material and conceptual relays between the embodied individual and large-scale environmental forces ... [C]onflict, risk, discord, and reflexivity are ... connotations of interconnectedness' (2014: 3, 4, 15). At the heart of the exploration, in *The People in the Trees*, of a narrator's encounter with a fundamentally strange landscape and ecosystem lies a questioning both of Norton's own legitimacy as an authorial subject proposing a linear narrative of scientific conquest, and, more generally, of a western and Enlightenment notion of Nature as a manageable 'other' from which the explorer-scientist distances himself in order to manipulate and exploit it at will, without consequence to his own entitled position. The text insists on the destructive consequences of unequal power relations between colonizer and colonized, and the very real and deadly impact of human action, despite a partial acknowledgement of the possibility of making kin with the non-human world. For the most part, the vibrancy of the non-human environment evokes panic and confusion in Norton, who unwittingly ascribes agency to the things the encounters: 'you felt for a minute frightened of the jungle, its voracious appetite and ambition, its hunger to consume every surface it encountered' (Yanagihara 2013: 82). Nature, in the novel, thus emerges as uncanny, repulsive, and powerful, something potentially able to shatter the very subject position that encounters it: 'the land is animated and hostile. Nature is not a backdrop for human action but a mode where the anthropocentric gaze is defeated' (Byrne 2017: 966).

Strikingly, Norton's ontological confusion, his confrontation with 'the imperturbability of nature, ... its unknowability, its fundamental lack of interest in humanity' (Yanagihara 2013: 99), and the negative affect the jungle triggers in him get closely tied to his generalized misogyny and fear of the boundless body. He explicitly compares the jungle to 'an overdressed woman parading her entire cache of sparkly jewels before [him]' (ibid.), and his frequent recourse to sexually charged vocabulary appears in close textual proximity to his female travel companion Esme's fertile and (to Norton) repugnant body:

---

²As Magdelena Zolkos puts it, 'Yanagihara narrates these situations as the workings of the affective forces of abjection, terror and disgust. This is because their common denominator is that they disrupt Norton's attachment to the masculine and colonial orders and to imperial knowledge claims' (2020: 156).

> [I] saw a crumpled blossom on the jungle floor ... Here the flowers were waxy and indistinguishable as flowers: where there should have been stamens there were grossly suggestive plasticky lips upon which bugs alighted to rest ... I saw that the flower was no flower at all, but rather a crumple of tissue, at its heart a smear of blood ... [A]round [Esme] seemed the sickening scent of menstrual blood. (100, 101)

Throughout the novel, Norton repeatedly expresses and enacts his disgust at the leaking (female, reproductive) body,[3] and its potentially devastating implications for the upholding of stable ontological boundaries between physical entities and their assumed animacy. The Manama fruit that fall from the trees, for instance, act upon his affective economy both through their confusion of clear-cut distinctions between lifeforms, and for their evocation of the boundless and sexualized body:

> Out of [the Manama fruit] squirmed a large writhing mass of grubs ... they looked like rivulets of suddenly animated ground beef, worming their way toward some sort of salvation ... [T]he air seemed to smell faintly of something human and unclean ... [Upon the Manama trunk was] a great swathe of blood ... As we moved closer, I saw that it was not blood but something living, so that it almost appeared a raw, exposed organ. (105, 106)

Norton's encounter with the material richness and sensory intensity of the jungle unsettles his ontological convictions and destabilizes clear-cut boundaries between colonizer and colonized. While he acknowledges the vibrancy and potential boundlessness of the material world that acts upon his body and senses – calling out to him as part of a vast network of kinship – he evaluates this thick material presence mostly in negative terms, as a loss of epistemological and ontological control ('Why must nothing obey the laws of nature?'), and decries the jungle's insistence on the 'existence of enchantment' (106).

These negative comments in Norton's account, however, are balanced by a sentimental fascination, sometimes bordering on identification, with the natural world he encounters, implying the breakdown of stable colonial dichotomies, and the possibility of kinship beyond the boundaries of the human. Not only does he acknowledge how the world acts upon him while he moves through it, but he also forms a particularly intimate bond with the opa'ivu'eke, a mysterious life-extending turtle. This animal, as Norton learns from Tallent, plays an important and sacred role in the islanders'

---

[3] For a thorough discussion of the relationship between masculinity and anxieties about the female body see, for example, Theweleit (1987).

mythology: the opa'ivu'eke can move between the realms of land and sea, and it seems to hold the secret to immortality that Norton is after (cf. 89–91). Norton's knowledge of the turtle's mythological role – as opposed to merely its scientifically decodable properties – in fact further contributes to unsettling his safely distanced relation to the space he assumes to be exploring and controlling: 'his view of the landscape changes from a mute and passive natural background into presence, sentience' (Byrne 2017: 973). Over the course of the story, the turtle becomes a symbolic focalizer of many of the concerns negotiated in the novel. As Karen Tei Yamashita puts it, Yanagihara 'captures here the idea of the turtle as a magical but also an inscrutable being upon whose back we climb hoping to find our destiny' (2018: 603). Determined to unravel the turtle's secret by scientific means, and prepared to disregard both the natives' mythological investment in the animals, and the precarious balance of the island's ecosystem, Norton is nevertheless sensitive to the affective charge and mutual recognition which characterize his encounter with one of the turtles:

> [T]he opa'ivu'ekes seemed to notice me … Their trust made my mission both easier and more difficult, and … I had to … remind myself of the necessity of what I was about to do … [The turtle] closed his yellow eyes as if in pleasure, as if I were petting him … Then it was time … A breeze licked its way between the trees, and as the opa'ivu'eke stretched his neck forward to partake in it, I flicked open the blade and brought it down on his neck. (Yanagihara 2013: 208, 209)

This moment, which is particularly disturbing for its juxtaposition of the moving encounter between turtle and human, and the brutal and calculated killing, exemplifies the ambiguous effect of Norton's disgusted and distanced colonial/scientific relation to the island. Although he continually experiences (and acknowledges) moments in which the porosity of the boundary that separates explorer from explored, colonizer from colonized, and subject from object of inquiry becomes porous, Norton opts, again and again, for keeping the boundary intact. Despite the fact that his own account makes room for an ontology which includes the possibility of non-human agency and human-non-human kinship, this kind of worldview repeatedly loses against the dominant narrative and self-image of the selfish, white, male explorer-scientist.

The ambiguous value of the blurring of the ontological and material boundaries between the human and the non-human becomes even more apparent in the novel's rendering of the mo'o kua'au, or 'dreamers', as the western explorers call them. These humans, having eaten the opa'ivu'eke's flesh, grow unusually old physically, while their minds and brains decay. In Norton's eyes, they are nothing more than scientifically intriguing specimen, whose kinship and ontological affinity with the non-human material world make them slightly disturbing to him, but also readily available as objects to be studied. In his first encounter with a mo'o kua'au woman, Norton only sees a 'thing on the floor', and uses the pronoun 'it' for the moving being, before recognizing a woman in her. It seems to him that 'she had once, long ago, been taught how to behave as a human and was slowly, steadily forgetting' (111). This 'forgetting' of recognizably human characteristics fundamentally unsettles the safety of the ontological paradigms upheld by Norton and the science he represents, because it signals an uncanny crossing of boundaries (between life and death, subject and object, human and non-human) and foregrounds the colonial and epistemological violence inflicted upon those that no longer count, or never have counted as part of the 'community of men'.

The mo'o kua'au are, in fact, doubly reduced by Norton's narrative authority: they are both exoticized and 'othered' by his supposedly disinterested colonial/scientific gaze, and framed as additionally disgusting because of the implication that they have regressed from a former status of humanity *back* to something else, thus inconveniently unsettling a narrative of human progress. Norton's most obvious attempt at fitting the mo'o kua'au into an ontological and epistemological (and imperial) framework he can process and control is his placing them, by means of language, outside of his own kinship group and in hierarchical relation to himself. He tries to make sense of the mo'o kua'au by associating them with non-human species and categories. He compares the woman's behaviour to that of a pig and a monkey, and likens her to a marionette which has to be given life from the outside (cf. 113). This process of ordering, however, inevitably fails, and the text repeatedly foregrounds Norton's association of the mo'o kua'au with the vibrant, leaking, and spilling natural world that so fascinates and disgusts him: '[t]hings clung to [the woman's hair]: chips of leaves and smears of dirt and fruit and shit; Tallent saw a hunono worm nestled in the hair above her vulva like an extraneous organ' (111).

By calling the mo'o kua'au 'dreamers', in effect giving them a non-native name, Norton and his fellow explorers establish a hierarchy which both explicitly marks the islanders as 'other' from the supposedly stable western subjects, and sets up a fantasy of dependence that completely ignores the native context in which these people exist: 'now that we named them as dreamers, now that we had cared for them, now that we considered them ours, something found and given meaning – it was somehow difficult to imagine them capable of living without us' (221). Here, too, the western explorers – and Norton's account in particular – replicate the 'benevolent' logic of the historical colonial narrative: as Pramod K. Nayar contends, 'the discourse of reform, rescue, native savagery, and Christian virtue constructed the contexts, justification, and ideological foundations for the moment of interventionist legislation, political decisions, and other colonial acts'

(2012: 161–2). By inscribing the 'dreamers' into a western epistemological framework, Norton and his colleagues construct their dependence on a narrative of hope for being 'saved'. Part of the colonial violence in Norton's account thus emerges from the imposition of a particular form of teleological temporality onto an environment and a people who had thus far existed outside such a logic. As Mindi McMann observes, '[r]eaders see, repeatedly, Norton's command of the island through language – through writing his memoir, and ... through his numerous acts of naming both the indigenous inhabitants and the children he later adopts and brings back to America' (2016: 101). The researchers establish this epistemological order despite their knowledge of the native term for the 'dreamers': mo'o kua'au, which translates as '"without throat." Although *kua'au* can also mean "friends" or "love." So, without friends, without love' (Yanagihara 2013: 95, emphasis in original). The U'ivuan name for the people who have eaten the flesh of the opa'ivu'eke thus evokes a much more complicated reality of the making and dissolution of bonds of kinship and structures of temporality. It also suggests a potential value of such an existence, which Norton's framing of the 'dreamers' as ill and degenerate could never account for. Beyond Norton's authorial and imperial account of the mo'o kua'au, which 'erases what constituted their central characteristic within U'iv[u]an society – that of withdrawal from the social structures of kinship, intimacy and companionship' (Zolkos 2020: 159) – this native understanding of their existence might very well allow for a different framing of the mo'o kua'au's dignity, value, and right to existence in forgetfulness and a state of dissolving structures of kinship.

Overall, the breakdown of the ontological distinctions human/animal, human/non-human, and animate/inanimate in Norton's account, while acknowledging the affective charge and impact of the vibrant material world, also becomes a means to reinforce colonial power-relations. As Magdalena Zolkos argues, 'the logic of appropriation "thingifies" the U'ivuan humans and non-humans, whereby they can be researched, commodified, rendered profitable, become recipients of humanitarian altruistic sentiments, and be subjected to violence' (2020: 158). However, although the colonial violence inflicted upon U'ivu does lead to big-scale destruction of the environment, the extinction of the opa'ivu'eke, and the destabilization of the island's practices of kinship and social life, the novel also gestures towards the limits of the human hubris embodied in Norton's account. Mindi McMann rightly observes that 'the island proves resistant to such violence, and ultimately, ... the opa-ivu'eke refuses to conform to Norton's narrative ... The turtle maintains its secret, and in refusing Norton's demands remains part of the "networks of intra-acting forces" that decenter the human and instead positions people as one of several material and discursive practices that converge to create meaning' (2016: 106, 107).

Imposing redemption: Narrative control and fascistic fascination

Where *The People in the Trees* establishes processes of colonial/scientific differentiation and narrativization, and the making, breaking, and maintaining of boundaries between those who count as kin and those who do not as a dominant theme in the story, it also foregrounds the fight over narrative control and the desire for teleological containment through its choice of perspective. By means of the construction of an extremely charismatic first-person voice which is, for the most part, our only entryway into the story and the events that unfold, the text lures its readers into following and identifying with this voice and its paranoid obsession with a teleological ordering of events. Norton's convictions and justifications, his judgements and psychopathic tendencies are hardly ever met by any check or foil. At the same time, however, the text manages to afford its readers indirect glimpses into different perspectives, and makes them aware that Norton's version of the story, his construction of a past, his evaluation of the present, and his place in a network of kinship characterized by abuse and violence, is not the only version. The novel thus makes explicit the power hierarchies reproduced by dominant narratives in general, and by the dominant narrative of neo-colonial science in particular.

Apart from a select few but very effective framing devices, the majority of the story is told by Norton himself, and the reading experience hinges upon a play with readerly fascination and scandalization. From the beginning, the text associates Norton's unwavering belief in his own greatness with futuristic projections of his own triumph at all cost: 'I was ... eager for a certain sort of greatness, the sort that seemed both possible and yet so distant' (Yanagihara 2013: 47). This fixation on personal success is less an open-ended expectation than an undoubting conviction akin to religious fanaticism, and it provides Norton and his narrative with a singular driving force. Its absolutist commitment to the telos of fulfilment emerges as the underlying reason for composing the compromised confessional account of his own life, for his increasing willingness to unlock the secret of eternal life, and for his supposedly benevolent but ultimately selfish and violent creation of a family through the adoption of a large number of children. The novel constructs Norton – through his own account – as an egomaniac and megalomaniac scientist-explorer, driven by his own desires and wishes: 'I wanted to write what I wanted, to answer what I wanted, to follow my every passion and curiosity' (240). He even comes to liken himself to a life-creating god: 'I had gone from being a pariah to being something of a god: I had become my own opa'ivu'eke, a creator of life and a granter of miracles, someone who had discovered something that made the impossible possible' (244).

Throughout his account of his own life, Norton repeatedly displays a cruel, unfeeling, and distant perspective on the human and more-than-human world surrounding him. Biological ties of filial kinship mean little to him. Instead, his mother's death from a bacterial infection only 'truly sparked [his] interest in disease' (27). Norton's decidedly clinical gaze remains a central theme throughout the novel, and it enables him to maintain the boundary between scientific subject and scientific object, and, more generally, between himself and the world around him. During his early days working with animals in a lab, he confesses that he 'rather enjoyed killing the mice' (54), and later, having brought back a group of mo'o kua'au to the United States, he remarks that they are 'not dissimilar to those dim white mice I had spent all those mornings killing: necessary, but not engaging in the least' (172). Since the narrative constructs Norton as mostly unempathetic, he becomes, as the novel's narrator, a particularly effective agent of the colonial/scientific project of separating the subject from the object of inquiry, and the imperialist explorer from any affinity with the colonized territory and its inhabitants. On one level, then, the novel foregrounds an accelerating logic of unfeeling, scientific/colonial violence inflicted in the expanding realms of Norton's influence. As Elanor Byrne puts it,

> Norton Perina's account of his lab exemplifies the island laboratory paradigm. The text is divided into three distinct areas that might be understood as three worlds where destruction can be unleashed: the life of the lab, the life of the island and the life in Perina's home in the United States, all of which Perina negotiates with a clinical, murderous and unsympathetic eye. (2017: 969)

While I generally agree with Byrne's analysis, I would argue that what makes the novel truly interesting, and Norton as its narrator so unescapably captivating is the fact that the novel itself complicates the straightforward progressive logic of ever increasing, unfeeling violence. Against the paranoid project of colonial objectification, the narrative pits reparative moments which show that Norton is indeed capable of being affected by his surroundings, of feeling intensely for other people, and even other non-human creatures, and of understanding, to an extent, his own role in the violent destruction of a society and ecosystem. It is thus not so easy, as Mindi McMann would have it, to conclude that Norton 'cannot show emotion or affection towards anyone or anything in the novel' (2016: 109). The text never allows the reader to fully distance themselves from its narrator as an unfeeling monster. Because of this very ambiguity, however, reparation, in this novel, emerges not primarily in the shape of real care and concern for others, but as painfully tied to the efficacy of the violent acts and narrative framings of a colonizing subject who is capable of seeing himself in others, but unwilling to draw moral conclusions from this that go beyond his own interest.

Most prominently in this respect, Norton's general lack of compassion with and of positive attachment to fellow beings stands in contrast to, on the one hand, sudden moments of pity for non-human animals, and, on the other hand, his intense homosocial attachment to his brother, and his curious homoerotic fascination with Paul Tallent. Having been offered a vuaka, a small monkey, for food in the jungle, Norton is haunted by the monkey's 'huge, sad eyes, ... and felt for a moment a despair so profound that [he] was momentarily unable to breathe' (Yanagihara 2013: 98). Similarly, upon witnessing the killing of a sloth in the village, he remembers its 'high, kittenish chirps that seemed to bother no one but [him]' (164). These rare moments of intense emotion, triggered by the suffering of another creature, serve as narrative disturbances in Norton's general self-fashioning as an unfeeling sociopath. They afford the reader the uncomfortable insight, offered throughout the novel by various different means, that the selfishness of male/white/colonial/scientific violence does not necessarily preclude the possibility of sentimental attachment; and, vice versa, that recognition of the self in the other as potential kin – as, for Norton, in the opa'ivu'eke, the vuaka, or the sloth – does not automatically undo structural power imbalances and individually and systemically inflicted violence.

Somehow even more unsettling, in this sense, are Norton's frequent references to his homosocial and homoerotic desires. Throughout his account, Norton's brother Owen remains one of his most important emotional anchors. At the same time, Norton's gradually explicit framing of his brother as openly gay, his own intense love for him, and his erotic, but never consumed desire for Tallent create a disturbing triangle of privileged homosocial desire between the novel's white men. At the same time, the text further aligns Norton's queer desires with his violation of the island's population. As Mindi McMann points out, '*The People in the Trees* presents a clear case of the interplay of sexual-colonial and environmental-scientific domination. Yanagihara demonstrates how white men often see these lands and their indigenous people as their own sexual, scientific, and mercantile playgrounds: places from which they can take what they want with no regard for the consequences' (2016: 94). The culmination of this nexus of sexual/colonial violence is Norton's paedophilic and potentially incestuous abuse and rape of his adopted children. The novel thus associates both an exclusively male, biological, filial relation (Norton and his brother), and the potentially queer kinship created through (homo)erotic desire (Norton and Tallent) with pain, betrayal, and (colonial) violence. Norton ultimately remains indifferent to the havoc his uncontrolled passions wreak. Insensitive both to his brother's siding with those who are not blood-kin (Norton's critics and the adopted child who finally accuses him of rape), and to the abused child's rage, he can only wonder at a dynamic that lies outside of his own understanding of the kind of loyalty he deems to deserve from those who are filial or adopted kin: '[m]y own brother, my twin, my constant, choosing a child over me. I could not fathom it, cannot fathom it still' (Yanagihara 2013: 344).

More generally, although, for the most part, Norton's memoir is a repelling account of blind and self-glorifying violence, Yanagihara enriches his narrative with rare but powerful moments of insight, in which he displays an acute awareness of his role in the island's destruction: 'we were the intruders, inserting ourselves rudely into a play in which we had no written part' (147). Ironically, Norton is in the process of writing this part for himself, a part which elevates him to protagonist, and grants him control of narrating the island's demise in his own terms and time. In consequence, the most extensive account of Norton's self-awareness provides only ambiguous reparation. Addressing his readers directly, thus drawing them into his own authorial present, and making them complicit in the knowledge he is about to divulge, he claims that '[y]ou know, we all know what happened next … [I]t is too difficult for me to make the story into what it ought to be: a saga in itself, a long death that spirals down slowly to the ground' (282). Norton thus frames the destruction of the island's indigenous ecology and culture as an inevitability already in the past, a telos that has been arrived at, and as a piece of common knowledge that cannot be changed, and can thus be narrated. His elegiac tone, while bearing witness to the destruction inflicted, simultaneously disavows the immediate impact of his own actions, and his continued participation, in the present, in perpetuating this violence. He displaces the violence temporally, turning it into a story (told in the past tense) that concerns neither him nor his assumed audience directly. As if to illustrate this point, what follows is a narrative enactment of this displacement through the invocation, in a decidedly archaic tone, of a long list of the island's exploitation, and, among other things, the opa'ivu'eke's extinction: '[s]hall I tell you …. Shall I tell you …. Shall I tell you …' (282–91).

While thus providing the reader with a very explicit account of the colonial violence that leads to the island's demise, Norton's first-person account can never become reparative in effect, because it remains trapped in his narrative attempt to free himself, in the act of telling, from any responsibility for the present and future he has created for the island. His 'archive of extinction' is thus fundamentally flawed and draws attention to 'the limits of the confessional mode, voicing a perpetrator whose account of his crimes discursively reproduces much of the violence to which he confesses' (Byrne 2017: 970). Although not altogether insensitive to the vibrancy of the world, Norton's evaluations and actions ultimately do not go beyond selfish justifications of harm and violence, inflicted by someone put in a powerful position through material, historical, and epistemological privilege. The narrative does allow for a few glimpses of self-consciousness, but these never lead to a full acknowledgement of Norton's destructive position in the web of things on the island and beyond: '[a]nd were it not for you, a small voice in my head said ..., the island would still be safe ... I did not go to destroy a people or a country ... Did I, however, end up doing so? It is not for me to decide. I did what any scientist would have done' (Yanagihara 2013: 274).

Yanagihara's choice of Norton as the only voice providing a substantial account of the events addressed in the novel forecloses any direct readerly access to the voices and opinions of other characters in the story. Although there are instances of direct speech on the part of, for example, Tallent or Esme Duff, the novel's focalization through an overt first-person narrator with an explicit agenda suggests that even instances of direct speech in this confessional report are filtered through Norton's memory and self-interest, heavily inflected by his homoerotic fascination with Tallent, and his misogynistic hate of Esme. Even more significantly, none of the instances of indigenous perspective that the novel has to offer emerge as direct, self-sufficient voices. Apart from being, like all other perspectives in the text, reported by Norton, indigenous knowledge and individual voices emerge, with the exception of a select few English-speaking guides and, later, the tragic dominance of English as the language of the colonizers on the island, as translations, reported and, we must assume, interpreted by Tallent and Norton. Although many of the conversations that involve indigenous characters appear in the text as if they were spoken in English, Norton himself repeatedly points out the necessity, both in the field and in his report, of translation (cf. 186). In effect, the textual erasure of self-sufficient indigenous voices from Norton's account, its reliance on translation, and Norton's explicit but belated realization of the culturally destructive consequences of the introduction of the English language to the island ('[Uva's] newly acquired English, and his pride in it ... made my skin prickle ..., and the enormity of the island's changes loomed large and clear in my mind' (277)) further foreground the epistemological and material power imbalance between colonizer and colonized that is one of the novel's most important themes. As Mindi McMann puts it,

> [w]hile the indigenous people in *The People in the Trees* do speak, ... their voices are often elided in the academic and imperial discourses of Norton, who ventriloquizes them. Norton writes the past – and the future – of U'ivu. In privileging Norton's authorial perspective in the novel, Yanagihara highlights the power of narrative and the systemic silencing of indigenous voices both in literature and in the environmental histories of their own countries. (2016: 97)

I agree that the novel's narrative foregrounding of the epistemological and cultural violence inflicted upon colonized populations contributes to the novel's evocation of an unfair struggle between the impossible (because not strategically future-oriented) hope of an indigenous people and ecosystem to continue to exist in the face of colonial intrusion and destruction, and the violently teleological creation of a profound material and cultural change by those in possession of the means to explore and exploit, and to tell the dominant narrative. At the same time, however, I would argue that even the novel's narrative positioning of Norton as all-dominating narrator leaves space for the reparative insight that, in the end, he cannot control the whole story. The island's foundation myth, for instance, even though filtered through Tallent's translation, has a profound and inadvertent effect on Norton. More generally, his confessional account remains checked by the overarching impact of the novel's very first pages, which, through the insertion of fictional newspaper articles, inform us of Norton's institutionally confirmed guilt of sexual abuse. However, and importantly, the novel at no point allows for the realization of the urgent hope – not futuristic, but fantastically projecting into the violently and irreparably changed past and present – that things might have turned out differently, that the story could have had a different ending, that the island's new and damaged present might just be an apocalyptic nightmare. Instead, and despite Norton's ultimate fall, the reader is left with the sobering realization that '[t]he triangulation of sexual abuse, exploitation of the people of U'ivu, and decimation of the environment are all sanctioned to varying degrees by larger economic and cultural locales, and more importantly, it continues to benefit Western interests' (McMann 2016: 110). That is, although the novel repeatedly foregrounds the ambiguous relational possibilities contained in Norton's reaction to the island's flora, fauna, and population, and although its first-person voice allows for reparative moments of mutual recognition, it ultimately confirms the historical efficacy of the paranoid colonial narrative which separates colonizing subject from colonized object, and which insists on violently imposing a teleological commitment to progress and modernity.

Framing colonial violence: Metafictional temporalities

Before turning to the way *The People in the Trees* negotiates the question of hope and temporality through the theme of immortality, I would like to briefly digress to discuss the novel's metafictional structure,[4] which further

---

[4] According to Patricia Waugh, 'metafiction is a term given to fictional writing which self-consciously and systematically draws attention to its status as an artefact in order to pose questions about the relationship between fiction and reality' (1984: 2). The more a narrative text foregrounds its own structure and strategies through metafictional elements, the more questions it asks about how we attempt to understand the world through narrative.

emphasizes its framing of colonial violence as epistemological violence. The metafictional elements serve to highlight the narrative work which allows Norton and his editor to enforce their paranoid politics of personal exculpation. In *The People in the Trees*, metafictional self-consciousness serves, in tandem with the use of narrative situation, to simultaneously perform and challenge the violent imposition of narrative authority on the novel's readers, and on its fictional objects of colonial and ecological exploitation.[5] The reader is forced to follow, witness, and emotionally experience the scandalous creation of Norton's self-righteous confessional account, its glorification and confirmation by his devoted editor Ronald Kubodera, and, more generally, the power of narrative control over the timing and pacing of omission and disclosure.

Norton's confessional account, including Ronald's editorial notes, preface, and postscript, is framed by only a few pages that do not form part of the two heavily inflected first-person narratives. Three short newspaper reports – two at the very beginning of the novel, and one between its 'official' ending and its epilogue – highlight the lack of heterodiegetic narration and diversity of perspective throughout the rest of the story. The articles' matter-of-fact tone both allows for an economical recounting of the most important events around which the story unfurls, and evokes a third, disinterested perspective: a public and readership that gets to judge and evaluate the two narrative voices. Significantly, the two pieces which begin the novel foreshadow the results of Norton's actions: his prison sentence for sexual abuse, and the fact that the opa'ivu'eke has gone extinct as a result of his research. This pre-empting of Norton's own confession further problematizes and delegitimizes his romantically charged elegy meant to redeem him from his implication in the violence inflicted on the island. At the same time, the newspaper pieces also quote several of Norton's apologists, who defend him as 'a prominent and highly respected member of the scientific community', 'an exemplary father and a brilliant mind', and 'a great mind and talent' (Yanagihara 2013: 3, 4). The reports thus also introduce the scientific community of (we can assume) men as a hegemonic apparatus of mutual defence and legitimation, and prepare the ground for Ronald's (and Norton's own) great apology, which emerges as a powerful act of narrative colonization, and as the projection of a possible future – through a dominant telling of the past – for one privileged individual at the cost of a whole civilization.

---

[5] Eleanor Byrne, in a similar line of argument, categorizes the novel as 'a form of postcolonial ecoGothic metafiction, [which] continually draw[s] attention to different narrative and discursive modes that contribute to (neo)colonial discourses that underpin the production of ecocidical dispassion, and an "anthropomyopic" vision that characterizes the US scientist who narrates the novel' (2017: 965).

Ronald's preface and epilogue, and his footnotes serve as a framing device which provides additional information about the events outside of the fictional space of Norton's own account, written in prison at Ronald's request. They add another layer to the grid of narration, power, and violence the novel sets up. The footnotes, in particular, also contribute to further destabilizing the reading experience: the 'combination of memoir and academic essay – the personal and the scholarly – undermines the reader's expectations of both genres' (McMann 2016: 93). At the same time, the scholarly pretence of Ronald's editorial effort serves to question the men's claim to legitimacy, since it quickly becomes clear that critical commentary is completely absent from the footnotes. Instead, they only add quasi-scientific noise, endless additions of fictional information, and references to external 'sources'. They increasingly emerge as distractions that halt the reading flow, and as insistent attempts to prevent the reader from judging Norton's actions. However, this excess of commentary also begs the reader to begin to question both Norton's own reliability, and Ronald's extreme bias. Ronald's own self-positioning within a dynamic of homosocial loyalty in his preface makes him as unreliable a narrator as Norton himself.[6] The more Norton's account shifts towards the apologetic, and the more his implication in the island's decline becomes explicit, the more Ronald's footnotes dominate the narrative as desperate attempts to redeem Norton's narrative. The most striking instance of this are Ronald's glosses of Norton's elegy ('Shall I tell you ...?'), in which he begins to give his own detailed account of the historical circumstances of the opa'ivu'eke's extinction and the mo'o kua'au's demise, taking over whole pages of the novel. This account renders yet another mode of temporality, one which frames the events of history in general, and a hegemonic scientific narrative in particular, unfortunate as they may be, as rational and inevitable, and in which the perpetrators – in this case Norton – are relieved of direct responsibility:

> This, however, is the story of science. A man discovers something. He doesn't know what it is or what it might solve ... To be a scientist is to learn to live all one's life with questions that will never be answered, with the knowledge that one was too early or too late ... The fact remains: Norton did as much as he could for the dreamers for as long as he could. He did far more than he was ethically or legally required to do for them. (Yanagihara 2013: 283, 284, 288)

---

[6] In the preface, Ronald defines his relationship to Norton as follows: 'I am proud ... of the fact that after establishing a relationship as colleagues, we began an equally intense one as friends' (Yanagihara 2013: 5). Over the course of the novel, Norton's own account qualifies this claim since he never once even mentions Ronald.

The footnotes, then, reproduce the homosocial network of colonial privilege and desire which also emerges in Norton's account itself. They serve to highlight the role the discourse of science plays in the marginalization and silencing both of the objects and victims of science, and of those voices that might tell a different story. Esme, for instance, who, in Norton's account, features mainly as a trigger of his disgust at all things female, literally gets pushed to the margins/footnotes in the novel's dominant reports of events and causality: Ronald, annotating Norton's account of the a'ina'ina ceremony, the ritual rape of boys on Ivu'ivu, dismisses her published study of the island's culture as 'a fairly sentimental memoir' (170), while admitting that she does not mention the a'ina'ina, and that her report diverges from Norton's in several other points. While thus serving as a further attack on a female voice which disrupts the smooth construction of Norton and Ronald's dominant narrative of teleological necessity, the novel here also offers a very rare reparative glimpse into a different perspective, one which explicitly delegitimizes Norton's voice, and positions him as aggressor: 'Perina would prove almost singlehandedly to be the source of the island's undoing ... [H]e was, in my opinion, always more interested in achieving personal immortality, no matter the cost to the people he had to exploit in order to do so' (170).

Throughout the novel, the footnotes both highlight and deconstruct the power of hegemonic discourse to determine who is heard, who gets to free themselves from responsibility, and who is excluded from the right to speak, and from the right to go on living. The novel achieves this effect by making visible both the rhetorics and the politics of exclusion. The most striking instance of this is Ronald's decision to edit a piece out of Norton's narrative, in which he admits to having raped one of his adoptive sons. Within Norton's report itself, the omission of this episode is tucked away in an inconspicuous footnote of Ronald's: '[t]here is a section following this that I have, as an editor, elected to excise' (339). It is only after the end of Norton's report, and after Ronald's own epilogue, in which he invokes something of a homosocial fugitive utopia for Norton and himself ('We are happy here, the two of us' (351)), that the story's self-appointed curator decides to provide his readers with the censored part. Dismissing it as 'a curious little footnote' (353), and downplaying Norton's violent actions as acts of love, the novel nevertheless ends with Norton's account of his rape of Vi.

Structurally, *The People in the Trees* thus productively disturbs its protagonists' attempts at being in control of their own story, at erasing voices of dissent, and at providing one linear account the telos of which must be Norton's absolution at all costs. Instead, the novel's metafictional structure fragments and halts the reading experience and forces the reader to question its narrators' pursuit of a bearable past and a utopian future for themselves at the price of silencing, wounding, and killing those outside of their narrow network of privileged homosocial relations.

An end without end: In pursuit of immortality

In *The Interview Magazine*, Yanagihara and Adam Leith Gollner[7] discuss *The People in the Trees* and their shared fascination with the science of and the human belief in immortality. Yanagihara, evoking Frank Kermode's famous *Sense of an Ending*, emphasizes that, to her, both life and literature only acquire meaning through the prospect of life's definite end: '[o]ne of the reasons that life is bearable is because it's going to end soon. One of the main concerns of fiction is how do we make a life of 85 years or so meaningful' (Gollner 2013). In *The People in the Trees*, the pursuit of immortality emerges as yet another ambiguous point of reference: it is both that which cheats life of its final telos and meaning, and that which itself becomes the telos which drives Norton (and others) into an increasingly violent and destructive obsession. His yearning for eternal life becomes the driving force behind his scientific endeavours, his creation of an unusually large adoptive family, and, finally, his self-glorification in the telling of his own story. In the novel, the tension between death and eternal life is embedded in a general concern with the ambiguity of time and temporality, and, ultimately, the question where and when hope can be found.

For Norton, his attempts to unlock the opa'ivu'eke's secret to eternal life are explicitly tied to the possibility of actual, physical immortality. His obsession has, however, further temporal implications. It also caters to Norton's need to know, in the present, that he has secured for himself, as an exceptional human being, a place of god-like fame in a future yet to come, a future fantastically extending far beyond his own physical existence: 'I ... could not help but project my thoughts into the future, for I knew with certainty that I had found something spectacular, something bound to change science and society forever. I had found nothing less than immortality itself' (Yanagihara 2013: 215). Norton's whole worldview, and his perception of his own place and destiny in it, hinges upon a paranoid conception of scientific progress, and on an individualistic notion of heroic self-inscription into the annals of fame and history which, for him, determine the meaning and value of human existence.

While *The People in the Trees* is thus, on one level, a detailed exploration of the violence and damage a worldview like Norton's can inflict if found in those in positions of structural privilege and power, the novel also provides a multitude of reparative foils to its protagonist's notion of temporality and

---

[7]In 2013, Gollner published *The Book of Immortality: The Science, Belief, and Magic Behind Living Forever*, in which he explores the human obsession with immortality in different religions, contemporary occult practices, and scientific endeavours.

individualism. Throughout Norton's account of his visits to the island of Ivu'ivu, linear, colonial time gets interrupted and disturbed, and time itself seems to take on an agency of its own: '[t]ime then seemed to yank into a long, zinging string, vibrating with a terrible, indiscernible significance as if it were itself alive, a witness to what I might do next' (125). Despite his fundamental reliance on the workings of western time and history, Norton admits to feeling the lure of this alternative temporality:[8] when his first stay on Ivu'ivu approaches its end, he admits to 'the shock of time itself, its sudden reappearance and relevance in our lives. Here, time twirled itself into long, spiralling whorls, defying biology and evolution ... And yet the definition of time we had to obey was the one determined in parts of the world where people consulted clocks and made and kept appointments' (213). Once again, as in the context of his disgust at the jungle, Norton's perspective oscillates ambiguously between a fascination with and interest in what he encounters, and an exoticization of and distancing from these very same things. Throughout, the novel allows Norton moments of being genuinely affected, while ultimately having him stick with what makes his character coherent: his ultimate faith in the powers of individuality and teleology.

Culturally, too, the society Norton and his colleagues encounter seems to exist more or less outside and independent of a western notion of history. For instance, it does not draw social meaning from recorded events or individual actions: 'there were very few recorded events on Ivu'ivu: they had here no notion of the king, no notion of time, no notion of history' (141). What emerges as most strange and 'other' to the team of scientists studying the Ivu'ivuans is their firm embeddedness in the present. This temporal orientation manifests itself, for example, in their own ostracizing of the mo'o kua'au, those individuals who have eaten the opa'ivu'eke's flesh, and have begun their decent into mental decay. To a significant extent, their outsider status is framed as the result of their loss of a grasp on the present and on their social connections within and beyond it, while physically, they continue into an indeterminate future. Similar to his belated realization of the destructive consequences of his actions for the island's ecosystem, Norton very aptly analyses the cultural implications of the arrival, with the armies of scholars, investors, and pharmaceutical companies, of colonial, western time to the island:

---

[8]Interestingly, it is Tallent – the character generally most associated with a 'genuine' interest in Ivu'ivuan culture, and the one who later, in fact, literally disappears from the story altogether – who proves to be most attached to western temporality during his time on Ivu'ivu: 'I was impressed that Tallent had all along been keeping track of time; he even produced from his rucksack a small calendar, and seeing the days ticked off by a pencil mark made our stay on the island feel somehow both longer and more real' (Yanagihara 2013: 221). One angle on this is that Tallent, as opposed to Norton, does not unquestioningly immerse himself in an exoticizing acceptance of another aspect of the 'foreign' and 'tropical'.

It was an island of waiters, where once waiting had been a foreign concept. This had never been a culture obsessed with the past, and why should it have been? Nothing ever changed. But now that everything had, all its inhabitants could think about was what they had lost. And so they remained frozen in their vigilance, toggling between hope and despair, waiting for their world to be restored. (294)

Like the survivors of the cataclysms that are a defining element of post-apocalyptic fiction, the Ivu'ivuans become witnesses to a loss they cannot process, eternally attached, with painful nostalgia, to a bygone past. Their only remaining hope is the restoration of that which can never come back. In effect, they are forced to adopt a paranoid relation to temporality and unlearn – as victims of colonial violence – the potential for reparation and healing in the present. The novel's painful irony is that it is Norton himself who voices these insights. And the fact that he is capable of them makes his inability to unlearn his own paranoid attachment to a narrative of innocence and inevitability even more apparent.

Another affinity with post-apocalyptic fiction to be found in *The People in the Trees* – and another one which foregrounds questions of temporality and belonging – is the inclusion of the zombie-like mo'o kua'au. Even before the team's 'discovery' of these undying people, Norton notices the absence of death itself on the island: 'I had not witnessed a death the entire time I had been in the village' (223). Norton's evaluation of the consequences of eating the opa'ivu'eke's flesh – in contrast to the natives' own take on things – clearly positions the resulting mental decay within an almost theological framework of divine punishment for tasting a forbidden fruit: 'I had already proven that the opa'ivu'eke could prolong life; now I had to discover how it might do so without delivering in tandem its terrible punishment' (242). To Norton, the mo'o kua'au are disturbing because, like the zombie, they walk the 'uncanny valley' between life and death. They defy familiar notions about a human lifespan and the temporal relation of an individual to history. Realizing that one of the mo'o kua'au must be 176 years old, Norton's first reaction is denial: '"[h]e can't be," I protested, the panic rising up, nearly choking me' (143). Although the pursuit of immortality lies at the heart of Norton's endeavours, his encounter with a people who actually lack the telos of physical decay is disturbing to him, because what the mo'o kua'au lose in the process is their individuality and their memory. They become, in effect, creatures of pure present-ness: 'it was a parody of immortality … Bit by bit, [their mind] disintegrated – first the memory, then the social nuances, then the senses, and then finally speech – until all that was left was the body … Surely there must be an end to this life, for there is an end to every life' (202, 203).

Like the zombies in *The Walking Dead*, the mo'o kua'au are suspended between the human and the no-longer-human, and they evoke the human obsession with individualism and immortal fame that is Norton's main driving force. For although he claims that '[t]here is a point – for me, it arrived perhaps a few years ago – when, without even realizing it, you switch over from craving more life to being resigned to its end' (203), his science, the adoption of his children, and his confessional report all bear witness to his desire to leave behind a mark, one not characterized by real care and concern for his human and non-human surroundings, but by the megalomaniac belief in his own genius and innocence. Strikingly, Norton explicitly frames the destruction that the scientists ultimately bring to the islands in temporal terms, as 'just another Micronesian ruin, once so full of hope' (289), and as the advent of endings: '[y]ou know, we all know what happened next. There were endings, but none of them were happy ... [I]t is too difficult for me to make the story into what it ought to be: a saga itself, a long death that spirals down slowly to the ground' (282). Colonial time here becomes apocalyptic time, but the end has already come, while Norton, as post-apocalyptic witness and prophet, positions himself outside of the framework of responsibility, writing himself out of the story.

In the end, the novel's most powerful image of the ambiguous and unknowable hope for an eternal present is the turtle: '[t]hey will let you live forever. Like they promised' (178). In *The People in the Trees*, this mythological promise emerges as a hope which can be misappropriated if understood as a mere resource for individual fulfilment at the cost of care for the network of vibrant things that share this world. Yanagihara herself foregrounds the turtle's mystery and vulnerability, and its non-human relation to temporality and teleology when explaining her reasons for choosing this animal as the novel's central image: '[t]hey're so self-possessed and self-contained and there's something wise and mysterious about them. I also like that they are prehistoric animals. They live for a tremendously long time, they keep their counsel, and they haven't really developed evolutionarily at all in the past couple thousand years. They're such gentle animals too, and I thought that added a pathos' (Gollner 2013). The novel repeatedly associates the opa'ivu'eke's exposure and ultimate extinction with concrete environmental damage inflicted by selfish acts of scientific curiosity and colonial violence, and, through the turtle's explicit mythological charge, with the epistemological and ontological devastation of Christian Revelation, defamiliarized through its embeddedness in local belief. When the three U'ivuan guides accompanying Norton, Tallent, and Esme to Ivi'ivu see an opa'ivu'eke for the first time, Norton realizes why this encounter distresses them so much, foreshadowing, in his own report, the destruction that will unfold: 'gods are for stories and heavens and other realms; they are not to be seen by men. But when we encroach on their world, when we see what we are not meant to see, how can anything but disaster follow' (Yanagihara 2013: 104).

Paranoid adoption: Children, time, and colonialism

In many ways, then, *The People in the Trees* presents the damaging impact of the paranoid narrative of colonial violence, which pits the self-exculpation of the individual, white, male explorer-subject against the survival of an indigenous ecosystem, culture, and (human and non-human) network of kinship. Reparation, understood as a deviation from the single story, as the possibility of sideway glances at and from perspectives outside the dominant one, and as a real acknowledgement of pain, suffering, and the entanglement of everything and everyone in complex networks of relationality, only ever emerges, in the novel, in indirect, roundabout ways. Yanagihara constructs Norton's account and his narrative voice so that it allows for a high level of insight into the dynamics of his own and others' destructive actions, while never leading to any real acknowledgement of responsibility. Tallent, too, becomes one of the voices that get to speak the truth of the imminent change which the arrival of colonial time and scientific exploitation will bring to the island as a result of Norton's discovery of the opa'ivu'eke's role in the mo'o kua'au's extended lifespan: 'it's over for them ... [E]very pharmaceutical company is going to go over there and try to capture those turtles. Not to mention every anthropologist and every botanist, herpetologist, you name it. Ivu'ivu as we know it is over' (Yanagihara 2013: 246). None of these insights, however, gets to unfold its reparative potential within the confines of Norton's report: he always manages to integrate each in the toxic logic of his own story, the single telos of which remains his own moral absolution.

Norton's refusal to embrace his own role in the complex network of neo-colonial relations, and the destructive ripples his own actions send through the material and affective world becomes most obvious in his adoption of over forty children from U'ivu, and his subsequent sexual abuse of some of them. His account of these adoptions fits seamlessly into his overarching narrative of teleological progression towards lasting fame and importance. His successive acquisition of non-biological offspring reads as a story of addiction, of a compulsive drive towards an ever-greater progeny he can shape according to his wishes. Strikingly, Norton's retelling of how he got to adopt the children runs parallel in phrasing to his elegiac account of the island's destruction:

> Shall I tell you how Muiva was my first child ... Shall I tell you ... that I began to want to repeat it again and again? Shall I tell you of how I began to adopt other children ... Shall I tell you how with each new child I acquired, I would irrationally think, *This is the one. This is the one who will make me happy. This is the one who will complete my life. This is the one who will repay me for years of looking.* (290, 291, emphasis in original)

Norton's quest to finding the 'perfect' child thus mirrors and reproduces his scientific and colonial quest to finding immortality and fame in the exoticized ecosystem of U'ivu: 'part of his disillusionment with parenting, combined with a compulsion to undertake more adoptions, follow from the failure to realize his fantasy of an encounter with an idealized native child – pure, uncivilized, and innocent' (Zolkos 2020: 154). The children, like Norton's science and his will to fame, both serve his need to endlessly push his own story towards some unreachable goal and represent the phantasmic telos itself: the revelation of his life, the fulfilment of his paranoid race towards the future. Unable to escape this paranoid logic, Norton is nevertheless able to question the meaning of his compulsively apocalyptic creation of offspring: 'I began to wonder seriously whether I had something of a tic … Why was I incapable of stopping? What was I hoping each new one might provide me that the previous thirty-odd had not? What was it that I wanted?' (Yanagihara 2013: 310). Taking the children out of their native environment – the destruction of which Norton contributed to – and claiming to benevolently give them a new and better life in America reproduces the structures of inequality inscribed in their own and his body to begin with, and emerges as an obsessive extension of his pursuit of eternal life though the ultimately selfish acquisition of non-biological offspring. At the same time, Norton appropriates a stance of cultural and moral relativism in order to enable an exoticizing and idealizing perspective on the ritual raping of boys which he witnesses on Ivu'ivu, and to justify his own sexual desire for some of his adopted children: 'I did not feel it was my position to pass judgement on the ritual … [I]t made me rethink certain assumptions I'd always had about childhood, and sex in general, and how there was no single correct attitude to either … [M]y time on Ivu'ivu taught me that all ethics or morals are culturally relative' (171). In the context of this book's argument, this rhetorical move is particularly striking for its perversion of the reparative potential implied in making kin. Norton here attempts to excuse his own actions by seemingly occupying a 'reparative' position which acknowledges the ambiguity of morality and ethics. He invokes a radical epistemological openness that exoticizes a non-western culture as 'innocent' in order to frame 'western' sexual morals as paranoid. Norton's privileged position in the novel's fictional world, however, exposes his argument as a convenient pose, since it obscures the workings of the power hierarchies inherent in the relationship between Norton and the islanders, between adults and children, and between Norton and his adopted offspring. His invocation of cultural relativism, precisely because it is put to work in the name of the preservation of sexual/colonial power, only serves to legitimize Norton's paranoid claim to truth and innocence. It becomes reparative only in the sense of guaranteeing coherence to his own worldview, while reproducing the structures of domination ingrained in his role as colonial explorer and exploiter: 'Norton views the people of Ivu'ivu as a means to satisfy his own curiosity – intellectual in the case of the turtle, sexual in the case of the Ivu'ivuans. Sex is an integral element of colonialism and a key tool of imperial oppression' (McMann 2016: 102).

The only character who opposes Norton's dominant narrative and his practice of colonial kin making is Vi, who, by refusing the name given to him by Norton, 'hold[s] the mirror back onto the colonizer' (Zolkos 2020: 164). In the end, the one place from which the novel's potential for resistance emerges is arguably Vi's 'personification of anti-colonial politics of resistance, and [his] disruption of [Norton's] fascistic desires for colonial appropriation' (165). Norton's fight with and rape of Vi foregrounds how the white colonizer-subject exerts power by attempting to determine the ontological status of the colonized 'other'. From the start, Norton doubts Vi's humanity, and explicates a worldview in which good and evil are irrelevant categories which fade away behind the colonial effort of turning 'savages' into 'humans'. Norton enacts colonial violence through language by reducing Vi to a 'little beast', a 'wretched monster', a 'beastly insect', and, finally, a 'thing', a 'nothing': '[y]ou are nothing. I gave you meaning. I gave you a life' (Yanagihara 2013: 337). Once again, the act of 'thingification' serves to implement the colonizer's power to grant and take away an ontological status that warrants morally considerate treatment, and the fundamental difference between those who count as human (and thus valuable) and those who do not.

The novel's biggest scandal, which finally shatters the reader's trust in the possibility of ultimate decolonial resistance, is its ending. Although Norton is sent to prison on charges of child abuse, the novel's metafictional structure provides a moment of strategic suspense when Ronald introduces the footnote indicating an omission, which is only revealed at the very end of the book. In it, the reader witnesses Norton's rape of Vi, which Norton describes as accompanied by feelings of both joy and anger, and which he frames as an act of love and personal bodily cleansing:

> I wondered if [Victor] felt as I did, as if my very insides were being scooped out and held aloft, the harsh, cold wind rushing through the cavity of my poor, filthy body, cleansing it and carrying away its impurities, scattering them to the night air … [I whispered] that I would punish him, that I would break him, that I would force him to behave. And then … I would find myself uttering words of love and longing and making him promises I had never made before … Later, when he accused me, I was shocked. For I loved him, you see, loved him despite everything. (361)

In Norton's framing of the rape, he reiterates the tension between repulsion and libidinal commitment that also characterizes his disgusted reactions to the island's flora and fauna. Through his violent transgression, Norton thus once again attempts to stabilize the porous boundaries between colonial subject and colonized object, and to confirm his authority over the teleological narrative of his own life. Vi, however, not only epitomizes the novel's many child characters who suffer the physical and mental consequences of sexual/colonial violence, but he is also the only character and the only voice that speaks back. His resistance to Norton's attempts at imposing a name on him, his renitent desire to narrate his own story, and, finally, his public accusation of Norton become the novel's strongest reparative motif.

The People in the Trees, then, emerges as a complicated and painful conglomeration of ontologies and epistemologies that acknowledges the potential kinship of all things and the unpredictability of agency in an intricately entangled network of human and non-human networks. At the same time, the novel foregrounds, by means of narrative voice and the deployment of metafictional structure, the violence and harm inherent in the ongoing reality of neo-colonial relations, and the unequal distribution of agency in a context determined by histories of exploitation and privilege. Most importantly, it invokes the awful effectiveness of a paranoid narrative which aims to exclude and destroy the voices that could tell a different story, and which lose their livelihood in the name of individuals and institutions that profit from the paranoid preservation of the status quo of post- and neo-colonial power relations. Read in this light, *The People in the Trees* enables an understanding of reparation as a project that needs to be in conversation with decolonial thinking and politics, with anti-teleological temporalities, and with critical epistemologies and ontologies which unsettle the paranoid logic of colonial time and paranoid futurism.

6

Beyond repair: Friendship and the end of hope in *A Little Life*

There is probably hardly another novel published in recent years that has provoked such heated debate and such wildly diverging critical responses as Hanya Yanagihara's *A Little Life* (2015). While Garth Greenwell, reviewing the book for *The Atlantic*, hails it as 'the most ambitious chronicle of the social and emotional lives of gay men to have emerged for many years' (2015), other critics denounce Yanagihara's melodramatic prose and lack of realism. Brigid Delaney, in *The Guardian*, perplexedly confesses to her own obsession with the book, despite the fact that its 'prose is a little patchy and the plot is at times almost operatic in its hysteria' (2016). It seems that it is precisely Yanagihara's employment of melodrama and a 'hysterical' writing style that contribute significantly to the novel's impact on its readers. A hybrid of the 'high-brow' contemporary American novel in the tradition of Donna Tartt and Jonathan Franzen, and of a seemingly outdated sensationalism reminiscent of nineteenth-century genre fiction, the novel certainly strikes a chord in its readership: people either intensely idolize the book, or outright refuse to finish it. *A Little Life*, then, sits uncomfortably among its fellow twenty-first-century American novels. To some critics, it seems, in style and effect, to belong to a different decade and literary tradition altogether. As Alex Preston puts it, '[i]t is a serious book, taking itself seriously in what seems to me a very American, very 90s manner' (2015). Stacy Gillis points out how it clearly inscribes itself into traditions 'of the Bildungsroman, of the fairy tale, and of the gothic' (2015). At the same time, as John Powers observes, the novel's greatest provocation, which makes it an intriguing case study for this book's line of argument, might well be its firm and consistent refusal of redemptive hope, and, as such, of one of the tenets of US-American culture: 'America is hooked on stories of redemption and rebirth ... We just love tales about healing' (2015). This is, however, exactly the kind of story *A Little Life* refuses to tell, leading, for many readers, to a strongly emotional and conflicted reading experience, which E. Alex Jung goes so far as to call 'masochistic' (2018).¹

The impassioned critical responses the novel has provoked indicate that something fundamental is at stake here, both in terms of the book's themes, and in terms of its effects. *A Little Life* is concerned with the dynamics of male friendship and love in contemporary US-American, upper-middle-class, urban culture, with the individual and social effects of trauma and pain, and, most importantly, with the possibility of things not getting better, not being made right again. Its damaged protagonist 'demands that we ask whether life is always worth living, whether some wounds are so deep as to be unrepairable' (Kidd 2015). The story follows four male friends living in New York City – Jude, Willem, JB, and Malcom – roughly from their time as college freshmen until their fifties. Jude is the novel's enigmatic central character, who is traumatized, physically disabled, and seemingly unknowable. The reader witnesses Jude's struggle with life and his success as a corporate litigator, and is presented with memories from his childhood, in which he was abused by several men. All four protagonists, in different ways, embody a teleology of success paradigmatically condensed in the national ethos of the 'American Dream'. Yet, on a different level, the novel also tells a story that has no future, a story beyond the hope for improvement – and this denial of things necessarily getting better in favour of focusing on an ethics of care is, I argue, where the novel's reparative potential lies.

In light of its thematic negotiations of questions of belonging and temporality, and its prominent place in and impact on both literary debate and wider popular culture, I want to engage with *A Little Life* as something of a culmination point of the concerns I have been tracing throughout this book. Hope and kinship, in this novel, emerge as traumatic wounds of contemporary US-American culture. The heterosexual, reproductive, and economically productive family unit implicitly remains a privileged reference point but is largely absent from the text. It gets replaced by a world of male-homosocial relations which, on the one hand, reproduces the paranoid register of (male) prosperity and success which still permeates contemporary US culture; it also, however, allows for fluid notions of male-homosocial care, love, and desire that emerge as a reparative foil to the persistent widespread dominance of masculinist ideology and homophobia. In this story, which, despite its strong subtext of Christian eschatology, ultimately negates the satisfaction of healing and redemption, hope, once

---

¹Joseph R. Worthen critically addresses the extremely emotional reception of the novel as paradigmatic of a contemporary tendency to consider literature 'empathy training' (2020: 58). The quality of a novel is judged on the basis of its ability to evoke strong emotional reactions in the reader: '[i]n effect, these readers are rating their own emotional responses instead of the production of the text which informs them' (61).

again, appears as a turning-away from the prescriptive logic of naïve optimism, and towards both the acknowledgement of enduring pain and the reparative potential of care, even and especially when there might be no brighter future on the horizon.

I will begin my analysis of the book by considering its treatment of temporality and knowledge, and how a-historicity contributes to its overall effect, arguing that the novel's narrative gaps and absences – of the HIV/AIDS crisis, 9/11, and (largely) historically situated homophobia and racism – produce a heightened awareness of these missing histories, and a nostalgic commitment to wilful ignorance. I will then consider the role of queer forms of friendship, love, and care, and how these intersect with privilege and the narrative logic of individual success, arguing that the novel's modes of kin-making rely on the erasure of economic hardship and the realities of oppression. Finally, I will move towards thinking about how trauma and physical pain, in *A Little Life*, structure the logic of the protagonists' relation to temporality and teleology, opting for a social and structural approach to trauma over the pathologizing logic of psychiatric diagnosis. Hope, I contend, emerges, in the novel, as a queer affect that relies on the registers of melodrama, the fairy tale, and camp sentimentality in order to sidestep political sincerity. Through affective excess, it opens up a reparative potential which explodes the confines of realist fiction, and reverberates with queer fantasies of pain, care, and post-identity that must sit uncomfortably and provokingly within the actual historical realities and traumas which still shape contemporary US culture.

Time, narrative, and knowledge

A Little Life stands in a peculiar relation to time and temporality. The narrative situation is fairly conventional: a heterodiegetic linear narrative alternating between the four friends' perspectives while increasingly privileging Jude and Willem's point of view is interspersed with flashbacks to Jude's childhood and adolescence, and with first-person accounts by Harold, Jude's mentor and adoptive father, from some unspecified future that foreshadow Jude and Willem's ultimate death (cf. Cummins 2015). What is more striking is the story's relation to history, which does not mirror the progressive linearity of its characters' lives. Set in New York City in some unspecified present over the course of several decades, 'the novel is stridently ahistorical[,] … set in a perpetual almost-now' (Preston 2015), and none of the specificities of recent US history in general and New York in particular find their way into the novel's fictional world. Most prominently, although its characters most likely must be passing the turn of the millennium at some point, 9/11 never occurs. Other, more stretched-out histories feature in an indirect and allusive fashion: state-sanctioned oppression of queer people, for example, is, in one off-hand dialogue, relegated to the past (cf. Yanagihara 2015: 533), and even identity politics as such are vaguely framed as belonging to bygone times (cf. 585).

The absence of historical context is so peculiar as to inevitably provoke irritation, and almost all critics of the book have remarked upon and contemplated this oddity.[2] One effect of these historical ellipses is that they infuse the story with a certain timelessness which places it in a liminal position between the specificities of realist fiction and the generalizing tendencies of fairy tales,[3] and it also manifests in what Scott Herring calls the novel's 'characterological nondevelopment' (2021: 139). As Mariam Digges points out, this fairy-tale quality, which is further enforced by Jude's unlikely path of unending suffering, provokes readers to expect the satisfactions of the teleological script of 'happily-ever-after', a paranoid wish whose fulfilment the book manages to deny again and again, making room for thinking about what, in the absence of a happy ending, can provide characters and readers with reparative sustenance (cf. 2016). Yanagihara herself admits to her fascination with the 'stubborn lack of redemption' in fairy tales, fables, and folk tales, and confirms her intention, in this text, 'to meld the psychological specificity of a naturalistic contemporary novel with the suspended-time quality of a fable' (Kavanagh 2015). Where the post-apocalyptic stories discussed earlier in this book use the temporal suspension of an imagined global cataclysm to make room for fictional renegotiations of structures of belonging, Yanagihara employs the ahistorical register of the fairy tale to create a fictional world that feels familiar enough to the contemporary reader to be able to directly relate to its concerns, but also generalized enough to depart from the realities of its actual, historically stratified setting. This strategy enables the novel to imbue its concern with male friendship and love with a utopian quality, without ever losing touch with the violent histories of racism and homophobia which remain the story's unspoken foil.

The narrative's play with historical gaps and silences is mirrored and enriched by a similar concern with knowledge and ignorance about the past in both the novel's characterization of its protagonist Jude and its use of flashbacks. In many ways, paranoid epistemologies structure much of the reading experience of *A Little Life*. Most strikingly, although the novel is

---

[2]Sara Baume, for example, compliments the novel's 'dismissal of history', its lack of female characters, and its 'superabundance of gay men' as a bold move in contemporary fiction, which makes the book, she argues, 'strangely timely in its timelessness' (2015); and Sean McCann reads the novel's a-historicity as symptomatic of its characters' insular concern with only themselves and their small circle of wealthy and privileged friends and acquaintances (cf. 2016).
[3]The novel itself repeatedly frames its characters' lives and development in terms of their narrative affinity with the conventions of the fairy tale (cf. Yanagihara 2015: 99, 146, 565).

clear about Jude's desperate unwillingness to share his past experiences – the physical and sexual abuse that caused his trauma – with anyone, the reader is forced to witness these events in flashbacks scattered throughout the story. The reader becomes a voyeur, and complicit in finding out the secrets Jude, paranoid and traumatized, means to keep hidden. In Jude, the novel presents a character that complicates any easy answer to the question whether knowledge or ignorance might be the more reparative practice. At an early point in the novel, JB expresses the friends' fundamental lack of knowledge about Jude: 'we never see him with anyone, we don't know what race he is, we don't know anything about him. Post-sexual, post-racial, post-identity, post-past ... The post-man. Jude the Postman' (Yanagihara 2015: 107). While this passage, on the one hand, ironically evokes the kind of post-identitarian politics the novel idealizes in its refusal to treat sexuality and race as associated with personal struggle or discrimination,[4] it also foregrounds Jude's undeterminable past and origin as an ambiguous blank space that becomes the site of a struggle over who has the authority to know, tell, and own his past. Much of Jude's narrative energy is spent managing knowledge about him, which, as we will see later, becomes intimately bound to and inscribed in his body.

From his early childhood in a Catholic monastery, the physical and psychological violence done to Jude is associated with other people's control over his relation to his own past, present, and future. One of the brothers, when asked by Jude about his origins, authoritatively binds him to his dependent situation by denying him reliable access to his origins: '[y]ou came, and you're here now, and you should concentrate on your future, and not on the past' (165). This lack of access to his own past and origins becomes, for Jude, both debilitating and his life's (and the novel's) main obsession. While, as a child, he comes to believe that he cannot find kinship in an adoptive family because '[t]here were simply too many unknowns' (166), control over the knowledge of his violent childhood and adolescence also becomes his means of creating an identity for himself which he believes guarantees that he will not be rejected by his friends. As such, Jude's enigmatic nature and unknown background work in two directions. On the one hand, forgetting and denial serve Jude as a reparative form of dealing with his trauma, and the novel matches Jude's lack of family with an almost unlikely array of reparative practices of making kin, being friends, getting adopted, and being loved. On the other hand, Jude's secretive nature is also a trigger for his friends' – and the reader's – paranoid curiosity.

---

[4] Alex Preston fittingly calls the novel's setting 'a kind of utopia of alterity where, at least in hipster New York, everyone is a minority – usually several minorities at once – and revels in his (and it is almost always his – Yanagihara often seems like the only woman involved) otherness' (2015).

Race, in particular, becomes a conflicted reference point that exemplifies the way in which, in *A Little Life*, access to individual and collective pasts becomes traumatically fragmented. The novel calls for an ethical consideration of who gets to know and tell a past, and what is at stake in witnessing such telling. Read in the wider context of US-American history, Jude's lack of biological kin and the detailed accounts of his frequent abuse, understood as not separate but related issues, become uncomfortable reminders of the violence done to Black slaves in the past, and of the ongoing violence against people of colour in the present, especially in a novel in which, as Janet Maslin puts it, 'race becomes a nonissue' (2015). In the text itself, race is only ever explicitly referred to as one of the mysteries that make up Jude's identity (cf. Yanagihara 2015: 7, 68, 139), or, self-deprecatingly, in pseudo-serious debates between JB and Malcom – both characters of colour – about their respective lack of commitment to the cause of Black collective and individual identity (cf. 10, 67). Race is thus both foregrounded and associated with epistemological uncertainty. For Jude and his sense of identity – and for the novel as a whole – what is at stake is the unspoken history of colonial violence against Black people and people of colour, and how this history is intimately linked to questions of kinship and origin. As Achille Mbembe points out it in his *Critique of Black Reason*,

> [f]or Blacks confronted with the reality of slavery, loss is first of a genealogical order. In the New World, the Black slave is legally stripped of all kinship. Slaves are, in consequence, 'without parents'. The condition of kinlessness is imposed on them through law and power ... [T]he racial community was a community founded on the memory of a loss – a community of the kinless. (2017: 33, 34)

Although *A Little Life* emphasizes the importance and reparative qualities of queer communities of care and of kinship based on friendship rather than on biological generation and 'blood relation', it also retains, as a subtle but crucial subtext, the trauma and violence of a specific history in which lack of knowledge about individual and collective origins becomes, first and foremost, a great and ongoing loss. Here, the formation of non-biological and non-filial relations is not a choice, but a violently imposed necessity, and ignorance and the need to improvise kinship provide, in this context, no room for reparation.

The management of knowledge and the question as to how to relate to epistemological imbalances is also what fundamentally structures and characterizes friendship in the novel. Indeed, for the circle of friends that has formed around Jude, abstinence from a paranoid wish for more knowledge about Jude and his past is what makes their friendship possible:

> [T]his was part of the deal when you were friends with Jude: ... [y]ou let things slide that your instincts told you not to, you scooted around the edges of your suspicions. You understood that proof of your friendship lay in keeping your distance, in accepting what was told you, in turning and walking away when the door was shut in your face instead of trying to force it open again. (Yanagihara 2015: 84)

Throughout the novel, Jude's wish to keep his traumatic past to himself and stay in control of knowledge he himself considers shameful determines the story's dynamics of friendship, which emerge as negotiations of the epistemological and temporal depth that friendship requires in order to provide reliability and kinship. Jude's stubborn resistance to his friends' curiosity, combined with the narrative betrayal of Jude's secrets on the part of the novel itself, raises two urgent questions: what degree of knowledge about the other does an intimate relationship require, and what relational effects will the disclosure or non-disclosure of this knowledge have?

Jude's practices of self-harm, in particular, illustrate the tension between respect for his privacy and a possible responsibility, on the part of his friends and chosen family, to uncover his secrets as an ethical conundrum. While Willem frames the always deferred act of asking the 'right' questions as possibly 'reparative, or at the very least preventative' (87), Jude himself repeatedly refers to his friends' chosen ignorance as the very condition of their functioning friendship: '[h]e was grateful, then, for his friends, and for how relatively little they had mined from him, how they had left him to himself' (141). One of the central questions raised in *A Little Life*, then, is under which conditions knowledge or ignorance is the more caring, responsible, and reparative practice, and who has the right to determine access to their own past, or denial thereof. The novel does not finally answer this question, but it introduces the possibility that friendship can provide contexts of care and kinship which exclude the confessional mode. The characters gradually grow into an (always fragile, but functional) practice in which they leave behind their past conviction that '[w]ithholding the details of your life from your friends was considered first a sort of mystery and then a kind of stinginess, one that it was understood would preclude true friendship' (707). For Jude, at least, this possibility, despite (or because of) the effects of trauma that shape his relationship to his own past, provides reparative access to structures of kinship which sustain him outside of and beyond the context of a therapeutic confrontation with his past suffering.

The novel itself does not give its readers the option of positioning themselves in a similar fashion. Much of the tension which Yanagihara sets up in the novel's narrative construction stems from the contrast between Jude's 'sense of violation' (197) at the prospect that other people will witness the violence done to him in the past, and the book's unrelenting uncovering, through flashbacks, of these very episodes. The novel thus interpellates the reader as intruder and voyeur, and questions the ethics of a reading practice trained in wanting to position the lives of (fictional and non-fictional) others in a past, present, and possible future densely packed with biographical detail. This discomfort, in turn, makes room for considering ignorance and sustained opacity as reparative practices which can be as fundamental to the workings of kinship in some contexts as knowledge and the sharing of intimacies are in others.

Queer kinship and the effects of privilege

The workings and dynamics of male friendship presented in *A Little Life* have been among those aspects of the novel that critics have responded to most strongly. Put simply, the public was surprised to be confronted with a fictional group of male friends acting in an almost exclusively male-homosocial environment for whom toxic masculinity and homophobia are no issues at all, and who provide an amount of care and emotional work for each other that seems to be a positively surprising oddity in the novel's contemporary critical environment.[5] As such, the novel fantasizes one version of the dissolution of the patriarchal and homophobic restrictions to male homosocial bonds theorized by Eve Sedgwick (1985). Sedgwick argues, in reference to René Girard, Gayle Rubin, and others, that modern western masculinity, as she investigates it in the nineteenth-century English novel, relies on a triangulation of male homosocial desire – which is necessary for the political functioning of patriarchal culture[6] – through women and thus heterosexual 'deflection'. Read in the context of this historical trajectory, *A Little Life* navigates its characters out of this modern paradigm not by affirming any stable form of gay sexual identity, but by reverting to the fantasy of a lost continuum in which male homosocial relations were untainted by the charge of perversion. In the process, the novel (almost) altogether eliminates women as signifiers in the relevant economies of family, friendship, love, and work, and this absence of (major) female characters

---

[5] Brigid Delaney, for example, comments that '[f]riendship is the solace in *A Little Life*, as it is in any life riven with anxiety, and it is rendered so exquisitely lifelike here – replete with beauty and dark currents – that it almost approximates the real thing' (2016); and Mariam Digges observes that '[t]he warmth with which Yanagihara paints the relationship between these four, particularly the affection between Willem and Jude, fills the reader with delight' (2016).

[6] As Sedgwick puts it, 'in any male-dominated society, there is a special relationship between male homosocial (*including* homosexual) desire and the structures for maintaining and transmitting patriarchal power: a relationship founded on an inherent and potentially active structural congruence' (1985: 25, emphasis in original).

haunts the text's all-male reparative register. At the same time, critics often disregard the fact that the affective intensity of the bond between Jude and his friends also constitutes itself against the stark foil of Jude's violent past, in which abusive monks, male social workers, and an effeminate doctor provide a dark mirror to the utopic network of male-homosocial care that tries to redeem Jude from his past.

To a large extent, friendship, in *A Little Life*, serves as a substitute for the biological family, and as the central facilitator for creating structures of kinship in a contemporary urban environment. Yanagihara herself emphasizes her belief in the centrality of friendship as the most creative form of commitment in today's society: 'friendship is the one relationship available to us in which the laws and limits are defined only by the participants ... When we choose a friend, and choose the terms of that friendship, we are exercising our rights of freedom and our rights as humans' (Rentzenbrink 2015). In the novel, many of the important forms of kinship outside the biological family emerge from ties of friendship: from mentorship through friendship to adoptive parenthood in the case of Harold and Jude; and from friendship to romantic relationship in the case of Willem and Jude. For Yanagihara, friendship takes precedence over other forms of publicly recognized relationships, because '[s]ociety depends on coupledom, for all sorts of reasons; it's good for social order and good for the economy. Friendships aren't in the same way' (ibid.).

While Yanagihara implies that kinship based on friendship exists, at least to a degree, outside the normalizing logics of social convention and capitalist production, the reparative effects of the bonds between the protagonists of *A Little Life* also and crucially depend on the social and economic privileges of the novel's characters. And this privilege, in turn, depends on the care members of the privileged class can and do extend to each other. As Sean McCann points out,

> [t]he message of ... [*A Little Life*] is that the fortune and happiness of the privileged depend on the private assistance they graciously extend to each other. In brief hopeless moments ... such privileged people feel bad when they realize that not everyone can be so lucky ... For the fortunate and privileged ... what matters most to the project of a successful life is neither the powers of the state nor the liberties of the market. The crucial factor rather is the way the wealthy guard their status by mutually caring for and protecting and extending benefits to each other. (2016)

McCann's analysis provides additional context for understanding the dynamics of hope and kinship in the novel. While most critics focus on the affective intensity of the characters' personal relations, a critical engagement with the social implications of the book's reality adds an important angle which exposes the elitism that supports its small fictional world. These dynamics call for a more detailed analysis, not least because they productively complicate any easy appropriation of the text as, for example, the 'great gay novel' (Greenwell 2015) of our time.

In her analysis of queer affect, Sara Ahmed argues that the normative scripts of heterosexuality inscribe themselves into bodies and spaces, and not only delineate which lives become liveable and which do not, but also guarantee the reproduction of what becomes manifest as 'society': 'the coupling of man and woman becomes a kind of "birthing," a giving birth not only to new life, but to ways of living that are already recognisable as forms of civilisation' ([2004] 2014: 144). Queerness, as a deviation from the heterosexual norm, then emerges, literally and figuratively, as 'the failure to reproduce, and as a threat to the social ordering of life itself' (145). *A Little Life*, I argue, effectively uncouples queerness and queer relationships from antisocial representation. Instead of figuring the antithesis to the social and political as such, as Lee Edelman would have it, queerness, in this novel, produces and reproduces a plethora of affects that bind individuals to one another through queer variations of friendship, love, pain, and chosen and adopted relations of kin. In the process, it works towards a positive representation of queer forms of kinship. However, its elitism and deliberate blindness to the workings of heterosexism in its own cultural context come at the price of a certain loss of queerness' critical potential.

The novel productively multiplies representations of liveable alternatives to the normative script of the heteroreproductive family, which lingers at the narrative margins to be both nostalgically claimed and perpetually rejected by the novel's protagonists. Like in *The Road* and *The Walking Dead*, however, the heterosexual nuclear unit remains a persistent object of nostalgic longing, and the foil against which all other iterations of kinship are measured. For Jude, the wish to 'acquire' a mother and a father forms part of his childhood desire for a 'normal' life and a home, and it stays with him until his wish's fulfilment in his adoption by Harold and his wife Julia as an adult. When, as a teenager, he is once almost adopted by a couple, his (thwarted) hope to become part of their family is closely tied to his hope for a fresh start, a break with his past, and the acquisition of a new identity: '[c]ould it be possible that he was entering this house as one person and then, as if the place were enchanted, transformed into another? ... [H]e would be Cody Leary, who would have parents, and a room of his own, and would be able to make himself into whomever he chose' (Yanagihara 2015: 216). Similarly, after his adoption as an adult, Jude associates his newly achieved position within the generational dynamic of filial relations with a hope for redemption and a publicly recognized place in the world: he is 'thrilled to have been claimed as another's in public, to finally be a member of the tribe of sons and daughters' (344). It is striking, however, that this framing of the nuclear family as telos works, for Jude, only in a retrogressive fashion: even as an adult, he wants to become someone's child, never someone's parent.

Instead of trying to 'do better' by potential children of his own, he remains melancholically attached to 'fixing' a past which denied him a 'functioning' family.

Filial generation, in *A Little Life*, is also bound to apocalyptic temporality. Harold reflects upon parental love for a child as 'a singular love, because it is a love whose foundation is not physical attraction, or pleasure, or intellect, but fear' (186). For him, the death of a child – and Harold sees two of his children die – is akin to apocalyptic revelation, an event which divides time into a before and after, and which presents the fulfilment of fear's anticipatory energy: 'finally, the moment you have been expecting, been dreading, been preparing yourself for since the day you became a parent, has come. *Ah*, you tell yourself, *it's arrived. Here it is*' (187, emphasis in original). In a similar fashion, the way the novel associates both Harold's parental care for Jude and the protagonists' friendship with the excessive drive to save Jude from himself produces an anticipatory tension that grinds against the reparative potential of care for someone who does not 'get better'; and this tension is resolved in the telos of Jude's ultimately successful suicide. However, like in most post-apocalyptic fiction, nothing is revealed in the end. What counts, and what becomes the locus of hope are the iterations of care and relationality that make up the novel's affective structure.

Even more central to this structure than the novel's concern with filial ties is its reparative portrayal of male-male friendship and romantic love, especially in Jude and Willem's relationship. Where Jude's adoptive entrance into the temporal logic of filial relations gives him a place within the privileged cultural narrative of generational belonging, his relationships with his friends, and with Willem in particular, provide him and the others with a context of care, and with an identity *as* friends which exists outside their respective (and, for Jude, traumatic) biographies and individual pasts. As Willem puts it, 'to Jude, he wasn't an actor: he was his friend, and that identity supplanted everything else' (494–5). Similarly, Jude reflects that 'Willem had been the first person who loved him, the first person who had seen him not as an object to be used or pitied but as something else, as a friend' (726–7).

While the novel thus embeds its reparative energies in relationships based on chosen kinship, friendship, love, and care, it also binds its hopeful and promissory energies to its characters' professional ambitions and their gradual access to and inhabiting of a world of luxury and aestheticization. The four friends' lives develop along a teleology of professional success which structures, within the context of the novel's general timelessness, the story's narrative temporality. Where Jude divides his own life into a time before and after the event that physically disabled him, he also regards his own and his friends' professional lives as split between a time before and after a breakthrough moment which led to their exceptional individual success:

[A]fter [the exhibition] 'Frog and Toad', something shifted for JB, the way that [the film] *The Sycamore Court* had shifted things for Willem, the way that the Doha museum had shifted things for Malcom, even the way – if he was to be boastful – that the Malgrave and Baskett suit had shifted things for him. It was only when he stepped outside his firmament of friends that he realized that that shift, that shift they had all hoped for and received, was rarer and more precious than they even knew. (655, emphasis in original)

While, on one level, hope, in *A Little Life*, gets untied from the teleological script of heteroreproductivity, on another level, the telos of the American promise of the self-made man places teleology as much at the centre of its narrative dynamic as the inevitability of Jude's ultimate death. The novel thus produces a tension between its general temporal stagnation and the sideways pull of queer relationality, and the progressive and unidirectional logic of its protagonists' unlikely path to fame and fortune.

Similarly, the story oscillates between the spatial abstractions of its de-historicized urban setting, and the binding of its hopeful energies to the descriptive detail of domestic space, expensive interior design, art, and other luxury items. Much of the novel's action takes place in and revolves around the domestic spaces that the protagonists live in, and which, for the most part, Malcom, the star architect, designs and builds for them. Filled with exclusive furniture and hung with expensive fine art, these spaces, which Yanagihara evokes in a lot of descriptive detail, seem to place the novel's characters in the unreality of the glossy pages of upscale homes and gardens magazines. They become the spatial expression of the friends' hope for a better life, an externalization of the promise of success through labour and ambition. As Harold puts it in one of his first-person retrospections in reference to Jude's last apartment, 'I had always thought it a hopeful place, with its high ceilings, its cleanliness, its visibility, its promise of transparency' (403). The text here conflates Jude's longing for a cleansing from his past – which finds expression in his literal excessive cleaning of his living space – with Harold and the others' ongoing wish to penetrate Jude's protective layers and learn about his past. In the end, however, this investment of luxurious domestic spaces with hopes for safety and peace is exposed as a fantasy when Jude is violently raped in his own home.

The novel's coupling of reparative forms of care and belonging with the teleological script of economic ascendance and cultural and aesthetic privilege not only confirms Sean McCann's reading of the text, but also highlights the dynamics of exclusion which a project of (fictional) emancipation can reproduce. Where Sara Ahmed, in reference to queer bodies, points out that '[t]he availability of comfort for some bodies may depend on the labour of others, and the burden of concealment' ([2004] 2014: 149), the novel presents a context in which the comfort of queer bodies and queer forms of kinship themselves come to depend not only on economic privilege, but also on the narrative conflation of moral deprivation with, for example, male effeminacy (in the case of Dr Traylor) or lack of cultural refinement (in the case of the guardians in the home Jude spends part of his youth in). As McCann aptly puts it, '[t]he predatory figures of *A Little Life* are nearly all the socially marginal poor or working class. The good and kind are rich' (2016, emphasis in original).

The reparative vision of unconditional and unquestioned care and queer relationality presented in *A Little Life*, then, sits uncomfortably within a context which binds such care and concern to economic and cultural privilege. To an extent, the novel's aesthetic appeal and plausibility rest on the creation of a fairy-tale world that disregards the violence of capitalism, and on aligning a gay male sensibility with a certain aesthetic elitism. On the other hand, the novel does reference historical realities, albeit in an indirect fashion. The formations of queer kinship portrayed, and the unconditional care that Jude's friends extend to a damaged (queer) man both provide reparative relief from the realities of a culture which often works to disable and disavow the importance of such networks of queer relationality, and evoke, without mentioning them explicitly, 'the communities of care formed by LGBT people in response to the AIDS crisis' (Greenwell 2015). The impact of collective and individual forms of trauma thus crucially shapes the novel's rendering of relationality.

Trauma, pain, and temporality

In *An Archive of Feelings*, Ann Cvetkovich proposes an understanding of trauma as first and foremost a social and cultural phenomenon, rather than as primarily an individual psychopathology. Recounting the Marxist framing of modernity and capitalism as fundamentally traumatizing experiences as such, she theorizes trauma as 'a social and cultural discourse that emerges in response to the demands of grappling with the psychic consequences of historical events ... I want to think about trauma as part of the affective language that describes life under capitalism ... as a collective experience that generates collective responses' (2003: 18, 19). This supra-individual approach to trauma is very productive for understanding the relationship between trauma, temporality, and relationality in *A Little Life*. A straightforward approach to reading trauma in the novel might very plausibly resort exclusively to clinical and individualized framings of PTSD and find many of its symptoms in Jude. However, I am less concerned with reading the novel's protagonist as an example of 'realist' clinical psychologies rendered in fiction than in drawing on understandings of trauma as a social and cultural process in order to highlight the ways in which the novel frames both temporality and relationality in traumatic terms. For Cvetkovich, one of the crucial elements of traumatic intersubjectivity is the role of witnessing, which is 'fraught with ambivalence rather than fulfilling the melodramatic fantasy that the trauma survivor will finally tell all and receive the solace of being heard by a willing and supportive listener' (22). In the novel, the relationships between Jude and his friends and chosen family are as much shaped by and constructed around the friends' role as witnesses and carers, as by Jude's own confrontations with (and evasion of) his traumatic past.

The novel's affective economy – in terms of both its rendering of relationships between its characters, and its framing of the reading experience itself[7] – is structured around the complex dynamics of witnessing; and these, in turn, structure its narrative rendering of temporality. Jude's own relation to his past and present is marked by the tension between remembering and forgetting, and, within the formal context of the novel, these temporal relations become both moral concerns and aesthetic structuring principles.[8] As Hannah Dyer observes, '[t]he novel's structure, in which present moments can only be explained by flashbacks to historical events, mimics the temporal structure of traumatic experience, wherein evidence of a disturbed past cannot be integrated and so it agitates the present' (2020: 88). While a disruptive relation to linear temporality has long been considered to be a central element of a clinical understanding of trauma as PTSD,[9] I want to propose a reading of Jude that takes his insistence on self-determination at face-value. Such a reading considers the consequences of what a liveable life under the conditions of trauma can look like beyond the scripts and expectations of therapy, while acknowledging the traumatic fragmentation

---

[7]As Jonas Kellermann argues, in the case of *A Little Life*, the reading experience itself can be understood as a form of 'compassionate witnessing': 'Yanagihara enforces unto the reader a form of literary witnessing which ... manages to convey to the reader the affective incommensurability of Jude's trauma, thus blurring the lines not only between trauma narratives and narratives about trauma, but also between competing theoretical conceptions of literary trauma' (2021: 335).
[8]Joshua Pederson especially foregrounds, in reference to trauma's relation to narrative, the affinity of traumatic and elliptical narration, and the centrality of unspeakability in relation to traumatic events: '[s]ometimes, trauma marks narrative with gaps and silence. At other times, narrative flows around trauma like a river past a hillock. In other words, a trauma narrative might only be indirectly related to the event itself' (2018: 102); and Silke Arnold-de Simine observes that '[t]rauma cannot be contained by verbal exegesis but spills out in uncontrollable images and is part of a fragmented and cyclical temporality. Trauma texts are therefore characterized by gaps, silences, and fragmentations, symptoms of "disremembering," which testify to the trauma' (2018: 141).
[9]As Lisa Diedrich points out, 'PTSD in its original clinical instantiation might be considered a disorder of time, or put differently: PTSD disorders a person's experience of temporality. In PTSD, the past is not past, and thus the present and future are precarious temporalities – the past threatens to crowd out the present and swallow up the future' (2018: 85).

of temporality as a narrative structure which can enable the positioning of a subject in the world. A 'merely' pathologizing – if clinically adequate – reading of Jude's individual psychology would not be able to account for the rich array of reparative practices that emerge from the novel's rendering of kinship, and from its relation to dynamics of telling and not-telling.

Jude's perspective on his own past is paranoid and obsessive, and it determines his understanding of time, dividing his life into segments of 'before' and 'after'. For example, thinking back to his abusive relationship with Brother Luke, who prostitutes Jude as a boy and lures him into a sexual relationship that makes it impossible for him to enjoy sex as an adult,[10] Jude reflects that 'he became obsessed in spells with trying to identify the exact moment in which things had started going so wrong, as if he could freeze it, preserve it in agar, hold it up and teach it before a class: *This is when it happened. This is when it started*' (Yanagihara 2015: 175, emphasis in original). Where Harold evokes apocalyptic time to capture the experience of parental love and loss, Jude similarly aims for narrative structure in locating a temporally specific event that would give meaning – albeit painful – to his present. More importantly, however, where the novel elaborately provides the reader with narrative accounts of past events in Jude's life, Jude himself is unable – with the significant exceptions of two long confessions, one to a female social worker as a child, one to Willem towards the end of the book – to actually narrate these events. This unspeakability, in turn, crucially structures the relationships between Jude and others: '[h]is past, his fears, what was done to him, what he has done to himself – they are subjects that can only be discussed in tongues he doesn't speak … [N]ow, what he doesn't say makes him stranger, an object of pity and even suspicion' (339). While Jude frames his traumatic inability to narrate his life in a linear fashion as a social deficiency – and thus performs an elliptical kind of communication which evokes the unspeakability of the cataclysmic event in post-apocalyptic narration – the novel itself foregrounds a different dynamic: traumatic temporality, with all its gaps, silences, and repetitions, is what ultimately enables the formation of kinship and structures of care in the novel. Jude's enigmatic past and identity are as much a source of irritation for his friends as they fascinate them. And the care they extend to him depends not primarily on narrative explanation – in fact, the sustained tension between the paranoid wish to know and the reparative move to hold back curiosity is the main driving force of their friendships – but is based on Jude's immediate needs in the present.

These needs manifest themselves in, on, and through Jude's body, which is visibly marked by physical abuse. The very corporeality of the way Jude's

---

[10]Emma V. Miller points out, in her discussion of trauma and sexual violence, that 'rape victims could comprise the greatest percentage of PTSD diagnoses' (2018: 227).

body speaks his past better than he ever could in words enables reparative processes of kin-making and care in the present without resorting to the narrative confessional mode. It also stands in uncomfortable contrast to the reading experience, in which the reader is unrelentingly confronted with very detailed reports of how Jude became (physically and mentally) who he is as an adult. The reader is thus forced into the shameful position of having to witness the abuse that Jude himself would rather not tell. This tension foregrounds the possibility that the confessional mode – and its attendant array of paranoid epistemologies – might not be the only viable form of relationality under conditions of trauma. In a similar vein, Elaine Scarry, in *The Body in Pain*, describes the relationship between physical pain and language as a tension between intimate certainty and the impossibility of communication. This tension runs parallel to the conflicted relationship between telling and psychological trauma, and also has profound intersubjective implications: 'pain comes unsharably into our midst as at once that which cannot be denied and that which cannot be confirmed … Physical pain does not simply resist language but actively destroys it' (1985: 4).

In *A Little Life*, physical pain serves two purposes. On the one hand, Jude's constant discomfort elevates him to an almost saintly status, which contributes to the novel's overall allegorical effect: it evokes the suffering of Christ and the eschatological notion of pain as a 'passage to salvation' (Fifield 2015: 117). On the other hand, although pain is, as Peter Fifield puts it, 'stubbornly personal' (ibid.), Jude's agony also becomes a facilitator for kinship: care for Jude's scarred and aching body emerges as a contested site over which his friends form their affective investment in him and in each other. His body and its scars speak his past despite himself and contribute to thwarting his efforts to live in the present and not let his past surface. At one point in the novel, he dreams of having the scars on his back removed, and with them 'all evidence of his time in the home and in Philadelphia, … documentation of those years erased from his body. He tried so hard to forget, he tried every day, but as much as he tried, there it was to remind him, proof that what he pretended hadn't happened, actually had' (Yanagihara 2015: 287). Jude's body also becomes a locus of hope and its disappointment when, for instance, as a young man, he is promised by a surgeon that his painful spasms 'may not be this severe in the future … The spine has wonderful reparative qualities' (115), only to be told, as an adult, by his friend and doctor Andy that '[i]t's not going to get better, Jude; as you get older, it'll get worse' (153). Andy's care for Jude's body, in particular, becomes paradigmatic of Jude's friends' hopeful investment in his (physical and mental) improvement against all odds – and against Jude's own unwillingness to let himself be fixed: 'Andy's job was to make people better: Andy saw him the way he saw a mangled tax law, as something to be untangled and repaired – whether *he* thought he could be repaired was almost incidental' (158, emphasis in original).

Jude's conflicted relationship with his own body, and especially his practices of self-harm continuously work against his friends' efforts to lead him towards betterment. And this tension fundamentally structures the novel's relationships. Jude's cutting, a coping mechanism he repeatedly emphasizes to not be able to live without, becomes a part of his secretive character which he pits against his friends' paranoid curiosity. As Harold puts it in reference to Jude's bag of razors, 'he had found somewhere to conceal it, somewhere I would never again discover it' (411). The cutting also forms a central part of the dynamic of Willem and Jude's relationship: '[s]ometimes the cutting has no place in their relationship. And sometimes it *is* their relationship' (554, emphasis in original). In Jude's practices of self-harm, the novel not only renders a graphic portrayal of the possible mental and physical consequences of trauma, but also foregrounds the moral ambivalence of the friends' desire to 'fix' Jude. While Harold, Willem, and the others perform much of their care for Jude through the paranoid prevention of his cutting, for Jude himself, the cutting also constitutes an element which represents his independence, and which defies his objectification in his friends' teleological narrative of improvement: '[p]eople had always decided how his body would be used, and although he knew that Harold and Andy were trying to help him, the childish, obdurate part of him resisted: he would decide. He had such little control of his body anyway – how could they begrudge him this?' (434). This resistance on Jude's part emerges, over the course of the novel, as a curiously reparative current that – violently and destructively – evokes Edelman's polemical embracing of the death drive, and of queerness as the antithesis of the social as such. Jude's persistent self-harming, and his ultimately successful suicide fly in the face of the novel's other narrative threads: its tale of ambition and success, its rendering of queer formations of kinship, and its characters' investment in the betterment of one saintly sufferer. Amy Rushton follows a similar line of argument in her reading of *A Little Life*, in which she contextualizes its representation of suicidal depression within the logic of neoliberal teleology:

> [F]ictional narratives of suicidal depression can disrupt neoliberal approaches to wellbeing ... [The novel's] emphasis on community is at odds with the neoliberal fixation on individualism and demands for self-responsibility: ... [it shows] that individualism is a convenient yet morally bankrupt dumping ground for responsibility, instead offering community and radical empathy as strategies for resistance to an inhumane and irresponsible neoliberal society. (2019: 196)

Reparation here emerges not as lasting physical or psychological betterment, but in the form of practices of care that enable the formation of community and kinship. Witnessing, in the novel, thus becomes a painful activity, one that confronts both characters and readers with having to acknowledge the value of care and community without the promise of a better future. The novel's provocation lies in its unrelenting and unabashed representation of physical and psychological violence which forces the reader to share its trauma.[11] However, what renders the reading experience bearable (for some), and what might plausibly explain, within the logic of the novel itself, the relative absence of desperation is its juxtaposition of pain and suffering with the reparative potential of kinship and community based on love, friendship, and the willingness to witness. As Yanagihara herself puts it,

> [a]s regards sexual violence, well, were we to avoid that topic, it'd mean avoiding not only much of art, but also history itself: it'd mean avoiding the world. Much as I hope the reader is there in this book to bear witness to Jude's life and his suffering, we equally owe it as humans to witness other humans' suffering as well, and not turn away because it makes us uncomfortable. (Kavanagh 2015)

On yet another level, trauma, in *A Little Life*, emerges as a social and cultural phenomenon. While the novel repeatedly references the sexually transmitted diseases that Jude has caught from the time Brother Luke sold him to male 'clients', these diseases remain oblique and unspecified, mostly serving to highlight Jude's self-hatred: '"[t]he things I've done," he said, "the diseases I have from them." He stumbled, hating himself. "It's disgusting; I'm disgusting" ... [H]e had to tell Willem about his diseases. "When you have sex in the future, you'd better make sure you always disclose beforehand," one of the doctors in Philadelphia had told him, years ago' (Yanagihara 2015: 221, 545). The association of diseases caught from abusive same-sex sexual activity with guilt and shame places the novel in an ambiguous position vis-à-vis AIDS literature. On the one hand, this indirect treatment of the relationship between gay male sexuality and disease[12] and its association with negative affect and social stigma reproduces the mystification of homophobic agitation in the early years of the AIDS crisis, and the ongoing trauma that still marks queer communities today. On the other hand, the novel counterbalances these traumatic and shameful silences with a sense of kinship that also evokes the communities of care so crucial in the past and present history of AIDS, and thus a collective history of trauma which, as Ann Cvetkovich puts it, 'resists the melodramatic structure of an

---

[11]Emma V. Miller points out the conflict at the heart of fiction about sexual trauma: 'literary fictional accounts of sexual violence have served a crucial role in bringing the sufferings of victims to public attention ... However, the effectiveness of literature in this respect has its own problems, and even in the domain of the arts there are limits to what people have been willing to accept on their bookshelves or to bear in performance' (2018: 229).

[12]As Garth Greenwell observes, '*A Little Life* avoids the familiar narratives of gay fiction. Yanagihara approaches the collective traumas that have so deeply shaped modern gay identity – sickness and discrimination – obliquely, avoiding the conventions of the coming-out narrative or the AIDS novel' (2015).

easily identifiably origin of trauma. Once the causes of trauma become more diffuse, so too do the cures, opening up the need to change social structure more broadly rather than just fix individual people' (2003: 33).

Although, in the end, the novel does go through the motions of the confessional narrative, and Jude discloses his past first to Willem and then, in letters after his suicide, to Harold and Julia, it also remains wary of the effects of such a confession. Jude's reports to his family never appear, in the text itself, as first-person accounts; the episodes that unfold his past to the reader stubbornly stick to a heterodiegetic voice, and thus never force Jude to identify with a past he constantly tries to keep at bay. In fact, the only character in the book who ever gives account of himself in his own voice is Harold, whose first-person segments are the only parts in the narrative that directly witness and confess to another character (the dead Willem) and, by extension, to the reader. Within the story itself, despite their ongoing curiosity, Jude's friends repeatedly express their ambiguous feelings towards their potential access to Jude's past. Early in the book, Harold admits that he 'knew nothing good lay behind his silence, and as much as [he] didn't want to hear what the story was, [he] wanted to hear it as well' (Yanagihara 2015: 397); and at the very end of the novel, he questions the value of Jude's final 'coming out': '[a]ll those answers I had wanted about who and why he was, and now those answers only torment' (813).

Alongside the morally and affectively ambiguous dynamics of knowledge and ignorance, forgetting and confessing in the context of trauma, the novel suggests the possibility that those practices which are often firmly placed in the vicinity of the pathological, such as repression, denial, or melancholy, might provide crucial sustenance to some subjects and their social networks. For instance, Jude's unwillingness to 'properly' mourn Willem after his sudden death in a car crash appears less as a pathology waiting to be treated, but as a plausible choice for this particular fictional character in this particular situation: '[a]t least no one tells him that he should move on. He doesn't want to move on, he doesn't want to move into something else: he wants to remain exactly at this stage, forever ... Denial is what sustains him' (728). Framing the libidinal identification with the lost object – which Freud theorizes as characteristic of the melancholic (cf. [1917] 1949: 437) – as a reparative practice for himself, Jude's refusal to move on evokes the impossibility to mourn queer loss that fails the scripts of socially viable relationality,[13]

---

[13] As Sara Ahmed points out in her discussion of the relationship between queer loss, grief, and melancholia, 'queer lives have to be recognised as lives in order to be grieved ... [and] queer losses were among the losses excluded from the public cultures of grief ... [M]elancholia should not be seen as pathological; the desire to maintain attachments with the lost other is enabling, rather than blocking new forms of attachment. Indeed, some have argued that the refusal to let go is an ethical response to loss ... In this model, keeping the past alive, even as that which has been lost, is ethical: the object is not severed from history, or encrypted, but can acquire new meanings and possibilities in the present' ([2004] 2014: 156, 157, 159).

and foregrounds 'melancholy as a form of mourning that should not be pathologized' (Cvetkovich 2003: 47). Trauma, then, in *A Little Life*, becomes a site on which normative expectations in relation to histories of pain and suffering are questioned. It opens up perspectives on the reparative potential of the impossibility to 'properly' narrate traumatic pasts and presents, and on the ambiguous dynamics of witnessing and caring in the face of ignorance and enduring pain, and in contexts in which things do not get better.

Hope as queer affect

In her exploration of the social and political workings of affect, Sara Ahmed discusses how social norms shape bodies, the things bodies can do, and how they can relate to each other in space. Queerness – and, in particular, queer forms of kinship – in this context, becomes a physically manifest resistance to normative bodily regulations that promises potential and possibility:

> [I]t is in 'not fitting' the model of the nuclear family that queer families can work to transform what it is that families can do. The 'non-fitting' or discomfort opens up possibilities, an opening up which can be difficult and exciting ... The hope of queer is that the reshaping of bodies through the enjoyment of what or who has been barred can 'impress' differently upon the surfaces of social space, creating the possibility of social forms that are not constrained by the form of the heterosexual couple. ([2004] 2014: 154, 165)

Hope, in *A Little Life*, I argue, emerges exactly from the novel's queer investment in the non-normative potentialities of bodies and identities, and the ways in which they relate to each other. Although they bear the marks of trauma and violence, the novel's fictional subjects repeatedly position themselves in relation to each other in queer and caring ways, and create utopic forms of kinship which sidestep the logic of the reproductive couple and the nuclear family. While the text concerns itself in detail with the individual and social effects and consequences of pain and trauma, it balances these negative affects with an equally pronounced exploration of reparative dynamics of kinship, love, and care. Almost as devoid of female characters as *The Road*, *A Little Life* has its protagonists leave behind toxic masculinity and homophobia in favour of fluid notions of what it means to be there for each other. Even though Jude eventually defies his friends' paranoid hope for him to 'get better' and have a future, hope becomes possible, again and again, in the story's incessant renegotiations of care and concern.

Friendship, in the novel, emerges as the most privileged site of hope, not in the sense of teleological improvement, but as an integration of the individual into a world of relationality. As Jude puts it to Felix, the troubled (and friendless) young boy he tutors, 'I went to college, and I met people who, for whatever reason, decided to be my friends, and they taught me – everything, really. They made me, and make me, into someone better than I really am' (Yanagihara 2015: 240). While friendship thus becomes the somewhat predictable counterweight to Jude's antisocial and suicidal tendencies, the novel decidedly queers this (male) friendship by imbuing it with a potential for romantic love more akin to premodern forms of male–male intimacy than to the modern, heterosexist split between friendship and (heterosexual) love.[14] As Willem reflects at an early point in the novel, '[w]hy wasn't friendship as good as a relationship? Why wasn't it even better? It was two people who remained together, day after day, bound not by sex or physical attraction or money or children or property, but only by the shared agreement to keep going, the mutual dedication to a union that could never be codified' (257). In the process of Jude and Willem's shifting relationship, which more and more comes to resemble coupledom, both keep reflecting on this shift; but while they express certainty that their friendship has moved beyond the boundaries of what they understand 'friendship' to be, they never frame themselves as a gay couple either. Instead, they keep their relationship deliberately unspecified, defying the expectations of both straight normativity and gay identity politics: '[t]he word "friend" was so vague, so undescriptive and unsatisfying ... But now they were inventing their own type of relationship, one that wasn't officially recognized by history or immortalized in poetry or song, but which felt truer and less constraining' (645). The novel's curious dodging of explicitly gay identities places its politics in a liminal and convoluted temporality: seemingly at once 'post-identitarian' (through privilege) and pre-Stonewall, with added premodern reminiscences, this fictional rendering of male-homosocial relationality and kinship sits provocatively suspended in-between different social and political iterations of the possibility of male intimacy. The text's shying away from any affirmative form of gay identity makes it both stubbornly apolitical, and available to appropriation by those readers who see in its very lack of agonizing identity politics a queer utopia which projects into a longed-for time 'after' or beyond identity politics. Hope, in this sense, emerges as an affect that is both nostalgic and romantic, and which longs for a timeless time in which the history of gay emancipation can either be taken for granted, or be imagined to never have been necessary in the first place.

What makes hope queer, in *A Little Life*, however, is not simply the fact that the novel concerns itself with non-normative forms of male friendship and love, but also its formal recourse to strategies of melodrama and

---

[14]On the historical development of friendship and pre-modern forms of homosocial intimacy between friends see, for example, Bray (2003).

camp,¹⁵ which sensationalize the reading experience, and provide a possible explanation for the book's largely positive reception by a specifically gay male readership. As Garth Greenwell puts it, '[t]o understand the novel's exaggeration and its intense, claustrophobic focus on its characters' inner lives require recognizing how it engages with aesthetic modes long coded as queer: melodrama, sentimental fiction, grand opera' (2015). This queer melodramatic mode emerges in the way the novel juxtaposes moments of intensely positive emotion with an almost unlikely array of injustice and scandalizing violence thrown at its protagonists. Its sentimentality finds expression in Jude's countless apologies, and its campiness arises, for example, in the nickname 'Judy', adopted for Jude by his friends. The novel's self-conscious reference to Jude's namesake St. Jude, '[t]he patron saint of lost causes' (Yanagihara 2015: 236), too, oscillates between realist detail, embedded in the sadistic structures of Jude's upbringing in a Catholic monastery, and a tongue-in-cheek symbolism which highlights his allegorical status as Christ-like sufferer and hopeless lost cause, around whom his friends construct their affective investments. Accordingly, when Willem gives Harold and Julia a statue of the saint, Jude self-consciously wonders 'if the brothers had intended it as he was certain others saw it: as a mockery; as a diagnosis; as a prediction' (ibid.). Within the logic of the story, the recurring reference to St. Jude works as a realist element that can plausibly be integrated into Jude's biography; as a symbolic choice for the novel, however, the patron saint of lost causes, his metafictional function as a figuration of Jude's role as lost and hopeless cause, and his actual appearance as a statue also become exaggerated gestures full of ironic surplus meaning easily appropriated by a camp sensibility – not least because of its evocation of camp's queer affinity with the Catholic veneration of saints like St. Sebastian.

The novel's central site of melodramatic tension, however, is the conflict between Jude's stubborn refusal of help, and his friends' unrelenting extension of care, love, and friendship. Jude's unwillingness to work towards betterment becomes, for the other characters as for the reader, a source of affective involvement.¹⁶ Andy, for example, constantly despairs over Jude's

---

¹⁵Notoriously eluding definition, camp, as a queer form of aesthetic production and appropriation, has often been associated with 'lowbrow' art forms, kitsch, and formal excess. Fabio Cleto, in reference to Susan Sontag's seminal essay, points out the centrality, for camp, of a certain 'aesthetic taste for the vulgar and the appreciation of kitschy middle-class pretensions … The transgressiveness of camp relies in its privilege of the secondary and derivative, among which Kitsch and pop, of serial reproduction over the original, showing that the secondary is always already copy of a copy' (1999: 10, 20). The heightened affective economies of melodrama make it a formal tradition that can easily be appropriated by a camp sensibility.
¹⁶As Alison Edwards puts it, Jude's 'sense of self, guilt, and rejection of his own strengths leave the reader, along with his friends, desperately hoping for his redemption but without any visible way to achieve it' (2016).

'perplexing and infuriating unwillingness to take proper care of himself, his maddening refusal to see a therapist, and his bizarre reluctance to take pain medication that would probably improve his quality of life' (155). Although feelings of infuriation and perplexity also accompany, for many readers, any engagement with the novel itself, the text refuses fulfilment of the paranoid wish for Jude to buy into the logic of therapeutic and medical treatment, and of physical and mental improvement: 'it remains mistrustful of the overarching apparatus of psychology and its guiding principles of long-term amelioration' (Herring 2021: 143). *A Little Life* goes to great lengths to establish, again in the language and mode of heightened melodrama, Jude's plausible right to refuse this narrative of teleological betterment. In a fight with Willem over Jude's cutting, Jude explicates his claim to his own broken body and to his own fragmented story: '"[s]top trying to fix me, Willem", Jude spits back at him. "What am I to you? Why are you with me anyway? I'm not your goddamned charity project. I was doing just fine without you"' (599). Jude's stubbornness and his claim to determining his own (fictional) life beyond the teleological narrative of becoming 'sane' and 'healthy' put into stark relief his friends' paranoid attempts to help him. Their love, and their 'steadfast … hope that their love can heal him' (Valdez Quade 2016) thus, on the one hand, become futile (and at times hardly believable) investments, but they also get imbued with a beauty which stems from the melodramatic extremes and the pathos that characterize the novel's relationships. As Nicole Lee puts it, Jude's 'friends' love – real, selfless love – is the thing that could save him, if only he would let it … But sometimes people are beyond repair' (2015).

Aside from the central tension between Jude's refusal to get better and the love and care extended by his friends, a moment of high melodrama arises in Willem's death. The novel establishes, over long narrative stretches, the possibility that Jude and Willem might actually find something like equilibrium in their queer relationship, only to destroy this possibility in a completely unforeseeable and deliberately provocative move. The chapter aptly called 'The Happy Years' contains the novel's greatest potential for queer identification with an idealized 'post-gay' (albeit also asexual) male-male relationship, but it ends with Willem's (and Malcom and his girlfriend's) death in a car crash (cf. Yanagihara 2015: 712). This sudden death puts into stark relief one of the novel's most emotionally charged expressions of love, spoken by Willem to Jude only about thirty pages before Willem's death:

> 'Who am I?' And then he hears … Willem's whispered incantation. 'You are Jude St. Francis. You are my oldest, dearest friend. You are the son of Harold Stein and Julia Altman. You're the friend of Malcom Irvine, of Jean-Baptiste Marion … You're a swimmer, you're a baker, you're a cook … You were treated horribly. You came out on the other end. You were always you'. (689)

By authoritatively naming Jude as kin, by placing him in relation to others, to what he does, and to his past, Willem gives Jude orientation and hope not for a future, but for the slight possibility of staying alive in the here and now. Willem and Jude's relationship thus emerges as 'informed by homonormative privilege yet untethered from social norms of psychotherapeutic betterment' (Herring 2021: 142). This short paragraph epitomizes the novel's politics of hope and kinship, and its impact is melodramatically heightened by Willem's sudden death, which further foregrounds the fragility of such hope without a future.

The novel's contextualization of queer male relationships within formal evocations of melodrama, and its 'hysterical' pitting of a male-homosocial utopia beyond identity politics and toxic masculinity against the harsh presence of loss and pain can help explain a certain gay male readership's fascination with the text. In an interview with *Vulture*, Antoni Porowski, one of the protagonists of the 2018 Netflix reboot of *Queer Eye*, admits to his utopic identification with the novel's inflated tension between the extremes of positive and negative emotions:

> I feel like it's actually ... an idealized future because of the fluidity of [the characters'] sexual path ... They treat [sexuality] like anything else, which is the world I want to live in ... There's a universality there that I feel a lot of people, gay people in particular, [can relate to] ... And just dealing with unconditional love, losing a parent, and sharing the bond of that pain together – and of course, I'm drawn to pain – we all relate to that. (Jung 2018)

While putting an emphasis on the novel's utopic rendering of male relationality, Porowski also specifically appropriates the text's pain as a shared gay experience. Invoking the dynamics of community that arise from similar biographical narratives in the context of a homophobic society, Porowski explains the creation, through the reading experience, of a gay male community with the novel's affective charge:

> I think we all have a little bit of Jude and Willem inside of us ... I think if you have had a life of pain – and I can relate to a lot of the story – it really makes you appreciate the good that you have in life as well ... I'm a highly sensitive, very emotional person, and the book, like the show [*Queer Eye*] gave me a lot of opportunities to cry. (ibid.)

It is clear – and Porowski must be aware of this – that he probably does not actually identify with the extreme forms of violence and suffering portrayed in the book, and the 'we' he foregrounds is fraught with ambiguity: 'we' cannot all identify with the experience of one character who lives through an unlikely array of physical and psychological abuse, and another one who becomes an almost saintly and eternally patient friend and lover. At the same time, Jude's symbolic potential as the Christ-like sufferer, who, like Jesus, becomes the innocent martyr onto whose body is inscribed all the suffering and evil in the world, and who has to die so that the world can heal, easily lends itself to sentimental appropriation.[17] As such, Porowski's reading exemplifies a privileged perspective on the text, which selects for those aspects that foreground the novel's fairy-tale, allegorical character rather than reading it as a realistic representation of sexual violence and abuse. The implicit exaggeration, however, is telling: putting an emphasis on gay male sentimentality and queerness' affinity with melancholy and pain, Porowski's appropriation of *A Little Life* itself becomes something of a camp performance, a melodramatic pose that serves to reference a tradition of queer community associated with aesthetic hyperbole and extreme emotionality. This kind of appropriation also, however, ignores both the novel's blatant elitism and its unabashed stereotyping of its 'villain' characters. Most strikingly, Dr Traylor, the last person to abuse Jude as a boy, is described as 'a man a little shorter than he, and thin, but with a sloping stomach and fertile, swelling hips' (Yanagihara 2015: 620). This clichéd rendering of an effeminate queer sexual predator sits awkwardly with enthusiastic readings of the book as 'the most ambitious chronicle of the social and emotional lives of gay men to have emerged for many years' (Greenwell 2015).

The efficacy of the queer affect of hope, then, in *A Little Life*, comes at the price of the novel's producing its own exclusions and dynamics of othering. Its formal oscillation between the conventions of realism and the stylizations of fairy tale and melodrama – what Scott Herring calls its 'psychological unrealism' (2021: 145) – invites affective identification and emotional investment as much as it refuses to be comfortably appropriated. In its characters' politics and convictions, the novel 'hysterically' juxtaposes extreme forms of destructive self-indulgence with countless iterations of unconditional love and care. Hope thus emerges as an ambiguous queer affect that has no fixed telos. For Jude, who calls himself 'an optimist' (Yanagihara 2015: 164), the knowledge that he can end his own life itself becomes a form of hope: '[o]nce he had decided, he was fascinated by his own hopefulness, by how he could have saved himself years of sorrow by

---

[17]Scott Herring argues that the novel's potential for queer identification also emerges from its formal and thematic suspicion of long-term commitment, in both the romantic and the medical sense: 'the book's generic noncompliance, nonpsychological characterology, and unrealistic narrative strategies connect with iterations of queer and lesbian feminist US politics thanks to its formalized suspicion toward therapeutic well-being and ingrained queer fears over institutionalization' (2021: 146).

just ending it – he could have been his own savior' (444).¹⁸ At the same time, hope, in the novel, is bound to the forms of friendship and love that keep Jude alive. As Stacy Gillis puts it, '[t]here is love and hope in *A Little Life* … hope left by the knowing of someone, of being friends. The hope also of loving one another well enough, although perhaps not the complete love we might have desired' (2015). This tension, which the novel never resolves, is what provides a truly queer perspective on the multidimensionality of hope and its relation to structures of kinship.

The right to be lonely

Hope, in *A Little Life*, is associated as much with the building and maintaining of structures of kinship as with their dissolution. The novel's tying of its utopian energies to acts of sustaining solidarity, friendship, and love in the present instead of investing in teleological futurism is checked by a decidedly antisocial current. Jude's struggle to stay alive with and for his friends and chosen family always retains the possibility that he will reclaim teleology for himself. His goal, however, will not be a brighter future, but an end to his existence within a web of relations¹⁹ – and this possibility, too, claims space within the reparative. Throughout the novel, we see Jude move back and forth between a socially induced fear of loneliness, and his wish to be left alone. Strikingly, Jude's anxiety in this respect is always tied to a fear of old age, and of not being able to take care of himself:

> How could he tell Harold of his deepest fears: his loneliness, of becoming the old man with a catheter and a bony, bare chest? How could he tell Harold that he dreamed not of marriage, or children, but that he would someday have enough money to pay someone to take care of him if he needed it, someone who would be kind to him and allow him privacy and dignity. (Yanagihara 2015: 275)

In this passage, Jude, on the one hand, positions himself against the logic of reproductive futurism (no marriage, no children); on the other hand, his

---

[18] Amy Rushton calls this the 'strangely utopian impulse of suicidal depression' (2019: 207). While I agree with her analysis that Jude's hope is bound to suicide as an option, and that this is why 'the denial of death is so damaging to Jude', I do not read this hope, as Rushton does, as primarily bound to 'faith in the future' (ibid.). Instead, I see the option of suicide as something that sustains Jude in the present, and binds him to life as something he can bear.

[19] Yanagihara herself emphasizes the centrality of death as the necessary telos of Jude's story: 'I always knew that the book would be his slow awakening to the fact that he's just too damaged to recover, that he is, in a fundamental sense, irreparable … I don't think Jude's story could've ended any other way' (Rentzenbrink 2015).

fear of loneliness specifically projects into his own future, and onto a future self that, given his health, he is not likely to ever become. Loneliness thus becomes not so much an indicator (ex negativo) of the reparative potential of sociality, but of a fear of the future loss of self-sufficiency and independence. As the story progresses, this fear moves further into the background, and Jude more and more claims his right to be left alone: '[p]lease. I'm tired. I need to be left alone' (763; cf. also 771, 772, 792).

On a more abstract level, the novel indicates Jude's generally loose connection to the world of social relations through bracketing the story with two references to Gustav Mahler's lied 'Ich bin der Welt abhanden gekommen'. Singing it to a judge at a job interview, Jude reflects that 'he understood, primally almost, the concept of losing, of loosing oneself from the world, of disappearing into a different place, one of retreat and safety, of the twinned yearnings of escape and discovery' (125–6). Towards the book's ending, he remembers the song when he has almost given himself up after Willem's death: '[n]ow, as he lies in bed, he hears the old lied murmur to him. *"I have become lost to the world,"* he sings quietly, *"in which I otherwise wasted so much time"*' (777, emphasis in original). Losing oneself to the world appears here as both predicament and desire, and the lied's positive evocation of the solitary quiet of worldly detachment and even death aptly captures Jude's ethereal existence, and foreshadows his suicide. Although the penultimate chapter ends with Jude making one final effort at staying alive and present for his friends and family – 'I have decided to stay' (794) – in the space between this chapter and the last, told one last time by Harold in retrospect to the dead Willem, Jude kills himself after all. This event, which divides the novel's stagnating time once more into a before and after, is not narrated. It leaves the reader with the ambiguous insight that hope can lie in new beginnings and final endings, and that kinship's reparative potential, too, has its limits.

Even before Jude's suicide, the tension between the novel's social and anti-social energies implies that the wish to be lonely, to exist outside the structures of solidarity, love, and kinship which Jude's friends extend to him can be as reparative to some as the need to be social is for others. In 'The Right to Be Lonely', Denise Riley, reacting to what she considers the recent proliferation of new family forms and 'the resulting residue of everyone else' (2002: 2) who refuse to exist in such structures, takes a stand against an idealization of kinship, even when it is expanded beyond the limits of the biological nuclear family: 'that thing, the Family, will, in its terrible iconicity, exceed my capture of it' (7). As an alternative, she posits that

> 'the right to be lonely' could also suggest the hope of being alone, yet understood as also social even within one's solitariness ... [T]here's a stronger solitude that refuses to be understood as merely presocial and that rejects the benevolent will to make everything, and it too, familial.

This solitude groans at the prospect of being tenderly ushered into the domain of the new social; its bearers are in no constellation, but tolerate being units of one. (9)

A Little Life goes to great lengths to spell out the reparative potential of queer formations of kinship based on care, love, and friendship, but it always contrasts these dynamics with a strong antisocial drive which never lets the narrative escape into the fulfilment of some fairy-tale fantasy of a male-homosocial utopia. In fact, I would argue that the novel only works because it does not allow for such fulfilment. The reparative vision of hope located in queer structures of belonging which the story proposes acquires its pathos through the novel's refusal to let this hope stabilize in some actually realized utopian future.[20] Readerly investment then comes to lie both with a hope for Jude's impossible betterment, *and* for an end to his suffering in death. As Amy Rushton puts it, '[t]he novel's conclusion aims to provoke radical empathy in the reader, simultaneously dreading but wishing for Jude's end. After all, Jude's death not only releases him from the relentless narrative but also the reader' (2019: 209).

While the novel thus, in tandem with its anti-progressive and anti-futuristic tendencies, produces its own teleological drive towards conclusion, this drive, in turn, is checked by a certain circularity implied by the fact that the story begins and ends on Lispenard Street in the timeless and ahistorical New York that is its setting (cf. Yanagihara 2015: 3, 739). Like *Cloud Atlas*, *A Little Life* combines the satisfaction of a narrative drive towards conclusion – 'a sense of inevitability and finality which is deeply satisfying despite its emotional complexity' (Edwards 2016) – with a notion of non-linear, repetitive temporality, a dynamic which locates hope both in the relief of teleological finality characteristic of the novel form, and in the mythological and ahistorical space and timelessness of the fairy tale.

The book's title is referred to three times throughout the story. Asking himself how he got into the abusive relationship with Caleb, Jude wishes for an escape from the temporal drift that is the result of ones own decisions: '[h]e had wanted … to close his eyes and reel back time … He would have … kept living his little life; he would have never known the difference' (Yanagihara 2015: 361). Brother Luke urges the young Jude 'to show a little life' (473) with his 'clients', determining his conflicted attitude towards sexuality. And this is what Jude remembers when he tries to make his relationship with Willem work: 'he would try – as Brother Luke had once asked him – to show a little life, a little enthusiasm' (547). Yanagihara

---

[20] Alex Preston makes a similar point, arguing that 'the novel is brilliantly redeemed by Yanagihara's insistence on Jude's right to suffer' (2015).

herself meant the title to refer to the fact that '[w]e have such small lives, all of us. And this is the story of one of those lives' (Valdez Quade 2016). While she thus foregrounds the universalizing tendencies of her novel's fairy-tale qualities, the references to the title in the text itself also epitomize the story's rendering of the relationship between hope and kinship as fraught with pain and trauma. At the same time, *A Little Life* constructs a fictional world in which hope emerges in places without a future, with full acknowledgement of the fact that some wounds will not heal, and some damage cannot be fixed. Hope thus becomes an improvised queer affect which is fundamentally tied to uncertainty, but which also finds expression in myriad forms of care and its (im)possibilities.

Coda

In this book, I have traced a tendency, in contemporary fiction, to locate hope in the potentiality of an extended present, and to align this kind of hope with a performative notion of kinship in the sense of spontaneous, improvised, and contingent acts of care and concern. I argued that this interplay between a decidedly non-futuristic utopian spirit and reconfigurations of structures of belonging which sidestep an exclusive focus on the nuclear family not only manifests itself as a discernible theme in recent novels, films, and television series, but also resonates with concerns in contemporary critical theory. Most noticeably, queer theory has, for a long time, been asking how queer subjectivity and the anti-normative thrust of queerness as such relate to notions of reproduction, generation, teleology, and linearity. I took my cue from queer theory's investment in negativity to argue that these insights gained from queerness' affinity with anti-futurism, failure, and a stubborn presentism should not be dismissed prematurely in the service of a renewed interest in queer relationality and utopianism. Instead, I proposed that non-futurity and anti-teleology are not by definition opposed to the work of building connections. Putting queer theory into conversation with other kinds of recent critical writing, I foregrounded a more general line of thought in contemporary critical thinking that is sceptical of blindly optimistic investments in a better future, and calls attention to the patient work of making kin and forging connections in the here and now. In particular, I wanted to show how this concern with making kin in and for the present manifests itself in theorizations of the place of criticism and critique in contemporary culture. Debates about reparative and postcritical hermeneutics productively resonate with theoretical and fictional endeavours to foreground the present as a plane of hopeful potential in precarious times on which lines of association and attachment can form, proliferate, and dissolve. Overall, the theoretical framework that guided my analyses of fictional texts was meant to draw attention to a particular kind of cultural mood and critical modality which speculate about the nature of hope and the possibility of belonging under devastating conditions.

Post-apocalyptic fiction, as the genre probably most readily associated with anxieties about the end of the world as we know it, provided a starting point for my investigation into the dynamics of temporality and belonging in fictional discourse. Contemporary post-apocalyptic narratives lend themselves particularly well to this sort of analysis because they are, in essence, fictional experiments in social and temporal world building. Their premise of a cataclysmic destruction of established structures and their often bleak and ambiguous relation to futurity enable negotiations of the tension between a nostalgic commitment to rebuilding and a radical investment in the contingent possibilities of the here and now. Where the past is gone and the future uncertain, these stories speculate about how human subjects will orient themselves towards each other and the world, and about how hope can attach either to the paranoid scripts of reproductive futures or to forms of solidarity and cooperation outside, beyond, and in addition to large-scale political structures and the nuclear family. I engaged with Cormac McCarthy's *The Road* to foreground the important role of child characters in post-apocalyptic narratives. Where the father clings to his will to survival in a devastated world by remaining attached both nostalgically to the past and to a (probably illusionary) future for his son, the child himself repeatedly escapes the father's paranoid scripts, which divide the world into family and enemy, and insists on taking the risk of reaching out to others without knowing or hoping that his world (or even his own life) has a future beyond the immediate next step. AMC's *The Walking Dead* provided me with additional perspectives on the dynamics of in- and outgroup formation in a post-apocalyptic scenario. The undead 'walkers' in the series call attention to the work of delineating who counts as kin and worthy of care and protection, and who does not. Over the course of the eight seasons I addressed in this chapter, the series holds on to the symbolic primacy of the nuclear family, but also speculates about what family can come to mean when biogenetic connection and the social and cultural foundations that give family a stable symbolic place break down. It engages queerness as a mood which asks uncomfortable questions about the violence inherent in the work of deciding who is friend and kin and who is enemy, and this mood manifests itself in the series' unruly children, its doomed queer characters, and the undead themselves.

I went on to consider contemporary speculative fiction as a genre which addresses not only possible futures, but also the potentialities of connection in the present and across time and space. I suggested that narratives which speculate about global connection and the possibilities of a new humanist sincerity both manage to make use of a dystopian setting in order to present a positive message of universal human connection, and remain sentimentally attached to a conservative notion of cosmopolitanism. I read David Mitchell's *Cloud Atlas* as an ultimately optimistic metafictional experiment in human understanding across time and space. The novel's thematic and narrative preservation of the tension between linear and circular notions of time productively disturbs the teleological thrust of both narrative and history, while the story also remains caught between a commitment to anti-imperialism and individual emancipation, and a conservative notion of family and belonging. Similarly, Netflix's web television series *Sense8* invests in a speculative reinvention of family and kinship which spans the globe in a way that only becomes possible by opting for an uncritical take on global inequality and postcolonial geographies. Both *Cloud Atlas* and *Sense8* are ambitious fictional experiments that attempt to globalize kinship by engaging a notion of universal humanism, and by foregrounding history and narrative as an ongoing and crowded present.

Finally, I suggested that Hanya Yanagihara's first two novels are paradigmatic examples of a pervading pessimism in recent cultural production. I proposed an understanding of pessimism as a particular form of realism, one which acknowledges the pain of structural and individual violence and the trauma shaping individual biographies and larger social and cultural processes, while also opening up narrative spaces of resistance and reparation that foreground the hopeful potential of care. These novels also, however, address the limits of healing and the possible corruption of kinship where power is abused. *The People in the Trees* makes use of its neo-imperialist first-person narrative voice in order to explore both what it can mean to move from exoticization towards making kin with the 'other', and how such recognition does not necessarily entail a process of decolonization if the power structures between human and non-human, and between colonizer and colonized remain intact. *A Little Life*, finally, renders a fictional setting almost devoid of any notion of historical progression as a foil to its story of male friendship. The novel works with contrasting extremes in pitting the bleakness and depression of individual psychological and physical trauma against the reparative potential of friendship, love, and care. Hope here manifests itself in structures of kinship which transcend easy categorization into family, romance, or friendship, and which make it possible to go on living in the here and now. It also, however, emerges as the acknowledgement that reparation might lie in accepting that kinship cannot heal all wounds, and that sometimes it is enough to attend to those who, in the end, might have no future.

Overall, then, the notion of hope I have attempted to trace and assemble in my theoretical considerations and close readings is quite sober; and the improvised nature of kinship in which this sort of hope becomes manifest remains ambiguously situated in-between individual liberation and empowerment and the possibility of neglect and abuse. This is no coincidence. One of the aims of this book has been to deviate from dominant accounts of hope-as-optimism and kinship-as-family, while also abstaining from focusing exclusively on queer utopian writing which presents chosen families and networks of care *within* a framework of future-oriented temporality. In doing so, I foregrounded a strand of popular theoretical and fictional speculation that seeks sustenance from acts of solidarity, friendship, love, support, and care without either subscribing to a narrative of teleological betterment, or presenting viable large-scale alternatives to the current state of affairs. As such, the body of texts I have explored in this book must surely irritate all those who call for new grand narratives and political utopias in these times of crisis. The stubborn presentism, scepticism, and pessimism I have traced over the course of the preceding chapters, however, have hopefully emerged as no less engaged with urgent questions of survival, of a good life and a good death, and of the consequences of global and local, social and personal devastation than more obviously 'political' fiction and theory. My intention was to provide a perspective on contemporary cultural production that can account for the constructive negotiations of temporality and belonging in texts which refuse to subscribe to a narrative of progressive futurity and social cohesion. As such, this book is meant to contribute to a conversation about the insights gained from turning our attention to local dynamics that can have large-scale repercussions, to reparation which emerges from the acknowledgement of pain, and to the here and now as a temporal plane of possibility and potential agency.

There are, of course, several directions which remain unexplored, and which could guide future analyses along the lines I have suggested here. Some of the fault lines I have only been able to hint at in my readings certainly warrant further consideration, most obviously, perhaps, the questions of postcolonial globality and a renewed interest in universal humanism briefly addressed in the chapters on *Cloud Atlas*, *Sense8*, and *The People in the Trees*, and the implications of economic privilege and precarity contained in both *Sense8* and *A Little Life*. What are the pitfalls of universalizing, in the interest of global understanding, regimes of temporality and a language of all-embracing mutuality? And how do the stratifications produced by global capital determine the temporal structures of individual lives and the lines along which kinship can and cannot form? In these last few pages, I would like to briefly explore the latter question in reference to two recent films which both originated outside the anglophone cultural sphere I have been focusing on, but have resonated intensely with international critics and audiences, and are thus global phenomena in their own right. Both films, released only one year apart, frame kinship as fundamentally entangled with the economic necessities of contemporary capitalist society, and investments in futurity as a privilege of the rich. They thus contextualize the nexus of hope and kinship in a way that complicates the association of non-linear temporality and creative forms of kin making with liberation and (queer) emancipation.

The Japanese drama *Shoplifters* premiered at the 2018 Cannes Film Festival, where it won the Palme d'Or, and it went on to receive numerous national and international awards. According to director Hirokazu Koreeda, he intended this film to continue an artistic exploration, started in his earlier work, of 'what makes a family: is it blood, or is it the time we spend together as family? In this film, I further that notion. It's about whether we can form a family beyond blood relations' (qtd. in Wise 2018). Set in present-day Tokyo, *Shoplifters* follows the fate of a family formed out of both choice and necessity: Osamu, a day labourer who loses his job at a construction site after injuring his leg; his wife Nobuyo, who later also loses her job at a laundry; Aki, who works as a stripper and is introduced to a colleague of Osamu's as Noboyu's sister from another mother; Shota, a boy who steals from shops with Osamu, who, in turn, tries to get Shota to acknowledge him as his father; and Hatsue, an old woman who owns the house the group live in, whose dead husband's pension they live off, and who everybody calls 'Grandma'. Early on in the film, Osamu and Noboyu encounter Yuri, a little girl from the neighbourhood, who is neglected and abused by her parents, and they take her with them to Hatsue's place. The film is an exploration of the consequences of financial precarity, in contemporary capitalist society, for the individual and collective lives of the poor. It negotiates the tension between aspects of economic necessity and emotional sustenance which shapes the group's improvised family structure. For instance, although Osamu and Nobuyo live with Hatsue mainly because she provides them with a house to live in and a minimum of money, and although they hide her death from the authorities in order to be able to continue living at her place and withdrawing her pension, it is clear that Hatsue chooses to indulge her adopted family for their company and emotional care. While her only remaining relatives – her husband's son from an affair and his wife – only tolerate irregular visits and give her money out of a sense of guilty conscience, her new family are a real source of happiness for her: shortly before she dies, the audience see her silently express her gratitude to the others during a visit to the beach, where the six of them happily inscribe themselves into a public image of family. At the same time, the characters' indulgence in performatively appropriating the structures of a nuclear family also regularly grinds both against the economic and social realities which always threaten to invade their precarious construct, and against the ambiguity of the power relations within and beyond the group. While Osamu, for example, tries to coax Shota into calling him 'Papa' and acknowledging Yuri as his sister, Shota remains reluctant and starts asking questions about the circumstances of his being 'saved'/kidnapped by the couple as a small boy. In the end, it is also Shota who initiates the turning point that leads to the family's dissolution: in an attempt to save Yuri from becoming a thief like himself, he jumps from a bridge and breaks his leg, letting himself get caught by the police. Although Osamu and Nobuyo try to escape with Aki and Yuri, they are confronted by the authorities. In consequence, Hatsue's death is revealed, Yuri is returned to her birth parents, and Aki finds out that Hatsue has been receiving money from her parents, who turn out to be Hatsue's husband's son and his wife. In addition, the audience learn that Osamu and Nobuyo had previously killed Nobuyo's abusive first husband. Nobuyo takes the blame for everything that has happened and goes to prison. In the end, then, the improvised family succumbs to the rules of the system, and its individual members are reintegrated into their 'proper' place: Osamu alone and in ongoing poverty; Nobuyo in prison; Aki presumably back with her parents; Shota in an orphanage and in school; and Yuri back with her birth parents, who continue to neglect and abuse her. The film at no point glorifies the protagonists' choices: their improvised family does not become manifest as a better alternative to established forms of kinship. What the film does address, however, is the mercilessness with which the capitalist system and the laws of bourgeois society disregard and eradicate the contingent structures from which its poor protagonists draw both economic and emotional sustenance. Their kind of family has no place in a world that privileges blood relation over protection from abuse (as in the case of Yuri), and which can only see the crimes committed and the rules broken by the poor, while unable and unwilling to address the existential needs of people whose only hope is to build fragile and temporary structures of kinship for themselves in order to survive and to aspire to some form of community.

The South Korean black comedy *Parasite* resonates, in many ways, with the reception history and thematic concerns of *Shoplifters*. It premiered, one year after *Shoplifters*, at the 2019 Cannes Film Festival, also won the Palme d'Or, and received even more national and international awards, among them – as the first Korean film – the Academy Award for Best International Feature Film and – as the first non-English-language film – the Academy Award for Best Picture. Like *Shoplifters*, *Parasite* addresses the relationship between kinship and economic precarity, and the possibility to sustain a livelihood and to have dreams as a poor person in a hyper-capitalist society. The film follows the poor Kim family as they navigate their way from a dependence on precarious, underpaid labour into well-paid positions in the household of the rich Park family. Where *Shoplifters* revolves around a chosen family that breaks back down into its constituent parts, *Parasite* reverses this movement. In order to be able to work for the Parks, the Kims pretend not to be related and to be individually qualified employees: Ki-woo, the son, enters the Park's house pretending to be a student who can teach their daughter English; Ki-jung, the Kims' daughter, is introduced by Ki-woo as a university-educated psychologist and art therapist; Ki-jung, in turn, recommends their father, Ki-taek, as a qualified chauffeur; and, finally, their mother Chung-sook joins them as the Parks' housekeeper. Most strikingly, the Kims' collective pretence not only pits them against their working-class 'rivals' – they have to get rid of the Parks' chauffeur and housekeeper in order to refill these positions – but is also surprisingly effective: in their upper-class arrogance, the Parks never check on their new employees' background, but exclusively trust in word-of-mouth recommendations. The Kims' performances as well-educated, vaguely middle-class service workers put them in a position of epistemological advantage over their naïve employers, who they regularly make fun of. However, over the course of the film, the shameful secret of poverty quite literally emerges from the hidden dark and catapults the poor back into precarity. Moon-gwang, the former housekeeper, has been hiding her husband Geun-sae in the house's secret bunker for years. And when Moon-gwang and Geun-sae realize the Kims' pretence, a fight over their respective secrets ensues which finally leads to both Moon-gwang's and Ki-jung's violent deaths, and Ki-taek's self-imprisonment in the bunker. *Parasite* relies on powerful symbols to foreground the classism and economic precarity that determine its poor protagonists' lives: rain and sewer water floods their subterranean flat, which contrasts sharply with the Parks' safely dry property; a decorative stone given to the Kim family by a well-off friend's grandfather emblemizes the frivolity of the rich, and almost kills Ki-woo after he, in turn, decides to go and kill Geun-sae with it to protect his own family's secret; and the Parks repeatedly notice – and are disgusted by – the Kims' smell as a distinctive and persistent marker of class which threatens to expose them as a family. The film thus implies that the Kims' fantasy of upward social mobility based on pretence and (theatrical) improvisation is doomed to finally succumb to the combined pressure of violent competition (with fellow infiltrators) and the secret of poverty which is always in danger of being swept to the surface. The family's performance necessitates spontaneous adaptation and precludes a long-term temporal perspective. Accordingly, *Parasite* explicitly frames teleological hope as a privilege of the rich: when asked by his children whether he has a plan – at a point when the family have already been exposed to Moon-gwang and Geun-sae – Ki-taek responds that the only plan that cannot go wrong is one that does not exist, implying that poor people like themselves can only live from day to day. Ironically, the film ends with Ki-woo committing to the plan of working hard and getting rich in order to buy the Parks' former home and free his father from his confinement in the bunker. If there is any telos at all that this diminished family can invest in, it is the goal of upward mobility, reached by sticking to the rules of the game. *Parasite*'s very last shot shows Ki-woo back in the family's dilapidated downstairs flat, and the audience is left with the impression that his long-term plan is probably no more than a pipe dream.

Both *Shoplifters* and *Parasite* thus address the temporality of hope and the contingent nature of kinship in explicit reference to economic privilege and precarity. They demonstrate that capitalism forces subjects into its own regimes of temporality, and that lived forms of kinship – whether within or beyond the structures of the nuclear family – is crucially determined by outside factors. Where most of the texts I engaged with in this book avoid addressing this issue either by presupposing large-scale systemic destruction – as in the case of *The Road* and *The Walking Dead* – or by unabashedly associating the reparative potential of creative kin-making with the freedom of economic privilege – as in *Sense8* and *A Little Life* – these films could serve as a starting point to begin a conversation about the entanglement of hope, kinship, and capitalism in contemporary society and in the contemporary cultural imagination.

The larger question implied here is under which material conditions and in which systemic circumstances a reparative re-imagining of kinship and a deviation from established teleologies becomes imaginable, feasible, and sustainable, and what role fiction and the cultural imagination can play in all this. I have traced some of the tendencies in recent fictional and theoretical discourse which, I believe, begin to address these issues. This line of thinking offers multiple openings for further investigation besides the one cursorily hinted at above. How precisely are repairing, reparation, and reparative reading entangled? What is the history of this entanglement? How can we address the religious languages, religious insinuations, and religious echoes in much post-apocalyptic, speculative, and pessimistic contemporary literature? What does this proliferation of religious language mean for a wider understanding of religion today? What is the significance of the missing mother who haunts many of the texts discussed in this book? How does her absence relate to a revaluation of philosophies of natality? Is there a way in which these texts with all their reproductive and anti-reproductive politics also suggest that we can and should become pregnant with each other and with our shared potentialities? These and many more questions emerge from the argumentative strands laid out in this book, and I hope many more questions can now be raised than have been answered. Any conclusions drawn from my considerations must necessarily remain provisional.

What I do hope to have shown is that a pervasive future-sceptic sense of urgency runs as a common theme through recent fiction and theory, and that this sense of a charged present and an intense investment in processes of making kin along lines of family, friendship, love, and care are often mutually constitutive. As such, this book is intended to be an intervention in contemporary debates about queer temporality, affect, and the social uses of contemporary fiction. It is also a book about the (counterintuitively) intense pleasures of the pessimistic mode, and about the realization that there is a future to be lived in the present. On a more methodological level, I hope that readers will also have come to share my conviction that the value of a critical attitude which attends to the nuances and ambivalences of individual texts in patient close readings should not be underestimated. In essence, my aim has been to propose an ethics of careful listening-to and feeling-with fictional texts and the characters that inhabit their worlds. Such a critical mode is crucial to my more general argument in favour of an attentive turn towards the potentialities of the present. If hope is to have any meaning today, these texts suggest, it must be rethought and reformulated not as a principle, but as a possibility; it must be realized in the present if it is to be realized at all – not as a system of beliefs but as a practice of connecting and caring.

REFERENCES

Adams, Tim (2015), 'Hanya Yanagihara: "I wanted everything turned up a little too high"', *The Guardian*, 26 July. Available online: https://www.theguardian.com/books/2015/jul/26/hanya-yanagihara-i-wanted-everything-turned-up-a-little-too-high-interview-a-little-life (accessed 29 September 2020).

Adorno, Theodor ([1967] 2019), *Aspekte des neuen Rechtsradikalismus*, Berlin: Suhrkamp.

Agamben, Giorgio (2009), *What Is an Apparatus? And Other Essays*, Stanford: Stanford University Press.

Ahmed, Sara ([2004] 2014), *The Cultural Politics of Emotion*, Edinburg: Edinburgh University Press.

Andersen, Tore Rye (2021), 'Storytelling after the End: Plotting a Course through Cormac McCarthy's *The Road*', *The Cormac McCarthy Journal*, 19 (1): 67–84.

Appiah, Kwame Anthony (2016), 'There Is No Such Thing as Western Civilisation', *The Guardian*, 09 November. Available online: www.theguardian.com/world/2016/nov/09/western-civilisation-appiah-reith-lecture (accessed 14 June 2021).

Arnold-de Simine, Silke (2018), 'Trauma and Memory', in J. Roger Kurtz (ed), *Trauma and Literature*, 140–52, Cambridge: Cambridge University Press.

Asante, Godfried, Noorie Baig, and Shuzhen Huang (2019), '(De)Politicized Pleasures and the Construction of (White) Queer Utopia in Netflix's *Sense8*', *Queer Studies in Media & Popular Culture*, 4 (3): 319–34.

Assmann, Aleida (2011), *Ist die Zeit aus den Fugen?*, München: Hanser.

Atwood, Margaret (2011), *In Other Worlds: SF and the Human Imagination*, London: Virago.

Barker, Chris, and Emma A. Jane (2016), *Cultural Studies: Theory and Practice*, London: SAGE Publications.

Bateman, Benjamin (2018), *The Modernist Art of Queer Survival*, Oxford: Oxford University Press.

Batty, Nancy, and Robert Markley (2002), 'Writing Back: Speculative Fiction and the Politics of Postcolonialism', Introduction, *Ariel*, 33: 5–14.

Baumann, Zygmunt (2017), *Retrotopia*, Cambridge: Polity.

Baume, Sara (2015), Review of *A Little Life*, by Hanya Yanagihara. *The Irish Times*, 08 August. Available online: www.irishtimes.com/culture/books/review-a-little-life-by-hanya-yanagihara-1.2308932 (accessed 08 June 2020).

Bayer, Gerd (2015), 'Perpetual Apocalypses: David Mitchell's *Cloud Atlas* and the Absence of Time', *Critique*, 56: 345–54.

Benjamin, Walter ([1940] 1992), 'Über den Begriff der Geschichte', in Rolf Tiedemann (ed), *Sprache und Geschichte: Philosophische Essays*, 141–54, Ditzingen: Reclam.

Bennett, Jane (2010), *Vibrant Matter: A Political Ecology of Things*, Durham: Duke University Press.

Bentley, Nick (2018), 'Trailing Postmodernism: David Mitchell's *Cloud Atlas*, Zadie Smith's *NW*, and the Metamodern', *English Studies*, 99 (7): 723–43.

Berardi, Franco (2011), *After the Future*, Gary Genosko and Nicholas Thoburn (eds), Edinburgh: AK Press.

Berger, Brigitte (1998), 'The Civilization-Building Role of the Nuclear Family in Historical Perspective', *International Journal on World Peace*, 15 (2): 21–30.

Berger, James (1999), *After the End: Representations of Post-Apocalypse*, Minneapolis: University of Minnesota Press.

Berger, James (2015), 'Propagation and Procreation: The Zombie and the Child', in Barbara Gurr (ed), *Race, Gender, and Sexuality in Post-Apocalyptic TV and Film*, 149–63, Basingstoke: Palgrave Macmillan.

Berlant, Lauren (2011), *Cruel Optimism*, Durham: Duke University Press.

Bernini, Lorenzo (2017), *Queer Apocalypses: Elements of Antisocial Theory*, Basingstoke: Palgrave Macmillan.

Bersani, Leo (1987), 'Is the Rectum a Grave', *October*, 43: 197–222.

Bersani, Leo (1995), *Homos*, Cambridge, MA: Harvard University Press.

Bishop, Kyle William (2013), 'Battling Monsters and Becoming Monstrous: Human Devolution in *The Walking Dead*', in Marina Levina and Diem-My T. Bui (eds), *Monster Culture in the 21st Century: A Reader*, 73–85, London: Bloomsbury Academic.

Bishop, Kyle William (2015), '"I always wanted to see how the other half lives": The Contemporary Zombie as Seductive Proselyte', in Laura Hubner, Marcus Leaning, and Paul Manning (eds), *The Zombie Renaissance in Popular Culture*, 26–38, Basingstoke: Palgrave Macmillan.

Bloch, Ernst ([1954] 2016), *Das Prinzip Hoffnung*, 10th edition, Berlin: Suhrkamp.

Bovermann, Philipp (2019), 'Wir sind untröstlich: Warum Melancholie die einzig angemessene Reaktion auf die drohende Katastrophe ist', *Süddeutsche Zeitung*, 22/23 June: 15.

Boxall, Peter (2013), *Twenty-First-Century Fiction: A Critical Introduction*, Cambridge: Cambridge University Press.

Bradway, Tyler (2021), 'Queer Narrative Theory and the Relationality of Form', *PMLA*, 136 (5): 711–27.

Bradway, Tyler and Elizabeth Freeman (2022), 'Introduction: Kincoherence/Kinaesthetics/Kinematics', in Tyler Bradway and Elizabeth Freeman (eds), *Queer Kinship: Race, Sex, Belonging, Form*, 1–22, Durham: Duke University Press.

Bray, Alan (2003), *The Friend*, Chicago: University of Chicago Press.

Brown, Kevin (2016), 'Finding Stories to Tell: Metafiction and Narrative in David Mitchell's *Cloud Atlas*', *Journal of Language, Literature and Culture*, 63 (1): 77–90.

Brown, Wendy (1993), 'Wounded Attachments', *Political Theory*, 21 (3): 390–410.

Buschendorf, Christa (2008), '*The Highpriest of Pessimism*': *Zur Rezeption Schopenhauers in den USA*, Heidelberg: Winter.

Butler, Judith (2002), 'Is Kinship Always Already Heterosexual?' *Differences: A Journal of Feminist Cultural Studies*, 13 (1): 14–44.

Butler, Judith (2015), *Notes toward a Performative Theory of Assembly*, Cambridge, MA: Harvard University Press.

Butler, Judith (2022), 'Kinship beyond the Bloodline', in Tyler Bradway and Elizabeth Freeman (eds), *Queer Kinship: Race, Sex, Belonging, Form*, 25–47, Durham: Duke University Press.

Byrne, Eleanor (2017), 'Ecogothic Dislocations in Hanya Yanagihara's *The People in the Trees*', *Interventions*, 19 (7): 962–75.

Callens, Melissa Vosen (2016), 'I Ain't No Hollaback Girl!', in Wayne Yuen (ed), *The Ultimate Walking Dead and Philosophy: Hungry for More*, 153–64, Chicago: Open Court.

Canavan, Gerry (2017), '"We are the walking dead": Race, Time, and Survival in Zombie Narrative', in Sarah Juliet Lauro (ed), *Zombie Theory: A Reader*, 413–32, Minneapolis: University of Minnesota Press.

Caradec, Julian (2020), 'The Value of the Suffering Child in Cormac McCarthy's *The Road*', *The Cormac McCarthy Journal*, 18 (2): 113–27.

Caserio, Robert L., Lee Edelman, Jack Halberstam, José Esteban Muñoz, and Tim Dean (2006), 'The Antisocial Thesis in Queer Theory', *PMLA*, 121 (3): 819–28.

Castiglia, Christopher (2017), 'Hope for Critique?', in Elizabeth S. Anker and Rita Felski (eds), *Critique and Postcritique*, 211–29, Durham: Duke University Press.

Castro, Heather L., and Dave Beisecker (2016), 'They Just Want Me to Be Like Them', in Wayne Yuen (ed), *The Ultimate Walking Dead and Philosophy: Hungry for More*, 165–73, Chicago: Open Court.

Chamberlin, Christopher (2022), 'Akinship', in Tyler Bradway and Elizabeth Freeman (eds), *Queer Kinship: Race, Sex, Belonging, Form*, 203–26, Durham: Duke University Press.

Chatman, Seymour (1978), *Story and Discourse: Narrative Structure in Fiction and Film*, Ithaca: Cornell University Press.

Cheung, Alexis (2017), 'An Interview with Hanya Yanagihara', *The Believer*, 20 November. Available online: https://believermag.com/an-interview-with-hanya-yanagihara/ (accessed 29 September 2020).

Childs, Peter, and James Green (2011), 'The Novels in Nine Parts', in Sarah Dillon (ed), *David Mitchell: Critical Essays*, 25–47, Canterbury: Gylphi Limited.

Ciuraru, Carmela (2013), 'Bitter Fruit', *The New York Times*, 27 September. Available online: https://www.nytimes.com/2013/09/29/books/review/the-people-in-the-trees-by-hanya-yanagihara.html (accessed 28 June 2021).

Cleto, Fabio (1999), 'Introduction: Queering the Camp', in Fabio Cleto (ed), *Camp: Queer Aesthetics and the Performing Subject*, 1–42, Edinburgh: Edinburgh University Press.

Cloud Atlas (2012), [film] dir. Tom Tykwer and The Wachowskis, USA: Anarchos Productions.

Coker, Wincharles (2014), 'Beyond Self Containment: On the Politics of Identity and Culture in a "Glocal" Society', *International Journal of Society, Culture & Language*, 2 (1): 53–62.

Coleman, Marilyn J., and Lawrence H. Ganong (2014), 'Introduction', in Marilyn J. Coleman and Lawrence H. Ganong (eds), *The Social History of the American Family: An Encyclopedia*, xxxi–xxxv, Los Angeles: SAGE Publications.

Coleman, Rebecca (2016), 'Austerity Futures: Debt, Temporality and (Hopeful) Pessimism as an Austerity Mood', *New Formations*, 87: 83–101.

Coronil, Fernando (1992), 'Can Postcoloniality Be Decolonized? Imperial Banality and Postcolonial Power', *Public Culture*, 5 (1): 89–108.

Cortiel, Jeanne (2015), 'Travels with Carl: Apocalyptic Zombiescape, Masculinity and Seriality in Robert Kirkman's *The Walking Dead*', in Peter Freese (ed), *The Journey of Life in American Life and Literature*, 187–204, Heidelberg: Universitätsverlag Winter.

Cummins, Anthony (2015), Review of *A Little Life*, by Hanya Yanagihara, *The Telegraph*, 20 August. Available online: www.telegraph.co.uk/books/what-to-read/a-little-life-by-hanya-yanagihara-review (accessed 08 June 2020).

Cvetkovich, Ann (2003), *An Archive of Feelings: Trauma, Sexuality, and Lesbian Public Culture*, Durham: Duke University Press.

Dannenberg, Nadine (2017), '"I'm not so sure humanity's worth saving": Zum Zusammenhang von Zombies, Männlichkeit und Kapitalismuskritik in *The Walking Dead* (2010-) und *Z Nation* (2014-)', *Feministische Studien*, 2: 339–48.

De Cristofaro, Diletta (2018), '"Time, No Arrow, No Boomerang, but a Concertina": *Cloud Atlas* and the Anti-Apocalyptic Critical Temporalities of the Contemporary Post-Apocalyptic Novel', *Critique: Studies in Contemporary Fiction*, 59 (2): 243–57.

De Cristofaro, Diletta (2020), *The Contemporary Post-Apocalyptic Novel: Critical Temporalities and the End Times*, London: Bloomsbury Academic.

DeCoste, D. Marcel (2012), '"A thing that even death cannot undo": The Operation of the Theological Virtues in Cormac McCarthy's *The Road*', *Religion & Literature*, 44 (2): 67–91.

Delaney, Brigid (2016), '*A Little Life*: Why Everyone Should Read This Modern-Day Classic', *The Guardian*, 19 January. Available online: www.theguardian.com/books/2016/jan/20/a-little-life-why-everyone-should-read-this-modern-day-classic (accessed 08 June 2020).

Delfino, Robert A., and Lea R. Lesinski (2016), 'Carol's Transformation', in Wayne Yuen (ed), *The Ultimate Walking Dead and Philosophy: Hungry for More*, 175–87, Chicago: Open Court.

Derrida, Jacques ([1980] 1999), 'On a Newly Arisen Apocalyptic Tone in Philosophy', in Peter Fenves (ed), *Raising the Tone of Philosophy: Late Essays by Immanuel Kant, Transformative Critique by Jacques Derrida*, 117–71, Baltimore: Johns Hopkins University Press.

Derrida, Jacques (1995), 'Passages – from Traumatism to Promise', in Elisabeth Weber (ed), *Points ... Interviews, 1974-1994*, 372–95, Stanford: Stanford University Press.

Di Leo, Jeffrey R. (2019), 'What Is Critique without Pessimism? Postcritique, Neoliberalism, and the Future of the Humanities', *The Comparatist*, 43: 6–25.

Diedrich, Lisa (2018), 'PTSD: A New Trauma Paradigm', in J. Roger Kurtz (ed), *Trauma and Literature*, 83–109, Cambridge: Cambridge University Press.

Dienstag, Joshua Foa (2006), *Pessimism: Philosophy – Ethic – Spirit*, Princeton: Princeton University Press.

Digges, Mariam (2016), 'Hanya Yanagihara's *A Little Life* May Be the Toughest Book You'll Ever Read', *SBS*, 25 May. Available online: www.sbs.com.au/topics/voices/culture/article/2016/05/24/hanya-yanagiharas-little-life-may-be-toughest-book-youll-ever-read (accessed 08 June 2020).

Dillon, Sarah (2011), 'Introducing David Mitchell's Universe: A Twenty-First Century House of Fiction', in Sarah Dillon (ed), *David Mitchell: Critical Essays*, 3–23, Canterbury: Gylphi Limited.

Duggan, Lisa (2002), *The New Homonormativity: The Sexual Politics of Neoliberalism*, Durham: Duke University Press.
DuMont, Andy (2012), 'Luminous Deceptions: Contingent Community and Aesthetic Form in Cormac McCarthy's *The Road*', *The Cormac McCarthy Journal*, 10 (1): 56–75.
Dunlop, Nicholas (2011), 'Speculative Fiction as Postcolonial Critique in *Ghostwritten* and *Cloud Atlas*' in Sarah Dillon (ed), *David Mitchell: Critical Essays*, 201–23, Canterbury: Gylphi Limited.
Dyer, Hannah (2020), *The Queer Aesthetics of Childhood*, New Brunswick: Rutgers University Press.
Edelman, Lee (2004), *No Future: Queer Theory and the Death Drive*, Durham: Duke University Press.
Edwards, Alison (2016), Review of *A Little Life*, by Hanya Yanagihara, *Kettle Mag*, 2 August. Available online: https://www.kettlemag.co.uk/review-a-little-life-by-hanya-yanagihara (accessed 08 June 2020).
Edwards, Caroline (2011), '"Strange Transactions": Utopia, Transmigration and Time in *Ghostwritten* and *Cloud Atlas*', in Sarah Dillon (ed), *David Mitchell: Critical Essays*, 177–200, Canterbury: Gylphi Limited.
Edwards, Caroline (2019), *Utopia and the Contemporary British Novel*, Cambridge: Cambridge University Press.
'Eine Sache für Profis' (2019), *Spiegel ONLINE*, 10 March. Available online: https://www.spiegel.de/politik/deutschland/christian-lindner-schueler-sollen-in-freizeit-fuer-klimaschutz-demonstrieren-a-1257086.html (accessed 19 August 2019).
Elrod, James M. (2019), '"I Am Also a We": The Interconnected, Intersectional Superheroes of Netflix's *Sense8*', *Panic at the Discourse: An Interdisciplinary Journal*, 1 (1): 47–57.
Eng, David L. (2010), *The Feeling of Kinship: Queer Liberalism and the Racialization of Intimacy*, Durham: Duke University Press.
Eng, David L. (2014), 'Reparations and the Human', *MLA Profession*, March. Available online: https://profession.mla.org/reparations-and-the-human (accessed 7 March 2022).
Felski, Rita (2015), *The Limits of Critique*, Chicago: University of Chicago Press.
Fernández, Laura (2018), 'Transnational Queerings and *Sense8*', in Frederick Luis Aldama (ed), *The Routledge Companion to Gender, Sex and Latin American Culture*, 222–30, London: Routledge.
Fifield, Peter (2015), 'The Body, Pain and Violence', in David Hillmann and Ulrika Maude (eds), *The Body in Literature*, 116–31, Cambridge: Cambridge University Press.
Fledderjohann, Matthew (2013), 'How to Continue: Existence through Beckettian Ritual in McCarthy's *The Road*', *The Cormac McCarthy Journal*, 11 (1): 44–58.
FP Staff (2017), 'The Exchange: Why Americans Can't Cope with Trauma', *Foreign Policy*, 11 January. Available online: https://foreignpolicy.com/2017/01/11/the-exchange-why-americans-cant-cope-with-trauma-meghan-orourke-hanya-yanagihara-the-long-goodbye-a-little-life/ (accessed 29 September 2020).
Fraser, Nancy (2017), 'Progressive Neoliberalism versus Reactionary Populism: A Hobson's Choice', in Heinrich Geiselberger (ed), *The Great Regression*, 40–8, Cambridge: Polity.

Freeman, Elizabeth (2010), *Time Binds: Queer Temporalities, Queer Histories*, Durham: Duke University Press.

Freud, Sigmund ([1913] 1961), 'Totem und Tabu', in Anna Freud, Edward Bibring, Willi Hoffer, Ernst Kris, and Otto Isakower (eds), *Sigmund Freud: Gesammelte Werke Band 9*, Frankfurt am Main: S. Fischer Verlag.

Freud, Sigmund ([1917] 1949), 'Trauer und Melancholie', in Anna Freud, Edward Bibring, Willi Hoffer, Ernst Kris, and Otto Isakower (eds), *Sigmund Freud: Gesammelte Werke Band 10*, 428–46, Frankfurt am Main: S. Fischer Verlag.

Freud, Sigmund ([1931] 1963), 'Über die weibliche Sexualität', in Anna Freud, Edward Bibring, Willi Hoffer, Ernst Kris, and Otto Isakower (eds), *Sigmund Freud: Gesammelte Werke Band 14*, 517–37, Frankfurt am Main: S. Fischer Verlag.

Garforth, Lisa (2019), 'Environmental Futures, Now and Then: Crisis, Systems Modeling, and Speculative Fiction', *Osiris*, 34: 238–57.

Gebauer, Carolin (2020), 'Dreading the Future: The Ethical Implications of Contemporary Speculative Fiction', *DIEGESIS: Interdisciplinary E-Journal for Narrative Research*, 9 (1): 20–38.

Gencarella, Stephen Olbrys (2016), 'Thunder without Rain: Fascist Masculinity in AMC's *The Walking Dead*', *Horror Studies*, 7 (1): 125–45.

General Assembly of the United Nations (2020), *Declaration on the Commemoration of the Seventy-Fifth Anniversary of the United Nations*. 21 September. Available online: https://www.un.org/pga/74/wp-content/uploads/sites/99/2020/07/UN75-FINAL-DRAFT-DECLARATION.pdf (accessed 02 February 2021).

Gentleman, Rye (2019), '"I Am Not Just a Me but I'm Also a We": Algorithmic Culture and Netflix's *Sense8*', *TDR/ The Drama Review*, 63 (4): 139–51.

Gerasopoulos, Vassilis (2018), '*Sense8*: Aspiring for "a Different Story about Difference"', *MAI: An Intersectional Journal*, 12 September. Available online: https://maifeminism.com/sense8-aspiring-for-a-different-story-about-difference/ (accessed 26 January 2021).

Gilarek, Anna (2015), 'The Temporal Displacement of Utopia and Dystopia in Feminist Speculative Fiction', *Explorations: A Journal of Language and Literature*, 3: 34–46.

Gill, R. B. (2013), 'The Uses of Genre and the Classification of Speculative Fiction', *Mosaic: A Journal for the Interdisciplinary Study of Literature*, 46 (2): 71–85.

Gillis, Stacy (2015), Review of *A Little Life*, by Hanya Yanagihara, *The Conversation*, 12 October. Available online: https://theconversation.com/review-a-little-life-by-hanya-yanagihara-48928 (accessed 08 June 2020).

Gollner, Adam Leith (2013), 'The Science of Immortality', *The Interview Magazine*, 11 October. Available online: https://www.interviewmagazine.com/culture/hanya-yanagihara-x-adam-leith-gollner (accessed 28 June 2021).

Gonnermann, Annika (2019), 'The Concept of Post-Pessimism in 21st Century Dystopian Fiction', *The Comparatist*, 43: 26–40.

Grasshoff, Friederike Zoe (2020), 'Jetzt geht's los', *Süddeutsche Zeitung*, 19/20 September: 51.

Gray, Richard (2010), 'Cormac McCarthy – *The Road*', in Jan Nordby Gretlund (ed), *Still in Print: The Southern Novel Today*, 119–24, Columbia: University of South Carolina Press.

Greeley, Stephen Brett (2012), 'Monsters of Modernity', in Wayne Yuen (ed), *The Walking Dead and Philosophy: Zombie Apocalypse Now*, 167–76, Chicago: Open Court.
Greenwell, Garth (2015), '*A Little Life*: The Great Gay Novel Might Be Here', *The Atlantic*, 31 May. Available online: www.theatlantic.com/entertainment/archive/2015/05/a-little-life-definitive-gay-novel/394436 (accessed 08 June 2020).
Guterres, António (2020), 'We Are All in This Together: Human Rights and COVID-19 Response and Recovery', *United Nations Secretary-General*, 23 April. Available online: https://www.un.org/sg/en/content/sg/statement/2020-04-23/we-are-all-together-human-rights-and-covid-19-response-and-recovery-video-message-the-secretary-general-delivered (accessed 02 February 2021).
Halberstam, Jack (2005), *In a Queer Time and Place*, New York: New York University Press.
Halberstam, Jack (2008), 'The Anti-Social Turn in Queer Studies', *Graduate Journal of Social Science*, 5 (2): 140–56.
Halberstam, Jack (2011), *The Queer Art of Failure*, Durham: Duke University Press.
Haraway, Donna J. (2016), *Staying with the Trouble: Making Kin in the Chthulucene*, Durham: Duke University Press.
Herring, Scott (2021), 'Never Better: Queer Commitment Phobia in Hanya Yanagihara's *A Little Life*', in Scott Herring and Lee Wallace (eds), *Long Term: Essays on Queer Commitment*, 134–54, Durham and London: Duke University Press.
Hicks, Heather J. (2016), *The Post-Apocalyptic Novel in the Twenty-First Century: Modernity beyond Salvage*, London: Palgrave Macmillan.
Hillmann, David, and Ulrika Maude (2015), 'Introduction', in David Hillmann and Ulrika Maude (eds), *The Body in Literature*, 1–9, Cambridge: Cambridge University Press.
Hollm, Jan (2015), 'Post-Apocalyptic Dystopia: Cormac McCarthy, *The Road* (2006)', in Eckart Voigts and Alessandra Boller (eds), *Dystopia, Science Fiction, Post-Apocalypse: Classics – New Tendencies – Model Interpretations*, 379–93, Trier: Wissenschaftlicher Verlag Trier.
Holloway, Daniel (2017), 'New 2017-18 TV Shows Are Mostly White and Male', *Variety*, 19 May. Available online: https://variety.com/2017/tv/news/new-2017-18-tv-shows-no-diversity-1202436493/ (accessed 26 January 2021).
Hölscher, Lucian (2016), *Die Entdeckung der Zukunft*, Göttingen: Wallstein.
Hopf, Courtney (2011), 'The Stories We Tell: Discursive Identity through Narrative Form in *Cloud Atlas*', in Sarah Dillon (ed), *David Mitchell: Critical Essays*, 105–26, Canterbury: Gylphi Limited.
Horn, Eva (2014), *Zukunft als Katastrophe*, Frankfurt am Main: S. Fischer.
Hortle, Luke (2016), 'David Mitchell's *Cloud Atlas* and the Queer Posthuman', *Literature Interpretation Theory*, 27 (4): 253–74.
Houser, Heather (2014), *Ecosickness in Contemporary U.S. Fiction: Environment and Affect*, New York: Columbia University Press.
Huber, Irmtraud (2014), *Literature after Postmodernism: Reconstructive Fantasies*, London: Palgrave Macmillan.

Hubner, Laura, Marcus Leaning, and Paul Manning (2015), 'Introduction', in Laura Hubner, Marcus Leaning, and Paul Manning (eds), *The Zombie Renaissance in Popular Culture*, 3–14, London: Palgrave Macmillan.

Huebert, David (2017), 'Eating and Mourning the Corpse of the World: Ecological Cannibalism and Elegiac Protomourning in Cormac McCarthy's *The Road*', *The Cormac McCarthy Journal*, 15 (1): 66–87.

Isaacson, Johanna, Madeline Lane-McKinley, and Kenan Sharpe (2015), Roundtable on *Sense8*, by Lili and Lana Wachowski, *Blindfieldjournal*, 14 August. Available online: https://blindfieldjournal.com/2015/08/14/roundtable-sense8/ (accessed 26 January 2021).

Iyer, Pico (2007), 'The 2007 TIME 100: David Mitchell', *TIME*, 07 May. Available online: http://content.time.com/time/specials/2007/time100/article/0,28804,1595326_1595332_1616691,00.html (accessed 25 May 2021).

Jackson, Holly (2014), *American Blood: The Ends of the Family in American Literature, 1850–1900*, Oxford: Oxford University Press.

Jameson, Frederic (2008), *The Ideologies of Theory*, London: Verso.

Jeffries, Stuart (2013), 'David Mitchell: "I Don't Want to Project Myself as This Great Experimenter"', Interview with David Mitchell, *The Guardian*, 08 February. Available online: https://www.theguardian.com/books/2013/February/08/david-mitchell-project-great-experimenter (accessed 18 January 2021).

Johns-Putra, Adeline (2016), '"My job is to take care of you": Climate Change, Humanity, and Cormac McCarthy's *The Road*', *MFS Modern Fiction Studies*, 62 (3): 519–40.

Jung, E. Alex (2018), '*Queer Eye*'s Antoni Porowski Goes Deep on *A Little Life*', *Vulture*, 23 February. Available online: www.vulture.com/2018/02/queer-eye-antoni-porowski-a-little-life.html (accessed 08 June 2020).

Justice, Daniel Heath (2008), '"Go Away, Water!" Kinship Criticism and the Decolonization Imperative', in Craig S. Womack, Daniel Heath Justice, and Christopher B. Teuton (eds), *Reasoning Together: The Native Critics Collective*, 147–68, Norman: University of Oklahoma Press.

Kamada, Roy Osamu (2013), 'Monstrous Citizenships: Coercion, Submission, and the Possibilities of Resistance in *Never Let Me Go* and *Cloud Atlas*', in Marina Levina and Diem-My T. Bui (eds), *Monster Culture in the 21st Century: A Reader*, 163–75, London: Bloomsbury Academic.

Kaplan, E. Ann (1997), *Looking for the Other: Feminism, Film, and the Imperial Gaze*, London: Routledge.

Kavanagh, Adalena (2015), 'A Stubborn Lack of Redemption', Interview with Hanya Yanagihara, *Electric Literature*, 21 May. Available online: www.electricliterature.com/a-stubborn-lack-of-redemption-an-interview-with-hanya-yanagihara-author-of-a-little-life (accessed 08 June 2020).

Keegan, Cáel M. (2016), 'Tongues without Bodies: The Wachowskis' *Sense8*', *TSQ: Transgender Studies Quarterly*, 3 (3–4): 605–10.

Kellermann, Jonas (2021), 'Witnessing Trauma in Hanya Yanagihara's *A Little Life*', *Critique: Studies in Contemporary Fiction*, 62 (3): 334–46.

Kelly, Adam (2010), 'David Foster Wallace and the New Sincerity in American Fiction', in David Hering (ed), *Consider David Foster Wallace: Critical Essays*, 131–46, Los Angeles: Sideshow Media Group Press.

Kempner, Brandon (2012), 'The Optimism of *The Walking Dead*', in Wayne Yuen (ed), *The Walking Dead and Philosophy: Zombie Apocalypse Now*, 141–54, Chicago: Open Court.

Kermode, Frank (1967), *The Sense of an Ending: Studies in the Theory of Fiction*, Oxford: Oxford University Press.

Kidd, James (2013), Review of *The People in the Trees*, by Hanya Yanagihara, *The Independent*, 21 December. Available online: www.independent.co.uk/arts-entertainment/books/reviews/review-the-people-in-the-trees-by-hanya-yanagihara-9015493.html (accessed 16 November 2022).

Kidd, James (2015), 'Over the Top, beyond the Pale, and Quite Simply Unforgettable', Review of *A Little Life*, by Hanya Yanagihara, *The Independent*, 08 August. Available online: www.independent.co.uk/arts-entertainment/books/reviews/a-little-life-by-hanya-yanagihara-book-review-over-the-top-beyond-the-pale-and-quite-simply-10445791.html (accessed 08 June 2020).

Kimzey, Blake (2013), 'The People in the Trees', *Washington Independent Review of Books*, 28 August. Available online: www.washingtonindependentreviewofbooks.com/index.php/bookreview/the-people-in-the-trees (accessed 16 November 2022).

Kirkman, Robert, Charlie Adlard, Tony Moore, and Cliff Rathburn (2001), *The Walking Dead: Compendium One*, Portland: Image Comics.

Knepper, Wendy (2016). 'Toward a Theory of Experimental World Epic: David Mitchell's *Cloud Atlas*', *Ariel: A Review of International English Literature*, 47 (1): 93–126.

Kozma, Alicia (2013), 'Leave It All Behind: The Post-Apocalyptic Renunciation of Technology in *The Walking Dead*', in Murali Balaji (ed), *Thinking Dead: What the Zombie-Apocalypse Means*, 63–96, New York: Lexington Books.

Kraatila, Elise (2019), 'Conspicuous Fabrications: Speculative Fiction as a Tool for Confronting the Post-Truth Discourse', *Narrative Inquiry*, 29 (2): 418–33.

Krause, Steffi (2017), 'Kartografie einer Geschichte: Analyse selbstreflexiver Erzählelemente und der Medialität in *Cloud Atlas*', *Kodikas/Code*, 40 (1–2): 102–15.

Kucała, Bożena (2018), 'The Eternal Recurrence of (Hi)Story: David Mitchell's *Cloud Atlas*', *Studia Litteraria Universitatis Iagellonicae Cracoviensis*, 13 (2): 107–15.

Labuschagne, Dalene (2019), 'Storytelling in David Mitchell's *Cloud Atlas*: Archiving the Future-to-Come', *Scrutiny 2*, 24 (2–3): 4–25.

Latour, Bruno (2004), 'Why Has Critique Run Out of Steam? From Matters of Fact to Matters of Concern', *Critical Inquiry*, 30: 225–48.

Laubender, Carolyn (2019), 'Beyond Repair: Interpretation, Reparation, and Melanie Klein's Clinical Play-Technique', *Studies in Gender and Sexuality*, 20 (1): 51–67.

Lauro, Sarah Juliet (2017), 'Introduction: Wander and Wonder in Zombieland', in Sarah Juliet Lauro (ed), *Zombie Theory: A Reader*, vii–xxiii, Minneapolis: University of Minnesota Press.

Lawrence, Nicholas (2020), 'Cannibalism, Terminus, and Ambivalent Frontier Mythology in AMC's *The Walking Dead*', *South Atlantic Review*, 85 (3): 116–31.

Le Guin, Ursula K. (2009), Review of *The Year of the Flood*, by Margaret Atwood, *The Guardian*, 29 August. Available online: https://www.

theguardian.com/books/2009/aug/29/margaret-atwood-year-of-flood (accessed 02 February 2021).

Lee, Nicole (2015), '"A Little Life", by Hanya Yanagihara, Inspires and Devastates', *The Washington Post*, 10 April. Available online: www.washingtonpost.com/entertainment/books/book-world-a-little-life-by-hanya-yanagihara-inspires-and-devastates/2015/04/09/de04604c-d573-11e4-a62f-ee745911a4ff_story.html (accessed 08 June 2020).

Levina, Marina, and Dien-My T. Bui (2013), 'Introduction: Toward a Comprehensive Monster Theory in the 21st Century', in Marina Levina and Dien-My T. Bui (eds), *Monster Culture in the 21st Century: A Reader*, 1–13, London: Bloomsbury Academic.

Light, Claire (2015), '*Sense8* and the Failure of Global Imagination', *The Nerds of Color*, 10 June. Available online: https://thenerdsofcolor.org/2015/06/10/sense8-and-the-failure-of-global-imagination/ (accessed 26 January 2021).

Livingston, Robert Eric (2001), 'Glocal Knowledges: Agency and Place in Literary Studies', *PMLA*, 116 (1): 145–57.

Lothian, Alexis (2018), *Old Futures: Speculative Fiction and Queer Possibility*, New York: New York University Press.

Love, Heather (2009), *Feeling Backwards: Loss and the Politics of Queer History*, Cambridge MA: Harvard University Press.

Lovegrove, James (2012), 'The World of the End of the World: Apocalyptic and Post-Apocalyptic Fiction', in Keith Brooke (ed), *Strange Divisions and Alien Territories: The Sub-Genres of Science Fiction*, 97–111, London: Palgrave Macmillan.

Machinal, Hélène (2011), '*Cloud Atlas*: From Postmodernity to the Posthuman', in Sarah Dillon (ed), *David Mitchell: Critical Essays*, 127–54, Canterbury: Gylphi Limited.

Marshall, Kate (2015). 'What Are the Novels of the Anthropocene? American Fiction in Geological Time', *American Literary History*, 27 (3): 523–38.

Martin, Theodore (2017), *Contemporary Drift: Genre, Historicism, and the Problem of the Present*, New York: Columbia University Press.

Maslin, Janet (2015), 'Review: "A Little Life", Hanya Yanagihara's Traumatic Tale of Male Friendship', *The New York Times*, 30 September. Available online: www.nytimes.com/2015/10/01/books/review-a-little-life-hanya-yanagiharas-traumatic-tale-of-male-friendship.html (accessed 08 June 2020).

Mbembe, Achille (2017), *Critique of Black Reason*, Durham: Duke University Press.

McCann, Sean (2016), '"I'm So Sorry": *A Little Life* and the Socialism of the Rich', *Post 45: Contemporaries*, 06 March. Available online: www.post45.org/2016/06/im-so-sorry-a-little-life-and-the-socialism-of-the-rich (accessed 08 June 2020).

McCarthy, Cormac (2007), *The Road*, New York: Vintage.

McEleney, Corey (2019), 'Reading to the Letter: No Future and the Question of Rhetoric', *GLQ: A Journal of Lesbian and Gay Studies*, 25 (3): 431–55.

McFarlane, Anna (2017), '*Sense8* (review)', *Science Fiction Film and Television*, 10 (1): 149–53.

McMann, Mindi (2016), '"There were endings, but none of them were happy": Exploitation and Authority in Hanya Yanagihara's *The People in the Trees*', *Paradoxa*, 28: 91–111.

McMorran, Will (2011), '*Cloud Atlas* and *If on a Winter's Night a Traveller*: Fragmentation and Integrity in the Postmodern Novel', in Sarah Dillon (ed), *David Mitchell: Critical Essays*, 155–75, Canterbury: Gylphi Limited.

Menninghaus, Winfried (2003), *Disgust: The Theory and History of a Strong Sensation*, Albany: State University of New York Press.

Mezey, Jason Howard (2011), '"A Multitude of Drops": Recursion and Globalization in David Mitchell's *Cloud Atlas*', *Modern Language Studies*, 40 (2): 10–37.

Miller, Carl F. (2014), 'The Cultural Logic of Post-Capitalism: Cormac McCarthy's *The Road* and Popular Dystopia', in Gisèle Marie Baxter, Brett Josef Grubisic, and Tara Lee (eds), *Blast, Corrupt, Dismantle, Erase: Contemporary North-American Dystopian Fiction*, 32–40, Waterloo: Wilfrid Laurier University Press.

Miller, Emma V. (2018), 'Trauma and Sexual Violence', in J. Roger Kurtz (ed), *Trauma and Literature*, 226–38, Cambridge: Cambridge University Press.

Miller, Julie (2017), 'Netflix Revives *Sense8*: Read Lana Wachowski's Heartwarming Letter', *Vanity Fair*, 29 June. Available online: https://www.vanityfair.com/hollywood/2017/06/netflix-sense8-lana-wachowski (accessed 4 October 2018).

Mincheva, Dilyana (2018), '*Sense8* and the Praxis of Utopia', *Cinephile*, 12 (1): 32–9.

Mitchell, David (2004), *Cloud Atlas*, London: Sceptre.

Mohanty, Chandra Talpade (1984), 'Under Western Eyes: Feminist Scholarship and Colonial Discourses', *Boundary 2: An International Journal of Literature and Culture*, 12 (3): 333–58.

Morgan, Lewis Henry (1871), *Systems of Consanguinity and Affinity of the Human Family*, Washington, DC: Smithsonian Institution.

Morgenstern, Naomi (2014), 'Postapocalyptic Responsibility: Patriarchy at the End of the World in Cormac McCarthy's *The Road*', *Differences: A Journal of Feminist Cultural Studies*, 25 (2): 33–61.

Mulvey, Laura (1975), 'Visual Pleasure and Narrative Cinema', *Screen*, 16 (3): 6–18.

Muñoz, José Esteban (2009), *Cruising Utopia: The Then and There of Queer Futurity*, New York: New York University Press.

Murdock, George Peter (1949), *Social Structure*, New York: Macmillan.

Murray, Heather (2010), *Not in This Family: Gays and the Meaning of Kinship in Postwar North America*, Philadelphia: University of Pennsylvania Press.

Nayar, Pramod K. (2012), *Colonial Voices: The Discourses of Empire*, Hoboken: Wiley-Blackwell.

Ng, Lynda (2015), 'Cannibalism, Colonialism and Apocalypse in Mitchell's Global Future', *SubStance*, 44 (1): 107–22.

Noble, Alan (2011), 'The Absurdity of Hope in Cormac McCarthy's *The Road*', *South Atlantic Review*, 76 (3): 93–109.

Noetzel, Justin T. (2014), 'Underworlds of Despair and Hope in Cormac McCarthy's *The Road*', in Susan M. Bernardo (ed), *Environments in Science Fiction: Essays on Alternative Spaces*, 120–36, Jefferson: McFarland.

O'Mahony, Lauren, Melissa Merchant, and Simon Order (2021), 'Necropolitics in a Post-Apocalyptic Zombie Diaspora: The Case of AMC's *The Walking Dead*', *Journal of Postcolonial Writing*, 57 (1): 89–103.

Paech, Joachim (1997), *Literatur und Film*, Stuttgart: J.B. Metzler.

Parasite (2019), [film] dir. Bong Joon-ho, South Korea: Barunson E&A.

Parker, Jo Alyson (2010), 'David Mitchell's Cloud Atlas of Narrative Constraints and Environmental Limits', in Jo Alyson Patker, Paul A. Harris, and Christian Steineck (eds), *Time, Limits and Constraints*, 201–17, Leiden: Brill Academic Publishing.

Parker, Jo Alyson (2015), 'From Time's Boomerang to Pointillist Mosaic: Translating *Cloud Atlas* into Film', *SubStance*, 44 (1): 123–35.

Parsemain, Ava Laure (2019), *The Pedagogy of Queer TV*, London: Palgrave Macmillan.

Pederson, Joshua (2018), 'Trauma and Narrative', in J. Roger Kurtz (ed), *Trauma and Literature*, 97–109, Cambridge: Cambridge University Press.

Polanki, Gautama (2018), 'The Iterable Messiah: Postmodernist Mythopoeia in *Cloud Atlas*', *C21 Literature: Journal of 21st-Century Writings*, 6 (3): 1–26.

Powers, John (2015), '"A Little Life": An Unforgettable Novel about the Grace of Friendship', *NPR*, 19 March. Available online: www.npr.org/2015/03/19/394050118/a-little-life-an-unforgettable-novel-about-the-grace-of-friendship?t=1591628984852 (accessed 08 June 2020).

Powning, Jacob M (2020), '"Dreams so rich in color. How else would death call you?" An Exploration of the Ending in Cormac McCarthy's *The Road*', *The Cormac McCarthy Journal*, 18 (1): 26–36.

Preston, Alex (2015), 'Relentless Suffering', Review of *A Little Life*, by Hanya Yanagihara, *The Guardian*, 18 August. Available online: www.theguardian.com/books/2015/aug/18/a-little-life-hanya-yanagihara-review-man-booker-prize (accessed 08 June 2020).

Pudney, Eric (2015), 'Christianity and Cormac McCarthy's *The Road*', *English Studies*, 96 (3): 293–309.

Pye, Danee, and Peter Padraic O'Sullivan (2012), 'Dead Man's Party', in Wayne Yuen (ed), *The Walking Dead and Philosophy: Zombie Apocalypse Now*, 107–16, Chicago: Open Court.

Quart, Alissa (2005), 'Happy Endings: The Post-Nuclear Family According to Don Roos', *Film Comment*, 31 (4): 48.

Radhakrishnan, Rajagopalan (2019), 'The Epistemology of Pessimism', *The Comparatist*, 43: 41–67.

Rai, Amit S. (2013), 'Ontology and Monstrosity', in Marina Levina and Diem-My T. Bui (eds), *Monster Culture in the 21st Century: A Reader*, 15–31, London: Bloomsbury Academic.

Rambo, Shelly L. (2008), 'Beyond Redemption? Reading Cormac McCarthy's *The Road* after the End of the World', *Studies in the Literary Imagination*, 41 (2): 99–120.

The Rd. (2013), [Synchronized two-channel video installation] Christoph Draeger, Switzerland.

Reed, Darren, and Ruth Penfold-Mounce (2015), 'Zombies and the Sociological Imagination: *The Walking Dead* as Social-Science Fiction', in Laura Hubner, Marcus Leaning, and Paul Manning (eds), *The Zombie Renaissance in Popular Culture*, 124–38, London: Palgrave Macmillan.

Rentzenbrink, Cathy (2015), Interview with Hanya Yanagihara, *Foyles*, 26 August. Available online: www.foyles.co.uk/hanya-yanagihara (accessed 08 June 2020).

Rickel, Jennifer (2015), 'Practice Reading for the Apocalypse: David Mitchell's *Cloud Atlas* as Warning Text', *South Atlantic Review*, 80 (1–2): 159–78.
Ricoeur, Paul (1970), *Freud and Philosophy: An Essay on Interpretation*, New Haven: Yale University Press.
Ricoeur, Paul (1985), *Time and Narrative: Volume 2*, Chicago: University of Chicago Press.
Riley, Denise (2002), 'The Right to be Lonely', *Differences: A Journal of Feminist Cultural Studies*, 13 (1): 1–13.
The Road (2009), [film] dir. John Hillcoat, USA: Dimension Films.
Rodríguez, Richard T. (2013), 'Making Queer Familia', in Donald E. Hall and Annamarie Jagose, with Andrea Bebell and Susan Potter (eds), *The Routledge Queer Studies Reader*, 324–32, London: Routledge.
Rohy, Valerie (2018), 'Queer Narrative Theory', in Matthew Garrett (ed), *The Cambridge Companion to Narrative Theory*, 169–82, Cambridge: Cambridge University Press.
Rosenberg, Charles E. (1975), 'Introduction: History and Experience', in Charles E. Rosenberg (ed), *The Family in History*, 1–11, Philadelphia: University of Pennsylvania Press.
Round, Julia (2012), 'The Horror of Humanity', in Wayne Yuen (ed), *The Walking Dead and Philosophy: Zombie Apocalypse Now*, 155–66, Chicago: Open Court.
Rubin, Gayle (1975), 'The Traffic in Women: Notes on the "Public Economy" of Sex', in Rayna R. Reiter (ed), *Toward an Anthropology of Women*, 157–210, New York: Monthly Review Press.
Rushton, Amy (2019), 'A Bubble in the Vein: Suicide, Community, and the Rejection of Neoliberalism in Hanya Yanagihara's *A Little Life* and Miriam Toews's *All My Puny Sorrows*', in Sharae Deckhard and Stephen Shapiro (eds), *World Literature, Neoliberalism, and the Culture of Discontent*, 194–213, London: Palgrave Macmillan.
Ryan, Matthew (2008), 'Hope Is Critical: Cormac McCarthy's *The Road*', *Arena Journal*, 31: 151–62.
Ryan, Maureen (2017), 'A Troubling Trend in Cancellations: Are Inclusive Shows in Danger?' *Variety*, 01 June. Available online: https://variety.com/2017/tv/opinion/canceled-shows-2017-sense8-get-down-underground-sweet-vicious-1202450885/ (accessed 26 January 2021).
Sahlins, Marshall (2013), *What Kinship Is – And Is Not*, Chicago: University of Chicago Press.
Said, Edward W. ([1978] 2003), *Orientalism*, London: Penguin.
Sarris, Andrew (1971), 'Literature and Film', *The Bulletin of the Midwest Modern Language Association*, 4 (1): 10–15.
Scarry, Elaine (1985), *The Body in Pain: The Making and Unmaking of the World*, Oxford: Oxford University Press.
Schleusener, Simon (2017), 'The Dialectics of Mobility: Capitalism and Apocalypse in Cormac McCarthy's *The Road*', *European Journal of American Studies*, 12 (3): 1–14.
Schneeberger, Aaron Francis (2019), 'The Genre Spaces of David Mitchell's *Cloud Atlas*', *College Literature*, 46 (3): 543–72.
Schneider, David M. (1984), *A Critique of the Study of Kinship*, Ann Arbor: University of Michigan Press.

Schoene, Berthold (2010), *The Cosmopolitan Novel*, Edinburgh: Edinburgh University Press.
Scruton, Roger (2010), *The Uses of Pessimism: And the Danger of False Hope*, London: Atlantic Books.
Sedgwick, Eve Kosofsky (1985), *Between Men: English Literature and Male Homosocial Desire*, New York: Columbia University Press.
Sedgwick, Eve Kosofsky (1997), *Novel Gazing: Queer Readings in Fiction*, Durham: Duke University Press.
Sedgwick, Eve Kosofsky (2003), *Touching Feeling: Affect, Pedagogy, Performativity*, Durham: Duke University Press.
Sense8 (2015–2018), [TV series] cr. The Wachowskis, USA: Anarchos Productions.
Shaw, Deborah (2017), '*Sense8* and Sensibility: How a TV Series Is Transcending Geographical and Gender Borders', *The Conversation*, 25 May. Available online: https://theconversation.com/sense8-and-sensibility-how-a-tv-series-is-transcending-geographical-and-gender-borders-77377 (accessed 26 January 2021).
Shin, Haerin (2017), 'Engineering the Techno-Orient: The Hyperrealization of Post-Racial Politics in *Cloud Atlas*', in Isiah Lavender III (ed), *Dis-Orienting Planets: Racial Representations of Asia in Science Fiction*, 131–43, Jackson: University Press of Mississippi.
Shoop, Casey, and Dermot Ryan (2015), '"Gravid with the Ancient Future": *Cloud Atlas* and the Politics of Big History', *SubStance*, 44 (1): 92–106.
Shoplifters (2018), [film] dir. Hirokazu Koreeda, Japan: AOI Promotion.
Skrimshire, Stefan (2011), '"There is no God and we are his prophets": Deconstructing Redemption in Cormac McCarthy's *The Road*', *Journal for Cultural Research*, 15 (1): 1–14.
Snediker, Michael D. (2009), *Queer Optimism: Lyric Personhood and Other Felicitous Persuasions*, Minneapolis: University of Minnesota Press.
Søfting, Inger-Anne (2013), 'Between Dystopia and Utopia: The Post-Apocalyptic Discourse of Cormac McCarthy's *The Road*', *English Studies*, 94 (6): 704–13.
Stack, Carol B. (1974), *All Our Kin: Strategies for Survival in a Black Community*, New York: Harper & Row.
Stroup, John, and Glenn W. Shuck (2007), *Escape into the Future: Cultural Pessimism and Its Religious Dimension in Contemporary American Popular Culture*, Waco: Baylor University Press.
Sullivan, Nell (2013), 'The Good Guys: McCarthy's *The Road* as Post-9/11 Male Sentimental Novel', *Genre*, 46 (1): 79–101.
Temko, Christine (2014), 'Speaking in the Face of Disintegration: Absurdism and the Persistence of Empathy in the Dimming Dialogues of Cormac McCarthy's *The Road*', *English Text Construction*, 7 (2): 151–77.
Tenga, Angela, and Jonathan Bassett (2016), '"You kill or you die, or you die and you kill": Meaning and Violence in AMC's *The Walking Dead*', *The Journal of Popular Culture*, 49 (6): 1280–300.
Theweleit, Klaus (1987), *Male Fantasies. Volume 1: Women, Floods, Bodies, History*, Minneapolis: University of Minnesota Press.
Theweleit, Klaus (1989), *Male Fantasies. Volume 2: Male Bodies: Psychoanalyzing the White Terror*, Minneapolis: University of Minnesota Press.
Thunberg, Greta, Luisa Neubauer, Kyra Gantois, Anna Taylor, and Anuna De Wever (2019), 'We don't want your hope. We want you to take action',

Frankfurter Allgemeine, 15 March. Available online: https://www.faz.net/-gqe-9kumx (accessed 19 August 2019).

Trimm, Ryan (2018), 'Spirits in the Material World: Spectral Worlding in David Mitchell's *Ghostwritten* and *Cloud Atlas*', *C21 Literature: Journal of 21st-Century Writings*, 6 (3): 1–28.

Tsang, Philip (2018), 'Allegory of the Global Anglophone: Interconnectedness and Sublimity in *Cloud Atlas*', *Novel: A Forum on Fiction*, 51 (3): 399–416.

Valdez Quade, Kirstin (2016), Interview with Hanya Yanagihara, *National Book Foundation*, February. Available online: www.nationalbook.org/hanya-yanagihara-interviewed-by-kirstin-valdez-quade (accessed 08 June 2020).

Varela, Anna (2020), 'COVID-19 Transmission "Webs" Show How We're All Connected', *Futurity*, 14 April. Available online: https://www.futurity.org/covid-19-transmission-networks-2337002/ (accessed 02 February 2021).

Vinney, Cynthia, and Caryn Wiley-Rapoport (2016), '"Look at the Flowers": Female Evolution in the Face of the Zombie Hordes of *The Walking Dead*', in Barbara Brodman and James E. Doan (eds), *The Supernatural Revamped: From Timeworn Legends to Twenty-First Century Chic*, 207–18, Madison: Farleigh Dickinson University Press.

Vint, Sherryl (2013), 'Abject Posthumanism: Neoliberalism, Biopolitics, and Zombies', in Marina Levina and Diem-My T. Bui (eds), *Monster Culture in the 21st Century: A Reader*, 133–46, London: Bloomsbury Academic.

Voigts, Eckart (2015), 'Introduction: The Dystopian Imagination – An Overview', in Eckart Voigts and Alessandra Boller (eds), *Dystopia, Science Fiction, Post-Apocalypse: Classics – New Tendencies – Model Interpretations*, 1–7, Trier: Wissenschaftlicher Verlag Trier.

The Walking Dead (2010–22), [TV series] cr. Frank Darabont, USA: Idiot Box Productions.

Warner, Alan (2006), 'The Road to Hell', *The Guardian*, 04 November. Available online: https://www.theguardian.com/books/2006/nov/04/featuresreviews.guardianreview4 (accessed 02 May 2021).

Waugh, Patricia (1984), *Metafiction: The Theory and Practice of Self-Conscious Fiction*, London: Methuen.

Wegner, Phillip E. (2020), *Invoking Hope: Theory and Utopia in Dark Times*, Minneapolis: University of Minnesota Press.

Weston, Kath (1991), *Families We Choose: Lesbians, Gays, Kinship*, New York: Columbia University Press.

West-Pavlov, Russell (2020), 'Kith and Kin', in Gero Bauer, Anya Heise-von der Lippe, Nicole Hirschfelder, and Katharina Luther (eds), *Kinship and Collective Action in Literature and Culture*, 35–42, Tübingen: Narr Francke Attempto.

White, Christopher T. (2015), 'Embodied Reading and Narrative Empathy in Cormac McCarthy's *The Road*', *Studies in the Novel*, 47 (4): 532–49.

Wiemann, Dirk (2017), 'David Mitchell, *Cloud Atlas* (2004)', in Christoph Reinfandt (ed), *Handbook of the English Novel, 1900-2015*, 498–517, Berlin: De Gruyter.

Wise, Damon (2018), 'Japanese Director Hirokazu Kore-eda Returns to Exploring Family Dynamics in Surprise Palme D'Or Winner *Shoplifters*', *Deadline*, 19 May. Available online: https://deadline.com/2018/05/shoplifters-hirokazu-kore-eda-palme-dor-cannes-video-interview-1202394721/ (accessed 23 June 2021).

Wittenberg, David (2018), 'Time', in Matthew Garrett (ed), *The Cambridge Companion to Narrative Theory*, 120–31, Cambridge: Cambridge University Press.

Womack, Ytasha (2013), *Afrofuturism: The World of Black Sci-Fi and Fantasy Culture*, Chicago: Chicago Review Press.

Wood, James (2000), 'Human, All Too Inhuman: On the Formation of a New Genre: Hysterical Realism', *The New Republic*, 23 July. Available online: https://newrepublic.com/article/61361/human-inhuman (accessed 29 September 2020).

Worthen, Joseph R. (2020), '*A Little Life* and Empathy Aptitude Reading', *Reception: Texts, Readers, Audiences, History*, 12: 54–70.

Wright, Geoffrey A. (2017), 'Hobbes, Locke, Darwin, and Zombies: The Post-Apocalyptic Politics of Survival in AMC's *The Walking Dead*', *Quarterly Review of Film and Video*, 34 (2): 148–70.

Xiang, Zairong (2020), 'COVID-19: On the Epistemic Condition', *Open Democracy*, 06 April. Available online: https://www.opendemocracy.net/en/can-europe-make-it/covid-19-epistemic-condition/ (accessed 02 February 2021).

Yamashita, Karen Tei (2018), 'Literature as Community: The Turtle, Imagination & the Journey Home', *The Massachusetts Review*, 59 (4): 597–611.

Yanagihara, Hanya (2013), *The People in the Trees*, London: Atlantic Books.

Yanagihara, Hanya (2015), *A Little Life*, New York: Anchor Books.

Young, Stephanie L., and Art Herbig (2020), '"I Am Also a We": Exploring Queer Worldmaking in *Sense8*', *QED: A Journal in GLBTQ Worldmaking*, 7 (2): 69–93.

Yuen, Wayne (2016), 'Carol Didn't Care', in Wayne Yuen (ed), *The Ultimate Walking Dead and Philosophy: Hungry for More*, 193–203, Chicago: Open Court.

Zalloua, Zahi (2019), 'Editor's Column: Pessimistic Times', *The Comparatist*, 43: 1–5.

Zibrak, Arielle (2012), 'Intolerance, A Survival Guide: Heteronormative Culture Formation in Cormac McCarthy's *The Road*', *Arizona Quarterly: A Journal of American Literature, Culture, and Theory*, 68 (3): 103–28.

Ziegler, John R. (2018), *Queering the Family in* The Walking Dead, London: Palgrave Macmillan.

Zolkos, Magdalena (2020), 'Hanya Yanagihara's *The People in the Tress* and Post-Colonial Trauma Criticism', *Textual Practice*, 34 (1): 147–68.

INDEX

Adorno, Theodor W. 50
Afrofuturism 110
Agamben, Giorgio 4
Ahmed, Sara 154–6, 210, 212, 219–20
anthropocentrism 17, 29, 33, 132, 179
apocalypse 44, 46–8, 58, 71, 97, 112, 118, 120, 122, 124, 126, 130–1, 168, 189, 196, 198, 215 (*see also* post-apocalypse)
    apocalyptic revelation 21
    pre-apocalypse 93
    pre-a. world 51, 54, 56, 63–4, 68, 73, 84, 93, 96
    pre-apocalyptic social structures 86
    zombie apocalypse 78, 82–4, 86, 89–90, 95, 97, 99–101
Assmann, Aleida 2–3
Atwood, Margaret 107–8

Bateman, Benjamin 5
Baumann, Zygmunt 2–3
belonging
    (un-)b. and capitalism 32
    b. and care 2, 5, 10, 13–17, 22–3, 38, 49, 101, 165, 168–9, 212
    b. and community 3, 20, 84
    b. and family 19, 31, 78, 86, 99, 157, 233
    (un-)b. and heterosexism 32
    indigenous b. 20
    b. and kinship 156
    b. and morality 80
    possibility of b. 231
    b. and reciprocity 13
    (non-)reproductive structures of b. 53
    socially meaningful b. 16
    b. and solidarity 104
    b. and temporality 5–6, 22, 24, 28–9, 33–4, 43–50, 52, 132, 150, 163, 169, 195, 202, 232, 234
    b. and time 2, 21, 34
Benjamin, Walter 7–8
Bennett, Jane 32–3
Berardi, Franco 1–2
Berger, James 46–8, 78, 94
Berlant, Lauren 13
Bernini, Lorenzo 79–80
Bersani, Leo 9
Black Mirror (TV series) 77
Bloch, Ernst 7–9, 11–12
Bradway, Tyler 15, 35
Brown, Wendy 158–9
Butler, Judith 15, 18, 144

cannibalism 57–62, 67, 69, 74, 83, 87, 129
capitalism 2, 8–9, 15, 32, 42, 54–5, 58, 83, 132, 148, 152, 157–8, 162–4, 174, 209, 213, 234–8
Castiglia, Christopher 27, 31
care (*see also* belonging)
    c. and community 93, 101, 213, 217–18
    c. and concern 2–3, 16, 18, 22–4, 41, 50, 168–9, 171, 185, 196, 213, 220, 231
    ethics of c. 71, 202, 220, 231
    c. and family 238
    c. and friendship 203, 222, 228, 233–4, 238
    homosocial c. 203, 209
    c. and kinship 207, 216–17, 220
    c. and love 203, 220, 222–3, 225, 228, 233–4, 238

networks of c. 156, 196, 233
c. for others 60, 65, 69–70, 81, 140, 146, 215–17, 226
parental c. 93, 211
c. and protection 84, 86, 232
c. and queer relationality 213
c. and reproduction 15
c. and responsibility 7
c. and sexuality 18
catamite 57–8, 60–1, 74
child
  c. abuse and rape 41, 172, 186, 197, 199, 202, 205–6, 209, 215–16, 225, 235
  c. as the carrier of hope and futurity 59–60, 65, 67, 70–1, 94, 101
  death of a c. as apocalyptic revelation 95, 211
  the figure of the C. 11, 18, 22, 31, 45, 49, 52, 63, 65, 70, 74–5, 78, 94–6, 133 (*see also* Edelman, Lee)
  Freud's c. 59
  c. as killer 97
  c. as object of paranoid protection 94, 98
  the perfect c. 198
  prophetic c. critic 97
  zombie c. 94–5, 99
Christianity 41–2, 53, 57, 62, 72, 74, 127, 182, 196, 202, 216, 222, 225
climate (*see also* devastation; environment)
  c. catastrophe 9, 45
  c. change 3, 52, 123, 168
  c. crisis 32, 44–5
  c. emergency 10, 29
Cloud Atlas (novel by David Mitchell) 6, 34, 38, 40, 111, 112, *113–35*, 150, 228, 232–34
Cloud Atlas (film by The Wachowskis and Tom Tykwer) 6, 40, 135–38, 139–40
coloniality 3, 20, 25, 41, 78, 83, 110, 123, 132, 134, 141, 143–6, 150, 162, 175–87, 189–90, 192, 194–200, 206
  anti-c. 135, 199
  de-c. 19–20, 104, 110, 199–200
  neo-c. 78, 190, 200
  post-c. 134, 140, 143, 146–7, 162–3, 190, 233–4
community (*see also* care; indigeneity; reparation)
  c. of belonging 2–3, 20, 84
  c. of colour/black c. 18
  gay and lesbian c. 17, 224
  global c. 104, 147–8
  human c. 72, 82, 84, 95, 104–5, 140
  c. of men 51, 61, 182
  queerness and c. 11–12, 30, 35, 206, 218, 225
  racial c. 206
  c. of readers and storytellers 125, 130–2
  reproduction and c. 94
  scientific c. 190
  slave c. 78
  temporality and c. 28, 31
  trans-/international c. 141, 145, 162
Contagion (film by Steven Soderbergh) 106
contemporary (*see also* fiction)
  c. crisis 34
  c. critical theory 22, 28–9, 52, 108, 231
  c. culture 3–4, 6, 9–10, 15, 20, 22, 28, 40–1, 47–9, 54–5, 78, 82, 104, 110–11, 163, 168, 231, 234, 238
  c. identity politics 111, 139
  non-contemporaneity 4 (*see also* Edwards, Caroline)
  c. popular culture 80
  c. society 17, 81, 88, 234, 238
  c. US culture 171, 202–3
  c. zeitgeist 2
cosmopolitanism 132, 150, 232
  c. in British fiction 115
  cosmopolitan novel 114
crisis (*see also* climate)
  contemporary c. 14–15, 34
  cultural, political, social c. 42, 44, 48
  c. in the early twenty-first-century 37

environmental c. 14, 109
global/global health c. 38, 44, 106
HIV/AIDS c. 203, 213, 218
post-apocalyptic c. 57
critique (*see also* postcritique)
   contemporary critical modalities 52
   c. epistemologies 200
   paranoid c. modalities 24
   c. race theory 15
   c. reading/thinking/writing 12, 23, 26, 231
   reparative c. attitude/modalities/ position 24–7 (*see also* Sedgwick, Eve K.)
   c. temporalities 115
   c. theory 22, 28–30, 32, 173–4, 231
culture 19, 36–7, 48, 150, 169, 171, 201–2
Cvetkovich, Ann 213–14, 218, 220

De Cristofaro, Diletta 46, 48, 115, 119, 121–2, 124, 135
DeLillo, Don 172
democracy
   anti-democratic practices 50
   d. collaboration 90
   European democracy 123
   d. governance 89
   liberal d. 158
   d. of moments 171
   non-democratic spaces 83
Derrida, Jacques 47, 50
devastation (*see also* climate; crisis)
   cultural d. 33
   ecological/environmental/global d. 17, 21, 33, 45, 53, 55, 108–9
   epistemological and ontological d. of Christian Revelation 196
   social d. 13, 17, 33, 53, 75, 234
diversity 15, 41, 107, 139–42, 145, 147–51, 156, 163–4
   kinship and d. 142
docta spes 8, 12, 14 (*see also* Bloch, Ernst)
Draeger, Christoph 53, 74–5
dystopia 46–7, 52, 77, 109, 114, 124 (*see also* fiction)

Edelman, Lee 10–11, 13, 22, 28, 31, 45, 51–2, 61, 133, 210, 217
Edwards, Caroline 4, 124–5
Eng, David 19, 24–5
Enlightenment 116, 118, 135, 179
environment (*see also* climate; crisis; devastation)
   environmental catastrophe/collapse/ crisis/damage/destruction 14, 34, 109, 126, 196
ethics
   e. of care in *The Road* and *A Little Life* 71, 202, 206–7, 219
   e. in *Cloud Atlas* 116–18
   e. and fiction 238
   gendered meaning of e. 58
   e. of kin and futurity in *The Road* 52
   e. and kinship 21
   e. in *The People in the Trees* 198, 207, 219
   pessimistic e. 173
   e. and philosophical pessimism 169
   reparative e. in *The Road* 69
   e. and reparative reading 27, 33
   e. in *The Walking Dead* 81, 93, 96
family
   f. and belonging 19, 31, 86, 99
   chosen f. 17, 151
   chosen f. in *A Little Life* 201–26
   chosen f. in *The Road* 67–75
   chosen f. in *Sense8* 139–141, 148, 151–4
   chosen f. in *The Walking Dead* 82, 85–7, 99–100
   f. and kinship 7, 15, 19, 150–7
   f. and nation in the US 14–15, 19, 78
   nuclear/biological/heterosexual/ heteronormal/reproductive f. 10, 14–15, 17–19, 41, 49–53, 62, 64, 72–3, 78, 86–9, 91, 97, 100, 104, 132, 141, 151, 154, 202, 210, 235, 237
   pre-apocalyptic f. 84
   queer/gay f. 18, 100, 151

INDEX

fascism 91, 184, 199
   fascistic ideologies 81–2
   fascist masculinity 91–2
fatherhood 14, 88–9, 92, 94
   the paranoid father in *The Road* 63–72, 75
   f. in *Sense8* 140–161
   father-son dyad in *The Road* 40, 51–62, 65
   f. in *The Walking Dead* 68–75, 77–92, 94–9
Felski, Rita 23–4, 26
femininity 88, 92–3
   post-apocalyptic f. 92–3
   reproductive f. 60
feminism 108, 164
   feminist research/theory 15, 29
   queer and lesbian feminism 225
   f. utopia 37
   The Walking Dead as a feminist text 92
fiction
   apocalyptic f. 78, 92
   contemporary f. 38, 10–17, 22, 27, 29–30, 36–7, 39, 42, 47, 50, 114, 116, 122, 132, 164–5, 204, 231, 238
   dystopian f. 40, 46–7, 77, 106, 109, 124–5, 174
   fictional worldmaking 129
   gay f. 218
   narrative f. 5, 23, 34–6, 41
   post-apocalyptic f. 6, 19, 39–40, 43, 45–9, 53, 55, 75, 77, 87, 90, 93, 96, 103–4, 122, 195, 204, 211, 215, 232, 238
   science f. 106–11, 139–41, 145, 152, 156–7
   speculative f. 6, 37, 40, 103–4, 106–11, 139–40, 165, 232, 238
   theory of f. 17, 37–8
   US f. 19, 38
Fraser, Nancy 164
Freeman, Elizabeth 15, 30–1, 157
Freud, Sigmund 22, 59, 153, 219
Fridays for Future 39, 44–5
future
   futures 2–3, 7, 10, 13–14, 72, 105–6, 108–11, 120, 132–4, 232

futurism 21, 50, 52, 226
   anti-futurism 9, 12, 45, 49, 231
   futuristic hope 1–2, 7–8, 11, 14, 41, 52, 56, 59, 61–2, 78, 80, 89, 93–8, 101, 123, 132–3, 170, 220, 224
   no future 10–12, 80 (*see also* Edelman, Lee)
   paranoid f. 53, 63, 71, 75, 100, 200
   post-apocalyptic/dystopian f. 33, 75, 114
   queer f. 11, 14, 29, 133
   reproductive f. 10–11, 52, 60, 62, 65, 73, 78, 84, 93, 97, 99–101, 132–4, 137, 226

gender and sexuality 36, 41–2, 57–8, 92, 94, 111, 140–1, 143–5, 147, 155, 163
glocality 145–6
God
   belief in G. 52, 67, 71
   the child as a g. 71
   death of G. 67, 71, 74
   G. as the father 65
   life-creating g. 184
   g.-like 193
   G.'s will 67, 71
   Goddess 118, 120, 134
Ghostwritten (novel by David Mitchell) 113
Guterres, Antonio 105

Halberstam, Jack 9–10, 12, 31–2, 36
Haraway, Donna J. 21, 34, 45, 49, 108
hermeneutics 20, 23, 25, 33, 36, 168
   h. and method 26
   paranoid h. 24 (*see also* Sedgwick, Eve K.)
   post-critical h. 23, 173–4, 231 (*see also* Felski, Rita; postcritique)
   queer h. 39
   reparative h. 24, 32–3, 38–9 (*see also* reparation; Sedgwick, Eve K.)
   h. of suspicion 22, 33 (*see also* Ricoeur, Paul)

heteronormativity 143
  heteronormative culture/existence/
    ideals/model/order 11, 18, 29,
    61–2, 151, 157
  h. family 21, 52, 153
  h. generation 63, 68
  h. and patriarchy 20
heterosexuality 10, 20, 94, 101, 137,
    208, 210 (see also family)
  heterosexual couple/love/
    relationship/romance 73, 99,
    115, 133, 136, 220–1
  non-heterosexuality 99–100
  heterosexual norms 101, 151,
    210
Hicks, Heather J. 47, 49, 122, 130–1
Hillcoat, John 6, 72–4
HIV/AIDS 10, 146, 203, 213, 218
Hobbes, Thomas 126
Hölscher, Lucian 2–3
homophobia 41, 81, 141, 202–4, 208,
    218, 220, 224
hope 7–14 (see also Bloch, Ernst; care;
    child; future)
  h. and connection/community
    111–12, 145, 150, 158, 236
  h. and kinship as conceptual
    framework 27
  h. vs. optimism 7, 12, 28, 168
  paranoid h. 53, 63, 98, 220
  post-apocalyptic h. 96
  h. in the present 2, 5, 8, 13–4, 21,
    27, 32, 64, 132, 135, 138–9,
    162, 174, 224, 231, 233
  queer h. 10–11, 38, 103, 203,
    220–3, 228–9
  hopeful reading 22, 27, 31
  reparative h. 14, 31, 49, 52–3, 62,
    75, 79, 173, 228
  teleological h. 42, 67–8, 79, 84, 93,
    99, 105, 117, 121, 170, 228
  h. and temporality 7–8, 12–13, 39,
    57, 95, 139, 189
  h. vs. utopia 4, 27
Horn, Eva 47–9, 51
Huber, Irmtraud 5, 116–17
humanism 134
  anthropocentric h. 33
  h. in *Cloud Atlas* 133, 232

  defunct h. 115
  false h. 84
  Enlightenment h. 118, 135
  global/universal h. 3, 20, 41, 105,
    111, 113, 135, 139, 158, 163,
    233–4
  h. and human rights 126
  humanist optimism 134
  ideal of h. 86
  liberal h. 118, 133, 143
  limits of h. 40
  new h. 38, 112, 115, 118, 140, 145,
    170
  non-western h. 143
  postmodernism and h. 116
  radical h. 53
humanity 17, 41, 58, 78, 83–4, 88, 105,
    107, 112, 115, 126, 179, 182,
    199
  h. and children 60
  h. in *Cloud Atlas* 116–18
  h.'s collective death 122
  future of h. 3, 9, 96, 106
  inhumanity/lack of h. 133, 172
  kinship as the common h. 41
  limits of h. 51
  the planet as the body of h. 61
  survival of h. 104, 114

identity politics 10, 111, 139, 158–9,
    164, 204, 221, 224
If on a Winter's Night a Traveller
    (novel by Italo Calvino) 114
indigeneity
  indigenous community/nations/
    people 20, 126, 186, 188
  i. culture/ecosystem 188, 197
  i. kinship 20
  i. knowledge 188
  i. literature 20
  i. perspective 188
  i. theorist/theories 19–20
Industrial Revolution 61
internet 105, 144, 146, 158

Jameson, Frederic 37
Jupiter Ascending (film by
    The Wachowskis) 139
Justice, Daniel Heath 19

Kaplan, E. Ann 145
Kelly, Adam 115
Kermode, Frank 193
kinship *14–22* (*see also* belonging; care; family)
   k. beyond the boundaries of the human 180–1, 197, 200
   biological/generational/male-male/reproductive k. 16, 25, 41, 70, 91–2, 151, 185
   k. and capitalism 234, 236, 238
   conservative/conventional/traditional k. 7, 15–17, 152, 155
   k. in contemporary fiction 11
   k. and feminism 15
   indigenous k. 20
   non-western k. 19–20
   queer k. 15, 17–18, 30, 41, 139–40, 150–2, 155, 157, 186, 208–10, 212–13, 217, 228, 234
   k. and race 15, 19, 206
   reparative k. 31, 50, 75, 207–8, 215, 218, 227–8, 220, 237–8
   sexual k. 143
   k. and temporality 6, 24, 38, 58, 183
Kirkman, Robert 77, 97
Klein, Melanie 23–5
Kore-eda, Hirokazu 234–5

Lacan, Jacques 10–11
Latour, Bruno 23
Le Guin, Ursula K. 107
LGBTIQ 17, 164, 213
A Little Life (novel by Hanya Yanagihara) 6, 38, 41, 169, 173, 201–29, 233–5, 238
Lothian, Alexis 13–4, 108, 110
Love, Heather 29

Mahler, Gustav 227
Martin, Theodore 4
Marxism 22, 213
masculinity 41, 60, 88, 180
   cowboy m. 97
   fascist m. 91–2
   m. and friendship/love 201–26
   m. and homophobia 202, 208, 210, 224
   imperialist m. 145
   militant m. 90–2, 99
   modern western m. 208
   scientific/imperial m. 177, 179
   survivalist m. 62, 88
materialism
   historical m. 7–8
   new m. 6, 28–9, 32
Mbembe, Achille 206
McCarthy, Cormac 6, 40, 46, 50–2, 54–60, 62–6, 68, 70, 72, 75, 87, 89, 98, 104, 232
Menninghaus, Winfried 177
metafiction 6, 113, 115, 125, 129, 173, 189–90
metalepsis 113–14, 127–31, 135
Mitchell, David 6, 34, 37, 40, 111–17, 119–21, 123–35, 139, 232
monstrosity 40, 61, 77–80, 82–4, 87–8, 90, 95–6, 99–101
Morgan, Lewis Henry 16
motherhood 14, 57–62, 67–8, 74, 87–9, 92–7, 137, 140, 146, 150–2, 154, 160–1, 185, 235–6, 238
Muñoz, José Esteban 11–12
Murray, Heather 17
mutuality of being 14, 16, 21, 125, 234 (*see also* Sahlin, Marshall)

Nayar, Pramod K. 176, 178, 182
neoliberalism 55, 141, 162–4, 174, 217
Nietzsche, Friedrich 121
nonnormativity 35

the Other 32–3, 44, 46, 68–9, 95–6, 110, 173, 175–9, 181–3, 185–6, 195–7, 199–200, 233

pacifism 85, 98
Pale Fire (novel by Vladimir Nabokov) 176
pandemic
   global p. 10, 39, 87–8, 104–6, 168
   Covid-19 p. 39, 104–6
Parasite (film by Bong Joon-ho) 42, 236–7

paranoia 9, 12, 23–5, 28, 34, 39, 41, 49–50, 59, 63–5, 67, 72, 74–5, 88, 90, 94, 98, 100–1, 128, 163, 173–5, 185, 190, 193, 195, 198, 200, 202, 204–6, 215, 217, 220, 223, 232 (*see also* future; hope; Sedgwick, Eve K.)
  critical p. 24, 26
  p. narrative 11, 15, 63, 71, 175, 189, 195, 197
  paranoia and the reparative 23–6, 52–3, 57, 75, 91–2, 100, 173, 215 (*see also* Sedgwick, Eve K.)
  paranoia and violence 88, 91–2, 101
  paranoid epistemology 23, 93, 96, 204, 216
  paranoid teleology 78, 184
  p. reading 23, 150 (*see also* Sedgwick, Eve K.)
patriarchy 89, 91, 94, 97, 101, 145 (*see also* family; masculinity)
  p. culture 145, 208
  p. masculinity and violence 91–2
  p. narratives 41
  patriarchal family 14–15, 19, 88
  patriarchy and homophobia 208
  patriarchal leadership 89
The People in the Trees (novel by Hanya Yanagihara) 6, 34, 38, 41, 73, 173, *175–200*, 233–4
pessimism 3, 5, 7, 9, 24, 26, 37, 39, 108, 117, 134–5, 165, 169–74, 233–4, 238
  Afro-P. 172
  hopeful pessimism 174–5
  hysterical p. 41, 167–8
  pessimistic critique 28–9
  philosophical p. 169–71, 174
  reparative position of p. 32
Porowski, Antoni 224–5
post-apocalypse 48–50, 59, 78–9, 89, 95, 96–7, 101 (*see also* apocalypse; crisis; femininity; fiction; future; hope; motherhood; storytelling)
  post-apocalyptic prophet 196
  post-a. social relations 80–2

post-a. struggle for survival 47
post-a. values 96
post-a. world 52, 59, 63, 75, 78–9, 84, 88, 90, 94, 99, 124–5, 232
postcritique 22–3, 173 (*see also* critique; Felski, Rita; reparation)
postcritical attitude/reading/ thinking/hermeneutics/writing 6, 22–3, 26–7, 30, 37, 173–4, 231
postmodernism 5, 20, 115–17

Quart, Alissa 157
queer 11, 13, 18, 25, 38, 42, 79, 99, 132, 134, 143, 146, 151–6, 169, 203, 206, 212, 219–26, 228–9, 231–2 (*see also* future; hope; kinship)
  q. anti-normativity 17, 35
  the q. art of failure 31 (*see also* Halberstam, Jack)
  q. community (of care) 30, 35, 206, 218, 225
  q. emancipation 17–18, 29, 99, 155, 234
  q. (and reparative) hermeneutics 39
  q. negativity 9–11, 26, 29–30, 35, 52, 79, 158
  q. studies 23, 42
  q. temporality 10, 28, 30, 35, 134, 157–9, 238
  q. theory 6, 9–10, 14–15, 17–18, 26, 28–9, 32, 35, 37, 52, 231
  q. time and belonging 34
  q. utopia 11–12, 29, 37, 143, 221, 233
  the zombie and the q. 80, 84
queerness 9–12, 14, 18, 30–1, 35–6, 38, 40, 49, 99–101, 156–9, 210, 217, 220, 225, 231–2
  q. in *The Walking Dead* 99–101

race/racism 15, 18–21, 41, 49, 55–6, 81, 83, 104–5, 110–11, 117–18, 123, 126, 138, 141, 143, 147, 155, 162, 171–2, 203–6
  anti-racism 164
Rai, Amid S. 79
The Rain (TV series) 77

reparation 7, 12–13, 24–6, 45, 49, 55, 57, 62, 66, 68, 72, 80, 88, 93–4, 98, 101, 108, 168, 185, 187, 189, 195, 197, 200, 206, 217, 226, 233–3, 238 (*see also* hope; kinship; postcritique)
- r. community/connection 80, 90–1, 100–1, 173, 218
- r. epistemology 23, 25, 31
- r. future 7, 67, 97
- r. group building/kin-making/solidarity 42, 68–72, 90, 93, 98, 198, 216, 237
- r. hermeneutics 23–4, 32, 38–9, 173–4, 231
- r. power of love and friendship 173
- r. reading 6, 22–3, 25–7, 30–33, 37, 174, 238 (*see also* postcritique; Sedgwick, Eve K.)
- reparative belonging and care 101, 150, 165, 168, 203, 211–13, 216, 220, 228, 233
- r. temporality 50, 52, 150, 173, 193

Ricoeur, Paul 22, 34
Riley, Denise 227
The Rd. (video installation by Christoph Draeger) 53, 74–5
The Road (novel by Cormac McCarthy) 6, 38, 40, 46, 50, 51–72, 75, 87, 89, 93, 97–8, 210, 220, 232, 237
The Road (film by John Hillcoat) 6, 50, 72–5
Robinson Crusoe (novel by Daniel Defoe) 116
Rodríguez, Richard T. 19
Rohy, Valerie 35
Rubin, Gayle 16, 208
Rushdie, Salman 172

Sahlins, Marshall 16, 125
Said, Edward W. 1
Scarry, Elaine 216
Schneider, David M. 16
Schoene, Berthold 115, 118, 122, 127

Schopenhauer, Arthur 171
Scruton, Roger 170–1
Sedgwick, Eve Kosofsky 23–6, 39, 35, 52, 128, 151, 208
Sense8 (TV series by The Wachowskis and J. Michael Straczynski) 6, 38, 40–1, 111–12, *139–65*, 233–4, 238
Shoplifters (film by Hirokazu Kore-eda) 42, 234–7
sinthomosexual 11, 61 (see also Edelman, Lee)
slavery 15, 18, 56, 60–1, 78, 117, 120, 126, 206
Smith, Zadie 117, 172
Snediker, Michael D. 12–13
socialism 8–9
Soylent Green (film by Richard Fleischer) 116
Stack, Carol B. 18
storytelling 27–8, 34, 153, 157
- s. across media 36
- contemporary s. 28, 36, 111
- imaginative s. 27, 108
- literary s. 113
- metafictional s. 6
- non-linear s. 158
- oral s. 114
- popular s. 36, 171
- post-apocalyptic s. 39, 49
- speculative s. 39, 108, 111
- utopian and dystopian s. 106

Straczynski, J. Michael 111, 139
symbolism 10, 17, 74, 127–9, 133, 137, 222

teleology (*see also* hope)
- apocalyptic t. 122
- t. and fiction 11–12
- non-teleological philosophy of love 169
- non-t. readings 72
- non-/anti-t. temporalities 22–3, 35, 100
- teleology and temporality 3, 22, 35, 46, 53, 64, 121, 183, 196, 200, 203

temporality (*see also* apocalypse; belonging; community; hope; kinship; queer; teleology)
  ambiguous t. 80, 115, 117–18, 129, 193
  apocalyptic t. 48, 132, 134, 211
  circular t. 33, 40, 108, 115, 117, 120–2, 129, 132, 134, 136, 214, 228, 233
  t. in fiction 11, 33–5, 107–8
  linear t. 10, 35, 40, 72, 110, 115, 117, 120–2, 129, 132, 134, 136, 161, 170, 174, 177, 194, 214, 233
  repetitive/non-linear t. 174, 218, 228, 234
  trauma and t. 169
Theweleit, Klaus 91, 180
Thunberg, Greta 44–5
Tomkins, Sylvan 23
trans* 139–44, 150, 155
trauma 30, 55, 57, 159, 168–70, 173, 202–3, 205–7, 213–20, 229, 233
Tykwer, Tom 6, 40, 111, 115, 135

United Nations 44, 104–5
utopia 1–5, 8–11, 26, 29–31, 34, 37, 39, 41, 45, 48, 52, 64, 99, 105

The Wachowskis 40, 111, 115, 135, 139, 162
The Walking Dead (graphic novel by Robert Kirkman) 77–8, 82, 99
The Walking Dead (TV series by AMC) 6, 38, 40, 50, 69, *77–101*, 104, 195, 210, 232, 237
Wallace, David Foster 172
The War of the Worlds (novel by H. G. Wells) 107
Verne, Jules 108
Waugh, Patricia 189
Wegner, Philipp E. 27
Weston, Kath 17
Wood, James 41, 172
Westworld (film by Michael Crichton) 77

Yanagihara, Hanya 6, 34, 41, 167–9, 171–5, 179, 181, 183–4, 186–8, 190–1, 193–4, 196–9, 201, 204–10, 212, 214–16, 218–19, 221–3, 225–6, 228, 233

zombies 40, 69, 77–84, 86–90, 92, 94–97, 99–101, 176, 195
  z. as carriers of futuristic hope 101
  z. as everybody's hope and future 96
  z. as kin 99